I0754637

MENTAL PHILOSOPHY;

EMBRACING THE THREE DEPARTMENTS OF THE

INTELLECT, SENSIBILITIES, AND WILL.

BY THOMAS C. UPHAM, D.D.,

PROFESSOR OF MENTAL AND MORAL PHILOSOPHY IN BOWDOIN COLLEGE; MEMBER OF THE ACADEMY OF METAPHYSICAL AND ETHICAL SCIENCES; AUTHOR OF "ÆSTHETIC AND MORAL LETTERS," "THE INTERIOR LIFE," "DIVINE UNION," ETC.

IN TWO VOLUMES.

VOL. I.: THE INTELLECT,

WITH AN APPENDIX ON LANGUAGE.

NEW YORK:

HARPER & BROTHERS, PUBLISHERS,

FRANKLIN SQUARE.

1869.

PREFACE.

In preparing the following work, I trust I have felt, in some degree, the responsibility which obviously ought to attach to such an attempt. It has been my object, aided by the views and researches which have characterized the labours of various philosophical sects, to give a condensed, but just and impartial, account of most of the leading principles of Mental Philosophy, so far as they appear to be ascertained and recognised at the present time. The Work, accordingly, is essentially Eclectic in its character; and, as such, can neither incur the discredit, nor claim the honour, of belonging exclusively to any of the great Philosophical Schools, although it does not hesitate to acknowledge its indebtedness to all. In connexion with a cordial application of the Eclectic principle, which has laid open to me the truth wherever it may be found, and under whatever name, I have felt it important to adhere as closely as possible to the rules of Inductive philosophizing, in opposition to that excess of bold conjecture and unchastened speculation which have too often perplexed and deformed mental inquiries. And in doing this I have been obliged to submit my conclusions everywhere to the subjective test of my own mental experience and operations, as developed within the sphere of my personal consciousness. In this way I have hoped, with Divine assistance, to prepare a Work which, together with some important views that might, perhaps, properly be considered original, should select, arrange, and systematize the doctrines of a multitude of writers; and which, while it might commend itself with some degree of confidence to the philosopher, should, at the same time, be accordant, as sound Philosophy ever will be, with the principles and interests of correct morals and religion. The aspect of the times evidently demanded that the attempt should be made by somebody. There is no question that a Work of this kind, especially in connexion with the mental training of young persons, has for some time been greatly needed. But whether I have succeeded, in a task of so much difficulty and requiring so much care, in meeting the reasonable expectations and wishes of the friends of mental science, I must leave to others to decide.

The reader will notice that the Work proceeds, after a brief discussion of the doctrine of Primary Truths, and a few other preparatory views, upon the basis of a threefold division of the mind, viz., the INTELLECT, the SENSIBILITIES, and the WILL. This general division, which, notwithstanding its obvious importance, has not generally been made prominent in philosophical writers, and has even been rejected by some, is strictly adhered to throughout. In the view of the writer it is a fundamental one, without which there is no adequate foundation for morals, æsthetics, or religion. From this general division other subordinate arrangements and classifications, some of which are peculiar to the present Work, naturally and easily flow. And thus the reader will find the whole subject opening itself connectedly and symmetrically, and in such a manner as to present, in its completed outline, not merely a disjointed congeries of philosophical facts, but the regularity and beauty of a philosophical system. The general division of the Sensibilities is into the Natural or Pathematic and Moral. Under the head of the MORAL SENSIBILITIES, I have examined the subject of conscience at some length and in various points of view, and cannot but hope that some of the difficulties which have hitherto attended it have been removed, and that the whole subject is placed, to some extent, in a consistent and satisfactory light. In many other respects, particularly in the classification of the Emotions and the Desires, and their relation to each other, and in some of the doctrines contained in the portion on the Will, the reader will find some important views, which I suppose he will not be likely to find, in the form in which they are now presented, in other philosophical works.

This work, in its original form, appeared a number of years since, and has passed through successive editions. It has been favourably received by the public; perhaps as much so as other philosophical works. Nevertheless, desirous of rendering it as perfect as possible, I have recently subjected it to re-examination and revision, and accordingly it appears now in a somewhat new form, in some respects condensed and in others enlarged, and with the results of the author's latest inquiries and emendations.

THOMAS C. UPHAM.

New York, Sept., 1869.

CONTENTS.

INTRODUCTION.

CHAP. I.—PRIMARY TRUTHS.

CHAP. II.—IMMATERIALITY OF THE MIND.

CHAP. III.—LAWS OF BELIEF.

CHAP. IV.—GENERAL CLASSIFICATION.

DIVISION FIRST.

THE INTELLECT OR UNDERSTANDING.

INTELLECTIVE OR INTELLECTUAL STATES OF THE MIND.

PART FIRST.

THE EXTERNAL OR SENSUOUS INTELLECT.

INTELLECTUAL STATES OF EXTERNAL ORIGIN.

CHAP. I.—ORIGIN OF KNOWLEDGE IN GENERAL.

CHAP. II.—THE POWER OF SENSATION.

CHAP. III.—PERCEPTION, OR THE PERCEPTIVE POWER.

CHAP. IV.—THE SENSES OF SMELL AND TASTE.

CHAP. V.—THE SENSE OF HEARING.

CHAP. VI.—THE SENSE OF TOUCH.

CHAP. VII.—THE SENSE OF SIGHT.

CHAP. VIII.—OF RELIANCE ON THE SENSES, AND IDEALISM.

CHAP. IX.—HABITS OF SENSATION AND PERCEPTION.

CHAP. X.—MUSCULAR HABITS.

CHAP. XI.—THE CONCEPTIVE POWER.—CONCEPTIONS.

CHAP. XII.—SIMPLICITY AND COMPLEXNESS OF MENTAL STATES.

CHAP. XIII.—ABSTRACTION.—THE ABSTRACTIVE POWER.

CHAP. XIV.—GENERAL ABSTRACT IDEAS.

CHAP. XV.—OF THE POWER OF ATTENTION.

DIVISION FIRST.

THE INTELLECT OR UNDERSTANDING.

INTELLECTIVE OR INTELLECTUAL STATES OF THE MIND.

PART SECOND.

THE INTERNAL OR SUPER-SENSUOUS INTELLECT.

INTELLECTUAL STATES OF INTERNAL ORIGIN.

CHAP. III.—CONSCIOUSNESS.

CHAP. IV.—RELATIVE SUGGESTION OR JUDGMENT.

CHAP. V.—ASSOCIATION. (I.) PRIMARY LAWS.

CHAP. VI.—ASSOCIATION. (II.) SECONDARY LAWS.

CHAP. VII.—CASUAL ASSOCIATIONS. (I.) INTELLECTUAL.

DIVISION FIRST.

THE INTELLECT OR UNDERSTANDING.

INTELLECTIVE OR INTELLECTUAL STATES OF THE MIND.

PART THIRD.

IMPERFECT AND DISORDERED INTELLECTUAL ACTION.

CHAP. I.—CONNEXION OF THE MIND AND BODY.

CHAP. II.—EXCITED CONCEPTIONS OR APPARITIONS.

CHAP. III.—PARTIAL INSANITY.

CHAP. IV.—TOTAL INSANITY OR DELIRIUM.

APPENDIX ON LANGUAGE.

CHAP. I.—NATURAL SIGNS.

CHAP. II.—ORAL SIGNS, OR SPEECH.

CHAP. III.—WRITTEN SIGNS.

CHAP. IV.—CHARACTERISTICS OF LANGUAGES.

INTRODUCTION.

CHAPTER I.

PRIMARY TRUTHS.

§ 1. Importance of preliminary statements in Mental Philosophy.

WE propose in a few introductory chapters to give some preparatory statements, which will aid, it is hoped, in making the way easier and clearer for what is to follow. The subjects of these introductory chapters, different in their nature, but agreeing in having certain common relations, are Primary Truths, the Immateriality of the mind, Laws of belief, and the general Classification into the intellect, sensibilities, and will, which is the basis of all the subsequent inquiries. The first chapter is on the subject of primary truths. It is often highly important, in the investigation of a department of science, to state, at the commencement of such investigation, and whether the investigation be of a specific or more general nature, what things are to be considered as preliminary and taken for granted, and what are not. If this precaution had always been observed, which, where there is any room for mistake or misapprehension, seems so reasonable, many useless disputes would have been avoided, and the paths to knowledge, too often unnecessarily perplexed and prolonged, would have been rendered more direct and easy.

It is impossible to proceed with inquiries in the science of MENTAL PHILOSOPHY, as it will be found to be in almost every other, without a proper understanding of those fundamental truths which are necessarily involved in what follows. And it will, accordingly, be the object of this chapter to endeavour to ascertain some of them.

§ 2. Nature of such preliminary statements.

Those preliminary principles which may be found necessary to be admitted as the antecedents and conditions of all subsequent inquiries, will be called, for the sake of distinction and convenience, PRIMARY TRUTHS. Other names have been given them, such as the "principles of common sense," and the "primordial elements of the human understanding;" but this is the designation, which especially commends itself to acceptance, both for its simplicity and its peculiar appropriateness to the subject. But passing from the name to the thing, the question arises, What are these truths? And in what manner do we know them?

According to the view of the subject taken by Buffier, a judicious French writer, who has made it a matter of special inquiry, and has written a treatise upon it, and whose views are approved and adopted in the subsequent investigations of Dugald Stewart, *they are such, and such only, as can neither be proved nor refuted by other propositions of greater perspicuity.* And this seems to be not only a succinct, but a satisfactory account of them, since, if there were other propositions into which they could be resolved, and by means of which they could be made clearer, then they could no longer be regarded as Primary, but those other clearer propositions would have that character.

But it may be asked again, Are there any propositions of this kind? Are there any so clear, that the great instrument of human reasoning cannot render them more perspicuous? Can there not be a complete action of the human mind in all its parts without the laying down of any antecedent truths whatever, as auxiliaries in its efforts after knowledge?— The answer to such questions, however formidable they may at first appear, is by no means difficult. In the first place, every man, who investigates at all, often experiences doubts in his inquiries. He accordingly endeavours to render such doubtful views clearer by argument. He goes on from step to step, from one proposition to another; but, unless he at last finds some truth utterly too clear to be rendered more so by reasoning, he must evidently proceed, adding deduction to deduction without end. His resting-place, accordingly, is in those truths which are elementary, and which illuminate the understanding by their own light, and not by a light let in from any other source.

In the second place, the nature of reasoning itself leads to the same view. It is well understood, that there can be no process of reasoning, without involving the fact of a successive perception of relations. But it is hardly necessary to say, that there can be no feeling or perception of relation where there is but one object of contemplation.—Something, therefore, must, from the nature of the case, be assumed as the antecedent, the basis, or necessary condition of every such process.

§ 3. Of the name or designation given them.

We propose to call those propositions, which are so elementary as to be susceptible neither of proof nor of refutation from other propositions of greater clearness, PRIMARY TRUTHS. Such propositions are termed, in the first place, TRUTHS, since they are forced upon us, as it were, by our very constitution. They exist as surely as the mind exists, where they have their birthplace; they as certainly and as strongly control the convictions of men, as the demonstrations of geometry; and not of one man merely, or any particular set of men, but of all mankind; for the few who pretend to reject them in speculation, constantly retract and deny such rejection of them in their practice. And yet they are not the deductions of reasoning, laboriously wrought out by proposition added to proposition; but rather the natural and necessary revelations and announcements of our mental nature.

With sufficient reason, also, are the propositions in

question called PRIMARY; because, as would seem to follow from the very definition of them, they are the propositions into which all reasoning ultimately resolves itself, and are necessarily involved and implied in the various investigations of which the mind is capable, whether they relate to the great subject before us or to others. As has been intimated, there cannot possibly be a process of reasoning, without some first principle or admitted truth from which to start.

§ 4. Primary truth of personal existence.

The PRIMARY TRUTH which we are naturally led to consider first, is that of the reality of our personal existence. The proposition *that we exist* is a sort of corner-stone to everything else; the foundation of our knowledge; the place and basis from which the edifice must rise.—Without undertaking to prove this fundamental truth, we nevertheless fully recognise and admit it. In other words, it is a proposition antecedent to reasoning, but which, notwithstanding, fully and perfectly secures our belief. If we reason on the subject of personal existence, there is necessarily implied an I, a personal self, by whom the process of reasoning is conducted, and which renders all such reasoning nugatory. If we doubt concerning our personal existence, there is the same implication, since there can be no doubting unless there is some one to doubt. And, of course, there can be no one to doubt where there is no personal existence. That we exist, therefore, is a truth of nature, and not of argumentation. Nothing which comes within the reach of the human mind is more clearly defined to its perception, more thoroughly controlling and operative, and more raised above cavils and skepticism, whether rational or irrational, than this.

§ 5. Occasions of the origin of the idea or belief of personal existence.

It remains, however, a distinct subject of inquiry, Under what circumstances this elementary belief arises?—And, in answer to this inquiry, we may say with abundant confidence, if it be not the earliest, it is at least among the earliest notions which the mind is capable of forming. A kind Providence has not conceded to a conviction, so essential to our whole mental history, a dilatory and late appearance. But that same Providence has given a place as well as a time, an occasion as well as a period of its formation; and although it may be impossible for us ever to ascertain that occasion with certainty, we may at least conjecture.

We look, therefore, in our meditations on this topic, at man in the commencement of his existence. We see him suddenly called forth from a state where there was neither form, nor knowledge, nor power, endowed with such capabilities of thought and action, both internal and external, as his Creator saw fit to give. Thus brought into being, and thus fitted up for his destined sphere, we will suppose that some external object is for the first time presented to the senses. The result of this is, that there is an impression made on the senses; and then at once there is a change in the mind, a new thought, a new feeling. Although, as already suggested, there is room for different conjectures here, there is much reason to believe that this is the true occasion of the origin of the belief in question. The first internal experience, the earliest thought or feeling, is immediately followed by the notion of personal or self-existence, as the subject of this new thought or feeling. And this idea or conviction of personal existence, which arises at this very early period, is continually suggested and confirmed in the course of the successive duties, enjoyments, and sufferings of life.

Such has commonly been supposed to be the origin of the belief in question. We may as well suppose it to come into being in connexion with the first act of the mind, as with any subsequent act, although with less distinctness and strength than afterward. But whether this account of the origin of the conviction of our personal existence be the true one or not, we may still hold to the fact of the belief itself as something beyond doubt. We may also regard it as necessarily resulting from our mental constitution, and as wholly inseparable from our being.

§ 6. Primary truth of personal identity.

The second of those preliminary truths which we term primary is the proposition of our Personal Identity.—If the consideration of our personal existence naturally comes first in the order of time, that of the truth now before us is not secondary in point of importance. We can not dispense with either without unsettling the grounds of inquiry and belief, and barring the access to all knowledge whatever.

IDENTITY is synonymous with sameness. And both terms, when we consider them as standing for mental states in distinction from the objects or things which the mental states represent, are the names of simple states of the mind. Although, therefore, the meaning of the term Identity is as clear as that of other terms standing for simple ideas, and everybody is supposed to understand it, it is not susceptible of definition. The term is applied to various objects, and, among others, to men.—The word PERSONAL implies Self, and personal identity is, therefore, the identity of ourselves. But the term *self* is complex, embracing both mind and matter, and hence we are led to consider the distinct notions of mental and bodily identity.

I. MENTAL IDENTITY.—By this phrase we express the continuance and oneness of the thinking principle merely. The soul of man is truly a unit. It is not, like matter, separable into parts. It may bring, from time to time, new susceptibilities into action; but its essence is unchangeable. That which constitutes it a thinking and sentient principle, in distinction from that which is unthinking and insentient, never deserts it, never ceases to exist, never becomes other than what it originally was.

II. BODILY IDENTITY.—By these expressions we mean the sameness of the bodily shape and organization. This is the only meaning we can attach to them, since the materials which compose our bodily systems are constantly changing. The body is not a unit in the same sense the soul is. It was a saying of Seneca, that no man bathes twice in the same river; and still we call it the same, although the water within its banks is constantly passing away. And in like manner we ascribe identity to the human body, although it is subject to constant changes; meaning by the expressions, as just remarked, merely the sameness of shape and organization.

III. PERSONAL IDENTITY.—This form of expression is more general, or rather more complex and comprehensive, than either of those which have been mentioned. It has reference to both mind and matter, as we find them combined together in that complex existence which we term man or person. It is equivalent to what is conveyed by the two phrases of mental identity and bodily identity. But it is evident we cannot easily separate the two when speaking of men. And accordingly, when it is said that any one is conscious of, knows, or has a certainty of his personal identity, it is meant to be asserted that he is conscious of having formerly possessed the powers of an organized, animated, and rational being, and that he still possesses those powers. He knows that he is a human being now, and that he was a human being yesterday, or last week, or last year.—There is no mystery in this. It is so plain, no one is likely to misunderstand it, although we admit our inability to give a definition of identity.

§ 7. Reasons for regarding this a primary truth.

If personal identity be a primary truth, it is antecedent to argument, and is independent of it.—What grounds are there, then, for regarding it as such?

In the FIRST place, the mere fact that it is constantly implied in those conclusions which we form in respect to the future from the past, and universally in our daily actions, is of itself a decisive reason for reckoning it among the original and essential intimations of the human intellect. On any other hypothesis we are quite unable to account for that practical recognition of it in the pursuits of men, which is at once so early, so evident, and so universal.

The farmer, for instance, who looks abroad on his cultivated fields, knows that he is the same person who, twenty years before, entered the forest with an axe on his shoulder, and felled the first tree. The aged soldier, who recounts at his fireside the battles of his youth, never once doubts that he was himself the witness of those sanguinary scenes which he delights to relate. It is altogether useless to attempt either to disprove or to confirm to them a proposition which they believe and know, not from the testimony of others or from reasoning, but from the interior and authoritative suggestion of their very nature; and which, it is sufficiently evident, can never be eradicated from their belief and knowledge until that nature is changed.

A SECOND circumstance in favor of regarding the notion of personal identity as an admitted or primary truth, is, that men cannot prove it by argument if they would; and, if they do not take it for granted, must forever be without it. The propriety of this remark will appear on examination.—There evidently can be no argument, properly so called, unless there is a succession of distinct propositions. From such a succession of propositions, no conclusion can be drawn by any one, unless he is willing to trust to the evidence of memory. But memory involves a notion of the time past; and whoever admits that he has the power of memory, in however small a degree, virtually admits that he has existed the same at some former period as at present.

The considerations which we have now particularly in view, and which are greatly worthy of attention in connexion with the principle under examination, may, with a little variation of terms, be stated thus.

Remembrance, without the admission of our personal identity, is clearly an impossibility. But there can be no process of reasoning without memory. This is evident, because arguments are made up of propositions which are successive to each other, not only in order, but in point of time. It follows, then, that there can be no argument whatever, or on any subject, without the admission of our identity, as a point from which to start. What, then, will it avail to attempt to reason either for or against the views which are here maintained, since, in every argument which is employed, there is necessarily an admission of the very thing which is the subject of inquiry?

§ 8. There are original and authoritative grounds of belief.

Supposing men actually to exist, and to be conscious of the continuance and sameness of their existence, we are next to enter into the interior of their constitution, and to inquire after such elements of intelligence and action as are to be found there. The next proposition, therefore, which is to be laid down as fundamental and as preliminary to all reasoning is, that there are in men CERTAIN ORIGINAL AND AUTHORITATIVE GROUNDS OF BELIEF.

Nothing is better known than that there is a certain state of the mind which is expressed by the term BELIEF. As we find all men acting in reference to it, it is not necessary to enter into any verbal explanation. Nor would it be possible by such explanation to increase the clearness of that notion which every one is already supposed to entertain.—Of this belief, we take it for granted, and hold it to be in the strictest sense true, that there are original and authoritative grounds or sources; meaning by the term *original* that these grounds or sources are involved in the nature of the mind itself, and meaning by the term *authoritative* that this belief is not a mere matter of chance or choice, but naturally and necessarily results from our mental constitution, and is binding upon us.

Sometimes we can trace the state of the mind which we term belief, to an affection of the senses, sometimes to consciousness, sometimes to memory, and at others to human testimony. In all these cases, however, the explanation which we attempt to give of the origin of belief, is limited to a statement of the circumstances in which the belief arises. But the fact that belief arises under these circumstances, is ultimate, is a primary law; and, being such, it no more admits of explanation than does the mere feeling itself.

Many writers have clearly seen and defended the necessity of the assumption which has now been made. Mr. Stewart, among others, has expressed the opinion (Hist. Disser., pt. i., § ii.), that there is involved, in every appeal to the intellectual powers in proof of their own credibility, the sophism of reasoning in a circle or PETITIO PRINCIPII; and expressly adds, that, unless this credibility be assumed as unquestionable, the further exercise of human reasoning is altogether nugatory.—Not less decisive is the language of Sir James Mackintosh on this subject (Ethical Philosophy, sect. vi.): "Universal skepticism involves a contradiction in terms. *It is a belief that there can be no belief.* It is an attempt of the mind to act without its structure, and by other laws than those to which its nature has subjected its operations. To reason without assenting to the principles on which reasoning is founded, is not unlike an effort to feel without nerves or to move without muscles. *No man can be allowed to be an opponent in reasoning who does not set out with admitting all the principles, without the admission of which it is impossible to reason.* It is, indeed, a puerile, nay, in the eye of wisdom, a childish play, to attempt either to establish or to confute principles by argument, which every step of that argument must presuppose. The only difference between the two cases is, that he who tries to prove them can do so only by first taking them for granted; and that he who attempts to impugn them falls at the very first step into a contradiction from which he never can rise."

§ 9. Primary truths having relation to the reasoning power.

Man may be sure of the fact of his existence and of its permanency; he may be possessed of grounds of belief to a certain extent, such as have been mentioned; and still we may suppose him incapable of reasoning. His knowledge would be greatly limited, it is true, without that noble faculty, but he would know something; his consciousness would teach him his own existence; his senses convey to him intimations of external origin; the testimony of others furnish various facts that had come within their observation. But, happily, man is not limited to the scanty knowledge which would come in by these sources alone; he can compare and combine, as well as perceive and experience; and, by means of the propositions thus combined and compared together, is enabled to deduce conclusions.

But there is this worthy of notice, that the reasoning power, although it exists in man, and is a source of belief and a foundation of knowledge, is necessarily built upon principles which are either known or assumed.—This is seen in the most common and ordinary cases of the exercise of this susceptibility. And it will be found also on examination, that one assumption may be resolved into another, and again into another, until we arrive at certain ultimate truths which are at the foundation of all reasoning whatever. It is important, therefore, to inquire, what general assumptions, having particular reference to the reasoning power, and absolutely essential to its action, are to be made. And these will be found to be two in number; at least there are two only which are particularly worthy of notice: one having special relation to the past, and the other to the future.

§ 10. No beginning or change of existence without a cause.

The one which has a relation to the past, and is the foundation of all reasonings, having a reference to any period antecedent to the present moment, may be stated as follows: *that there is no beginning or change of existence without a cause.*—This principle, like others which have been mentioned, we may well suppose to be universally admitted. When any new event takes place, men at once inquire the cause; as if it could not possibly have happened without some effective or preparative antecedent.

And such being the general and unwavering reception of the principle before us, it would seem to follow clearly that there are grounds for it in the human constitution. A reliance on any principle whatever, so firm and general as is here exhibited, is not likely to be accidental. And when we inquire what these grounds are, we shall not fail to come to the conclusion, that the proposition in question is supported by an original intimation or feeling which is utterly inseparable from our mental nature, and which is made known to us by consciousness alone.—Although the feeling of belief, which is implied in the proposition that there is no beginning or change of existence without a cause, is an original one, directly resulting from our nature, still it is in our power to give some account of the circumstances in which it arises.

§ 11. Occasions of the origin of the primary truth of effects and causes.

The mind embraces the elementary truth which we are considering at a very early period. Looking round upon nature, which we are led to do more or less from the commencement of our being, we find everything in motion. Things which had no existence are raised into life; and new forms are imparted to what existed before. The human mind, which is essentially active and curious, constantly contemplates the various phenomena which come under its notice; observing not only the events and appearances themselves, but their order in point of time, their succession. And it is led in this way to form the belief (not by deduction, but from its own active nature), that every new existence and every change of existence are preceded by something, without which they could not have happened.

Undoubtedly the belief, as in many other cases, is comparatively weak at first, but it rapidly acquires unalterable growth and strength; so much so that the mind applies it without hesitation to every act, to every event, and to every finite being. And thus a foundation is laid for numberless conclusions, having a relation to whatever has happened in time past. It is true that the verbal proposition, by which our belief in this case is expressed, is not always, nor even generally, brought forward and stated in our reasonings on the past, but it is always implied.

This primary truth is an exceedingly important one. By its aid the human mind retains a control over the ages that are gone, and subordinates them to its own purposes. It is susceptible, in particular, of a moral and religious application. Let this great principle be given us, and we are able to track the succession of sequences upward, advancing from one step to another, until we find all things meeting together in one self-existent and unchangeable head and fountain of being. But there it stops. The principle will not apply to God, since He differs from everything else which is the object of thought, in being an existence equally without change and without beginning.

§ 12. Matter and mind have uniform and fixed laws.

It is necessary to assume also, particularly in connexion with the reasoning power, that matter and mind have uniform and permanent laws.

This assumption, as well as the preceding, is accordant with the common belief of mankind. All men believe that the setting sun will rise again at the appointed hour, that the decaying plants of autumn will revive in spring, that the tides of ocean will continue to heave as in times past, and the streams and rivers to flow in their courses. If they doubted, they would not live and act as they are now seen to do.

This belief in the uniformity and permanency of the laws of nature does not arise at once; but has its birth at first in some particular instance, then in others, till it becomes of universal application. In the first instance, the feeling in question, which we express in various ways by the terms anticipation, faith, expectation, belief, and the like, is weak and vacillating; but it gradually acquires strength and distinctness. And yet this feeling, so important in its applications, is the pure work of nature; it is not *taught* men, in the strict sense of that term, but is produced within them; the necessary and infallible product and growth of our mental being; a sort of inalienable gift of the Almighty to every man, woman, and child; arising in the soul with as much certainty and as little mystery as the notions, expressed by the words power, duration, right, wrong, truth, or other elementary states of the mind. It is true, it is an expectation or belief, directed to a particular object, and, therefore, is not easily susceptible of being expressed by a single term, as in the case of the ideas just referred to; but the circumstance of its being expressed by a circumlocution does not render the feeling less distinct or real than others.—As, therefore, the strong faith, which men entertain in the continuance of the laws of creation, is the natural and decisive offspring of that mental constitution which God has given us, there is good ground for assuming the truth of that to which this faith relates, and to regard it as a principle in future inquiries, that matter and mind are governed by uniform laws.

§ 13. This primary truth not founded on reasoning.

But perhaps it is objected, that we can arrive at the great truth under consideration without assuming it as something ultimate, as something resulting from our constitution; and that nothing more is wanting in order to arrive at it than a train of reasoning.—The sun, it is said, rose to-day, therefore he will rise to-morrow: Food nourished me to-day, therefore it will do the same to-morrow: The fire burned me once, therefore it will again.

But it demands no uncommon sagacity to perceive

that something is here wanting, and that a link in the chain of thought must be supplied in order to make it cohere. The mere naked fact that the sun rose to-day, without anything else being connected with it, affords not the least ground for the inference that it will rise again; and the same may be said of all similar instances. Now the link which is wanting in order to bind together the beginning and the end in such arguments as have been referred to, is the precise assumption which has been made, and which is held to be as reasonable as it is necessary, because it is founded on an acknowledged, universal, and elementary feeling of our nature. And we may here affirm with perfect confidence, that, without making this assumption, the power of reasoning cannot deduce a single general inference, cannot arrive at so much as one general conclusion, either in matter or mind, which has relation to the future. But the moment we make the assumption, a vast foundation of knowledge is laid. Grant that nature is uniform in her laws; then give us the fact that food nourished us to-day, or that the sun rose to-day, or any other fact of the kind, and it follows, with readiness and certainty, that what has once been will be again.—So that we must regard the principle of the permanency and uniformity of the laws of nature as something antecedent to reasoning, and not subsequent to it; a principle authorized and sustained by an ultimate, and not by any secondary action of the mind.

This subject will be better understood in connexion with the chapter on the Intuitional or Suggestional Power, and with what will be said in a future chapter on the subject of Assumptions in Reasoning.

CHAPTER II.

IMMATERIALITY OF THE MIND.

§ 14. On the meaning of the terms material and immaterial.

Another of those topics which may be deemed introductory and auxiliary to the main subject, is the question of the materiality or immateriality of the soul. In entering upon this inquiry, which is obviously too important to be altogether dispensed with, it will be necessary, in the first place, to explain the meaning of the leading terms.—The words MATERIAL and IMMATERIAL are relative, being founded on the observation of the presence or of the absence of certain qualities.—Why do we call a piece of wood, or of iron, material? It is because we notice in them certain qualities, such as extension, divisibility, impenetrability, and colour. And, in whatever other bodies we observe the presence of these qualities, we there apply the term. The term IMMATERIAL, therefore, by the established use of the language and its own nature, it being in its etymology the opposite of the other, can be applied only in those cases where these qualities are not found.

Hence we assert the mind to be immaterial, because, in all our knowledge of it, we have noticed an utter absence (or, perhaps, more properly, have always failed to detect the presence) of those qualities which are acknowledged to be the ground of the application of the opposite epithet. The soul undoubtedly has its qualities or properties, but not those which have been spoken of. Whatever we have been conscious of, and have observed within us, our thought, our feeling, remembrance, and passion, are evidently and utterly diverse from what is understood to be included under the term materiality.

Such is the origin of these two terms, and the

ground of the distinction between them. And, thus explained, they can hardly fail to be understood. We may, therefore, now proceed to state the evidence of the actual existence of that distinction between mind and matter which is obviously implied in every application of them. In other words, we are to attempt to show that the soul is not matter, and that thought and feeling are not the result of material organization.

§ 15. Difference between mind and matter shown from language.

Is it a fact that the being or existence called the SOUL is distinct and different from that existence which we call MATTER?—It is not unusual, in writings on the philosophy of the mind, to refer to the structure of languages in order to illustrate our mental nature; and, in respect to the question now before us, we are warranted in saying, in the first place, that Language, in general, is one proof of such distinction. In the preceding section we have seen the use of certain terms in our own language, and the grounds of it. All other languages, as well as our own, have names and epithets distinctly expressive of the two existences in question. This circumstance, when we consider that the dialects of men are only their thoughts and feelings imbodied, as it were, may be regarded as a decisive proof that the great body of mankind believe in both, and, of course, believe in a well-founded distinction between them.

That such is the belief of men generally, as clearly evinced by the structure of languages and in various other ways, will not, probably, be denied. It is a matter too evident to permit us to anticipate a denial. When, therefore, we take into view that there are grounds of belief fixed deeply and originally in our constitution, and that, in their general operation, they must be expected to lead to truth and not to error, we are unable to harbour the supposition, that men are deceived and led astray in this opinion; that they so generally and almost universally believe in the existence of what, in point of fact, does not exist.

§ 16. Their different nature shown by their respective properties.

Again, the distinction between mind and matter is shown by the difference in the qualities and properties which men agree in ascribing to them respectively.—The properties of matter are extension, hardness, figure, solidity, divisibility, and the like. The attributes of mind are thought, feeling, volition, reasoning, the passions. The phenomena exhibited by matter and mind are not only different in their own nature, but are addressed, considered as objects of perception, to different parts of our constitution. We obtain a knowledge of material properties, so far as it is direct and immediate, by means of the senses; but all our direct knowledge of the nature of the mental phenomena is acquired by consciousness.

Every one knows that the phenomena in question are not identical. There is no sameness or similitude, for instance, in what we express by the terms hardness and desire, solidity and hatred, divisibility and belief, extension and imagination. But let us look more at particulars. All matter is divisible. The smallest particle has its top and bottom, its right and left side, and may be regarded as susceptible of measurement. But what does consciousness testify in regard to the mental phenomena? Does it give us the least intimation that they are mechanically divisible? Is any man ever conscious of a half, quarter, or third of a hope, joy, or sorrow, actually cut asunder and set off from the remaining half, two thirds, or three quarters of such hope, joy, or sorrow? It is not only true that no one has had such experience, but no one ever conceives such experience possible. And as to extension, are we ever conscious of a thought, feeling, or volition as having length and breadth; as being, for instance, an inch in length and half an inch in breadth? There is nothing of the kind. Consciousness never gave, and it is not too much to say that it never will give, any such information. The properties or attributes of matter and mind, therefore, are entirely different. And as all persons hold it to be unphilosophical to ascribe attributes so different to the same subject, we conclude the subjects of them are not the same. And accordingly, we call the subject of one class of phenomena Mind, and that of the other Matter.

§ 17. The soul's immateriality indicated by the feeling of identity.

There is another somewhat striking consideration which may aid in evincing the immateriality of the soul. It is well known that the materials of which the human body is composed are constantly changing. The whole bodily system repeatedly undergoes, in the course of the ordinary term of man's life, a complete renovation; and yet we possess, during the whole of this period, and amid these utter changes of the bodily part, a consciousness of the permanency as well as of the unity of the mind. "This fact," remarks Mr. Stewart, "is surely not a little favourable to the supposition of mind being a principle essentially distinct from matter, and capable of existing when its connexion with the body is dissolved."

Truly, if the soul, like the body, were made up of particles of matter, and the particles were in this case, as in the other, always changing, we should be continually roving, as an old writer expresses it, and sliding away from ourselves, and should soon forget what we once were. The new soul, that entered into the same place, would not necessarily enter into the possession of the feelings, consciousness, and knowledge of that which had gone. And hence we rightly infer, from an identity in these respects, the identity or continued existence of the subject to which such feelings, consciousness, and knowledge belong. And as there is not a like identity or continued existence of the material part, we may infer, again, that the soul is distinct from matter.

§ 18. The material doctrine makes man a machine.

The doctrine that thought is the result of material organization, and that the soul is not distinct from the body, is liable, also, to this no small objection: that it makes the soul truly and literally a machine. If what we term mind be in truth matter, it is, of course, under the same influences as matter. But matter, in all its movements and combinations, is known to be subject to a strict and inflexible direction, the origin of which direction is exterior to itself. The material universe is truly an automaton, experiencing through all time the same series of motions, in obedience to some high and authoritative intelligence; and is so entirely subject to fixed laws, that we can express in mathematical formulas not only the state of large bodies, but of a drop of water or of a ray of light; estimating minutely extension and quantity, force, velocity, and resistance.

It is not thus with the human mind. That the mind has its laws is true; but it knows what those laws are; whereas matter does not. This makes a great difference. Matter yields a blind and unconscious obedience; but the mind is able to exercise a foresight; to place itself in new situations; to subject itself to new influences; to surround itself with new motives, and thus control, in a measure, its own laws. In a word, mind is free; we have the best evidence of it, that of our own consciousness. But matter, as we learn from all our observations of it, may justly be characterized as a slave. It does not turn to the right or left; it does not do this or that, as it chooses; it possesses no self-determining and self-moving element; but, the subject of an overpowering allotment, it is borne onward to the appointed mark by an inflexible destiny.—If these views be correct, we see here a new reason for not confounding and identifying these two existences.

§ 19. No exact correspondence between the mental and bodily state.

The train of thought in the last section naturally leads us to remark further, that there is an absence of that precise correspondence between the mental and bodily state which would evidently follow from the admission of materialism. Those who make thought and feeling the result of material organization, commonly locate that organization in the brain. It is there the great mental exercises, in the phraseology of materialists, are secreted, or are developed, or are brought out in some other mysterious way, by means of a purely physical combination and action. Hence, such is the fixed and unalterable nature of matter and its results, if the brain be destroyed, the soul must be destroyed also; if the brain be injured, the soul is proportionally injured; if the material action be disturbed, there must be an exactly corresponding disturbance of the mental action. The state of the mind, on a fair interpretation of this doctrine, is not less dependent on that of the body than the complicated motions of the planetary system are on the law of gravitation. But this view, whether we assign the residence of the soul to the brain or to any other part of the bodily system, does not appear to be accordant with fact. It is not only far from being approved and borne out, but it is directly contradicted by well-attested experience in a multitude of cases.

§ 20. Evidence of this want of exact correspondence.

We are desirous not to be misapprehended here. We readily grant that the mind, in our present state of existence, has a connexion with the physical system, and particularly with the brain. It is, moreover, obviously a natural consequence of this, that, when the body is injured, the mental power and action are in some degree affected; and this we find to be agreeable to the facts that come within our observation. But it is to be particularly noticed, that the results are just such as might be expected from a mere connexion of being; and are evidently *not* such as might be anticipated from an identity of being.

In the latter case, the material part could never be affected, whether for good or evil, without a result precisely corresponding in the mind. But, in point of fact, this is not the case. The body is not unfrequently injured when the mind is not so; and, on the other hand, the soul seems to be almost entirely prostrated when the body is in a sound and active state. How many persons have been mutilated in battle, in every possible way short of an utter destruction of animal life, and yet have discovered at such times a more than common greatness of mental power! How often, when the body is not only partially weakened, but is resolving, at the hour of death, into its original elements, and possesses not a single capability entire, the mind, remaining in undiminished strength, puts forth the energy and beauty of past days!

We are now speaking of injuries to our corporeal part, and of bodily debility in general; but if we look to the brain in particular, which is more intimately connected with the mental action than any other part of the bodily system, we shall find ourselves fully warranted in an extension of these views there. According to the system of the materialists, the soul does not merely exist and act in connexion with the body, but is identical with it. And not only this, they go further, and locate this identity in the brain, making the soul and the brain not merely connected together, but identically the same thing. But the objection to their views, which, in its general form, has already been made, exists here in full strength. If that organization, which they hold to result in thought and feeling, be identical with the brain, it must be diffused through the whole of that organ, or limited to some particular part. But it appears, from an extensive collection of well-authenticated facts, that every part of the brain has been injured, and almost every part absolutely removed, but without permanently affecting the mental powers, which is absolutely impossible if there be an identity of the two things. "Every part of that structure," says Dr. Ferriar, in a learned Memoir, "has been deeply injured or totally destroyed, without impeding or changing any part of the process of thought." He remarks again, after bringing forward a considerable number of well-authenticated facts, as follows: "On reviewing the whole of this evidence, I am disposed to conclude, that, as no part of the brain appears essentially necessary to the existence of the intellectual faculties, and as the whole of its visible structure has been materially changed without affecting the exercise of those faculties, something more than the discernible organization must be requisite to produce the phenomena of thinking."*

§ 21. Comparative state of the mind and body in dreaming.

The views of the two preceding sections receive some confirmation from the comparative state of the mind and body in dreaming.—In sound sleep, the senses sink into a state of utter and unconscious sluggishness; the inlet to everything external, as far as we can judge, is shut up; the muscles become powerless, and everything in the body has the appearance of death. It is true, the soul appears, for the most part, to be fallen into a like state of imbecility; but this is not the case in its dreams, which are known to take up no small portion of the hours of sleep. At such times it does not appear to stand in need of the same repose with the body; otherwise it would seek and possess it. On the contrary, when the powers of the body are utterly suspended, the soul is often exceedingly on the alert; it rapidly passes from subject to subject, attended sometimes with sad and sometimes with raised and joyful affections.

But this is not all: often, in the hours of sleep, the intellect exhibits an increased invention, a quickened and more exalted energy in all its powers. Many writers have remarked, that the conclusions of abstruse investigations have been suggested to them at such times. Not a few would conclude themselves persons of genius, if they could pronounce the arguments and the harangues in the awakened soberness of the morning, which they had framed in the visions of the night. Does not this state of things seem to indicate that there is a natural and fundamental dis-

* Memoirs of the Manchester Philos. Society, vol. iv.

tinction between the mental and the material part of man?

§ 22. The great works of genius an evidence of immateriality.

Now let us look at what mind, in man's awakened moments, is able to accomplish, and see if the results of its action, in its higher and nobler exercises, are such as we commonly expect from or ascribe to matter.—Look first at the kindred powers of memory and imagination. I am at this moment sitting in my chair, with a book and paper before me, and a pen in my hand. But my memory is aroused, my imagination takes wing, and my soul suddenly finds itself (at least considered in reference to its operations) in a far-distant place. I see distinctly before me the trees which shaded me, and the hills where I wandered in my childhood. The same waters flow before me, the same bright sun shines in the heavens; I see around me a multitude of familiar faces, and embrace, with all the vividness of early affections, my old companions. In this excursion of the soul, how many recollections have been revived! How many feelings have been restored! What pictures of natural and social beauty have been presented to the intellectual sight! But do we commonly, or can we, with any show of reason, ascribe this wonderful power, which transfers us in a moment to the distant and the past, to a mere mass of matter? I think not.

Look, again, at the powers of judgment and reasoning, and of imagination in its greater and more permanent efforts. In doing this, we are to keep in mind that those things which cannot be known directly and in their own essence, are known for the most part simply by their *results*. And in accordance with this view, which leads us to look from results to causes, I ask myself, What was it that originated and perfected the demonstrations of Euclid? Where was the authorship of the political institutions of Solon and Lycurgus, of modern England and France, and of that still greater effort of political wisdom, the American

Constitution? What was it that infused the breath of immortality into the Iliad and Odyssey? What was it that gave birth to the wonderful inventions and combinations of the Jerusalem Delivered, the Fairy Queen, and the Paradise Lost? Where shall we look for the origin of the Philippics of the Ancients, or, in later times, of the speeches of Fox and of the orations of Bossuet?

In these, and in all other cases where human genius has achieved its higher triumphs, we submit it to any one to say, whether mankind generally would be likely to ascribe their origin to a mere lump of matter? When men cast their eyes upon a piece of matter, they look simply for material herbage and flower, leaves and fruit; for something which is addressed, and addressed exclusively, to the taste and touch, the sight and smell; and not for political axioms and mathematical demonstrations, for flights of fancy and flashes of eloquence. We venture to assert, that the man who gives himself up to the influence of the vast conceptions imbodied in the works and institutions of human genius, will find it as difficult to attribute them to a purely material cause, as it is to adopt the theory of the atheist, and ascribe the beautiful and complicated machinery of the universe to a fortuitous concurrence of atoms.

§ 23. The doctrine of materiality inconsistent with future existence.

With the subject of the immaterial nature of the soul, that of its immortality is closely connected. It is true, the immortal existence of the soul does not follow with absolute certainty from the mere fact of its immateriality; but it is, at least, rendered in some degree probable. Certainly we have no direct evidence of the discontinuance of the soul's existence at death as we have of that of the body. What takes place at death is only a removal of the soul's action from our notice, but not, as far as we know, a cessation and utter extinction of it. The supposition, therefore, is a reasonable one, that the soul will continue to exist, merely because it exists at present, inasmuch as its immaterial nature does not require the suspension of its existence at death, and as we have no direct evidence of such an event.—Death, in the language of Mr. Stewart, only lifts up the veil which conceals from our eyes the invisible world. It annihilates the material universe to our senses, and prepares our minds for some new and unknown state of being.

But the opposite doctrine, that which asserts the materiality of the soul, so far from furnishing a presumption in favor of our future existence, seems to render immortality impossible. Those, who hold that thought and feeling are in some way the direct and positive result of material organization, are understood to admit that the soul (or, rather, what they speak of as the soul) dies with the body; and certainly they would be very inconsistent with themselves if they did not do so. Where, then, is that immortality, of which the light of nature as well as Revelation assures us?—We are aware of what the materialist will say here. We understand him to assert that a *new* soul will be created after death, either at the final resurrection or at some antecedent period, which will take the place in all respects of the old one which perished with the body. But there is an insuperable difficulty here. It is inconceivable (we assert it with entire confidence) that a soul, created subsequently in time, should be conscious of, or, rather, should recognise, mental operations and affections *as its own*, which operations and affections pertained, in point of fact, to another soul. Such a case would constitute an *origination* rather than a continuance of existence; it would not be *our* immortality, but that of another; the chain connecting the present with the future would be broken; and we, who are destined, on the system of materialism, to perish with the body, could not by any possibility participate in that future existence which is raised up to take the place of the present. Would there be any propriety or justice in bringing such new-created soul before the judgment-seat of the Supreme Being in reference to crimes or to virtues which in fact pertained to another soul! It is evident, since such a soul could not be conscious of or recognise a previous existence, simply because such existence had never taken place, it would not be a suitable object of praise and blame, reward and punishment, in reference to deeds done in the present life. So that it seems to be an inevitable conclusion, that the souls which are destined to come under the Divine adjudication, in other words which are made amenable to God's eternal law, which in its principles is the same in the future life as the present, must remain *permanent*, whatever may become of the body, until the fullness of the final sentence shall be passed upon them. But if the soul is material and dies with the body, then it is not permanent, and cannot be so. The immateriality of the soul, therefore, on the supposition of the body's being dissolved and destroyed at death, becomes the basis of its immortality. If the doctrine of immateriality falls, then that of immortality and of a future retribution falls with it.—All arguments, therefore, which go to sustain the soul's immortality and its liability to future judgment, indirectly support the doctrine of its immateriality. We add nothing further, excepting the single remark, that the distinction between the body and soul is either implied or asserted in various passages of the Scriptures; as, for instance, when we are directed "not to fear them which kill the body, but are not able to kill the soul."

CHAPTER III.

LAWS OF BELIEF.

§ 24. Of belief, its degrees, and its sources.

MAN is so constituted that, under certain circumstances, he naturally and necessarily believes, and has knowledge. As that state of mind which we term BELIEF is simple, and, consequently, undefinable, we have therefore a knowledge of it, not by verbal definition, but wholly by our own internal reflection or consciousness. Belief is always the same in kind or nature; but it admits of different degrees. We ascertain the existence of these differences of strength, which we express by various terms, such as presumption, probability, high probability, and certainty, by means of that same internal consciousness which assures us of the existence of the mere feeling itself.

In the chapter on Primary Truths, we had occasion to assert it as an indisputable principle, *that there are in men certain original and authoritative grounds of belief.* This is an important doctrine in mental philosophy, and one which is always to be kept in mind. It is perhaps proper, before we proceed further, to state some of those original principles by which our belief is thus naturally controlled.

§ 25. Of intuition, consciousness, and the senses, as grounds of belief.

The most marked and prominent of those grounds or laws of belief, which are understood to be original and ultimate in the mental constitution, are Suggestion or Intuition, Consciousness, the Senses, Memory, Testimony, Relative Suggestion, and Reasoning.

I.—Suggestion or Intuition. By means of this cognitive power we have a knowledge of certain elementary notions, such as the abstract conceptions of existence, mind, self-existence or self, personal identity, succession, duration, space, unity, number, power, right, wrong, and some others. All men possess these notions, all understand them; but if they are asked in what way they come to a knowledge of them, they can only say that, in virtue of the constitution of the mind itself, they are naturally and necessarily suggested.—The mind is so constituted, that they naturally and necessarily flow forth from it, and thus furnish the foundations of belief and knowledge.

II.—Consciousness. By means of that internal reflection which is denominated consciousness, we have a knowledge of our mental states, of the various perceptions, affections, and decisions of the mind. In regard to all such objects of knowledge, we are obliged to rest, ultimately, upon consciousness. The belief from this source is in the highest degree authoritative and decisive. It is impossible for us to disbelieve that the mind experiences certain sensations, or puts forth certain operations, whenever, in point of fact, that is the case; or to believe them to be otherwise than they in fact are.

III.—THE SENSES. The states of mind to which operations upon or affections of our senses give rise, are also, by our very constitution, the occasions or grounds of belief. By means of the senses, we have a knowledge, in particular, of the external, material world; of trees, and fields, and waters; of the sounds of the elements and the music of birds; of the sun, and moon, and stars, and all the various and beautiful forms of the tangible and visible creation. Men, prompted by the suggestions of their own mental nature, universally rely upon the senses in respect to everything which comes within their appropriate sphere. When one man states to another a report of what has happened at some time, the hearer yields to him a greater or less degree of credence, according to the circumstances. But if the narrator asserts that he saw or heard it with his own eyes or ears, that the affair actually came under the cognizance of his own senses, everybody deems such a statement satisfactory. What better evidence, they say, than that of his senses!

§ 26. Memory and Testimony considered as sources of belief.

IV.—Another original ground or law of belief is the Memory. So far as we are confident, or, rather, have no particular reason to doubt, that the original sensations and perceptions in any given case are correctly reported in the remembrance, the latter controls our belief and actions not less than those antecedent states of mind on which it is founded. "The evidence of memory," says Dr. Beattie, "commands our belief as effectually as the evidence of sense. I cannot possibly doubt, with regard to any of my transactions of yesterday which I now remember, whether I performed them or not. That I dined to-day, and was in bed last night, is as certain to me as that I at present see the colour of this paper. If we had no memory, knowledge and experience would be impossible; and if we had any tendency to distrust our memory, knowledge and experience would be of as little use in directing our conduct and sentiments as our dreams now are. Sometimes we doubt whether, in a particular case, we exert memory or imagination; and our belief is suspended accordingly: but no sooner do we become conscious that we *remember*, than conviction instantly takes place; we say, I am certain it was so, for I now remember I was an eye-witness."*

There remains, however, another inquiry: What is the origin of this confident reliance? And the reply here is, as in many other cases, It is our nature, our mental constitution; the will and ordinance of the Being who created us. Whatever may be said on the subject, there must be, and there are, certain original grounds, certain fundamental laws of belief, which, in every analysis of our knowledge, are fixed and permanent boundaries, beyond which we cannot proceed. And reliance on memory is one of them.

V.—Human Testimony. By this is commonly meant the report of men concerning what has fallen under their personal observation. And this forms another ground of belief. As to the fact that men readily receive the testimony of their fellow-beings, and that such testimony influences their belief and conduct, it cannot be denied. They thus universally yield credence to the statements of each other, unless something comes to their knowledge unfavourable to the credibility of the narrator, because it is natural or constitutional to do so. In other words, the very nature of our mental constitution, independently of the suggestions of reason and experience, leads us to be-

* Beattie's Essay on Truth, pt. i., ch. ii., § 4.

lieve what men assert. We are so constituted, that the very first sound of the human voice which reaches us calls into action a disposition on our part to admit the truth of whatever intelligence it conveys.—In support of this view (which, it may be remarked, has in its favour the weighty names of Reid and Campbell among others), reference may properly be made to what we observe in children. In the earliest period of life, as soon as the first gleams of intelligence are visible, they look with hope and fondness to those who support them; there seems to be no doubt, no suspicion, no want of confidence. This strong reliance discovers itself from time to time, as they advance towards youth; and, in the whole of the early part of our existence, is so distinct, strong, and operative, that men have given to it a specific name, in order to distinguish it from the more chastened credence of riper years. We speak of the caution and the convictions of manhood, and of the simplicity and CREDULITY of children.

§ 27. Objection to reliance on testimony.

It may be objected to the doctrine of reliance on human testimony, that we are liable to be led into mistakes by the statements of our fellow-men. This objection merits some attention; and the answer to it may be summed up in two particulars.—FIRST. The proportion of cases of deception, compared with those where we are not deceived, is very small. We admit that we may be disappointed and deceived sometimes, but not often, in comparison with the whole number of cases where we place reliance. Men are naturally disposed to speak the truth; it is much easier than to speak what is not true, for truth is at hand; but the practice of prevarication and misstatement requires labour and invention—besides jarring violently upon every honourable sentiment within us. So capable is this view of being sustained, that even those men who have brought upon themselves the infamy of being considered liars, probably utter the truth a hundred times where they utter a falsehood once.—SECOND. Admitting that we are liable to be led astray by means of testimony, still it is in our power, and is our duty, to take suitable precautions against this liability.—We are by no means required to place implicit confidence in it, without a regard to the circumstances under which it is given, and the character and opportunities of the person who gives it. Every one knows that there are in himself tendencies and principles which, in certain circumstances, may be brought in conflict with the more ennobling principle of truth; and that he is liable to error, even when he supposes himself to be seeking the truth, from the mere want of labour and care. And we may make use of this experience in judging of the testimony of others, since we may reasonably suspect in them the existence of similar tendencies and similar want of circumspection. It is therefore consistent with any suitable degree of reliance on testimony to satisfy ourselves whether the person who testifies possessed ample means of information; whether he made use of those means; and whether, in giving testimony, he may not be under the influence of interest or passion.

§ 28. Of judgment or relative suggestion as a ground of belief.

VI.—Another ground or law of belief, of such a nature as to be entitled to a distinct consideration, is RELATIVE SUGGESTION. By this phrase is expressed the power or susceptibility, by means of which we perceive the relations of objects. It is also called the JUDGMENT. What RELATIONS themselves are, it is unnecessary to attempt to define; no mere form of words can render the conception of them clearer to any person's comprehension than it is already supposed to be. All that needs be asserted is the mere fact, that, when the mind contemplates two or more objects, we naturally put forth other perceptions or feelings; we cannot avoid doing it. For instance, we feel or perceive such objects to be the same or different, like or unlike, equal or unequal, cause or effect, whole or part, attribute or subject, &c.

These new feelings, as well as the direct perceptions of the objects to which they relate, are occasions of belief. We not only believe the existence of the feelings or mental states themselves, but find ourselves unable to resist and exclude the belief of the actual existence and truth of that to which they correspond, viz., relations. The relations of things, it is true, are not objects directly addressed to the external senses; and as we cannot directly see them, nor hear them, nor feel them, they seem comparatively obscure. And yet we are so constituted, that the cognizance of them is utterly inseparable from a knowledge of those objects in respect to which they exist. If they are not perceivable by the outward senses, they are nevertheless perceivable by the mind, and are undoubtedly, in some important sense, real subjects of contemplation and knowledge.—Accordingly, RELATIVE SUGGESTION, the name of the susceptibility by means of which we become acquainted with relations, is properly regarded a LAW OF BELIEF.

§ 29. Of reasoning as a ground or law of belief.

VII.—All REASONING, both Moral and Demonstrative, and in whatever form it exists, is also an original foundation of belief. Relative suggestion and reasoning, or in other words judgment and ratiocination, are closely connected together, since every train of reasoning implies and involves a series of felt or perceived relations. Perceptions of relation may be regarded as the links which bind together such separate perceptions, facts, or truths, as come within the range of the subject reasoned upon, and without which they would inevitably remain in their original state of insulated and unavailable propositions. Truth is added to truth, feeling arises successive to feeling, until we arrive at the conclusion which invariably fixes our belief.

When, however, we assert, that the conclusions deduced from a process of reasoning invariably influence our belief, we should particularly keep in mind here that belief may exist in very various degrees. When the successive feelings which we have in a train of reasoning are all intuitive, and the propositions with which we commenced were certain, or were assumed as such, belief is, of course, of the highest kind. And this is always the case in demonstrations; for there we always begin with either known or assumed truths; and as the propositions compared together are entirely abstract, there seems to be no room for doubt or mistake. But in moral reasoning, although the mental process is the same, the conclusion is not necessarily true; the propositions contemplated are in general of a different character from what we find in demonstrative reasoning; and the conclusion will vary from mere presumption to absolute certainty, according to the nature of the facts laid before the mind.

But is it a fact, that Reasoning necessarily controls our convictions in any case? What evidence is there that our belief, in a greater or less degree, is naturally dependent on its conclusions?—If we can suppose such a question to be seriously put, a prompt and satisfactory answer is to be found in the general and in individual experience. No man has it in his power to refuse obedience to the decisions of reasoning; nor does he ever do it, except from an inability to embrace at once, and to balance the successive steps of the process. So far as he fully understands the elementary parts which enter into a just train of reasoning, and can estimate the relative bearing of one part on another, just so far his belief is naturally and necessarily affected.

It will naturally suggest itself, that the statements of this chapter are merely preparatory, and are not by any means to be accepted as full and exhaustive statements of the great cognitive powers and sources of knowledge, which are thus briefly and imperfectly described. They will be more fully considered when coming up again for examination in their appropriate place.

CHAPTER IV.

GENERAL CLASSIFICATION.

§ 30. The mind may be regarded in a threefold point of view.

It is undoubtedly true, that the human soul is to be regarded as constituting a nature which is one and indivisible; but still there is abundant reason for asserting that its nature can never be fully understood by contemplating it solely and exclusively under one aspect. There are, accordingly, three prominent and well-defined points of view in which the mind may be contemplated, viz., the Intellect, the Sensibilities, and the Will; otherwise expressed by the phrases INTELLECTUAL, SENTIMENTIVE or SENTIENT, and VOLITIONAL states of the mind. Whatever truly and appropriately belongs to the intellect, has something peculiar and characteristic of it which shuts it out from the domain of the sensibilities; and whatever has the nature of a volition, has a position apart both from the intellectual and the sentient. This is a fundamental arrangement, which, when properly and fully carried out and applied, includes the whole soul. To the one or the other of these general heads, everything involved in our mental existence may be referred. In fully exhausting, therefore, these topics, we may justly count upon having completed the exploration of the mental constitution.

§ 31. Evidence of the general arrangement from consciousness.

The general arrangement which has been spoken of, viz., into the INTELLECTUAL, SENTIMENTIVE, and VOLITIONAL states of the mind, appears to be susceptible of abundant illustration and proof. It is not our intention, however, to enter into the discussion of its correctness at much length; but merely to indicate, as briefly as possible, some of the grounds on which it has been made; premising, at the same time, that the whole of this work, while it is based in a good degree on this fundamental division, will be found to furnish incidental evidence throughout of its truth.

In proof of the propriety of the general arrangement in question, we may refer, in the first place, to Consciousness. In doing this we are, of course, obliged to presume that the reader understands what is meant by the term consciousness; and that he assents to the truth, so readily and generally acknowledged, that we have much of our knowledge of the mind by its aid. Mental philosophers assure us that we are enabled, by means of consciousness, to ascertain what thought and feeling are in themselves, and to distinguish them from each other. And if we are not willing to depend upon the information thus given us, if we reject its authority in the hopes of finding something more certain, we shall only be involved in greater difficulty; in the language of Condillac on this very subject, "we stray from a point which we apprehend so clearly that it can never lead us into error."* But if it be true that the existence and distinctive character of the mental acts are made known, in a good degree at least, by consciousness, and that we may justly and confidently rely on its testimony, we naturally inquire, What does it teach in the present case? And, in answering this question, we may safely appeal to any person's recollections, and ask, Whether he has ever been in danger of confounding a mere perception, a mere thonght, either with desires and emotions on the one hand, or with volitions on the other? Does not his consciousness assure him that the mental states, which we thus distinguish by these different terms, are not identical; that the one class is not the other; that they as actually differ from each other as association does from belief, or imagination from memory? —It may be objected, however, that we find ourselves perplexed and at a loss to explain, by any statement

* Origin of Knowledge, pt. i., ch. i.

in words, the precise difference in this case, whatever that difference may actually be. We readily admit the fact implied in this objection, but without admitting that it has any weight as proof against the distinction in question. No simple notion or feeling whatever is susceptible of a definition, of an explanation by mere words alone. And it cannot be expected of anything, whose own nature we cannot explain by words, that we can fully explain by a mere verbal statement its difference from other things.

It would seem, therefore, that we may rest in this inquiry upon men's consciousness; not of one merely, but of any and all men. The understanding stands apart from the rest. The will also has its separate and appropriate position. We may, at least, assert with full confidence, that no one is in danger of confounding volitions with intellections; that is to say, with the mere notions of the understanding. On this point there is certainly a general agreement. And yet our consciousness, if we will but attend to its intimations with proper care, will probably teach us, that the nature of a volition more nearly approaches that of a purely intellectual act than it does the distinctive nature of emotions and desires. It is undoubtedly true, that volitions may have aroused and excited antecedents, and may thus be very closely connected with the various affections; but in themselves they are cold and unimpassioned; they are purely executive or mandatory, and are as obviously free from any actual impregnation of appetite, sentiment, or desire, as the most abstract and callous exercises of the intellect.

§ 32. Evidence of the same from terms found in different languages.

We are enabled further to throw some light on this subject from a consideration of the terms which are found in various languages. Every language is, in some important sense, a mirror of the mind. Something may be learned of the tendency of the mental operations, not only from the form or structure of language in general, but even from the import of particular terms. There can be no hesitation in saying that every language has its distinct terms, expressive of the threefold view of the mind under consideration, and which are constantly used with a distinct and appropriate meaning, and without being interchanged with each other, as if they were synonymous. In other words, there are terms in all languages (meaning those, of course, which are spoken by nations somewhat advanced in mental culture) which correspond to the English terms INTELLECT, SENSIBILITIES, WILL. If such terms are generally found in languages differing from each other in form and in meaning, it is certainly a strong circumstance in proof that the distinction which we propose to establish actually exists. On the supposition of its having no existence, it seems impossible to explain the fact that men should so universally agree in making it. If, on the other hand, it does exist, it is reasonable to suppose that it exists for some purpose; and, existing for some purpose, it must, of course, become known; and, being known, it is naturally expressed in language, the same as any other object of knowledge. And this is what we find to be the case. So that we may consider the expression to be an evidence of the fact; the sign, an intimation and evidence of the reality of the thing signified.

§ 33. Evidence from incidental remarks in writers.

We now pass to other sources of evidence on this subject. No small amount of knowledge, bearing upon the capabilities and the character of the human mind, may be gathered from the incidental remarks of writers of careful observation and good sense. And accordingly, if we find remarks expressive of mental distinctions repeatedly made by such men, when they are not formally and professedly treating of the mind, it furnishes a strong presumption that such distinctions actually exist. Their testimony is given under circumstances the most favourable to an unbiased opinion; and ought to be received into the vast amount of evidence, drawn from a great variety of sources, which goes to illustrate the true nature of the soul. The popular author of Literary Hours has given, in one of his Works, an interesting biographical sketch of Sir Richard Steele. After remarking upon the inconsistencies of his life, his excellent resolutions, and his feeble performances, his successive seasons of riot and of repentance, he refers the cause of these inconsistencies to the feebleness of the will; and, in doing it, he incidentally, but very clearly, makes the distinction under consideration. "His misfortune, the cause of all his errors, was not to have clearly seen where his deficiencies lay; they were neither of the *head* nor of the *heart*, but of the *volition*. He possessed the wish, but not the power of volition, to carry his purposes into execution."* As we are not at liberty to suppose that so respectable a writer employs words without meaning, he must be regarded as intending to make the distinction which has been asserted to exist.

In Dr. Currie's well-written Life of Burns, it is asserted that the force of that remarkable poet lay in the powers of his understanding and the sensibilities of his heart. And the writer not only thus clearly indicates the distinction between the understanding or intellect and the heart, but in another passage, which undoubtedly discloses the key to the poet's character and conduct, he distinguishes both of them from the volitional power. The passage referred to is this: "He knew his own failings; he predicted their consequences; the melancholy foreboding was not long absent from his mind; yet his *passions* carried him down the stream of error, and swept him over the precipice he saw directly in his course. The fatal defect in his character lay in the *comparative weakness of his volition*, which, governing the conduct according to the dictates of the *understanding*, alone entitles it to be denominated rational."†

* Drake's Essays illustrative of the Tattler, Spectator, and Guardian, vol. i., p. 50.

† Currie's Life of Burns, Philadelphia ed., p. 62.

A recently-published Inquiry concerning the Indications of Insanity, in which are various sketches of personal history and character that illustrate certain traits of the mind, has the following statement: "Delinquents of this description are, perhaps, not unable to distinguish between what is right and what is wrong; but their *will* is not governed by their *understanding*, and they want the power of restraining themselves from that which, when committed, they are afraid to reflect upon. Their *will* remains; but it springs from depraved *sensations* and *emotions*, or from *passions* inordinate and unrestrained."*

A celebrated writer, in giving directions to his son as to the manner of conducting negotiations with foreign ministers, makes use of the following language: "If you engage his *heart*, you have a fair chance for imposing upon his *understanding* and determining his *will*."† This writer, as well as many others, employs the more common term heart to express the sensibilities; and he evidently uses language as if there were a known and admitted distinction between the intellectual, sentient, and voluntary parts of our nature; since he speaks of the control or regulation of the understanding as being, in the case under consideration, subsequent to the possession of the heart, and the determination of the will as subsequent to both, or, at least, as not identical with them.

In his Diary of private and personal experiences, under date of Jan. 12th, 1723, President Edwards, in speaking of the consecration which he felt it his duty to make of himself to God, and of the self-renunciation consequent upon it, says: "I can challenge no right in this *understanding*, this *will*, these *affections*, which are in me."

We might multiply passages of this kind to almost any extent, if our limits would permit it. And these passages, if the distinction for which we contend does not exist, must obviously convey erroneous ideas. This

* Conolly's Inquiries concerning the Indications of Insanity, &c., Lond. ed., p. 454.

† Chesterfield, Lond. ed., vol. iii., p. 137.

we cannot well suppose. On the contrary, we have not the least doubt that they express a great and important fact in our mental constitution; a fact which is at the basis of all true philosophy of the mind. A single extract more from Shakspeare (Hamlet, Act i., Sc. ii.) will close this class of evidences on this topic.

> "It shows a *will* most incorrect to heaven,
> A *heart* unfortified—
> An *understanding* simple and unschool'd."

§ 34. Further proof from various writers on the mind.

The distinction in question has also been fully recognized by various distinguished writers on the mind. The following passage is to be found in Mr. Locke: "Thus, by a *due consideration*, and *examining* any good proposed, it is in our power to raise our *desires* in a due proportion to the value of that good, whereby, in its turn and place, it may come to work upon the *will*, and be pursued. For good, though appearing, and allowed ever so great, yet, till it has raised *desires* in our minds, and thereby made us uneasy in its want, it reaches not our *wills*."* Here the threefold division in question is distinctly recognised. The due consideration and examining which are spoken of, imply an act of the intellect; the desires, which are subsequently raised, are appropriately ascribed to the sensibilities; and these last are followed by an act of the other part of our nature, viz., the will.

Mr. Hume, in his Dissertation on the Passions, has the following passage, which is clear enough in its import without comment: "It seems evident that *reason*, in a strict sense, as meaning the judgment of truth and falsehood, can never, of itself, be any *motive* to the *will*, and can have no influence but so far as it touches some *passion* or *affection*."

In the Essays on the Principles of Morality and Natural Religion, ascribed to Lord Kames, is a passage as follows: "He hath *appetites* and *passions* which prompt him to their respective gratifications;

* Essay on the Understanding, bk. ii., ch. xxi., § 46.

but he is under no necessity of blindly submitting to their impulse. For *reason* hath a power of restraint. It suggests motives from the cool views of good and evil. He deliberates upon these. In consequence of his deliberation, he *chooseth;* and here, if anywhere, lies our liberty."

Among writers more recent, who have insisted on this distinction with much earnestness and clearness, we may mention Sir James Macintosh. In some strictures on Dr. Price's Review of the Principal Questions in Morals, he has occasion to make a remark, the substance of which had been given before, and is repeated afterward, "that no perception or judgment, or other unmixed act of the *understanding*, merely as such, and without the agency of some intermediate *emotion*, can affect the *will*."*

A writer of our own country, who has furnished some valuable contributions to a knowledge of our mental structure, expresses himself thus: "Why do not philosophers consider all the operations of the understanding and the affections as constituting but one general class of operations, and as belonging to one faculty? The reason is, they see no similarity between intellectual perceptions and affections. A perception is not a feeling either of pleasure or pain, nor a desire. And pleasure, and pain, and desires, they clearly see, are not perceptions. Hence classing them together would be improper, and create confusion. It would be confounding things which differ, and destroying all those distinctions which are necessary to the acquirement of scientific knowledge. For a person has no more than a confused notion of things who does not make distinctions where there are differences, or point out the difference between one thing and another. As perceptions and affections generically differ, philosophers have distinguished them, and formed them into *distinct classes;* and so they have admitted the existence of two faculties. And for the same reason they admit two, they ought to grant there are

* General View of the Progress of Ethical Philosophy, p. 157.

three faculties. For, when we attend to the affections and to volitions, it is evident there is a generic difference between them. It is evident that pain, pleasure, and desires are not volitions, and have no similarity to those voluntary exertions which produce effects on the body, and in other things around us. For these affections do not immediately produce any external effects; they are effects themselves produced by the heart, and are either virtuous or vicious. For it has been shown, that vice and virtue belong to the heart only, and its operations or affections. There is, therefore, no more propriety in classing the affections and volitions together, than in making but one class of the affections and perceptions. The affections and volitions so widely differ, that they naturally divide themselves into two distinct general classes."*

It would be easy here, as in the case of writers not professedly and formally treating of mental philosophy, to multiply passages of the same import from numerous other inquirers into the mind, if it were thought necessary. The view thus taken by English and American writers is sustained by judicious metaphysicians of other countries, of which our limits will permit us to give only a single passage as an instance. The writer, after some remarks on the origin of the desires, hopes, and fears, proceeds as follows: "Ces affections internes sont ce que nous nommons *sentimens.* Ils diffèrent des sensations, en ce que les sensations ont leur source directement dans l'extérieur, tandis que les sentimens sont produits en nous seulement à l'occasion de l'exterieur, soit qu'il nous affecte actuellement, soit qu'il nous ait précédemment affectés. Ils resemblent aux sensations, en ce que, comme elles, *ils sont independans de notre volontè*, et non susceptibles d'être produits ou empêchés par nous. Qui peut, en effet, *désirer*, *espérer*, *craindre à volontè?*"†

* Burton's Essays on Metaphysics, Ethics, and Theology, p. 92.

† De La Libertè et de ses Differens Modes, par Augustin-François Théry.

§ 35. Classification of the intellectual states of the mind.

For the reasons which have been given, we find ourselves authorized, in the first place, in arranging the states, exercises, or acts of the mind (for these terms, the most general we can employ, will apply to all of these classes), under the three general heads of Intellectual, Sentimentive or Sentient, and Volitional. Our intellectual states of mind, together with their corresponding susceptibilities or powers, will first come under consideration. On looking attentively, however, at the intellectual part of our nature, we readily discover that the results which are to be attributed to it are susceptible of a subordinate classification, viz., into INTELLECTUAL or INTELLECTIVE STATES of External, and those of Internal origin.

It is presumed, that, on a little examination, this distinction will be sufficiently obvious. If the mind were insulated and cut off from the outward world, or if there were no such outward world, could we feel, or see, or hear? All those mental affections which we express when we speak of the diversities of taste and touch, of sound and sight, are utterly dependent on the existence and presence of something which is exterior to the intellect itself. But this cannot be said of what is expressed by the words truth, falsehood, opinion, intelligence, cause, obligation, effect, and numerous creations of the intellect of a like kind.

It is worthy of remark, that the subordinate classification which is now proposed to be made did not escape, in its essential characteristics, the notice of very ancient writers. We have the authority of Cudworth,* that those intellectual states which have an internal origin, bore among the Greeks the name of NOEMATA, *thoughts* or *intellections;* while those of external origin were called AISTHEMATA, *sensations.* Although this classification, the grounds of which cannot fail readily to present themselves, has been recognised and sanctioned, in some form or other, by numerous writers on the human mind, it is probable that some fu-

* Cudworth's Immutable Morality, bk. iv., ch. i.

ture opportunity will be found more fully to explain and defend it; the objections which have sometimes been made will not be overlooked; and it will readily be perceived, that we shall be better prepared for this proposed explanation, after having considered the relation which the mind sustains to the external world by means of the senses, and analyzed the knowledge which has its origin in that source.

Such are the topics which we have thought it necessary to bring to the reader's notice in these Introductory chapters. We do not see how they could well have been omitted; and they could not have found a place in the body of the work without producing some degree of confusion. With the basis which is thus laid, and with that divine assistance which is necessary to the success of all efforts, we proceed with increased hope and confidence in the investigation of the numerous and diversified problems which are involved in the analysis and history of the human mind.

DIVISION FIRST.

THE INTELLECT OR UNDERSTANDING.

INTELLECTIVE OR INTELLECTUAL STATES OF THE MIND.

PART FIRST.

THE EXTERNAL OR SENSUOUS INTELLECT.

INTELLECTUAL STATES OF EXTERNAL OR SENSUOUS ORIGIN.

CHAPTER I.

ORIGIN OF KNOWLEDGE IN GENERAL.

§ 36. Connection of the mind with the material world.

THE human mind has a nature and principles of its own; but, at the same time, it cannot properly be said that it is entirely independent in its action; that is to say, it undoubtedly has a connexion, more or less intimate and important, with other things. An entire separation of the soul and its action from everything else is merely a supposition, an hypothesis, which is not realized in our present state of being. What the soul will be in a future state of existence, is, of course, another inquiry. It is possible that it may be disburdened, more than it is in this life, of connexions and dependencies, and will possess more freedom and energy; but it seems to be our appropriate business at present to examine it as we find it here.

Confining our attention, therefore, to what now is, we proceed to say, that in our present existence Providence has obviously designed and established an intimate connexion between the soul and the material world. We have a witness of this in the mere fact of the existence of an external creation. Was all this visible creation made for nothing? Are the flowers of the garden and the wilderness formed merely to waste their sweetness on the air? Are all those varieties of pleasing sound, that come forth from animate and inanimate nature, uttered and breathed out in vain? Can we permit ourselves to suppose, that the symmetry of form everywhere existing in the outward world, the relations and aptitudes, the beauties of proportion, and the decorations of colours, exist without any object? And yet this must be so, if there be no connexion between the soul of man and outward objects. What would be proportion, what would be colour, what would be harmony of sound without the soul, to which they are addressed, and from which they are acknowledged to derive their efficacy? Where there is no soul, where there is a deprivation and want of the conscious spirit, there is no sight, no hearing, no touch, no sense of beauty. Everything around us, considered in its results, depends on the mind; the senses are merely the medium of communication, the conditions and helps of the perceptions, and not the perceptions themselves.—With such considerations we justify what has been said, that Providence designed, and that it has established an intimate connexion between the soul and the material world.

And there is another train of thought which leads to the same conclusion. On any other supposition than the existence of such a connexion, we cannot account for that nice and costly apparatus of the nerves and organs of sense with which we are furnished. Although we behold on every side abundant marks of the Creator's goodness in forms and varieties of existence without end, we may safely say he does nothing in vain. The question, then, immediately recurs, What is the meaning of the expenditure of the Divine goodness in the formation of the eye, in the windings and ingenious construction of the ear, and in the diffusion of the sense of touch? We cannot give a satisfactory answer to this question, except on the ground that there is a designed and established connexion between the mind and the material world. If we admit the existence of this connexion, everything is at once explained.

§ 37. Of the origin or beginnings of knowledge.

The Creator, therefore, established the relation between mind and matter; and if we are correct in the statements which are to follow, it will be found a striking and important fact, that, in this connexion of the mental and material world, we are to look for the commencement of the mind's activity, and for the beginnings of knowledge. The soul, considered in its relationship to external nature, may be compared to a stringed instrument. Regarded in itself, it is an invisible existence, having the capacity and elements of harmony. The nerves, the eye, and the senses generally are the chords and artificial framework which God has woven round its unseen and unsearchable essence. This living and curious instrument, which was before voiceless and silent, sends forth its sounds of harmony as soon as it is swept by outward influences. But this, it will be noticed, is a general statement; so general and indefinite, perhaps, that it will be necessary to descend to some particulars, which will more fully illustrate our meaning.

We proceed, therefore, to say specifically, that there are certain elementary notions, which seem to be involved in, and inseparable from, our very existence, such as self, identity, personality, and others. The supposition would be highly unreasonable that we can exist for any length of time without possessing them. It is certain that these notions are among the earliest which men form; and yet cautious and judicious inquirers into the mind have expressed the opinion, that even these do not arise except subsequently to an impression on the organs of sense.

Speaking of a being, whom, for the sake of illustration, he supposed to be possessed of merely the two senses of hearing and smelling, Mr. Stewart makes this remark: "Let us suppose, then, a particular sensation to be excited in the mind of such a being. The moment this happens, he must necessarily acquire the knowledge of two facts at once; that of the existence of the *sensation*, and that of *his own existence* as a sentient being."* This language clearly implies, that the notions of existence and of person or self are attendant upon, and subsequent to, an affection of the mind, caused by an impression on the senses. In his Essays he still more clearly and decisively advances the opinion, that the mind is originally brought into

* Philosophy of the Human Mind, vol. i., ch. i.—See also § 5 of this Work.

action through the medium of the senses, and that human knowledge has its origin in this way.—"All our simple notions," he says (Essay iii.), "or, in other words, all the primary elements of our knowledge, are either presented to the mind immediately by the powers of consciousness and perception, or they are gradually unfolded in the exercise of the various faculties which characterize the human understanding. According to this view of the subject, the sum total of our knowledge may undoubtedly be said to *originate* in sensation, inasmuch as it is by impressions from without that consciousness is first awakened, and the different faculties of the understanding put in action."*

Perhaps this subject, however, will always remain in some degree of doubt; and we have merely to say, that of the various opinions which have been advanced in respect to it, we give the preference to that which has been referred to, as supported by Stewart, De Gerando, and other judicious writers, without any disposition to assert its infallibility, and yet with the feeling that the preponderance of arguments is greatly in its favor. The mind, therefore, appears at its creation to be merely an existence, involving certain principles, and endued with certain powers, but dependent for the first and original developement of those principles and the exercise of those powers on the condition of an outward impression. But then it is to be remembered, that it is no sooner brought into action, than it finds new sources of thought and feeling in itself.

§ 38. Our first knowledge in general of a material or external origin.

Our doctrine, then, is (affirmed with as much assurance as is suitable in a case which perhaps can never be divested of some degree of obscurity), FIRST, that there is an established and close connection between

* Views similar to those of Mr. Stewart are maintained by De Gerando, in a Memoir entitled, *De la Generation des Connoisances Humaines.*

the mind and the material world; and, SECOND, that it is by means of this connexion, and through the mediumship and instrumentality of the senses, that the mind is first brought into action. And in further illustration and support of these views, we proceed now to some additional facts and arguments, which are entitled to a candid consideration, and which we think can hardly fail to be assented to.

What has been said will, in the first place, be found agreeable to each one's individual experience. If we look back to the early periods of life, we discover not merely that our ideas are then comparatively few in number, but that far the greater proportion of them are suggested by external objects. They are forced upon us by our immediate wants; they have relation to what we ourselves see, or hear, or touch; and only a small proportion are internal and abstract. As we advance in years, susceptibilities and powers of the mind are brought into exercise, which have a less intimate connexion with things external; and thoughts from within are more rapidly multiplied than from without. We have in some measure exhausted that which is external; and as the mind, awakened to a love of knowledge and a consciousness of its own powers, has at last been brought fully into action by means of repeated affections of the senses, a new world (as yet in some degree a TERRA INCOGNITA) projects itself upon our attention, where we are called upon to push our researches and gratify our curiosity.—This is the general experience, the testimony which each one can give for himself.

In the second place, what has been said finds confirmation in what we observe of the progress of the mind in infants and children generally. The course of things which we observe in them agrees with what our personal consciousness and remembrance, as far back as it goes, enables us to testify with no little confidence in our own case. No one can observe the operations of the mind in infants and children, without being led to believe that the Creator has instituted a connexion between the mind and the material world, and that the greater portion of our early knowledge is from an outward source.

To the infant its nursery is the world. The first ideas of the human race are its particular conceptions of its nurse and mother; and the origin and history of all its notions may be traced to its animal wants, to the light that breaks in from its window, and to the few objects in the immediate neighbourhood of the cradle and hearth. When it has become a few years of age, there are other sources of information, other fountains of thought, but they are still external and material. The child then learns the topography of his native village; he explores the margin of its river, ascends its flowering hills, and penetrates the seclusion of its valleys. His mind is full of activity; new and exalting views crowd upon his perceptions; he beholds, and hears, and handles; he wonders, and is delighted. And it is not till after he has grasped the elements of knowledge, which the outward world gives, that he retires within himself, compares, reasons, and seeks for causes and effects.

It is in accordance with what has now been stated of the tendencies of mind in children, that we generally find them instructed by means of sensible objects, or by pictures of such objects. When their teachers make an abstract statement to them of an action or event, they do not understand it; they listen to it with an appearance of confusion and vacancy, for the process is undoubtedly against nature. But show them the objects themselves, or a faithful picture of them, and interpret your abstract expressions by a reference to the object or picture, and they are observed to learn with rapidity and pleasure. The time has not yet arrived for the springing up and growth of thoughts of an internal and abstract origin.

§ 39. **Further proof of the beginnings of knowledge from external causes.**

In the third place, the history of language is a strong proof of the correctness of the position, that the mind is first brought into action by means of the senses, and acquires its earliest knowledge from that source. At first words are few in number, corresponding to the limited extent of ideas. The vocabulary of savage tribes (those, for example, which inhabit the American continent) is, in general, exceedingly limited. The growth of a language corresponds to the growth of mind; it extends itself by the increased number and power of its words, nearly in exact correspondence with the multiplication and the increased complexity of thought. Now the history of all language teaches us, that words, which were invented and brought into use one after another, in the gradual way just mentioned, were first employed to express external objects, and afterward were used to express thoughts of an internal origin. Some writer remarks, that among the Boschuanas of South Africa, who live in a parched and arid country, the word PULO, which literally signifies *rain*, is the only term they have to express a blessing or blessings. But there may be blessings internal as well as external; goods and joys of the mind as well as of the body; still, in the language of these Africans, it is all *rain;* the blessings of hope, and peace, and friendship, and submission, and all other modes of intellectual and sentient good, are expressed by this one term, because in their first and external experience it was employed as the name of an object of the highest external good.

There are multitudes of instances of this kind. Almost all the words in every language expressive of the susceptibilities and operations of the mind, may be clearly shown to have had an external origin and application before they were applied to the mind. Take certain terms in the English language, which are of Latin derivation. To IMAGINE, in its literal signification, implies the forming of a picture; to IMPRESS conveys the idea of leaving a stamp or mark, as the seal leaves its exact likeness or stamp on wax; to REFLECT literally means to turn back, to go over the ground again. These words cannot be applied to the mind in the literal sense; the nature of the mind will not admit of such an application; the inference therefore is, that they first had an external application. Now if it be an established truth, that all language has a primary reference to external objects, and that there is no term expressive of mental acts which was not originally expressive of something material, the conclusion would seem to be a fair one, that the part of our knowledge, which has its rise by means of the senses, is, as a general statement, first in origin. And the more so, when we combine with these views the considerations which have been previously advanced.

§ 40. The same subject further illustrated.

And, in the fourth place, it is not too much to say, that all the observations which have been made on persons who, from their birth, or at any subsequent period, have been deprived of any of the senses, and all the extraordinary facts which have come to our knowledge having a bearing on this inquiry, go strongly in favour of the views which have been given.—It appears, for instance, from the observations which have been made in regard to persons who have been deaf until a particular period, and then have been restored to the power of hearing, that they never previously had those ideas which naturally come in by that sense. If a person has been born blind, the result is the same; or if having the sense of sight, it has so happened that he has never seen any colours of a particular description. In the one case he has no ideas of colours at all, and in the other only of those colours which he has seen.—It may be said, perhaps, that this is what might be expected, and merely proves the senses to be a source of knowledge, without necessarily involving the priority of that knowledge to what has an internal origin. But then observe the persons referred to a little further, and it will be found, as a general statement, that the powers of their minds have not been unfolded; they lay wrapped up, in a great measure, in their original darkness; no inward light springs up to compensate for the absence of that which, in other cases, bursts in from the outward world. This circumstance evidently tends to confirm the principle we are endeavouring to illustrate.

Of those extraordinary instances to which we alluded as having thrown some light on the history of our intellectual acquisitions, is the account which is given in the Memoirs of the French Academy of Sciences for the year 1703, of a deaf and dumb young man in the city of Chartres. At the age of three-and-twenty, it so happened, to the great surprise of the whole town, that he was suddenly restored to the sense of hearing, and in a short time he acquired the use of language. Deprived for so long a period of a sense which in importance ranks with the sight and the touch, unable to hold communion with his fellow-beings by means of oral or written language, and not particularly compelled, as he had every care taken of him by his friends and relations, to bring his faculties into exercise, the powers of his mind remained without having opportunity to unfold themselves. Being examined by some men of discernment, it was found that he had no idea of a God, of a soul, of the moral merit or demerit of human actions; and what might seem to be yet more remarkable, he knew not what it was to die; the agonies of dissolution, the grief of friends, and the ceremonies of interment being to him inexplicable mysteries.

Here we see how much knowledge a person was deprived of merely by his wanting the single sense of hearing; a proof that the senses were designed by our Creator to be the first source of knowledge, and that without them the faculties of the soul would never become operative.

§ 41. Subject illustrated from the case of James Mitchell.

But the foregoing is not the only instance of this sort which ingenious men have noticed and recorded. In the Transactions of the Royal Society at Edinburgh (vol. vii., pt. 1) is a Memoir communicated by Dugald Stewart, which gives an account of James Mitchell, a boy born deaf and blind. The history of this lad, who laboured under the uncommon affliction of this double deprivation, illustrates and confirms all that has been above stated. He made what use he could of the only senses which he possessed, those of touch, taste, and smell, and gained from them a number of ideas. It was a proof of the diligence with which he employed the limited means which were given him, that he had, by the sense of touch, thoroughly explored the ground in the neighbourhood of the house where he lived, for hundreds of yards. But deprived of sight, of hearing, and of intercourse by speech, it was very evident to those who observed him, as might be expected, that his knowledge was in amount exceedingly small. He was destitute of those perceptions which are appropriate to the particular senses of which he was deprived; and also of many other notions of an internal origin, which would undoubtedly have arisen if the powers of the mind had previously been rendered fully operative by means of those assistances which it usually receives from the bodily organs.—Such instances as these, however they may at first appear, are extremely important. They furnish us with an appeal, not to mere speculations, but to fact. And it is only by checking undue speculation, and by recurring to facts, that our progress in this science will become sure, rapid, and delightful.*

§ 42. Illustration from the case of Caspar Hauser.

There is a recent instance, perhaps more decisive than has ever before occurred, and as melancholy as it is deeply interesting. We refer to the case of Caspar Hauser. I know that attempts have been made to throw discredit upon the statements and the

* The statements concerning the young man of Chartres are particularly examined in Condillac's Essay on the Origin of Knowledge, at Section fourth of Part first. The interesting Memoir of Stewart has recently been republished in the third volume of his Elements of the Philosophy of the Human Mind.

history of this young man. But, after much investigation, the facts have been so well established, that they may properly be received as throwing important light on the history of the human mind. It appears, from all that can be gathered on the subject, that this unfortunate lad was from infancy confined in a low and small apartment, which he sometimes called a cage. No light ever entered this little prison. Till his release in the seventeenth year of his age, he never saw the sky, nor the pleasant light of day, nor ever perceived any difference between day and night. Whenever he awoke from sleep, which was generally sound and at stated intervals, he found a loaf of bread and a pitcher of water near him. Sometimes the water was mixed with opium or some other intoxicating drug. Under the influence of this mixture, which was occasionally given him, he was suddenly cast into a profound slumber; and when he afterward awoke, he found that he had a clean shirt on, and that his nails had been cut. He never saw the face of the man who changed his clothing and brought him his food and drink. The only objects which he had to amuse himself with were two wooden horses and several ribands. These horses he believed to have a degree of life and sensibility. His only occupation was to move them backward and forward by his side, and to tie the ribands upon them in various positions. While in his little prison he never heard a human voice, nor any other sound except what he himself made in playing with his little wooden companions. Thus it was in a solitude and inactivity little less than that of the grave, he spent his infancy, childhood, and youth.

But it is unnecessary to go into all the particulars of this unfortunate young man's history. When he was released from his confinement in the year 1828, he was, as nearly as could be ascertained from the structure and developements of his body, about 17 years of age.—And what was the condition of his mind? He had no knowledge of language, excepting a few words, to which he seems to have attached scarcely any meaning. When he appeared, helpless and alone, in the streets of Nuremberg, the common questions of the police officers were put to him. What is your name? What is your business? Whence came you? But he had no perception of their import. He heard without understanding; he saw without perceiving; the tears stood in his eye; unintelligible sounds and sorrowful moans burst from his lips. He was entirely ignorant of all the common objects and occurrences of nature, and of all the usual customs and conveniences of life. Like the blind boy couched by Cheselden for the cataract, he was incapable of estimating the true direction and distance of things. The objects which were presented to his notice affected him as they do an infant or a little child. He endeavoured, for instance, to lay hold of all bright and glittering objects just as a child does; and when he could not reach them, or was forbidden to touch them, he cried. He was attracted by the brightness of an object; but he seemed incapable of distinguishing one object from another. When objects were brought very near to him, he generally gazed at them with a stupid look, which only in particular instances was expressive of curiosity and astonishment. He could not distinguish animated things from inanimate, but ascribed a degree of life to all. He had no ideas of family, of relationship and friendship, and would often ask for an explanation of what is meant by mother, brother, and sister. He had no moral or religious ideas; and even the sentiments of modesty and shame, so deeply implanted in the human breast and so easily called into action, seem never to have been excited in his bosom. In a word, his mind was essentially an unintelligent blank; and this merely because it had been shut out from any connexion with the outward world of men and nature. No basis had been laid for its operations; the power destined to bring it into action had never touched it; it was like some desert place of earth, where the sun never shone, and the breeze never blew, and the rain never descended, that presents to the eye of the beholder one unvaried surface of arid and withering desolation.

§ 43. Of connatural or innate knowledge.

The considerations of this chapter naturally bring us upon the question of innate or connatural knowledge. It was formerly maintained by certain writers, that there are in the minds of men ideas and propositions which are not acquired or taught at any time or in any way, but are coetaneous with the existence of the mind itself, being wrought into, and inseparable from it. It was maintained that they are limited to no one class, neither to the rich nor the poor, neither to the learned nor the ignorant, to no clime and to no country, but all participate in them alike. They were supposed to be characterized by three marks: FIRST, that they exist from the very beginning of the mind's existence; SECOND, that they are entirely distinct in themselves, and are the subjects of distinct consciousness from the time that they were called into being; and, THIRD, that, in being common to all men and all nations, they are universal. These propositions and ideas, being thus coetaneous with the existence of the soul, and being there established at the commencement of its existence by the ordinance of the Deity, were further regarded as the first principles of knowledge, and as the rules by which men were to be guided in all their reasonings about natural and moral objects.

From these innate and original propositions, the following may be selected as specimens of the whole: (1.) Of the natural kind. The whole is greater than a part: Whatever is, is: It is impossible for the same thing to be and not to be at the same time and in the same sense.—(2.) Of the moral kind. Parents must be honoured: Injury must not be done: Contracts should be fulfilled, and others of a moral nature.—(3.) Of the religious kind. There is a God:

God is to be worshipped: God will approve virtue and punish vice.

§ 44. The doctrine of innate knowledge not susceptible of proof.

The prominent argument brought forward by the supporters of the doctrine of innate knowledge was this, that all mankind, without exception, and from the earliest period of our being able to form an acquaintance with their minds, exhibit a knowledge of ideas and propositions of this kind, and that this universal knowledge of them cannot be accounted for, except on the ground of their being coetaneous with the mind's existence, and originally implanted in it. Our answer is briefly this. If we admit that all men are acquainted with them and assent to them, this by no means proves them innate, so long as we can account for this acquaintance and this assent in some other way. It is granted by all that the mind exists, that it is capable of action, and that it possesses the power or the ability of acquiring knowledge. If, therefore, in the exercise of this ability, which all admit it to have, we can come to the knowledge of what are called innate or connatural ideas and propositions, it is unnecessary to assign to them another origin, in support of which no positive proof can be brought.

But the truth is, that it does not appear that all men are acquainted with the ideas and propositions in question; and especially they do not exhibit such a distinct acquaintance with them from the first dawn of their knowledge, as would be the case if they were connatural in the mind. The supposed fact, on which the argument in support of innate knowledge is founded, has the appearance at least of being an assumption; it has never been confirmed by candid and careful inquiry, which ought to be done before it is made use of as proof; nor is it susceptible of such confirmation.

§ 45. The doctrine tried by the idea of a God.

Let us test the matter by a single case. Every enumeration of innate propositions embraces the following, That all men have a notion of a God; and undoubtedly, if there be any one which has a claim to universality and early developement, it is this. But, in point of fact, we know that all men are not acquainted with this notion; the testimony of travellers among uncivilized nations has been given again and again, that there is not such a universal acquaintance. It is true that all men have in themselves the elements from which the idea may be formed; but, owing to the peculiar circumstances of extreme depression and ignorance in which they are sometimes placed, there are some individuals in whom it is not developed; and perhaps whole tribes or classes of men, as some travellers have stated, in whom the developement is so indistinct and weak as to be hardly perceptible. There is also a class of unfortunate persons to be found in civilized and Christian nations (we have reference to the deaf and dumb, those in the situation of the young man at Chartres), who will throw light on this subject, if men will but take the trouble to examine those who have in no way received religious instruction. There is reason to believe that, in many cases, they will be found utterly without a knowledge of their Creator. We will give a single instance.

Massieu was the son of a poor shepherd in the neighbourhood of Bordeaux. Destitute from birth of the sense of hearing, and, as a natural consequence, of the power of speech, he grew up, and knew barely enough to enable him to watch his father's flocks in the fields. Although his capacity was afterward fully proved to be of the most comprehensive and splendid character, as it was not then drawn out and brought into action, he appeared in early life to be but little above an idiot. In this situation he was taken under the care of the benevolent Sicard, who was able, after great labour and ingenuity, to quicken by degrees the slumbering power of thought into developement and activity. Did his instructor suppose that Massieu was acquainted with the notion of a God?—Far from it; he had abundant evidence to the contrary; nor did he even undertake to teach him that vast idea for some time. He directed his attention at first to knowledge more obvious and accessible in its origin; he led him, in perfect consistency with what is required by the nature and laws of the mind, by easy steps from one degree of knowledge to another, till he supposed him capable of embracing the glorious conception of a First Cause. Then he contrived to arouse his attention and anxiety; he introduced him to a train of thought which would naturally bring him to the desired result; he had previously taught him the relation of cause and effect; and on this occasion he showed him his watch, and, by signs, gave him to understand that it implied a designer and maker; and the same of a picture, a piece of statuary, a book, a building, and other objects indicative of design. Then he held up before him a chain, showing him how one link was connected with, and dependent on, another; in this way he introduced into the mind of Massieu the complex notion of the mutual dependence and concatenation of causes. At last the full idea, the conception of a primary, self-existent, and self-energetic cause, the notion of a God, came like light from Heaven into his astonished and rejoicing soul. He trembled, says his historian; he was deeply affected, prostrated himself, and gave signs of reverence and adoration. And when he arose, he uttered by signs also, for he had no other language, these beautiful words, which his instructor declared he should never forget: Ah! let me go to my father, to my mother, to my brothers, to tell them of a God; they know him not.*

§ 46. The further discussion of this subject unnecessary.

Such facts and illustrations as have been given seem to settle this question. Our view, then, is this: The cognitive faculties, or those faculties which have relation to the origin of knowledge, may be regarded as INNATE; but the knowledge which is the result of the

* See the work of Sicard, entitled *Cours d'Instruction d'un Sourd-Muet de Naissance*, chap. XXV.

exercise of such faculties (and this is the case with all perceptions, all propositions, and all forms of knowledge whatever) is to be regarded, not as innate, but as ACQUIRED. And this view is consistent with the admission, that many of the ideas and propositions which are regarded as innate, arise at an early period, are nearly universal, and are of very great importance.

The further discussion of the subject here does not appear to be necessary. At the present time there is, with but few exceptions, much unanimity in relation to it. But those who wish to go more fully into a question which formerly attracted a good deal of attention, will find a more minute examination of it in the philosophical writings of Locke, Gassendi, and Leibnitz, and, more recently, in the works of De Gerando.

§ 47. Concluding remarks on the rise of knowledge by means of the senses.

Considering it, therefore, as sufficiently settled that there is no innate or connatural knowledge, whatever may be true of innate or connatural cognitive powers, we recur with increased confidence to the principle laid down in the beginning of this chapter, that the mind is first brought into action by the intermediation of the senses, and that the beginnings and the greater part of its earliest knowledge are from an external source.

Let us suppose a man entirely cut off from all outward material impressions, or, what is the same thing, with his senses entirely closed. It is very obvious, and the instances already brought forward clearly prove, that he would be entirely deprived of that vast amount of knowledge which has an immediate connexion with the senses. But this is not all; there are other ideas whose connexion with the senses is less immediate, of which he would not fail to be deprived, by being placed in the circumstances supposed. Even if he should possess the idea of existence, and of himself as a thinking and sentient being (although we cannot well imagine how this should be, independently of some impression on the senses), still we have no reason to believe that he would know anything of space, of motion, of the place of objects, of duration, of time. What could he know of time without a knowledge of day and night, the rising and setting sun, the changes of the seasons, or some other of its measurements! What could he know of motion while utterly unable to form the idea of place! And what could he know of place without the aid of the senses! And, under such circumstances, what reasoning would he be capable of, further than to form the single proposition, that his feelings, whatever they might be, belonged to himself! And we might go further, and ask, What would he know of himself?

Look at the subject in whatever way we will, we must, I think, at last come to the conclusion, that the connexion of the mind with the material world by means of the senses is the basis of our early mental history, and the only key that can satisfactorily unlock its explanation. This is the beginning. We are far from saying or believing that it is the end. The Sensational sources of knowledge come first; the Internal or Super-sensational make their appearance afterward. If there are cognitions or knowledges which come from below, there are others, which in their due time and place will be found to come from above. The doctrine of outward sources of knowledge does not exclude that of inward sources. And the whole truth will be found in that broad and comprehensive Eclecticism, which, while it discriminates between mind and matter, recognises the claims and relations of both, and combines Sensationalism and Intellectualism, the Sensuous and the Super-sensuous, in one conjoined and harmonious system.

CHAPTER II.

THE POWER OF SENSATION.

§ 48. Sensation a simple mental state originating in the senses.

IN connection with the general principles laid down in the Introductory chapters, and in the chapter on the Origin of Knowledge, which prepare the way, in a number of important respects, for what is to follow, we are ready to proceed to the investigation of the various mental powers and susceptibilities. And here we make two very brief remarks. FIRST, it will be found, in the history of the mind's development, that each power, each susceptibility, has its appropriate place. And the examination of a power out of the right place causes much perplexity; while the examination of it where it appropriately belongs throws light upon it and upon the other powers with which it is connected. Thus we cannot understand Perception without the antecedent knowledge of Sensation; we cannot understand the Conceptive power without the antecedent knowledge of that which perceives; the philosophical analysis of the Reasoning power implies the knowledge of the power of Memory, and so on. The examination of the powers in a reverse order, placing Perception before Sensation, the Reasoning power before Memory, and the power of Imagination before that which furnishes conceptive states, or even a slight deviation from the true order of arrangement in these and in other cases, produces more or less of perplexity and confusion. A SECOND remark is, that man is not only a cognitive being, a being made to acquire knowledge, but also an æsthetic or emotional, a moral, and active being; and, therefore, that his powers, as we shall be led to see, are very various in their character. And there are some important powers, which it is difficult to class either as perceptive or active, and which seem, in their position and functions, to be chiefly auxiliary to the prompt and definite action of others; such as the power of Habit and the power of Association. With these remarks we are prepared to enter upon the analysis before us.

In proceeding with the examination of the External or Sensational intellect, in distinction from the Internal or Supersensational intellect, the first cognitive power which presents itself to our notice is Sensation. This power is variously named Sensation, the Sensational power, and Sensationality. Owing to the imperfection of language, the word SENSATION sometimes means the mental power or faculty, and sometimes the result of the exercise of that power. The power is one thing, the result of the exercise of that power is another. But as we generally get the best idea of the powers or susceptibilities of the mind from an examination of the results to which they give rise, we shall proceed briefly to examine sensation, the mental state, in distinction from the sensational or sensuous power, with which it originates.

It is generally understood that sensation is a simple act or state of the mind, and, as a necessary result of its simplicity, that it is unsusceptible of definition. As these characteristics alone, however, would not separate it from many other mental states, it has this peculiarity to distinguish it, *that it is immediately successive to a change in some organ of sense, or, at least, to a bodily change of some kind.* But it is evident that, in respect to numerous other feelings, this statement does not hold good. They are immediately subsequent, not to bodily impressions, but to other states of the soul itself. Hence it is, that while we speak of the sensations of heat and cold, hardness, softness, and the like, we do not commonly apply this term to joy and sorrow, hatred and love, and other emotions and passions.

§ 49. All sensation is properly and truly in the mind.

Sensation is often regarded as something having a

position, and as taking place in the body, and particularly in the organ of sense. The sensation of touch, as we seem to imagine, is in the hand, which is the organ of touch, and is not truly internal; the hearing is in the ear, and the vision in the eye, and not in the soul. But it will at once occur, that this supposition, however widely and generally it may be made, is altogether at variance with those essential notions which we have found it necessary to form of matter. If the matter of the hand, of the eye, or ear, can have feeling in any degree whatever, there is no difficulty in the supposition, that the matter of the brain, or any other material substance, can put forth the exercises and functions of thought. But, after what has been already said on the subject of the mind's immateriality, this supposition is altogether inadmissible. All we can say with truth and on good grounds is, that the organs of sense are accessory to sensation and necessary to it, but the sensation or feeling itself is wholly in the mind. How often it is said, in the use of metaphorical language, that the eye sees; but the language, expressive of the literal and real fact is, that the soul sees, for the eye is only the organ, instrument, or minister of the soul in visual perceptions.

"A man," says Dr. Reid, "cannot see the satellites of Jupiter but by a telescope. Does he conclude from this that it is the telescope that sees those stars? By no means; such a conclusion would be absurd. It is no less absurd to conclude that it is the eye that sees or the ear that hears. The telescope is an artificial organ of sight, but it sees not. The eye is a natural organ of sight by which we see; but the natural organ sees as little as the artificial."

Among other things illustrative of the correctness of what has been said, there is this consideration also. The opinion that sensation is in the organ or some other material part, and not in the soul, is inconsistent with the fundamental and indisputable doctrine of mental identity. "When I say I see, I hear, I feel," says the same judicious author, "this implies that it is one and the same self that performs all these operations. And as it would be absurd to say that my memory, another man's imagination, and a third man's reason, may make one individual intelligent being, it would be equally absurd to say that one piece of matter seeing, another hearing, and a third feeling, may make one and the same percipient being."*

And again, it would not be out of place to illustrate the subject from what may be witnessed immediately after death, and before the decomposition and dissolution of the body. The eye still remains; the sense of hearing remains; the sense of touch and the other senses are there; but there is no vision, no hearing, no tactual sensation, because the senses are not complemented and made available by the presence of the soul.

Although the opinion that sensation is not in the mind but in the body, is unfounded, it is not, perhaps, surprising that such a belief should have arisen. If the hand be palsied, there is no sensation of touch; if the ear be stopped, there is no sensation of hearing; if the eye be closed, there is no vision; hence it happens, that when we have these sensations, we are led to think of the organ or part of the bodily system, with the affection of which they are connected. When we feel a pain arising from an external cause, it is a natural, and often a useful curiosity which endeavours to learn the particular place in the body which is affected. This, which we are generally able to ascertain, always arrests our attention more or less. In this way we gradually form a very strong association, and almost unconsciously transfer the place of the inward sensation to that outward part, with which we have so frequently connected it in our thoughts. Although this is clearly a mere fallacy, the circumstance of its being a plausible and tenacious one renders it the more necessary to guard against it.

* Reid's Intellectual Powers, Essay ii.

§ 50. Sensations are not images or resemblances of objects.

But while we are careful to assign sensations their true place in the mind, and to look upon what is outward in the body as merely the antecedents or causes of them, it is a matter of some consequence to guard against a danger directly the reverse of that which has been remarked on. We are apt to transfer to the sensation, considered as existing in the mind, some of those qualities which belong to the external object. But, in point of fact, our sensations are by no means copies, pictures, or images of outward objects; nor are they representations of them in any material sense whatever; nor do they possess any of their qualities.

It is true, we often think it otherwise; constantly occupied with external objects, when in the act of contemplation we retire within the mind, we unwarily carry with us the form and qualities of matter, and stamp its likeness on the thought itself. But the thought, whatever it may by the constitution of our nature be the sign of, has no form, and presents no image analogous to what are outwardly objects of touch and sight; nor has it form or image in any sense which we can conceive of. When, therefore, we have an idea of some object as round or square, we are not to infer, from the existence of the quality in the outward object, that the mental state is possessed of the same quality or attribute; when we think of anything as extended, it is not to be supposed that the thought itself has extension; when we behold and admire the varieties of color, we are not at liberty to indulge the presumption that the inward feelings are painted over, and radiant with corresponding hues. There is nothing of the kind; and the admission of such a principle would lead to a multitude of errors.

This subject is illustrated in the following manner by Dr. Reid, whom we have already had repeated occasion to refer to on the subject before us.—"Pressing my hand with force against the table, I feel pain, and I feel the table to be hard. The pain is a sensation of the mind, and there is nothing that resembles it in the table. The hardness is in the table, nor is there anything resembling it in the mind. Feeling is applied to both, but in a different sense; being a word common to the act of sensation, and to that of perceiving by the sense of touch.

"I touch the table gently with my hand, and I feel it to be smooth, hard, and cold. These are qualities of the table perceived by touch; but I perceive them by means of a sensation which indicates them. This sensation not being painful, I commonly give no attention to it. It carries my thought immediately to the thing signified by it, and is itself forgotten as if it had never been. But by repeating it, and turning my attention to it, and abstracting my thought from the thing signified by it, I find it to be merely a sensation, and that it has no similitude to the hardness, smoothness, or coldness of the table which are signified by it.

"It is indeed difficult, at first, to disjoin things in our attention which have always been conjoined, and to make that an object of reflection which never was so before; but some pains and practice will overcome this difficulty in those who have got the habit of reflecting on the operations of their own minds."*

§ 51. The connexion between the mental and physical change not susceptible of explanation.

External bodies operate on the senses before there is any affection of the mind, but it is not easy to say what the precise character and extent of this operation is. We know that some object capable of affecting the organ must be applied to it in some way either directly or indirectly, and it is a matter of knowledge also, that some change in the organ actually takes place; but further than this we are involved in uncertainty. All we can undertake to do at present is the mere statement of the facts, viz., the application of an external body, and some change in consequence of it in the organ of sense.

* Reid's Intellectual Powers, Essay ii.

Subsequently to the change in the organ, either at its extremity and outward developement, or in the brain, with which it is connected, and of which it may be considered as making a part, a change in the mind or a new state of the mind immediately takes place. Here also we are limited to the mere statement of the fact. We here touch upon one of those boundaries of the intellect which men are probably not destined to pass in the present life. We find ourselves unable to resolve and explain the connexion between mind and matter in this case, as we do in all others. All we know and all we can state with confidence is, that a mental affection is immediately subsequent to an affection or change which is physical.

CHAPTER III.

PERCEPTION, OR THE PERCEPTIVE POWER.

§ 52. Of the meaning and nature of perception.

We next come to the subject of Perception. We consider this power here, because this seems its proper place. It is obviously subsequent, in the history of the mind's developement, to the Sensational power, but is as clearly antecedent to many others which are to follow. This is the second cognitive power, and is variously denominated Perception, the Perceptive power, and Perceptivity. Its results, or the states of mind to which it gives rise, are called perceptions. And the power, as in other analogous cases, is most easily and satisfactorily understood from an examination of its results. It is hardly necessary to add that what we have to say here does not concern internal perception, but merely that which relates to objects exterior to the mind.

Perception, using the term in its application to outward objects, differs from sensation as a whole does from a part; it embraces more. It may be defined, therefore, an affection or state of the mind *which is immediately successive to certain affections of the organ of sense, and which is referred by us to something external as its cause.* In regard to the specific nature of this reference, namely, whether it involves some inductive process, or whether it is a purely instinctive tendency, there may be differences of opinion; but possibly and probably the truth may include a very simple mental process, which has the form of reasoning, but which is prompted and secured in its action by an implanted or instinctive tendency of the mind.

It will be recollected that the term SENSATION, when applied to the mind, expresses merely the state of the mind, without reference to anything external which might be the cause of it, and that it is the name of a truly simple feeling. Perception, on the contrary, is the name of a complex mental state, including not merely the internal affection of the mind, but also a reference to the exterior cause. Sensation is wholly within; but Perception carries us, as it were, out of ourselves, and makes us acquainted with the world around us. It is especially by means of this last power that material nature, in all its varieties of form and beauty, is brought within the range of our inspection. If we had but sensation alone, there would still be form and fragrance, and colour and harmony of sound, but it would all seem to be wholly inward. The mind would then become not merely what Leibnitz supposed it to be, a mirror of the universe; it would be to us the universe itself; we could know no other world, no other form of being. Perception or perceptivity prevents the possibility of such a mistake; operating in virtue of its own law of being and action, it undeceives and dissipates the flattering notion that all things are in the soul; it leads us to other existences, and, in particular, to the knowledge of the vast and complicated fabric of the material creation.

§ 53. Of the primary and secondary qualities of matter.

From what has been said, it will be noticed that

SENSATION implies the existence of an external material world as its cause, or at least as the occasion of its existence; and that PERCEPTION implies the same existence both as cause and object. As, therefore, the material world comes now so directly and closely under consideration, it seems proper briefly to advert to that subject. It is obvious we are ignorant, so far as the senses are concerned, of the subjective or real essence of matter. Our sensuous knowledge embraces merely its qualities or properties, and nothing more. Without proposing to enter into a minute examination of them, it will be proper to recall the recollection here, that the qualities of material bodies have been ranked by writers under the two heads of Primary and Secondary.

The PRIMARY QUALITIES are known by being essential to the existence of all bodies. They are extension, figure, divisibility, and solidity; and some writers have included motion. They are called PRIMARY for the obvious reason that all men embrace them in the notions which they form of matter, and that they are essential to its existence. All bodies have extension, all bodies have figure, all are capable of division, all possess the attribute of solidity.

By SOLIDITY in bodies (perhaps some would prefer the term RESISTANCE) is to be understood that quality by which a body hinders the approach of others between which it is interposed. In this sense, even water, and all other fluids, are solid. If particles of water could be prevented from separating, they would oppose so great resistance that it would be impossible for any two bodies, between which they might be, to come in contact. This was shown in an experiment which was once made at Florence. A quantity of water was enclosed in a gold ball, which, on the most violent pressure, could not be made to fill the internal cavity, until the water inside was forced through the pores.—There is reason also for that part of the arrangement which includes DIVISIBILITY. We cannot conceive of a particle so small as not to be susceptible of division. And to that small particle must belong not only divisibility, but the qualities of solidity, extension, and figure.

§ 54. Of the secondary qualities of matter.

The SECONDARY qualities of bodies are of two kinds: (1.) Those which have relation to the perceiving and sentient mind; (2.) Those which have relation to other bodies.

Under the first class are to be included sound, colour, taste, smell, hardness and softness, heat and cold, roughness and smoothness, &c. When we say of a body it has sound, we imply in this remark that it possesses qualities which will cause certain effects in the mind; the term sound being applicable by the use of language both to the qualities of the external object, and to the effect produced within. When we say it has colour, we always make a like reference to the mind which beholds and contemplates it; and it is the same of the other secondary qualities of this description.

The other class of secondary qualities (or properties, as they are not unfrequently termed), those which have relation to other material bodies, are exceedingly various and numerous. The material substance which, in relation to the mind, possesses the qualities of sound and colour, may possess also, in relation to other bodies, the qualities or properties of malleability, fusibility, solubility, permeability, and the like.

§ 55. Of the nature of mental powers or faculties, and their names.

One or two explanatory remarks may properly be made here. We are now considering the specific powers of the mind as they present themselves for examination in the respective general Departments to which they belong. But it is desirable to remember, that the powers or faculties, which it is necessary thus to make distinct objects of consideration, are not, on that account, to be regarded as distinct from the mind itself. They are not separate from the mind, but are included in it; and, psychologically considered, merely involve and imply the fact of the ability of the mind to act in a particular way; although it may properly be added, that the particular form of action is rendered possible, and is in some cases necessitated by the circumstances in which the mind is placed. It is to these varieties of action, manifesting themselves under different circumstances, but having a commonness of mental origin, that we give specific names; and speak, as I think, with entire propriety of the power of perception, of the conceptive power, of the powers, or faculties, or susceptibilities of the memory, imagination, reasoning, and the like. And without employing such specific names, no satisfactory analysis and history of the mind would be possible.

II. And further we confess to some reluctance in employing, to any great extent, new terms. Sometimes this is necessary, but not very often. As a general rule, it is better to employ the common and acknowledged phraseology, only taking care to limit and explain it so far as it may be liable to misapprehension, in consequence of a new and scientific application. "It looks too much like affectation," says Locke, speaking of the common and recognized forms of speech, "wholly to lay them by; and philosophy itself, though it likes not a gaudy dress, yet, when it appears in public, must have so much complacency as to be clothed in the ordinary fashion and language of the country, so far as it can consist with truth and perspicuity."

III. We are not to suppose, when we speak of a power or susceptibility of the mind, that, because the name of it is often a single word, the power itself is for that reason a single or simple thing, and unsusceptible of analysis. Some powers, such as the powers of Sensation and Intuition, appear to be simple. Others, such as Imagination and Reasoning, are obviously complex. In the latter there are a number of mental acts, comprehended under one name; and it is necessary, therefore, to analyze them, and to become acquainted with their parts, otherwise our notions will become confused, and often erroneous.

CHAPTER IV.

THE SENSES OF SMELL AND TASTE.

§ 56. Nature and importance of the senses as a source of knowledge.

In connexion with what has been said in the last two chapters on the powers of sensation and perception, it is desirable to keep clearly in the mind the precise relation of the senses to the origin, progress, and amount of our knowledge, and to possess, if possible, a correct understanding of their true value. In a certain sense, the possession of the bodily organs with which we are furnished is not essential and prerequisite to the possession of that knowledge which we are accustomed to ascribe to them. There is nothing unwarrantable and unreasonable in the supposition, that the knowledge which we have by their means might have been possessed without their aid, either immediately, or in some way altogether different. Their use and indispensableness in the acquisition of a certain portion of what men are permitted to know, is a matter of arrangement and appointment on the part of our Maker. It is undoubtedly an evidence of the correctness of this remark, that the Supreme Being has a full acquaintance with all those outward objects which present themselves to our notice, without being indebted to any material instrumentality and mediation. He perceives in another way, or, rather, all knowledge is inherent in, and originally and unalterably essential to, himself.

It is not so, as we have reason to believe, with any other beings, and certainly not with man. Although a great part of his knowledge relates to material things, he is so formed, and his constitution is so ordered, that he is wholly dependent for it on the senses.—Deprive him of the ear, and all nature becomes voiceless and silent; deprive him of the eye, and the sun and moon withdraw their light, and the universe becomes darkened like sackcloth; deprive him of the sense of touch, and he is then entirely insulated, and as much cut off from all communication with others as if he were the only being in existence.

§ 57. Of the connexion of the brain with sensation and perception.

It may perhaps be asked, Whether these views are intended to exclude the brain, as having a connexion with the senses in the results which are here ascribed to them? And this inquiry leads us to observe (what has been before alluded to), that the brain is a prominent organ in the material part of the process of sensation and of external perception. The senses evidently cannot be separated from the nervous system. But the substance which is found in the nerves, excepting the coat in which it is enveloped, is the same as in the brain, being of the same soft and fibrous texture, and in continuity with it. As a general statement, when the brain has been in any way injured, the inward sensation, which would otherwise be distinct on the presentation of an external body, is imperfect. Also, if the nerve be injured, or if its continuity be disturbed by the pressure of a tight ligature, the effect is the same; a circumstance which goes to confirm the alleged identity of substance in the two.

The brain, therefore, and whatever of the same substance is in continuity with it, particularly the nerves, constitute the *sensorial organ*, which, in the subordinate organs of taste, smell, sight, touch, and hearing, presents itself under different modifications to external objects. On this organ, the *sensorial*, as thus explained, an impression must be made before there can be sensation and perception.

An impression, for instance, is made on that part of the sensorial organ called the auditory nerve, and a state of mind immediately succeeds, which is variously termed, according to the view in which it is contemplated, either the sensation or the perception of sound.—An impression is made by the rays of light on that expansion of the optic nerve which forms what is called the RETINA of the eye, and the intellectual principle is immediately brought into that new position, which is termed visual perception, or a perception of sight.—The hand is impressed on a body of an uneven and rough surface, and immediately consequent on this application and pressure is that state of mind which is termed a sensation or perception of roughness.

§ 58. Order in which the senses are to be considered.

In considering those mental states which we possess by means of the senses, it is natural to begin with that sense which will cause us the least difficulty in the analysis of its results, and to proceed to others successively, as we find them increasing in importance. It may not be altogether easy to apply this principle with strictness, but it will answer all the purpose for which it is here introduced, if we consider the senses in the following order, the smell, taste, hearing, touch, and sight.

The mind holds a communication with the material world by means of the sense of smelling. All animal and vegetable bodies (and the same will probably hold good of other bodies, though generally in a less degree) are continually sending out effluvia of great subtilty. These small particles are rapidly and widely scattered abroad in the neighbourhood of the body from which they proceed. No percipient being can come within the circumference occupied by these continually moving and volatile atoms, without experiencing effects from it.

§ 59. Of the sense and sensation of smell.

The medium through which we have the sensations and perceptions of smell, is the organ which is termed the olfactory nerve, situated principally in the nostrils, but partly in some continuous cavities. When any odoriferous particles, sent from external objects, affect this organ, there is a certain state of mind produced, which varies with the nature of the odoriferous bodies. But we can no more infer, from the sensation itself merely, that there exists any necessary connexion between the smell and the external objects, than that there exists a connexion between the emotions of joy and sorrow and the same objects. It might, indeed, be suggested to us by the change in our mental states, that there must be some cause or antecedent to the change; but this suggestion would be far from implying the necessity of a *corporeal* cause.

How, then, does it happen that we are not merely sensible of the particular sensation, but refer it at once to some external object, to the rose or the honeysuckle? In answer, it may be remarked, if we had always been destitute of the senses of sight and touch, this reference never could have been made; but, having been furnished with them by the beneficent Author of our being, we make this reference by experience. When we have seen the rose, when we have been near to it and handled it, we have uniformly been conscious of that state of mind which we term a sensation of smell. When we have come into the neighbourhood of the honeysuckle, or when it has been gathered and presented to us, we have been reminded of its fragrance. And thus, having learned by experience that the presence of the odoriferous body is always attended with the sensations of smell, we form the habit, aided perhaps by some interior instinctive tendencies, of attributing the sensations to that body as their cause.

§ 60. Of perceptions of smell in distinction from sensations.

The mental reference spoken of in the last section is made with almost as much promptness as if it were necessarily involved in the sensation itself. It is at least so rapid, that we find ourselves unable to mark the mind's progress from the inward feeling to the conception of the outward cause. Nor is this inability surprising, when we consider that we have repeated this process, both in this and in analogous cases, from our earliest childhood. No object has ever been present to us, capable of operating on the senses, where this process has not been gone through. The result of this long-continued and frequent repetition has been an astonishing quickness in the mental action, so much so that the mind leaps outward with the rapidity of lightning, to be present with, and to comprehend the causes of the feeling within.

This view, it will be seen, helps in illustrating the nature of PERCEPTION, as distinguished from sensation. The outlines of that distinction have already been given; and every one of the senses, as well as that now under consideration, will furnish proofs and illustrations of it. Accordingly, when we are said to perceive the smell, or to have perceptions of the smell of a body, the rapid process which has been described is gone through, and the three things which were involved in the definition of Perception already given are supposed to exist: (1.) The presence of the odoriferous body, and the affection of its appropriate organ; (2.) The change or sensation in the mind; and (3.) The reference of the sensation to the external body as its cause.

§ 61. Of the sense and the sensation of taste.

The tongue, which is covered with numerous nervous papillæ, forms essentially the organ of taste, although the papillæ are found scattered in other parts of the cavity of the mouth. The application of any sapid body to this organ immediately causes in it a change or affection; and this is at once followed by a mental affection or a new state of the mind. In this way we have the sensations and perceptions, to which we give the names sweet, bitter, sour, acrid, and others.

Having experienced the inward sensation, the affections of the mind are then referred by us to something external as their *cause*. We do not, however, always, nor even generally, distinguish the qualities which constitute this cause by separate and appropriate designations; but express them by the names that are employed for the internal feeling, viz., sweetness, bitterness, sourness, &c. This reference of what is internally experienced to its external cause, is very rapidly made; so that we at once say of one apple it is sweet, and of another it is sour. Still it is to be kept in mind, that, in point of fact, it is subsequent, both in the order of nature and of time, to the mere sensation; although we may not be able, in consequence of its rapidity, to mark distinctly the progress of the mental action from the one to the other. As in the case of smells, which have already been remarked upon, the reference is the result of our former experience. We say of one body it is sweet, and of another it is sour, because we have ever observed that the mental states indicated by those terms have always existed in connexion with the presence of those bodies.

Whenever, therefore, we say of any bodies that they are sweet, bitter, sour, or apply any other epithets expressive of sapid qualities, we mean to be understood to say, that such bodies are fitted in the constitution of things to cause in the mind the sensations of sweetness, bitterness, and sourness, or other sensations expressed by denominations of taste. Or, in other words, that they are the established antecedents of such mental experiences, as there is, further than this, no necessary connexion between them.

§ 62. Design and uses of the senses of smell and taste.

It is not unprofitable to delay oftentimes, and contemplate the designs and uses which nature has in view in her works. Although the sense of smell may appear (and perhaps with sufficient reason) to be of less importance than the other senses and the other parts of the animal economy, it is not without its ends. There is evidently design in the position of the organ in reference to the effluvia, which are the direct subjects of its action, it being placed in the inside of the canal, where the air is continually forced in and out with every breath we draw. The organ is precisely adapted, both in its nature and its place, to its appointed medium of communication with other bodies; nor is this the only mark of design attending it. This sense is frequently a source of gratification; and although it is less keen and powerful in men than in many inferior animals, it still has power enough to afford much assistance in this respect, that it often warns us of the presence of objects which experience has found to be injurious to us. The remark has been justly made, that the senses both of taste and smell are of great use in distinguishing bodies that cannot be distinguished by our other senses. They are peculiarly quick and exact in their judgments, especially in discerning, before we can ascertain it in any other way, the beginning and progress of those changes which all bodies are constantly undergoing.

But in both of these senses design and utility are discoverable in reference to food in particular. While the sense of smell guards the entrance of the canal for breathing, the sense of taste has its station at the entrance of the alimentary canal. Hence the food which we consume undergoes the scrutiny of both; an intentional and benevolent provision for protecting men and the animal creation generally against the introduction of what would be noxious to them.

CHAPTER V.

THE SENSE OF HEARING.

§ 63. Organ of the sense of hearing.

FOLLOWING the order which has been proposed, we are next to consider the sense of HEARING. And, in proceeding to the consideration of this subject, the remark is a very obvious one, that we should be unable to hear if we had not a sense designed for and appropriate to that result. The air, when put strongly in motion, is distinctly perceived by the touch; but no impression which it could make on that sense would cause that internal feeling which is termed a sensation of sound. Our Creator, therefore, has taken care that these sensations shall have their own organ; and it is obviously one of precise and elaborate workmanship. The ear is designedly planted in a position where, with the greatest ease, it takes cognizance of whatever is going on in the contiguous atmosphere. When we examine it externally, we not only find it thus favorably situated, but presenting a hollowed and capacious surface, so formed as to grasp and gather in the undulations of air continually floating and in motion around it. Without, however, delaying to give a minute description of the internal construction of the ear, which belongs rather to the physiologist, it will answer our present purpose merely to add, that these undulations are conducted by it through various windings, till they are brought in a state of concentration, as it were, against the membrane called the TYMPANUM. It is worthy of notice, that on the internal surface of this membrane (the drum, as it is popularly called) there is a nerve spread out in a manner analogous to the expansion of the optic nerve at the bottom of the eye. Whether this nervous expansion be indispensably necessary to the result or not, it is certain that a pressure upon or affection of the tympanum by the external air is followed by a new state of the mind, known as the sensation or perception of sound.

§ 64. Nature of sonorous bodies, and the medium of the communication of sound.

When we leave the bodily organ, and, looking outward, inquire still further for the origin of the sensations which we have by means of the ear, we find them attributable ultimately to the presence and influence of the substances around us. Those undulations of air, which impinge upon the tympanum, and without which there is no sensation of sound, are caused by the vibrations or oscillations of the particles of certain bodies. The material substances which have this quality are termed sonorous, as wood, brass, iron, &c.; but it exists in different bodies in very various degrees.

The quality of sonorousness, therefore, in any substance, is properly a susceptibility of motion among its own parts. When it is forcibly struck, this motion exists first in itself, and is afterward communicated to the circumambient air. The movement of the air which is thus caused, is again communicated, like the concentric waves of water agitated by a stone thrown into it, to other portions successively, till it reaches the ear.

The air, accordingly, is the medium of communication between the sonorous body and the tympanum of the ear. It is true that many solid bodies are good conductors of sound as well as the atmosphere; but as portions of air, through which the vibratory motion must of course pass, are in all cases interposed between that organ and the sounding body, it is not necessary to dwell upon them here. It is sufficient for our present purpose merely to understand, that there is in every sounding body, in the first place, a vibratory motion among its own particles from some cause or other; that this vibration or undulation is communicated from the sounding body to the air, and from one portion of air to another, till it reaches the organ of hearing. Why the internal sensation should at once follow the completion of this process is another inquiry, which we do not undertake to explain. We have before us the antecedent and the consequent, the affection of the organ of hearing by an outward impulse, and the new mental state within; but the reason of this invariable connexion in two things that are entirely distinct and different, is a matter beyond our limited comprehension.

§ 65. Varieties of the sensation of sound.

The sensations which we thus become possessed of by the hearing, are far more numerous than the words and the forms of speech, having relation to them in different languages, would lead us to suppose. It will help to illustrate this subject if we recur a moment to the sense of TASTE. The remark has somewhere been made to this effect, and probably with much truth, that if a person were to examine five hundred different wines, he would hardly find two of them of precisely the same flavour. The diversity is almost endless, although there is no language which distinguishes each variety of taste by a separate name. It is the same in respect to the sensations of sound. These sensations exhibit the greatest variety, although the differences are too minute to be separated and distinctly represented by language.

These views will appear the less objectionable, when it is remembered that sounds differ from each other both in the tone and in the strength of the tone. It is remarked by Dr. Reid, that five hundred variations of tone may be perceived by the ear; also an equal number of variations in the strength of the tone; making, by a combination of the tones and of the degrees of strength, many thousands of simple sounds, differing either in tone or strength.

In a perfect tone, a great many undulations of elastic air are required, which must be of equal duration and extent, and follow each other with perfect regularity. Each undulation is made up of the advance and retreat of innumerable particles, whose motions are all uniform in direction, force, and time. Accordingly, there will be varieties also and shades of difference in the same tone, arising from the position and manner of striking the sonorous body, from the constitution of the elastic medium, and from the state of the organ of hearing.

Different instruments, such as a flute, a violin, and a bass viol, may all sound the same tone, and yet be easily distinguishable. A considerable number of human voices may sound the same note, and with equal strength, and yet there will be some difference. The same voice, while it maintains the proper distinctions of sound, may yet be varied many ways by sickness or health, youth or age, and other alterations in our bodily condition to which we are incident.

§ 66. Manner in which we learn the place of sounds.

It is a fact worthy of notice in respect to sounds, that we should not know, previous to all experience on the subject, whether a sound came from the right or left, from above or below, from a smaller or a greater distance. And this will appear the less surprising, when we remember, that the undulations of air are always changed from their original direction by the channels and the windings of the ear before they strike the tympanum. Abundant facts confirm this statement.

Dr. Reid mentions, that once, as he was lying in bed, having been put into a fright, he heard his own heart beat. He took it to be some one knocking at the door, and arose, and opened the door oftener than once before he discovered that the sound was in his own breast. Some traveller has related, that when he first heard the roaring of a lion in a desert wilderness, not seeing the animal, he did not know on what side to apprehend danger, as the sound seemed to him to proceed from the ground, and to enclose a circle, of which he and his companions stood in the centre.

It is by custom or experience that we learn to distinguish the place of things, and, in some measure also, their nature, by means of their sound. It is thus that we learn that one noise is in a contiguous room, that another is above our heads, and another is in the street. And what seems to be an evidence of this is, that when we are in a strange place, after all our experience, we very frequently find ourselves mistaken in these respects.

If a man born deaf were suddenly made to hear, he would probably consider his first sensations of sound as originally wholly within himself. But, in process of time, we learn not only to refer the origin of sounds to a position above or below, to the right or left, but to connect each particular sound with a particular external cause, referring one to a bell as its appropriate external cause, another to a flute, another to a trumpet.

§ 67. Application of these views to the art of ventriloquism.

We are naturally led to make a few remarks here in explanation of VENTRILOQUISM, a well-known art, by which persons can so modify their voice as to make it appear to their audience to proceed from different objects, distances, and directions. There is no peculiarity of structure in ventriloquists, as is often supposed; except that the capacity of the chest and the lungs is sometimes found to be greater than usual. It is also true, that the power and activity of the muscles, connected with the organs of speech and with the chest and lungs, is considerably increased by frequent exercise. Nevertheless, the great natural requisite on the part of the ventriloquist is to be able to mimic sounds; and he will be likely to succeed nearly in proportion to his skill in this particular. The secret, then, of his acoustic deceptions, supposing him to be capable of exact imitation, will be sufficiently understood by referring to the statement maintained in the preceding section, viz., That, previous to experience, we are unable to refer sounds to any particular external cause.

The sound itself never gives us any direct and immediate indication of the place, or distance, or direction of the sonorous body. It is only by experience, it is only by the association of place with sound, that the latter becomes an indication of the former. Now supposing the ventriloquist to possess a delicate ear, which is implied in his ability to mimic sounds, he soon learns, by careful observation, the difference which change of place causes in the same sound. Having in this way ascertained the particular modulations of sound, which, in accordance with the experience of men and the associations they have formed, are appropriate to any particular distances, direction, or object, it is evident, whenever he exactly or very nearly imitates such modulations, that the sounds must appear to his audience to come from such distance, object, or direction.

One part of the art, however, consists in controlling the attention of persons present, and in directing that attention to some particular place by a remark, motion, or some other method. If, for instance, the sound is to come from under a tumbler or hat, the performer finds it important to have their attention directed to that particular object, which affords him an opportunity for the exercise of all those associations which they have formed with any sound coming from a very confined place. All, then, that remains for him to do, is to give his voice a dull modulation and on a low key, which we know from our experience to be the character of confined sounds. Then there seems to be a voice speaking under a tumbler or hat; and if any person should, either intentionally or unintentionally, lift these articles up, the ventriloquist immediately utters himself more distinctly and freely, like a person who has been very much confined on being readmitted into the free and open air. It is also necessary, when his face is towards his auditors, that he should make use chiefly of the muscles of the throat; an outward and visible moving of the lips would much weaken the deception.

§ 68. Uses of hearing and its connexion with oral language.

Although, as in the cases just mentioned, the artifices of men may sometimes impose upon this organ and lead its decisions astray, it is one, in the ordinary calls for its exercise, of exceeding value. One of the distinguished benefits of the sense of hearing is, that, in consequence of it, we are enabled to hold intercourse with each other by means of spoken language, without which the advancement of the human mind must have inevitably been very limited. It is by means of speech that we express our feelings to the little company of our neighbours and our own family; and without it this pleasant and cheering intercourse must be almost entirely suspended. Not limited in its beneficial results to families and neighbourhoods, it has been the medium of the transmission of thought from age to age, from generation to generation. So that in one age has been concentrated the result of all the researches, the combination of the wisdom of all the preceding.

"There is, without all doubt," it has been observed, "a chain of the thoughts of human kind, from the origin of the world down to the moment at which we exist, a chain not less universal than that of the generation of every being that lives. Ages have exerted their influence on ages; nations on nations; truths on errors; errors on truths."

Whether oral language was an original invention of man, or whether, in the first instance, it was a power bestowed upon him by his Creator and coeval with the human race, the ear must, in either case, have been the primary recipient.—The faculty of speech, so necessary and so beneficial, could not have existed, either by invention or by communication, without the sense of hearing. And hence it happens, that all those who are born deaf are without speech. Their inability to speak is not in general the result of a defect in the organs of speech, but because they cannot hear others, and thus imitate the sounds they utter.

CHAPTER VI.

THE SENSE OF TOUCH.

§ 69. Of the sense of touch and its sensations in general.

We are next to consider the sense of TOUCH. The principal organ of this sense is the hand, although it is not limited to that part of our frame, but is diffused over the whole body. The hand principally arrests our attention as the organ of this sense, because, being furnished with various articulations, it is easily moveable by the muscles, and can readily adapt itself to the various changes of form in the objects to which it is applied.

The senses which have hitherto been examined are more simple and uniform in their results than that of the touch. By the ear we merely possess that sensation which we denominate hearing; we have the knowledge of sounds, and that is all. By the palate we acquire a knowledge of tastes; and by the sense of smelling we become acquainted with the odours of bodies. The knowledge which is directly acquired by all these senses, is limited to the qualities which have been mentioned. By the sense of touch, on the contrary, we become acquainted, not with one merely, but with a variety of qualities or attributes, such as the following: heat and cold, hardness and softness, roughness and smoothness, resistance, extension, and figure; and, in particular, it is in the application of this sense that we find an occasion furnished for the origin of the antecedent and more general notion of externality.

§ 70. Idea of externality suggested in connexion with the touch.

If man were possessed of the sense of smell alone, it would be found that the earliest elements of his knowledge consisted exclusively in sensations of odours. According, however, as these sensations were agreeable or disagreeable, he would acquire the additional ideas of pleasure and pain. And, having experienced pleasure and pain, we may suppose that this would subsequently give rise both to the feelings and the abstract conceptions of desire and aversion. But if he had no other sense, all these feelings would seem to him to be internal, not only in their experience, but their origin; in other words, to be mere emanations from the soul itself; and he would be incapable of referring them to an external cause.—If he were possessed of the sense of hearing alone, the result would be similar;

his existence would then seem to consist essentially of sounds, as in the other case it would be made up of odours; nor, indeed, by the aid of merely both these senses combined, would he be able to form an idea of externality or outness.

But this idea is a most important one; it is the connecting thought, which introduces us to an acquaintance with a new form of existence, different from that interior existence which we variously call by the names spirit, mind, or soul. This idea first arises in the mind, although it is not directly addressed to that sense, by means of the touch.

There is no question that the other senses might of themselves furnish a basis of considerable extent for the mental action. By means of their aid alone, such a developement of mind might take place, that we could perceive, think, compare, abstract, reason, and will. And although, under such circumstances, everything would seem to us to be internal, yet we should probably find the mental action unembarrassed and easy, and a source of pleasure. But, after a time, we decide to move the limbs in a particular direction, and to press the hand or some other part of the body through some hard and resisting substance. It is when we attempt to do anything of this kind, which calls the sense of touch into action, that we find the wonted series of thoughts disturbed, the desire checked, and the volition counteracted. It is probably at this precise position of the mind, with scarcely the interval of a momentary pause of wonder, that there arises vividly in the soul a new thought, a new state of mind, which we call the idea of externality or outness. It is the sense of touch which impinges upon the obstacle that stands in our way; and no other sense admits of this peculiar application. It is thus the means of partially disturbing the previous connexion and tendency of thought, and of giving occasion for the rise of the new idea which is under consideration. And this idea, called into existence under these circumstances, becomes associated with all those notions which we subsequently form of matter.—It may be of some importance to add here, that we shall have occasion to refer to this idea again in a subsequent chapter on the Intuitional or Suggestional power.

And the idea or thought, being thus originated on the appropriate occasion of its origin, and not by an arbitrary act of volition merely, but by the necessities of our mental existence, is an affirmation in the soul itself of the reality of that for which it stands, however difficult it may be to define or describe it. It is to be remembered, that externality is not a direct object of the touch, as extension and hardness are, but that the tactual sense simply furnishes the *occasion* on which it is formed.

§ 71. Origin of the notion of extension, and of form or figure.

The idea of EXTENSION has its origin by means of the sense of touch. When the touch is applied to bodies, when in the intermediate parts there is a continuity of the same substance, we necessarily form that notion. It is not, however, to be imagined that Extension, as it exists outwardly, and the corresponding notion in the mind, actually resemble each other. So far from any imitation and copying from one to the other, or resemblance in any way, there is a radical and utter diversity. As to outward, material extension, it is not necessary to attend to it here; our business at present is with the corresponding mental state. Nor will it be necessary to delay even upon that; the more we multiply words upon it, the more obscure it becomes. As it is a simple mental state, we cannot resolve it into others, and in that way make it clearer by defining it. We must refer in this case, as in others like it, to each one's personal experience. It will be better understood in that way than by any form of words.

The notion of extension is intimately connected with, and may be considered in some sort the foundation of, that of the FORM or figure of bodies.—Dr.

Brown somewhere calls the Form of bodies their relation to each other in space. And it is very true that the form of bodies involves the fact of the relation of their parts to each other. But we do not propose here to consider form in its outward existence, but only the idea or mental state which corresponds to it. The notion which we have of the form of things is subsequent, in the order of nature, to that which we have of their extension. The former could not exist without the antecedent existence of the latter. Both are simple; both are undefinable; and both are to be ascribed in their origin to the occasion furnished by the sense of touch.

§ 72. On the sensations of heat and cold.

Among the states of mind which are usually classed with the intimations of the sense under consideration, are those which are connected with changes in the temperature of our bodies. Some writers, it is true, have been inclined to dissent from this arrangement, and have hazarded an opinion that they ought not to be ascribed to the sense of TOUCH; but Dr. Reid, on the contrary, who gave to our sensations the most careful and patient attention, has decidedly assigned to them this origin. Among other remarks, he has expressed himself on this subject to this effect.

"The words HEAT and COLD," he remarks (Inquiry into the Human Mind, chap. v.), "have each of them two significations; they sometimes signify certain sensations of the mind, which can have no existence when they are not felt, nor can exist anywhere but in the mind or sentient being; but more frequently they signify a quality in bodies, which, by the laws of nature, occasions the sensations of heat and cold in us; a quality which, though connected by custom so closely with the sensation that we cannot without difficulty separate them, yet hath not the least resemblance to it, and may continue to exist when there is no sensation at all.

"The sensations of heat and cold are perfectly

known, for they neither are, nor can be, anything else than what we feel them to be; but the qualities in bodies which we call *heat* and *cold* are unknown. They are only conceived by us as unknown causes or occasions of the sensations to which we give the same names. But, though common sense says nothing of the nature of the qualities, it plainly dictates the existence of them; and to deny that there can be heat and cold when they are not felt, is an absurdity too gross to merit confutation. For what could be more absurd than to say that the thermometer cannot rise or fall unless some person be present, or that the coast of Guinea would be as cold as Nova Zembla if it had no inhabitants?

"It is the business of philosophers to investigate, by proper experiments and induction, what heat and cold are in bodies. And whether they make heat a particular element diffused through nature, and accumulated in the heated body, or whether they make it a certain vibration of the parts of the heated body; whether they determine that heat and cold are contrary qualities, as the sensations undoubtedly are contrary, or that heat only is a quality, and cold its privation; these questions are within the province of philosophy; for common sense says nothing on the one side or the other.

"But, whatever be the nature of that quality in bodies which we call *heat*, we certainly know this, that it cannot in the least resemble the sensation of heat. It is no less absurd to suppose a likeness between the sensation and the quality, than it would be to suppose that the pain of the gout resembles a square or a triangle. The simplest man that hath common sense does not imagine the sensation of heat, or anything that resembles that sensation, to be in the fire. He only imagines that there is something in the fire which makes him and other sentient beings feel heat. Yet as the name of *heat*, in common language, more frequently and more properly signifies this unknown something in the fire than the sensation occasioned by it, he justly laughs at the philosopher who denies that there is any heat in the fire, and thinks that he speaks contrary to common sense."

§ 73. On the sensations of hardness and softness.

"Let us next consider," continues the same writer, "HARDNESS and SOFTNESS; by which words we always understand real properties or qualities of bodies, of which we have a distinct conception.

"When the parts of a body adhere so firmly that it cannot easily be made to change its figure, we call it *hard;* when its parts are easily displaced, we call it *soft.* This is the notion which all mankind have of hardness and softness: they are neither sensations nor like any sensation; they were real qualities before they were perceived by touch, and continue to be so when they are not perceived: for if any man will affirm that diamonds were not hard until they were handled, who would reason with him?

"There is, no doubt, a sensation, by which we perceive a body to be hard or soft. This sensation of hardness may easily be had by pressing one's hand against a table, and attending to the feeling that ensues, setting aside, as much as possible, all thoughts of the table and its qualities, or of any external thing. But it is one thing to have the sensation, and another to attend to it and make it a distinct object of reflection. The first is very easy; the last, in most cases, extremely difficult.

"We are so accustomed to use the sensation as a sign, and to pass immediately to the hardness signified, that, as far as appears, it was never made an object of thought, either by the vulgar or by philosophers; nor has it a name in any language. There is no sensation more distinct or more frequent; yet it is never attended to, but passes through the mind instantaneously, and serves only to introduce that quality in bodies which, by a law of our constitution, it suggests.

"There are, indeed, some cases, wherein it is no difficult matter to attend to the sensation occasioned by the hardness of a body; for instance, when it is so violent as to occasion considerable pain: then nature calls upon us to attend to it; and then we acknowledge that it is a mere sensation, and can only be in a sentient being. If a man runs his head with violence against a pillar, I appeal to him whether the pain he feels resembles the hardness of the stone; or if he can conceive anything like what he feels to be in an inanimate piece of matter.

"The attention of the mind is here entirely turned towards the painful feeling; and, to speak in the common language of mankind, he feels nothing in the stone, but feels a violent pain in his head. It is quite otherwise when he leans his head gently against the pillar; for then he will tell you that he feels nothing in his head, but feels hardness in the stone. Hath he not a sensation in this case as well as in the other? Undoubtedly he hath; but it is a sensation which nature intended only as a sign of something in the stone; and, accordingly, he instantly fixes his attention upon the thing signified; and cannot, without great difficulty, attend so much to the sensation as to be persuaded that there is any such thing distinct from the hardness it signifies.

"But, however difficult it may be to attend to this fugitive sensation, to stop its rapid progress, and to disjoin it from the external quality of hardness, in whose shadow it is apt immediately to hide itself: this is what a philosopher by pains and practice must attain, otherwise it will be impossible for him to reason justly on this subject, or even to understand what is here advanced. For the last appeal, in subjects of this nature, must be to what a man feels and perceives in his own mind."

§ 74. Of certain indefinite feelings sometimes ascribed to the touch.

In connexion with these views on the sensations of touch, it is proper to remark, that certain feelings have been ascribed to that sense which are probably of a character too indefinite to admit of a positive and undoubted classification. Although they clearly have their place in the general arrangement which has been laid down, with the states of mind which we are now considering; that is to say, are rather of an external and material, than of an internal origin; still they do not so evidently admit of an assignment to a particular sense. Those sensations to which we now refer (if it be proper to use that term in application to them) appear to have their origin in the human system considered as a whole, made up of bones, flesh, muscles, the senses, &c., rather than to be susceptible of being traced to any particular part. Of this description are the feelings expressed by the terms uneasiness, weariness, weakness, sickness, and those of an opposite character, such as ease, hilarity, health, vigour, and the like.

§ 75. Relation between the sensation and what is outwardly signified.

We here return a moment to the subject of the relation between the internal sensation and the outward object; and again repeat that the mental state and the corresponding outward object are altogether diverse. This view holds good in the case of the secondary, as well as of the primary qualities of matter. Whether we speak of extension, or resistance, or heat, or colour, or roughness, there are, in all cases alike, two things, the internal affection and the outward quality; but they are utterly distinct, totally without likeness to each other. But how it happens that one thing, which is totally different from another, can nevertheless give us a knowledge of that from which it differs, it would be a waste of time to attempt to explain. Our knowledge is undoubtedly limited to the mere fact.

This is one of those difficult but decisive points in MENTAL PHILOSOPHY, of which it is essential to possess a precise and correct understanding. The letters which cover over the pages of a book are a very different thing from the thought, and the combinations of thought, which they stand for. The accountant's columns of numerals are not identical with the quantities and their relations which they represent. And so in regard to the mind; all its acts are of one kind, and what they stand for is of another. The mind, in all its feelings and operations, is governed by its own laws, and characterizes its efforts by the essential elements of its own nature. Nothing which is seen or heard, nothing which is the subject of taste, or touch, or any other sense, nothing material which can be imagined to exist in any place or in any form, can furnish the least positive disclosure either of its intrinsic nature or of the mode of its action.

What, then, is the relation between the sensation and the outward object, between the perception and the thing perceived? Evidently that of the sign and the thing signified. And as in a multitude of cases, the sign may give a knowledge of its object, without any other grounds of such knowledge than mere institution or appointment, so it is in this. The mind, maintaining its appropriate action, and utterly rejecting the intervention of all images and visible representations, except what are outward and material, and totally distinct from itself both in place and nature, is, notwithstanding, susceptible of the knowledge of things exterior, and can form an acquaintance with the universe of matter.

A misapprehension in this respect, the mistaken supposition of the mind's either receiving actual filmy images from external objects, or being itself transformed into the likeness of such images, has been, in times past, the source of much confusion and contention. But that opinion, however prevalent it may have been once, is mere hypothesis; it has not the slightest well-founded evidence in its favour. Still we can reject it wholly from our belief, and from all influence on our belief, only by guarding against early associations, by a rigid self-inspection, and by carefully separating the material and the immaterial, the qualities of mind and of matter.

CHAPTER VII.

THE SENSE OF SIGHT.

§ 76. Of the organ of sight, and the uses or benefits of that sense.

Of those instruments of external perception with which a benevolent Providence has favoured us, a high rank must be given to the sense of seeing. If we were restricted in the process of acquiring knowledge to the informations of the touch merely, how many embarrassments would attend our progress, and how slow it would prove! Having never possessed sight, it would be many years before the most acute and active person could form an idea of a mountain, or even of a large edifice. But by the additional help of the sense of seeing, he not only observes the figure of large buildings, but is in a moment possessed of all the beauties of a wide and variegated landscape.

The organ of this sense is the eye. On a slight examination, the eye is found to be a sort of telescope, having its distinct parts, and discovering throughout the most exquisite construction. The medium on which this organ acts are rays of light, everywhere diffused, and always advancing, if they meet with no opposition, in direct lines. The eye, like all the other senses, not only receives externally the medium on which it acts, but carries the rays of light into itself; and, on principles purely scientific, refracts and combines them anew.

It does not, however, fall within our plan to give a minute description of the eye, which belongs rather to the physiologist; but such a description, with the statement of the uses of the different parts of the organ, must be to a candid and reflecting mind a most powerful argument in proof of the existence and goodness of the Supreme Being. How wonderful, among other things, is the adaptation of the rays of light to the eye! If these rays were not of a texture extremely small, they would cause much pain to the organ of vision, into which they so rapidly pass. If they were not capable of exciting within us the sensations of colour, we should be deprived of much of that high satisfaction which we now take in beholding surrounding objects; showing forth, wherever they are to be found, the greatest variety and the utmost richness of tints.

§ 77. Statement of the mode or process in visual perception.

In the process of vision, the rays of light, coming from various objects and in various directions, strike, in the first place, on the pellucid or transparent part of the ball of the eye.

If they were to continue passing on precisely in the same direction, they would produce merely one mingled and indistinct expanse of colour. In their progress, however, through the crystalline humour, they are refracted or bent from their former direction, and are distributed to certain focal points on the retina, which is a white, fibrous expansion of the optic nerve.

The rays of light, coming from objects in the field of vision, whether it be more or less extensive, as soon as they have been distributed on their distinct portions of the retina, and have formed an image there, are immediately followed by the sensation or perception which is termed sight. The image which is thus pictured on the retina, is the last step which we are able to designate in the material part of the process in visual perception; the mental state follows, but it is not in our power to trace, even in the smallest degree, any physical connexion between the optical image and the corresponding state of the mind.—All that we can say in this case is, that we suppose them to hold to each other the relation of antecedent and consequent by an ultimate law of our constitution.

§ 78. Of the original and acquired perceptions of sight.

In speaking of those sensations and perceptions, the origin of which is generally attributed to the sense of sight, it is necessary to make a distinction between those which are ORIGINAL and those which are ACQUIRED. Nothing is properly original with the sense of sight but the sensations of colour, such as red, blue, yellow. These sensations (or perceptions, as they are otherwise called, when the internal feeling is combined with a reference to the external cause) are exceedingly numerous. In this respect, the intimations of the sense of sight stand on the same footing with those of taste and hearing; although distinctive names, in consequence of the difficulty of accurately separating and drawing the line between each, are given only in a few cases. All the sensations of colour are original with the sight, and are not to be ascribed to any other sense.

A part, however, of that knowledge, which we attribute to the sight, and which has the appearance of being immediate and original in that sense, is not so. Some of its alleged perceptions are properly the results of sensations, combined not only with the usual reference to an external cause, but with various other acts of the judgment. In some cases the combination of the acts of the judgment with the visual sensation is carried so far, that there is a sort of transfer to the sight of the knowledge which has been obtained from some other source. And not unfrequently, in consequence of a long and tenacious association, we are apt to look upon the knowledge thus acquired as truly original in the seeing power. This will suffice, perhaps, as a statement of the general fact, while the brief examination of a few instances will help to the more thorough understanding of those acquired perceptions of the sight which are here referred to.

§ 79. The idea of extension not originally from sight.

It is well known that there is nothing more common than for a person to say that he sees the length or breadth of any external object; that he sees its extent, &c. These expressions appear to imply (and undoubtedly are so understood) that extension is a direct object of sight. There is no question that such is the common sentiment, viz., that the outlines and surface which bodies permanently expand and present to the view, are truly seen. An opinion different from this might even incur the charge of great absurdity.

But, properly, the notion of extension, as we have already seen, has its origin in the sense of touch. Being a simple and elementary thought, it is not susceptible of definition; nor, when we consider extension as existing outwardly and materially, can we make it a matter of description without running into the confusion of using synonymous words. But, whatever it is (and certainly there can be neither ignorance nor disagreement on that point, however much language may fail of conveying our ideas), the knowledge of it is not to be ascribed originally to the sight.

The notion of extension is closely connected with externality. It is not possible to form the idea of extension from mere consciousness, or a reflection on what takes place within us. But making a muscular effort, and thus applying the touch to some resisting body, we first have the notion of outness; and either from the same application of that sense, or when we have repeated it continuously on the same surface, we have the additional notion of its being extended or spread out. If a man were fixed immoveably in one place, capable of smelling, tasting, hearing, and seeing, but without tactual impressions originating from a resisting body, he would never possess a knowledge of either. Having first gained that knowledge from the touch in the way just mentioned, he learns in time what appearance extended bodies (which are, of course, coloured bodies) make to the eye. At a very early period, having ascertained that all coloured bodies are spread out or extended, he invariably associates the idea of extension with that coloured appearance. Hence he virtually and practically transfers the knowledge obtained by one sense to another; and even, after a time, imagines extension to be a direct object of sight, when, in fact, what is seen is only a sign of it, and merely suggests it. An affection of the sense of touch is the true and original occasion of the origin of this notion; and it becomes an idea of sight only by acquisition or transference.

§ 80. Of the knowledge of the figure of bodies by the sight.

Views similar to those which have been already advanced will evidently apply to the figure of bodies. We acquire a knowledge of the figure or form of bodies originally by the sense of touch. But it cannot be doubted that this knowledge is often confidently attributed to the sense of sight as well as the touch. Although there is reason to believe that men labour under a mistake in this, it is not strange, when we trace back our mental history to its earlier periods, that such a misapprehension should exist.

A solid body presents to the eye nothing but a certain disposition of colours and light. We may imagine ourselves to see the prominences or cavities in such bodies, when in truth we see only the light or the shade occasioned by them. This light and shade, however, we learn by experience to consider as the sign of a certain solid figure.—A proof of the truth of this statement is, that a painter, by carefully imitating the distribution of light and shade which he sees in objects, will make his work very naturally and exactly represent not only the general outline of a body, but its prominences, depressions, and other irregularities. And yet his delineation, which, by the distribution of light and shade, gives such various representations, is on a smooth and plain surface.

It was a problem submitted by Mr. Molyneux to Mr. Locke, whether a blind man, who has learned the difference between a cube and a sphere by the touch, can, on being suddenly restored to sight, distinguish between them, and tell which is the sphere and which is the cube, by the aid of what may be called his *new* sense merely. And the answer of Mr. Locke was, in agreement with the opinion of Molyneux himself, that he cannot. The blind man knows what impressions the cube and sphere make on the organ of *touch*, and by that sense is able to distinguish between them; but, as he is ignorant what impression they will make on the organ of sight, he is not able, by the latter sense alone, to tell which is the round body and which is the cubic.

It was remarked, that solid bodies present to the eye nothing but a certain disposition of light and colours.—It seems to follow from this, that the first idea which will be conveyed to the mind on seeing a globe, will be that of a circle on a plain surface, but variously shadowed with different degrees of light. This imperfect idea is corrected in this way.. Combining the suggestions of the sense of touch with those of sight, we learn by greater experience what kind of appearance solid convex bodies will make to us. That appearance becomes to the mind the sign of the presence of a globe; so that we have an idea of a round body by a very rapid mental correction, whereas the notion first conveyed to the mind is truly that of a plain, circular surface, on which there is a variety in the dispositions of light and shade. It is an evidence of the correctness of this statement, that in paintings, plain surfaces, variously shaded, represent convex bodies, and with great truth and exactness.

It appears, then, that extension and figure are originally perceived, not by sight, but by touch. We do not judge of them by sight until we have learned by our experience that certain visible appearances always accompany and signify the existence of extension and of figure. This knowledge we acquire at a very early period in life; so much so, that we lose, in a great measure, the memory both of its commencement and progress.

§ 81. Measurements of magnitude by the eye.

What has been said naturally leads us to the consideration of MAGNITUDE. This is a general term for Extension, when we conceive of it not only as limited or bounded, but as related to and compared with other objects. Although we make use of the eye in judging of it, it is to be kept in mind, that the knowledge of magnitude is not an original intimation of the sight, but is at first acquired by the aid of touch. So well known is this, that it has been common to consider Magnitude under the two heads of tangible or real, and visible or apparent; the tangible magnitude being always the same, but the visible varying with the distance of the object. A man of six feet stature is always that height, whether he be a mile distant, or half a mile, or near at hand; the change of place making no change in his real or tangible magnitude. But the visible or apparent magnitude of this man may be six feet or two feet, as we view him present with us and immediately in our neighbourhood, or at two miles' distance; for his magnitude appears to our eye greater or less, according as he is more or less removed.

In support of the doctrine that the knowledge of magnitude is not an original intimation of the sight, but is at first acquired by the aid of touch, we may remark, that, in judging of magnitude by the sight, we are much influenced not merely by the visual perception, but particularly by comparison with other objects, the size of which is known or supposed to be known. "I remember once," says Dr. Abercrombie (Intellec. Powers, part ii., sect. 1), "having occasion to pass along Ludgate Hill, when the great door of St. Paul's was open, and several persons were standing in it. They appeared to be very little children, but, on coming up to them, were found to be full-grown persons. In the mental process which here took place, the door had been assumed as a known magnitude, and the other objects judged of by it. Had I attended to the door being much larger than any door that one is in the habit of seeing, the mind would have made allowance for the apparent size of the persons; and, on the other hand, had these been known to be full-grown persons, a judgment would have been formed of the size of the door."

Among the multitude of instances which might be adduced in illustration of the doctrine under notice, the following statement, to be found in the seventh number of the Edinburgh Journal of Science, is a somewhat striking one. In examining a dioramic representation of the inside of Rochester Cathedral, which produced the finest effect, from the entire exclusion of all extraneous light and of all objects, excepting those on the picture itself, the writer of the statement referred to was struck with an appearance of distortion in the perspective, which he ascribed to the canvass not hanging vertically. Upon mentioning this to the gentleman who exhibited the picture, he offered to walk in front of it, and strike its surface with the palm of his hand, to show that the canvass was freely suspended. Upon doing this, a very remarkable deception, or illusion rather, took place. As his hand passed along, it gradually became larger and larger till it reached the middle, when it became enormously large. It then diminished till it reached the other end of the canvass.

As the hand moved towards the middle of the picture, it touched the parts of the picture more and more remote from the eye of the observer; and, consequently, the mind referred the hand and the object in contact with it to the same remote distance; and, consequently, gave it a fictitious magnitude, corresponding with the visible figure it presented, combined with the supposition of its being placed at a distance. (See Edin. Journ. of Science, No. vii., p. 90, and Art. Science, Edin. Encyc.)

§ 82. Of objects seen in the mist, and of the sun and moon in the horizon.

In accordance with the above-mentioned principle, it happens, that objects seen by a person in a mist seem larger than life. Their faint appearance rapidly conveys to the mind the idea of being considerably removed, although they are actually near to us. And the mind immediately draws the conclusion (so rapidly as to seem a simple and original perception), that the object, having the same visible or apparent magnitude, and yet supposed to be at a considerable distance, is greater than other objects of the same class. So that it is chiefly the view of the mind, a law or habit of the intellect, which in this particular case gives a fictitious expansion to bodies; although it is possible that the result may in part be attributed to a difference in the refraction of the rays of light, caused by their passing through a denser and less uniform medium than usual.

These remarks naturally remind us of the well-known fact, that the sun and moon seem larger in the horizon than in the meridian. A number of reasons may be given for this appearance.—(1.) The horizon may seem more distant than the zenith, in consequence of intervening objects. We measure the distance of objects in part by means of those that are scattered along between, and any expanse of surface, where there are no such intervening objects, appears to us of less extent than it actually is. Now if the rays of light form precisely the same image in the eye, but the source of them is supposed to be further off in the horizon than in the zenith, such have been our mental habits, that the object in the horizon will probably appear the largest.—(2.) Another reason, which is sometimes assigned, of the enlarged appearance of the sun and moon in the horizon is, that the rays from them fall on the body of the atmosphere obliquely, and, of course, are reflected downward towards the beholder, and subtend a larger angle at his eye. Hence, as we always see objects in the direction of the ray just before it enters the eye, if we follow the rays back in the precise direction of their approach, they will present to the eye the outlines of a larger object as their source than they would if they had not been refracted.—When the atmosphere is not clear, but unusual masses of vapour are accumulated in it, whether immediately around us or anywhere else in the direction of the rays, the refraction is increased, and the object is proportionally enlarged. This circumstance helps to explain the fact of the enlargement not being uniform, but sometimes greater and at others less.—(3.) Our estimate of the size of the sun and moon is also affected by the simultaneous perception of other objects of known magnitude, which happen to be in the same direction. The setting sun, for instance, when it is seen through distant woods, appears much enlarged. The woods, in consequence of their distance, subtend but a small angle at the eye; but, being objects of known magnitude, they appear enlarged and nearly of their natural size in our conception of them. And as the sun fills a larger space in our eye than the separate trees which fall within its disk, it experiences in our conception an enlargement, precisely corresponding with the imagined or conceptive enlargement of the objects which are encircled by its rays. Just as in the case of a balloon, which, at a great elevation, crosses the disk of the sun or moon. The balloon is an object of known size and of great size; but, in fact, when seen at a great elevation, it is materially and visually a mere speck, although much enlarged *mentally*. Accordingly, when it passes over the disk of the sun or moon, those bodies will appear greatly enlarged, so as to correspond with our previous conceptions of the size of the body which their rays at that time encircle.—(The reader will find this subject more fully explained in Dr. Arnott's Elements of Physics, vol. i.)

§ 83. Of the estimation of distances by sight.

We are next led to the consideration of distances as made known and ascertained by the sight. By the distance of objects, when we use the term in reference to ourselves, we mean the space which is interposed between those objects and our own position. It might be objected, that space interposed is only a synonymous expression for the thing to be defined. Nevertheless, no one can be supposed to be ignorant of what is meant. Even blind men have a notion of distance, and can measure it by the touch, or by walking forward until they meet the distant object.

The perception of distance by the sight is an acquired and not an original perception, although the latter was universally supposed to be the fact until comparatively a recent period.

All objects in the first instance appear to touch the eye, but our experience has corrected so many of the representations of the senses before the period which we are yet able to retrace by the memory, that we cannot prove this by a reference to our own childhood and infancy. It appears, however, from the statement of the cases of persons born blind on the sudden restoration of their sight.—"When he first saw," says Cheselden, the anatomist, when giving an account of a young man whom he had restored to sight by couching for the cataract, "he was so far from making any judgment about distance, that he thought all objects touched his eye, as he expressed it, as what he felt did his skin; and thought no objects so agreeable as those which were smooth and regular, although he could form no judgment of their shape, or guess what it was in any object that was pleasing to him."

This anatomist has further informed us that he has brought to sight several others, who had no remembrance of ever having seen; and that they all gave the same account of their learning to see, as they called it, as the young man already mentioned, although not in so many particulars; and that they all had this in common, that, having never had occasion to move their eyes, they knew not how to do it, and, at first, could not at all direct them to a particular object; but in time they acquired that faculty, though by slow degrees.*

* Some doubts have been raised from time to time of the correctness of Cheselden's experiments and inquiries here referred to. For-

Blind persons, when at first restored to sight, are unable to estimate the distance of objects by that sense; but soon observing that certain changes in the visible appearance of bodies always accompany a change of distance, they fall upon a method of estimating distance by the visible appearance. And it would no doubt be found, if it could be particularly examined into, that all mankind come to possess the power of estimating the distances of objects by sight in the same way. When a body is removed from us and placed at a considerable distance, it becomes smaller in its visible appearance, its colours are less lively, and its outlines less distinct; and we may expect to find various intermediate objects, more or fewer in number corresponding with the increase of the distance, showing themselves between the receding object and the spectator. And hence it is that a certain visible appearance comes to be the sign of a certain distance.

Historical and landscape painters are enabled to turn these facts to great account in their delineations. By means of dimness of colour, indistinctness of outline, and the partial interposition of other objects, they are enabled apparently to throw back, at a very considerable distance from the eye, those objects which they wish to appear remote. While other objects, that are intended to appear near, are painted vivid in colour, large in size, distinct in outline, and are separated from the eye of the spectator by few or no intermediate objects.

§ 84. Estimation of distance when unaided by intermediate objects.

As we depend in no small degree upon intermediate objects in forming our notions of distance, it results,

tunately, Mr. Stewart has taken up the subject with his accustomed caution and candour in his Account of James Mitchell, a boy born deaf and blind. He shows to ample satisfaction, in a note near the commencement of that Narration, that the facts which have been brought forward in opposition to Cheselden may be satisfactorily explained, without any impeachment of the correctness of his statements or the justness of his conclusions from them.—See additional confirmations of this subject in the life of Caspar Hauser.

that we are often much perplexed by the absence of such objects. Accordingly we find that people frequently mistake when they attempt to estimate by the eye the length or width of unoccupied plains and marshes, generally making the extent less than it really is. For the same reason they misjudge of the width of a river, estimating its width at half or three quarters of a mile at the most, when it is, perhaps, not less than double that distance. The same holds true of other bodies of water, and of all other things which are seen by us in a horizontal position, and under similar circumstances.

We mistake in the same way, also, in estimating the height of steeples, and of other bodies that are perpendicular, and not on a level with the eye, provided the height be considerable. As the upper parts of the steeple out-top the surrounding buildings, and there are no contiguous objects with which to compare it, any measurement taken by the eye must be inaccurate, but is generally less than the truth.

Hence perhaps it is that a man on the top of a steeple appears smaller to those below than the same man would seem to the same person and at the same distance on level ground. A man on the earth's surface, placed at the same distance, would probably appear nearly of his actual size. As we have been in the habit of measuring horizontal distances by the eye, we can readily form a nearly accurate opinion whether the person be at a hundred feet distance, or more or less; and the mind immediately makes an allowance for this distance, and corrects the first visual representation of the size of the person so rapidly that we do not remember it. But, having never been in the habit of measuring perpendicular distances, the mind is at a loss, and fails to make that correction which it would readily, and, as it were, intuitively make in the case of objects on level ground. The mistake, therefore, of his supposed nearness, combined with this perplexity, causes the comparative littleness of the man on the steeple.

The fixed stars, when viewed by the eye, all appear to be alike indefinitely and equally distant. Being scattered over the whole sky, they make every part of it seem like themselves at an indefinite and equal distance, and therefore contribute to give the whole sky the appearance of the inside of a sphere. Moreover, the horizon seems to the eye to be further off than the zenith; because between us and the former there lie many things, as fields, hills, and waters, which we know to occupy a great space; whereas between us and the zenith there are no considerable things of known dimensions. And, therefore, the heavens appear like the segment of a sphere, and less than a hemisphere, in the centre of which we seem to stand.—And the wider our prospect is, the greater will the sphere appear to be, and the less the segment.

§ 85. Of objects seen on the ocean, &c.

A vessel seen at sea by a person who is not accustomed to the ocean, appears much nearer than it actually is, and on the same principles as already illustrated. In his previous observations of the objects at a distance, he has commonly noticed a number of intermediate objects interposed between the distant body and himself. It is probably the absence of such objects that chiefly causes the deception under which he labours in the present instance.

In connexion with what has been said, we are led to make this further remark, that a change in the purity of the air will perplex, in some measure, those ideas of distance which we receive from sight. Bishop Berkeley remarks, while travelling in Italy and Sicily, he noticed that cities and palaces, seen at a great distance, appeared nearer to him by several miles than they actually were. The cause of this he very correctly supposed to be the purity of the Italian and Sicilian air, which gave to objects at a distance a degree of brightness and distinctness which, in the less clear and pure atmosphere of his native country, could be observed only in those towns and separate edifices which were near. At home he had learned to estimate the distances of objects by their appearance; but his conclusions failed him when they came to be applied to objects in countries where the air was so much clearer.—And the same thing has been noticed by other travellers who have been placed in the like circumstances.

§ 86. Explanatory remarks.

We have now given a brief outline, first, of the power of Sensation or Sensationality, and, second, of the power of Perception or Perceptivity; together with some account of the senses, through which they respectively operate, and by means of which they are made available as sources or inlets of knowledge. The next faculty naturally presenting itself for consideration in the list of the faculties of the mind distinctively known as Cognitive, is the Conceptive power. But before we can reach this faculty, which is one of great importance, because without it the human mind would be limited in its inquiries to the sphere of objects actually present, we must delay a little upon the subject of the reliance which can be justly placed upon the senses; a subject which involves the acceptance or rejection of IDEALISM, a doctrine which, in limiting our knowledge to ideas or states of the mind, denies by implication any true knowledge of objects outside of ourselves.

II. There is also another subject, to which it is necessary that attention should early be given—that of HABIT. The term Habit indicates a law of the mind's action; and back of that law, inasmuch as law is only the form or mode of activity, there is and must be a principle or power. When spoken of as a power of the mind, as is often done and not without reason, Habit rejects the descriptive epithet of Cognitive; but I think may properly be denominated an Auxiliary power. And as its mighty influence is felt in all the three leading Departments under which the mind is to be considered, we shall lose nothing in giving it an early recognition.

Note.—In the well-known Natural History of Buffon, a writer distinguished alike for learning and eloquence, we have an account of the process by which the full use of the sight and of the other external senses is acquired. He invents a delightful recital, and puts it in the mouth of our first parent; and thus instructs us in the most abstruse subjects by an appeal to the imagination. His views, founded obviously on much inquiry and reflection, notwithstanding the imaginary circumstances in which he presents them, may be regarded as confirmatory of what has been said in these chapters on the uses and the comparative developement and reliableness of the senses.

CHAPTER VIII.

OF RELIANCE ON THE SENSES, AND IDEALISM.

§ 87. By means of sensations we have a knowledge of outward things.

In the third chapter of the Introduction it was remarked, that the states of mind to which operations upon or affections of our senses give rise, are, by our very constitution, the occasions or grounds of belief; and that it is by means of the senses we have a knowledge, in particular, of the external, material world. The new feelings, following an affection of the senses, are in some sense the occasions on which the active and curious mind moves out of the world of its own spiritual and immaterial existence, and becomes acquainted with matter. It is somewhat here as in the reading of a book. When we read a book, only certain coloured marks or lines, arranged in a particular order, are directly presented to our senses; but we find them connected with new states of mind, utterly distinct from the direct impression which they make. A piece of paper, written over with such coloured delineations, becomes to the soul a sign of the most various and exalted ideas; and in like manner, such is the constitution of our mental nature, it is found to be the case that certain new affections of the mind, provided they are caused by means of the senses, become the signs of various existences, which are wholly diverse from the feelings themselves. We experience the feelings, in other words the mental states, which all admit to be in themselves neither archetypes nor resemblances of anything whatever which is external to the soul; and then at once we become acquainted with a vast multitude of outward objects. On the authority of such feelings as are immediately consequent on an affection of the senses, all mankind, if the evidence of their general conduct and of their express declarations is to be regarded, believe in outward objects, as having a distinct and real existence, as having forms, properties, and relations.

§ 88. Objection to a reliance on the senses.

Nevertheless, without denying the fact of this general reliance on the senses as a ground of belief, an objection has been made to its being well placed. The objection, stated in a few words, is this, THAT OUR SENSES SOMETIMES DECEIVE US, AND LEAD US INTO MISTAKES.

In support of the objection, such instances as the following are brought forward.—The sun and moon appear to the spectator on the earth's surface to be a foot or two in diameter, and little more than half a mile high; a straight stick, thrust into the water, appears to us crooked, as seen by the eye in that position; a square tower at a distance is mistaken for a round one; a piece of ice for a stone; a brass coin for a gold one. Nor are such mistakes to be ascribed solely to the sense of sight; they are not unfrequently committed when we rely on the intimations of the taste and smell, the touch and hearing.—Various facts of the above kind have been brought forward to discredit the senses, and to prevent a reliance on them. It is not necessary to extend the enumeration of them, as these will serve for a specimen of the whole.

§ 89. The senses circumscribed or limited rather than fallacious.

That there are some apparent grounds for the objection which has been made to a full reliance on the testimony of the senses, it is not necessary to deny. It is nevertheless true, that the great mass of the alleged fallacies which have been brought forward in opposition to such reliance, are susceptible of a satisfactory explanation.—But before entering into particulars, it is requisite to make the general remark, that the senses are more properly circumscribed or limited than fallacious; and that they lead us astray, not so much by their own direct action as in consequence of our expecting too much of them. Now if we keep this in view, and moderate and chasten our expectations by the evidently limited nature of the senses, we shall find less to complain of.

The imperfect examination of the senses which we have just gone through, evinces the truth of this remark. It is the business, the appropriate function of the sense of smelling, to give us a knowledge of the odours of bodies. When we have these sensations, we may be led, from some principle of the mind, to look for the cause of them, but nothing more; we do not learn from it what the cause is. It is not pretended that this sense alone can give us the notion of an external odoriferous body. The sense of taste is equally limited with that of smell; but both, as far as they go, are grounds of knowledge, and do not deceive. It might, no doubt, be said, that they may be diseased, and thus mislead us; but the remarks of this section go on the supposition that the senses are in a sound state.—When we come to the sense of hearing, we find that the perceptions of sound have, in part, an acquired character. The reference of a particular sound to a particular external cause always implies the previous exercise of the touch, also the exercises of that principle of the mind which is termed association, and of an act of the judgment. But hearing, when in a sound state, is always a ground of belief and knowledge, as far as the mere sensation of sound is concerned, and so far can be most certainly trusted.

It is the appropriate business of the sense of sight,

against the testimony of which so many objections have been made, to render us acquainted with the colours of bodies. To say, therefore, that it leads us into errors in respect to solidity, extension, size, direction, or distance, is but very little, or, rather, nothing to the purpose. These are acquired perceptions, and have their origin in another sense, that of touch. The visual sensations are in these cases mere signs of the knowledge which we have from another source. When, therefore, we separate what belongs to the sight from what belongs to the touch, and distinguish between them, it is impossible to fix the charge of misrepresentation upon either.

And hence, on the question whether our senses mislead us, we are always to consider to which of the senses the particular things under review appropriately belong. And in many cases when we are searching after truth, it becomes us to call in the aid of all the senses, and not to consult one to the entire omission of the others. They all make parts of one great and wonderful system, and cannot be safely separated. When they are in a sound state; when the intellectual experiences, of which they are the origin, are properly discriminated; and, further, when the intimations of one sense are aided by those of another, and by the guidance of the reasoning power, which clearly ought not to be excluded, we may then confidently expect to be led by them into the truth, so far as our Creator designed that it should be made known to us.

§ 90. Some alleged mistakes of the senses owing to want of care.

If the course indicated at the close of the last section were always followed, the mistakes to which we are occasionally exposed would be much less frequent. But even when we refer to all the senses, and combine with this reference the deductions of reasoning, we may still err from want of care. Beyond all question, some of the mistakes ascribed to the senses are owing to premature inferences from them; to a want of caution, discrimination, and full inquiry. This particular view of the subject is illustrated as follows by Dr. Reid.—"Many things called the deceptions of the senses are only conclusions rashly drawn from the testimony of the senses. In these cases the testimony of the senses is true, but we rashly draw a conclusion from it which does not necessarily follow. We are disposed to impute our errors rather to false information than to inconclusive reasoning, and to blame our senses for the wrong conclusions we draw from their testimony.

"Thus, when a man has taken a counterfeit guinea for a true one, he says his senses deceived him; but he lays the blame where it ought not to be laid: for we may ask him, Did your senses give a false testimony of the colour, or of the figure, or of the impression? No. But this is all that they testified, and this they testified truly. From these premises you concluded that it was a true guinea, but this conclusion does not follow; you erred, therefore, not by relying upon the testimony of sense, but by judging rashly from its testimony. Not only are your senses innocent of this error, but it is only by their information that it can be discovered. If you consult them properly, they will inform you that what you took for a guinea is base metal, or is deficient in weight, and this can only be known by the testimony of sense.

"I remember to have met with a man who thought the argument used by Protestants against the Popish doctrine of transubstantiation, from the testimony of our senses, inconclusive; because, said he, instances may be given where several of our senses may deceive us; how do we know, then, that there may not be cases wherein they all deceive us, and no sense is left to detect the fallacy? I begged of him to know an instance wherein several of our senses deceive us. I take, said he, a piece of soft turf; I cut it into the shape of an apple; with the essence of apples I give it the smell of an apple; and with paint I can give it the skin and colour of an apple. Here, then, is a body, which, if you judge by your eye, by your touch, or by your smell, is an apple.

"To this I would answer, that no one of our senses deceives us in this case. My sight and touch testify that it has the shape and colour of an apple; this is true. The sense of smelling testifies that it has the smell of an apple: this is likewise true, and is no deception. Where, then, lies the deception? It is evident it lies in this, that because this body has some qualities belonging to the apple, I conclude that it is an apple. This is a fallacy, not of the senses, but of inconclusive reasoning."*

There are other instances where the subject might be placed in a true light. It is well known (to take an illustration not unfrequently referred to by writers) that the vibrations of a pendulum are affected by its geographical position, the latitude where it is. Before this fact was ascertained, a person might have employed a pendulum of a given length as a measure of comparative duration at two distant points on the globe's surface. And when he had done this, he might have been disposed to declare, on the authority of his senses and personal observation, that two portions of time, measured in different latitudes, were the same, although they were in fact different.

But here comes the question: Are his senses to blame for this mistake? Not at all. The testimony of the senses and of observation, as far as it went, was correct. The mistake is evidently to be attributed to erroneous deduction. The conclusion was bottomed on the great and undoubted principle of reasoning, that the laws of nature are uniform. But then there were mistaken assumptions in this particular case which vitiated the reasoning, viz., that the earth is circular and not a spheroid; and that the same quantity of the attractive force of the earth operates on the pendulum at every point on the earth's surface. Here is the foundation of the mistake; in certain facts precipitately assumed as grounds of reasoning, and in the deductions from them, and not in the senses.

* Reid's Intellectual Powers of Man, Essay ii.

§ 91. Of mistakes in judging of the motion of objects.

"Many false judgments," it is further remarked by Dr. Reid, "that are accounted deceptions of sense, arise from our mistaking relative motion for real or absolute motion. These can be no deceptions of sense, because by our senses we perceive only the relative motions of bodies; and it is by reasoning that we infer the real from the relative which we perceive. A little reflection may satisfy us of this.

"It was before observed, that we perceive extension to be one sensible quality of bodies, and thence are necessarily led to conceive space, though space be of itself no object of sense. When a body is removed out of its place, the space which it filled remains empty till it is filled by some other body, and would remain if it should never be filled. Before any body existed, the space which bodies now occupy was empty space, capable of receiving bodies, for no body can exist where there is no space to contain it. There is space, therefore, wherever bodies exist or can exist.

"Hence it is evident that space can have no limits. It is no less evident that it is immoveable. Bodies placed in it are moveable, but the place where they were cannot be moved; and we can as easily conceive a thing to be moved from itself, as one part of space brought nearer to, or removed further from another.

"This space, therefore, which is unlimited and immoveable, is called by philosophers *absolute space.* Absolute or real motion is a change of place in absolute space.

"Our senses do not testify the absolute motion or absolute rest of any body. When one body removes from another, this may be discerned by the senses; but whether any body keeps the same part of absolute space, we do not perceive by our senses. When one body seems to remove from another, we can infer with certainty that there is absolute motion; but whether in the one or the other, or partly in both, is not discerned by sense.

"Of all the prejudices which philosophy contradicts, I believe there is none so general as that the earth keeps its place unmoved. This opinion seems to be universal, till it is corrected by instruction, or by philosophical speculation. Those who have any tincture of education are not now in danger of being held by it, but they find at first a reluctance to believe that there are antipodes; that the earth is spherical, and turns round its axis every day, and round the sun every year. They can recollect the time when reason struggled with prejudice upon these points, and prevailed at length, but not without some effort.

"The cause of a prejudice so very general is not unworthy of investigation. But that is not our present business. It is sufficient to observe, that it cannot justly be called a fallacy of sense; because our senses testify only the change of situation of one body in relation to other bodies, and not its change of situation in absolute space. It is only the relative motion of bodies that we perceive, and that we perceive truly. It is the province of reason and philosophy, from the relative motions which we perceive, to collect the real and absolute motions which produce them.

"All motion must be estimated from some point or place which is supposed to be at rest. We perceive not the points of absolute space, from which real and absolute motion must be reckoned; and there are obvious reasons that lead mankind, in a state of ignorance, to make the earth the fixed place from which they may estimate the various motions they perceive. The custom of doing this from infancy, and of using constantly a language which supposes the earth to be at rest, may perhaps be the cause of the general prejudice in favour of this opinion.

"Thus it appears, that if we distinguish accurately between what our senses really and naturally testify, and the conclusions which we draw from their testimony by reasoning, we shall find many of the errors, called fallacies of the senses, to be no fallacy of the senses, but rash judgments, which are not to be imputed to our senses."

§ 92. Of mistakes as to the distances and magnitude of objects.

One class of the fallacies by means of the senses is made up of those errors we commit in our perceptions of the distance of objects. Our sight, it is said, often represents objects to be near which are distant, and objects to be distant which are near. That we often form erroneous judgments as to the distance of objects, is true; but it is a mistaken sentiment which ascribes these erroneous opinions to the misrepresentations of the sight in itself considered.

Take the case of the sun and moon. Those heavenly bodies, as they come under the cognizance of sight, appear not only very small, but also as being at no great distance. Still, in this very instance (although this is one of the cases most frequently referred to by the expositors of the alleged weaknesses and errors of the senses), it cannot be shown that there is any deception practised upon us by that sense. It has sufficiently appeared that extension, figure, the magnitude and the distance of bodies, are not direct objects of sight, and that our notions of them are not original in that sense, but are acquired. While, therefore, we have a direct acquaintance with colours by means of sight, it happens that, in estimating the distance of objects by the same sense, we are obliged to call in the aid of the intimations of the touch, and to make use also of comparison and judgment. And hence we are able to fix on this general principle, that the apparent magnitude of an object will vary with its distance.—It is clear, therefore, that there is no deception practised upon us. When, by such calculations as we are able to make, we have ascertained the distance of the sun and moon, then every one is satisfied that their apparent magnitude or their appearance to the eye is just such as it should be; and that the eye gives to us precisely the same representation as in any other instance of visible objects presented to it. It gives such a view of the object and of the distance of the object as it was designed to give; and teaches us here the same as it teaches us constantly.

(II.) Another class of errors are those of magnitude. The notions which we form on that subject also are acquired, and not original. We judge objects to be great or small in comparison with ourselves or with one another, and not in consequence of anything which is directly or immediately perceived in the objects themselves. We might call many objects small which happened to be of the size of a particular diamond, and yet not inconsistently speak of the diamond itself as a very large one; and this for the simple reason that our notions of large and small are not absolute but relative, and are formed by repeated acts of comparison. If there were but one object in creation besides ourselves, and if we could not reason from ourselves to that object, we could not possibly form any notion of its magnitude as distinct from the mere idea of extension. It is very clear, our senses could not, of themselves, authorize us to speak of such an object as large or small. Nor could it be done by reasoning, inasmuch as there are supposed to be no other objects with which to compare it.—These few remarks and illustrations can hardly fail to evince, that such mistakes as may exist in regard to the distance and magnitude of objects, are not exclusively attributable to the senses.

§ 93. The senses liable to be diseased.

There is one respect, however, in which it is perhaps true that we can speak with propriety of deceptions arising from the cause now under consideration. The body, as a whole, being liable to be diseased, the senses, as a part of the physical system, are of course not exempted from this liability. As a mere question of fact, it cannot be deemed a matter of doubt that the senses are often physically disordered, and at such times all persons are liable to be led astray by them. What is sweet to persons ordinarily, may appear bitter to one with a diseased palate; what is white to the mass of mankind, may appear of a yellow hue to one whose organ of sight is diseased; the physical condition of the sense of touch may be so perverted as to lead the diseased person to imagine he is made of glass or feathers instead of flesh and blood.

But it is surely enough to say, in respect to cases of this kind, that such is the condition of humanity, the sad but common allotment of mankind. What principle in our mental constitution is not liable to be perverted? What susceptibility is not liable to find its action suspended? In our general conduct, we rely, and very correctly, on the MEMORY; but the laws of memory may be disorganized by what may be termed a mental disease. We rely with equal readiness on the REASONING power; no one doubts that its conclusions are a ground of belief. But of what value is reasoning when uttered in the ravings of a madman, or when drawing its conclusions in a lunatic asylum?—It follows, therefore, if the senses deceive us in the case we are now attending to, the fault, if such it is to be considered, is not an exclusive one. It belongs to other parts of our nature also, not excepting its noblest and most trustworthy powers. And if we must reject the testimony of the senses simply because they are liable to be diseased, we must, for the same reason and in consistency with ourselves, reject the testimony of memory, of reason, and even of consciousness.

§ 94. On the real existence of a material world.

It will be noticed that, in what has been said, we have taken for granted the actual existence of an external, material world. Certain it is, that no man who has the ordinary constitution of a man, if he gives himself up to the instinctive tendencies of his nature, can doubt the reality of such an external, material creation. All external nature is operating upon us from the very moment of our birth, and giving origin, consistency, and strength to this belief. The resistance which bodies present to the touch when that sense is impressed upon them by the agency of the muscles, gives occasion for the distinct and important idea of externality; and with this idea the senses soon enable us to associate others, as extension, colour, form, and all material qualities and properties. In this way we become acquainted with what is called the outward world. And we are now prepared to assert explicitly, that this supposed outward world has an actual and independent existence.

But an objection is made here. It may be said that the mere fact of our having sensations or ideas of externality, extension, colour, and the like, does not necessarily involve and imply the true and actual existence of those things which they represent, or of which they are supposed and believed to be the effect. In other words, we may possess certain internal affections, and attribute them to something external and material as their cause; and we may truly and sincerely believe the reality of such a cause, while, in point of fact, it does not exist; and, consequently, our conviction of a truly existing material world may be a self-imposition and delusion.

It is this view which furnishes the basis of the doctrine known as IDEALISM. On this doctrine, which limits our knowledge to what is internal or subjective, and which therefore denies any real knowledge of the outward material world, a few remarks may properly be offered.

§ 95. Doctrine of the non-existence of matter considered.

The first remark which we have to make concerns the mere fact of belief. We have already made the declaration with confidence, that no man who has the ordinary constitution of a man can doubt of the reality of external, material things. It is no presumption to assert, that the belief of the reality of an external cause of our sensations is universal. This is the common feeling, the common language of all mankind. —Those who deny the propriety of relying on the evidence of the senses for the existence of the material world, and who deny such existence, should explain this belief. That such a belief exists cannot be denied; that it is a false belief, an unfounded conviction, ought not to be lightly asserted. It wars too much, as even a slight examination would suffice to show, with the sentiments of man's moral and religious constitution.

It is to be acknowledged with gratitude, that the great mass of mankind fully believe in the existence of the Deity, a being of perfect truth as well as benevolence. And this being is man's creator. But to create man so that he should be irresistibly led to believe in the existence of a material world when it did not exist, to create him with high capacities of thought, feeling, and action, and then to surround him with mere illusive and imaginary appearances, does not agree with that notion of God which we are wont to entertain. Mr. Stewart, in speaking of the metaphysical inquiries of Des Cartes, observes in relation to himself, that his reasonings led him to conclude, that God cannot possibly be supposed to deceive his creatures; and, therefore, that the intimations of our senses and the decisions of our reason are to be trusted to with entire confidence, wherever they afford us clear and distinct ideas of their respective objects.

In the second place, it will undoubtedly be admitted, that the sensations which have been spoken of have an existence. This existence, it is true, is wholly internal; but still the simple fact remains that they exist; our consciousness most decisively teaches us so. But it has been laid down as a primary truth, a first principle, that there is no beginning or change of existence without a cause. This is an elementary principle, placed as far above all objection and skepticism as any one can be, and evidently preliminary to the full exercise of reasoning.

And where, then, is the cause of these internal effects? What man, who denies the existence of the material world, is able to indicate the origin of these results? If, yielding to the suggestions of our nature and the requisitions of our belief, we seek for a cause external to ourselves, we find a satisfactory explanation; otherwise we may expect to find none of any kind.

§ 96. The senses as much grounds of belief as other parts of our constitution.

Furthermore, it must be admitted, as has already been particularly stated and shown, that there are certain original sources or grounds of belief in our constitution. To say otherwise would be to loosen and destroy the foundations of all knowledge, whether that knowledge has relation to matter or mind. But what evidence is there that there are such original sources of belief, or that any one thing in particular is the foundation of such belief more than any other thing? The answer is, our own internal consciousness and conviction, and this merely; we are conscious of belief, and are able to trace it to the occasions which give it rise.

Now if we carefully examine our minds, we shall find that the intimations of the senses as effectually cause belief as any other source of evidence whatever. Our consciousness, our internal conviction tells us, that our belief is as decisively regulated by the perceptions, derived through the senses, as by our intuitive or inductive perceptions; and that they are as much a ground of knowledge. We assert this with confidence; therefore, if the senses are not a ground of belief and knowledge, the way is fairly open for unlimited skepticism on all subjects. It will in this case be impossible to fix upon anything whatever which is to be received as evidence, and men must give up all knowledge of intellect as well as matter, and will be at once released from all moral obligation.

§ 97. Opinions of Locke on the testimony of the senses.

As the satisfactory understanding of this subject is of much practical importance, we shall close what has been said upon it by some passages from Mr. Locke. —"If, after all this," he says, in the Fourth Book of his Essay, "any one will be so skeptical as to distrust his senses, and to affirm that all we see and hear, feel and taste, think and do, during our whole being, is but the series and deluding appearances of a long dream, whereof there is no reality; and, therefore, will question the existence of all things, or our knowledge of anything; I must desire him to consider that, if all be a dream, then he doth but dream that he makes the question; and so it is not much matter that a waking man should answer him. But yet, if he pleases, he may dream that I make him this answer, that the certainty of things existing in *rerum natura*, when we have the testimony of our senses for it, is not only as great as our frame can attain to, but as our condition needs. For our faculties being suited not to the full extent of being, nor to a perfect, clear, comprehensive knowledge of things, free from all doubt and scruple, but to the preservation of us in whom they are, and accommodated to the use of life, they serve to our purpose well enough, if they will but give us certain notice of those things which are convenient or inconvenient to us. For he that sees a candle burning, and hath experimented the force of its flame by putting his finger in it, will little doubt that this is something existing without him, which does him harm, and puts him to great pain; which is assurance enough, when no man requires greater certainty to govern his actions by than what is as certain as his actions themselves. And if our dreamer pleases to try whether the glowing heat of a glass furnace be barely a wandering imagination in a drowsy man's fancy, by putting his hand into it he may perhaps be wakened into a certainty greater than he could wish, that it is something more than bare imagination. So that this evidence is as great as we can desire, being as certain to us as our pleasure or pain, *i. e.*, happiness or misery, beyond which we have no concernment, either of knowing or being. Such an assurance of the existence of things without us is sufficient to direct us in the attaining the good and avoiding the evil which is caused by them, which is the important concernment we have of being made acquainted with them."

CHAPTER IX.

HABITS OF SENSATION AND PERCEPTION.

§ 98. General view of the law of habit and of its applications.

WE proceed now, in accordance with an intimation at the close of the 7th Chapter, to the consideration of a great mental principle, generally known as the law of HABIT. We sometimes speak of Habit as a law, and sometimes as a power. The term law denotes a fixed line or mode of action; but if the action has a beginning, and if it tends to certain fixed results, which could not otherwise have existed, it implies the existence somewhere of power. But if it should be conceded, that it is proper to speak of Habit as a mental power (a view in support of which much might be said), it is not in any proper sense of the terms a Cognitive power; in other words, it does not directly and by its own action originate or increase our knowledge; but it oftentimes very greatly *aids* the action of the faculties of cognition as well as the emotional and other susceptibilities. And this is sufficient to justify us in speaking of it as one of the Auxiliary powers of the mind, and in giving it this early consideration.

But in this case as in others our attention will be directed chiefly to results. The result, which is involved in a Habit, is this: *That the mental action acquires facility and strength from repetition or practice.* The fact that the facility and the increase of strength implied in HABIT is owing to mere repetition, or what is more frequently termed practice, we learn, as we do other facts and principles in relation to the mind, from the observation of men around us, and from our own personal experience. And as it has hitherto been found wholly impracticable to resolve it into any general fact or principle more elementary, it may justly be regarded as something ultimate and essential in our nature.

The term Habit, by the use of language, indicates the facility and strength acquired in the way which has been mentioned, including both the result and the manner of it. As the law of habit has reference to the whole mind of man, the application of the term which expresses it is of course very extensive. We apply it to the dexterity of workmen in the different manual arts, to the rapidity of the accountant, to the coup d'œil or eye-glance of the military engineer, to the tact and fluency of the extemporaneous speaker, and in other like instances. We apply it also in cases where the mere exercise of emotion and desire is concerned; to the avaricious man's love of wealth, the ambitious man's passion for distinction, the wakeful suspicions of the jealous, and the confirmed and substantial benevolence of the philanthropist.

It is remarkable, that the law under consideration holds good in respect to the body as well as the mind. In the mechanical arts, and in all cases where there is a corporeal as well as mental effort, the effect of practice will be found to extend to both. Not only the acts of the mind are quickened and strengthened, but all those muscles which are at such times employed, become stronger and more obedient to the will. Indeed, the submission of the muscular effort to the volition is oftentimes rendered so prompt by habit, that we are unable distinctly to recollect any exercise of volition previous to the active or muscular exertion. It is habit which is the basis of those characteristic peculiarities that distinguish one man's handwriting from another's; it is habit which causes that peculiarity of attitude and motion, so easily discoverable in most persons, termed their gait; it is habit also which has impressed on the muscles immediately connected with the organs of speech, that fixed and precise form of action, which, in different individuals, gives rise, in part at least, to characteristics of voice. The habit in the cases just mentioned is both bodily and mental, and has become so strong, that it is hardly possible to counteract it for any length of time.—The great law of Habit, which is a Power as well as a Law, is applicable to all the leading divisions of our mental nature, the Intellect, the Sensibilities, the Will; and as we advance from one view of the mind to another, we shall have repeated occasion to notice its influence. In the remainder of this chapter, we shall limit our remarks to habit, considered in connexion with the Sensations and Perceptions.

§ 99. Of habit in relation to the smell.

We shall consider the application of the principle of Habit to the senses in the same order which has already been observed. In the first place, therefore, there are habits of Smell.—This sense, like the others, is susceptible of cultivation. As there are some persons whose power of distinguishing the difference between two or more colours is feeble, so there are some who are doubtful and perplexed, in like manner, in the discrimination of odours. And as the inability may be overcome in some measure in the former case, so it may be in the latter. The fact that the powers of which the smell is capable are not more frequently brought out and quickened, is owing to the circumstance that it is not ordinarily needed. It sometimes happens, however, that men are compelled to make an uncommon use of it, when, by a defect in the other senses, they are left without the ordinary helps to knowledge. It is then we see the effects of the law of Habit. It is stated in Mr. Stewart's account of James Mitchell, who was deaf, sightless, speechless, and, of course, strongly induced by his unfortunate situation to make much use of the sense we are considering, that his smell would immediately and invariably inform him of the presence of a stranger, and direct to the place where he might be; and it is repeatedly asserted, that this sense had become in him extremely acute.—"It is related," says Dr. Abercrombie, "of the late Dr. Moyse, the well-known blind philosopher, that he could distinguish a black dress on his friends by its smell."

In an interesting account of a deaf, dumb, and blind girl in the Hartford Asylum recently published, statements are made on this subject of a similar purport. —"It has been observed," says the writer, "of persons who are deprived of a particular sense, that additional quickness or vigour seems to be bestowed on those which remain. That blind persons are often distinguished by peculiar exquisiteness of touch, and the deaf and dumb, who gain all their knowledge through the eye, concentrate, as it were, their whole souls in that channel of observation. With her whose eye, ear, and tongue are alike dead, the capabilities both of touch and smell are exceedingly heightened. Especially the *latter* seems almost to have acquired the properties of a new sense, and to transcend the sagacity even of a spaniel."—Such is the influence of habit on the intimations of the sense under consideration.

§ 100. Of habit in relation to the taste.

The same law is applicable to the Taste. We see the results of the frequent exercise of this sense in the quickness which the dealer in wines discovers in distinguishing the flavour of one wine from that of another. So marked are the results in cases of this kind, that one is almost disposed to credit the story which Cervantes relates of two persons who were requested to pass their judgment upon a hogshead, which was supposed to be very old and excellent. One of them tasted the wine, and pronounced it to be very good, with the exception of a slight taste of leather which he perceived in it. The other, after mature reflection and examination, pronounced the same favourable verdict, with the exception of a taste of iron, which he could easily distinguish. On emptying the hogshead, there was found at the bottom an old key with a leathern thong tied to it.

Another practical view of this subject, however, presents itself here. The sensations which we experience in this and in other like cases, not only acquire by repetition greater niceness and discrimination, but increased strength (and perhaps the increased strength is in all instances the foundation of the greater power of discrimination). On this topic we have a wide and melancholy source of illustration. The bibber of wine and the drinker of ardent spirits readily acknowledge, that the sensation was at first only moderately pleasing, and perhaps in the very slightest degree. Every time they carried the intoxicating potion to their lips, the sensation grew more pleasing, and the desire for it waxed stronger. Perhaps they were not aware that this process was going on in virtue of a great law of humanity; but they do not pretend to deny the fact. They might, indeed, have suspected at an early period that chains were gathering around them, whatever might be the cause; but what objection had they to be bound with links of flowers; delightful while they lasted, and easily broken when necessary! But here was the mistake. Link was added to link, chain was woven with chain, till he who boasted of his strength was at last made sensible of his weakness, and found himself a prisoner, a captive, a deformed, altered, and degraded slave.

There is a threefold operation. The sensation of taste acquires an enhanced degree of pleasantness; the feeling of uneasiness is increased in a corresponding measure when the sensation is not indulged by drinking; and the desire, which is necessarily attendant on the uneasy feeling, becomes in like manner more and more imperative. To alleviate the uneasy feeling and this importunate desire, the unhappy man goes again to his cups, and with a shaky hand pours down the delicious poison. What then? He has added a new link to his chain; at every repetition it grows heavier and heavier; till that, which at first he bore lightly and cheerfully, now presses him like a coat of iron, and galls like fetters of steel. There is a great and fearful law of his nature bearing him down to destruction. Every indulgence is the addition of a new weight to what was before placed upon him, thus lessening the probability of escape, and accelerating his gloomy, fearful, and interminable sinking. We do not mean to say that he is the subject of an implacable destiny, and cannot help himself. But it would seem that he can help himself only in this way; by a prompt, absolute, and entire suspension of the practice in all its forms, which has led him into this extremity. But few, however, have the resolution to do this; the multitude make a few unwilling and feeble efforts, and resign themselves to the horrors of their fate.

Some years since there was a pamphlet published in England, entitled the Confessions of a Drunkard. The statements made in it are asserted on good authority to be authentic. And what does the writer say?—"Of my condition there is no hope that it should ever change; the waters have gone over me; but out of the black depths, could I be heard, I would cry out to all those who have but set a foot in the perilous flood. Could the youth, to whom the flavour of his first wine is delicious as the opening scenes of life, or the entering upon some newly-discovered paradise, look into my desolation, and be made to understand what a dreary thing it is when a man shall feel himself going down a precipice with open eyes and a passive will; to see his destruction, and have no power to stop it, and yet to feel it all the way emanating from himself; to perceive all goodness emptied out of him, and yet not be able to forget a time when it was otherwise; to bear about the piteous spectacle of his own self-ruin; could he see my fevered eye, feverish with last night's drinking, and feverishly looking for this night's repetition of the folly; could he feel the body of the death of which I cry hourly, with feebler and feebler outcry, to be delivered, it were enough to make him dash the sparkling beverage to the earth in all the pride of its mantling temptation."*

§ 101. Of habit in relation to the hearing.

There is undoubtedly a natural difference in the quickness and discrimination of hearing. This sense

* London Quarterly Review, vol. xxvii., p. 120.

is more acute in some than in others; but in those who possess it in much natural excellence, it is susceptible of a high degree of cultivation. Musicians are a proof of this, whose sensibility to the melody and concord of sweet sounds continually increases with the practice of their art.

This increase of sensibility in the perceptions of hearing is especially marked and evident when uncommon causes have operated to secure such practice. And this is the state of things with the Blind. The readers of Sir Walter Scott may not have forgotten the blind fiddler, who figures so conspicuously with verse and harp in Red Gauntlet; a character sufficiently extraordinary, but by no means an improbable exaggeration. The blind necessarily rely much more than others on the sense of hearing. By constant practice they increase the accuracy and power of its perceptions. Shut out from the beauties that are seen, they please themselves with what is heard, and greedily drink in the melodies of song. Accordingly, music is made by them not only a solace, but a business and a means of support; and in the Institutions for the Blind this is considered an important department of instruction.

Many particular instances on record, and well authenticated, confirm the general statement, that the ear may be trained to habits, and that thus the sensations of sound may come to us with new power and meaning. It is related of a celebrated blind man of Puiseaux in France, that he could determine the quantity of fluid in vessels by the sound it produced while running from one vessel into another. "Dr. Rush," as the statement is given in Abercrombie's Intellectual Powers, "relates of two blind young men, brothers, of the city of Philadelphia, that they knew when they approached a post in walking across a street, by a peculiar sound which the ground under their feet emitted in the neighbourhood of the post; and that they could tell the names of a number of tame pigeons, with which they amused themselves in a little garden, by only hearing them fly over their heads." Dr. Saunderson, who became blind so early as not to remember having seen, when happening in any new place, as a room, piazza, pavement, court, and the like, gave it a character by means of the sound and echo from his feet; and in that way was able to identify pretty exactly the place, and assure himself of his position afterward. A writer in the First Volume of the Manchester Philosophical Memoirs, who is our authority also for the statement just made, speaks of a certain blind man in that city as follows: "I had an opportunity of repeatedly observing the peculiar manner in which he arranged his ideas and acquired his information. Whenever he was introduced into company, I remarked that he continued some time silent. The sound directed him to judge of the dimensions of the room, and the different voices of the number of persons that were present. His distinction in these respects was very accurate, and his memory so retentive that he was seldom mistaken. I have known him instantly recognise a person on first hearing him, though more than two years had elapsed since the time of their last meeting. He determined pretty nearly the stature of those he was conversing with by the direction of their voices; and he made tolerable conjectures respecting their tempers and dispositions by the manner in which they conducted their conversation."

§ 102. Of certain universal habits based on sounds.

There are certain habits of hearing (perhaps we should say classes of habits) which all men, by the aid of the other senses, combined with that of the judgment, form at an early period of life. The first class of habits here referred to are those which have relation to the particular cause and the distance of sounds. The manner in which we learn these has been pointed out in a previous section (§ 66). The mere sensations of sound are entirely a distinct thing from the ideas of cause, place, and direction, which we generally combine with them. Owing to frequent repetition from early life, this combination is effected so rapidly, that we are unable to retrace the successive steps of the process, and the whole seems to be involved in a single sensation. Perhaps it may be said that the effect of repetition (that is to say, the HABIT) has more direct and special relation to the act of judgment, which combines the reference with the sensation, than to the sensation itself. However that may be, it may still be proper to speak of habits of hearing in the respect now under consideration, when we remember that the reference has been so long and closely interwoven with the sensation as to be apparently and practically, though not really, identical with it.

In respect to spoken language also, our habits are so laboriously and deeply founded, that we may almost consider ourselves as having a new sense superadded to that of hearing. In our ordinary conversation with others, we seem to hear the whole of what is said; nothing is lost, as we imagine. But that this is not the fact, and that we are sustained in such cases not wholly by an actual sensation of sound, but in part, at least, by an acquired power of HABIT, is evident from this. When we hear proper names, whether of persons, places, or natural objects, pronounced for the first time, we often hesitate in respect to them; are not certain that we possess the syllables intended to be conveyed, and ask for the repetition of them. We experience the same difficulty and uncertainty, as every one must have known who has tried it, when we hear a person read or converse in a foreign language. But when the conversation is in our own language, and relates to persons and objects we are acquainted with, it is altogether different, as has already been intimated. But what is the ground of the difference? Why are we perplexed in one case and not in the other?—In our intercourse with others in conversation, it almost constantly happens (at least as much so as on any other occasions), that the ear catches nothing but imperfect syllables, half-uttered words, sounds jumbled and commingled together; but we are nevertheless not commonly at a loss and perplexed, as in the cases before mentioned. By the aid of judgment, and the power of conception, whose action has in this case, by long repetition, formed itself into a prompt and decisive habit, we at once separate these confused elements, supply the breaks in their connexion, fill up the deficiencies, and make out a continuous and significant whole. And yet this is done so rapidly, and is so common, that in most cases we imagine there is nothing more than the pure and unmixed sensation.

§ 103. Application of habit to the touch.

The sense of touch, like the others, may be exceedingly improved by habit. The more we are obliged to call it into use, the more attention we pay to its intimations. By the frequent repetition, therefore, under such circumstances, these sensations not only acquire increased intenseness in themselves, but particularly so in reference to our notice and remembrance of them. But it is desirable to confirm this, as it is all other principles from time to time laid down, by an appeal to facts, and by careful inductions from them.

Diderot relates of the blind man of Puiseaux mentioned in a former section, that he was capable of judging of his distance from the fireplace by the degree of heat, and of his approach to any solid bodies by the action or pulse of the air upon his face. The same thing is recorded of many other persons in a similar situation;* and it may be regarded as a point

* It is a singular circumstance, that something similar to what is here stated of the ability of blind men to discover the nearness or distance of objects by changes in the resistance of the atmosphere, has been noticed by the naturalist Spallanzani in respect to bats. He discovered that bats, when perfectly blinded and afterward set at liberty, had the extraordinary faculty of guiding themselves through the most complicated windings of subterraneous passages, without striking against the walls, and they avoided with great skill cords, branches of trees, and other obstacles, placed by design in their way.

This ability is probably owing to an extreme delicacy in the wing, which is of a very large size in proportion to that of the animal, and well established, that blind people, who are unable to see the large and heavy bodies presenting themselves in their way as they walk about, generally estimate their approach to them by the increasing resistance of the atmosphere. A blind person, owing to the increased accuracy of his remaining senses, especially of the touch, would be better trusted to go through the apartments of a house in the darkness of midnight, than one possessed of the sense of seeing without any artificial light to guide him.

In the celebrated Dr. Saunderson, who lost his sight in very early youth, and remained blind through life, although he occupied the professorship of mathematics in the English University of Cambridge, the touch acquired such acuteness that he could distinguish, by merely letting them pass through his fingers, spurious coins, which were so well executed as to deceive even skilful judges who could see.*

The case of a Mr. John Metcalf, otherwise called Blind Jack, which is particularly dwelt upon by the author of the Article in the Memoirs just referred to, is a striking one. The writer states that he became blind at an early period; but, notwithstanding, followed the profession of a wagoner, and occasionally of a guide in intricate roads during the night, or when the tracks were covered with snow. At length he became a projector and surveyor of highways in difficult and mountainous districts; an employment for which one would naturally suppose a blind man to be but indifferently qualified. But he was found to answer all the expectations of his employers, and most of the roads over the peak in Derbyshire, in England, were altered by his directions. Says the person who gives this account of Blind Jack, "I have several times met

is covered with an exceedingly fine network of nerves. The bat, as it strikes the air with its wings, receives sensations of heat, cold, and resistance, and, in consequence, is enabled to avoid objects which would otherwise obstruct its flight, apparently in the same way that blind persons perceive a door or a wall by a change in the temperature or in the resistance of the air.

* Memoirs of Manchester Philos. Society, vol. i., p. 164.

this man, with the assistance of a long staff traversing the roads, ascending precipices, exploring valleys, and investigating their several extents, forms, and situations, so as to answer his designs in the best manner."

In the interesting Schools for the Blind which have recently been established in various parts of the world, the pupils read by means of the fingers. They very soon learn by the touch to distinguish one letter from another, which are made separately for that purpose of wood, metals, or other hard materials. The printed sheets which they use are conformed to their method of studying them. The types are much larger than those ordinarily used in printing; the paper is very thick, and, being put upon the types while wet, and powerfully pressed, the letters on it are consequently *raised*, and appear in relief. The pupils, having before learned to distinguish one letter from another, and also to combine them into syllables and words, are able, after a time, to pass their fingers along the words and sentences of these printed sheets, and ascertain their meaning with a good degree of rapidity.

Perhaps it may occasion some surprise when we add, that men may not only read by the touch, but may even find a substitute for the hearing in that sense. Persons who were entirely deaf have in some instances discovered a perception of the proportion and harmony of sounds.

"It will scarcely be credited," says an English writer, speaking of one in that situation, "that a person thus circumstanced should be fond of music; but this was the fact in the case of Mr. Arrowsmith. He was at a gentleman's glee club, of which I was president at that time, and, as the glees were sung, he would place himself near some article of wooden furniture, or a partition, door, or window-shutter, and would fix the extreme end of his finger nails, which he kept rather long, upon the edge of some projecting part of the wood, and there remain until the piece under performance was finished, all the while expressing, by the most significant gestures, the pleasure he experienced from the perception of musical sounds. He was not so much pleased with a solo as with a pretty full clash of harmony; and if the music was not very good, or I should rather say, if it was not correctly executed, he would show no sensation of pleasure. But the most extraordinary circumstance in this case is, that he was most evidently delighted with those passages in which the composer displayed his science in modulating the different keys. When such passages happened to be executed with precision, he could scarcely repress the emotions of pleasure which he received within any bounds; for the delight he evinced seemed to border on ecstasy."*

§ 104. Other striking instances of habits of touch.

The power of the touch will increase in proportion to the necessity of a reliance on it. The more frequent the resort to it, the stronger will be the habit; but the necessity of this frequent reference to it will be found to be peculiarly great where a person is deprived of two of his other senses. It is noticed of James Mitchell, whose case has been already referred to, that he distinguished such articles as belonged to himself from the property of others by this sense. Although the articles were of the same form and materials with those of others, it would seem that he was not at a loss in identifying what was his own. It will be recollected that he could neither see nor hear, and was, of course, speechless. He was obliged, therefore, to depend chiefly on the touch. This sense was the principal instrument he made use of in forming an acquaintance with the strangers who frequently visited him. And what is particularly remarkable, he actually explored by it, at an early period, a space round his father's residence of about two hundred yards in extent, to any part of which he was in the practice of walking fearlessly and without a guide whenever he pleased.

It is related of the deaf and blind girl in the Hart-

* London Quarterly Review, vol. xxvi., p. 404.

ford Asylum, that it is impossible to displace a single article in her drawers without her perceiving and knowing it; and that, when the baskets of linen are weekly brought from the laundress, she selects her own garments without hesitation, however widely they may be dispersed among the mass. This is probably owing, at least in great part, to habits of touch, by means of which the sense is rendered exceedingly acute.—Diderot has even gone so far as to conjecture that persons deprived of both sight and hearing would so increase the sensibility of touch as to locate the seat of the soul in the tips of the fingers.

§ 105. Habits considered in relation to the sight.

The law of habit affects the sight also. By a course of training this sense seems to acquire new power. The length and acuteness of vision in the mariner who has long traversed the ocean has been frequently referred to.—A writer in the North American Review (July, 1833) says he once "knew a man in the Greek Island of Hydra, who was accustomed to take his post every day for thirty years on the summit of the island, and look out for the approach of vessels; and, although there were over three hundred sail belonging to the island, he would tell the name of each one as she approached with unerring certainty, while she was still at such a distance as to present to a common eye only a confused white blur upon the clear horizon." There are numerous instances to the same effect, occasioned by the situations in which men are placed, and the calls for the frequent exercise of the sight. The almost intuitive vision of the skilful engineer is, beyond doubt, in most cases merely a habit. He has so often fixed his eye upon those features in a country which have a relation to his peculiar calling, that he instantly detects the bearing of a military position, its susceptibility of defence, its facilities of approach and retreat, &c.

No man is born without the sense of touch, but many are born without the sense of hearing; and, wherever this is the case, we are entitled to look for habits of sight. Persons under such circumstances naturally and necessarily rely much on the visual sense, whatever aids may be had by them from the touch. Hence habits; and these imply increased quickness and power wherever they exist. It is a matter of common remark, that the keenness of visual observation in the DEAF and DUMB is strikingly increased by their peculiar circumstances. Shut out from the intercourse of speech, they read the minds of men in their movements, gestures, and countenances. They notice with astonishing quickness, and apparently without any effort, a thousand things which escape the regards of others. This fact is undoubtedly the foundation of the chief encouragement which men have to attempt the instruction of that numerous and unfortunate class of their fellow-beings. They can form an opinion of what another says to them by the motion of the lips, and sometimes even with a great degree of accuracy. That this last, however, is common it is not necessary to assert; that it is possible, we have the testimony of well-authenticated facts. In one of his letters, Bishop Burnet mentions to this effect the case of a young lady of Geneva.—" At two years old," he says, " it was perceived that she had lost her hearing, and ever since, though she hears great noises, yet hears nothing of what is said to her; but, by observing the motion of the lips and mouths of others, she acquired so many words, that out of these she has formed a sort of jargon, in which she can hold conversation whole days with those who can speak her language. She knows nothing of what is said to her unless she sees the motion of their lips that speak to her; one thing will appear the strangest part of the whole narrative. She has a sister with whom she has practised her language more than with anybody else, and in the night, by laying her hand on her sister's mouth, she can perceive by that what she says, and so can discourse with her in the dark." (London Quarterly Review, vol. xxiv., p. 399.)

Such are the views which have been opened to us in considering the law of HABIT in connexion with the senses; and we may venture to say, with confidence, that they are exceedingly worthy of notice. There are two suggestions which they are especially fitted to call up. They evince the striking powers of the human mind, its irrepressible energies, which no obstacles can bear down. They evince also the benevolence of our Creator, who opens in the hour of misery new sources of comfort, and compensates for what we have not by increasing the power and value of what we have.

§ 106. Sensations may possess a relative as well as positive increase of power.

There remains a remark of some importance to be made in connexion with the general principle which has been brought forward, and as in some measure auxiliary to it; for it will help to explain the more striking instances of habits, if any should imagine that the fact of mere repetition is not sufficient to account for them. Our sensations and perceptions may acquire not only a direct and positive, but a relative and virtual increase of power.

This remark is thus explained. We shall hereafter see the truth of an important principle to this effect, that there will be a weakness of remembrance in any particular case in proportion to the want of interest in it. Now hundreds and thousands of our sensations and perceptions are not remembered because we take no interest in them. Of course they are the same, relatively to our amount of knowledge and our practice, as if they had never existed at all. But when we are placed in some novel situation, or when, in particular, we are deprived of any one of the senses, the pressure of our necessities creates that interest which was wanting before. Then we delay upon, and mark, and remember, and interpret a multitude of evanescent intimations which were formerly neglected. The senses thus acquire a very considerable relative power and value. And, in order to make out a satisfactory explanation of some instances of habits, it is perhaps necessary that this relative increase should be added to the direct and positive augmentation of vigour and quickness, resulting from mere repetition or exercise.

§ 107. Of habits as modified by particular callings or arts.

Hitherto it has been our chief object to examine habits in their relation to the senses separately; it is proper, also, to take a general view of them, as formed and modified by the particular callings and employments of men. Habits of perception are frequently formed under such circumstances, where all the senses are not only possessed, but where they exist with their ordinary aptitudes and powers. In consequence of the habits which he has been called upon to form by his particular situation, a farmer of a tolerable degree of experience and discernment requires but a slight inspection in order to give an opinion on the qualities of a piece of land, and its suitableness for a settlement. A skilful printer will at once notice everything of excellence or of deficiency in the mechanical execution of a printed work.—The same results are found in all who practise the fine arts. An experienced painter at once detects a mannerism in colouring, combinations and contrasts of light and shade, and peculiarities of form, proportion, or position, which infallibly escape a person of more limited experience.

Dr. Reid speaks on this subject in the following characteristic manner.—"Not only men, but children, idiots, and brutes, acquire by habit many perceptions which they had not originally. Almost every employment in life hath perceptions of this kind that are peculiar to it. The shepherd knows every sheep of his flock, as we do our acquaintance, and can pick them out of another flock one by one. The butcher knows by sight the weight and quality of his beeves and sheep before they are killed. The farmer perceives by his eye very nearly the quantity of hay in a rick, or of corn in a heap. The sailor sees the burden, the build, and the distance of a ship at sea, while she is a great way off. Every man accustomed to writing, distinguishes acquaintances by their handwriting as he does by their faces. And the painter distinguishes by the works of his art the style of all the great masters. In a word, acquired perception is very different in different persons, according to the diversity of objects about which they are employed, and the application they bestow in observing them."*

§ 108. The law of habit considered in reference to the perception of the outlines and forms of objects.

Before leaving the subject of Habit, considered as influencing Sensation and Perception, there is one other topic which seems to be entitled to a brief notice; we refer to the manner in which we perceive the outlines and forms of bodies. In discussing the subject of Attention, Mr. Stewart, in connexion with his views on that subject, introduces some remarks in respect to vision. He makes this supposition, That the eye is fixed in a particular position, and the picture of an object is painted on the retina. He then starts this inquiry: Does the mind perceive the complete figure of the object at once, or is this perception the result of various perceptions we have of the different points in the outline?—He holds the opinion, that the perception is the result of our perceptions of the different points in the outline, which he adopts as naturally consequent on such views as the following. The outline of every body is made up of points or smallest visible portions; no two of these points can be in precisely the same direction; therefore every point by itself constitutes just as distinct an object of attention to the mind, as if it were separated by some interval of empty space from all the other points. The conclusion therefore is, as every body is made up of parts, and as the perception of the figure of the whole object implies a knowledge of the relative situation of the different parts with respect to each other, that such

* Reid's Inquiry into the Human Mind, chap. vi., § 20.

perception is the result of a number of different acts of attention.

But if we adopt this view of Mr. Stewart, it is incumbent upon us to show how it happens that we appear to see the object at once. The various facts which have been brought forward in this chapter, appear to furnish us with a solution of this question. The answer is, that the acts of perception are performed with such rapidity, that the effect with respect to us is the same as if it were instantaneous. A habit has been formed; the glance of the mind, in the highest exercise of that habit, is indescribably quick; time is virtually annihilated; and separate moments are to our apprehension of them crowded into one.

§ 109. Notice of some facts which favour the above doctrine.

Some persons will probably entertain doubts of Mr. Stewart's explanation of the manner in which we perceive the outlines of objects; but there are various circumstances which tend to confirm it.—When we look for the first time on any object which is diversified with gaudy colours, the mind is evidently perplexed with the variety of perceptions which arise; the view is indistinct, which would not be the case if there were only one, and that an immediate perception. And even in paintings, which are of a more laudable execution, the effects at the first perception will be similar.

But there is another fact, which comes still more directly to the present point. We find that we do not have as distinct an idea, at the first glance, of a figure of a hundred sides, as we do of a triangle or square. But we evidently should, if the perception of visible figure were the immediate consequence of the picture on the retina, and not the combined result of the separate perceptions of the points in the outline. Whenever the figure is very simple, the process of the mind is so very rapid that the perception seems to be instantaneous. But when the sides are multiplied beyond a certain number, the interval of time necessary for these different acts of attention becomes perceptible.

We are then distinctly conscious that the mind labours from one part of the object to another, and that some time elapses before we grasp it as a whole.

§ 110. Additional illustrations of Mr. Stewart's doctrine.

These views and illustrations are still further confirmed by some interesting and, perhaps, more decisive facts. In 1807, Sir Everard Home, well known for his various philosophical publications, read before the Royal Society an account of two blind children whom he had couched for the cataract. One of these was John Salter. Upon this boy various experiments were made, for the purpose, among other things, of ascertaining whether the sense of sight does originally, and of itself alone, give us a knowledge of the true figure of bodies. Some of the facts elicited under these circumstances have a bearing upon the subject now before us. In repeated instances on the day of his restoration to sight, the boy called square and triangular bodies, which were presented to the visual sense merely, *round.* On a square body being presented to him, he expressed a desire to touch it. "This being refused, he examined it for some time, and said at last that he had found a corner, and then readily counted the four corners of the square; and afterward, when a triangle was shown him, he counted the corners in the same way; but, in doing so, his eye went along the edge from corner to corner, naming them as he went along." On the thirteenth day after the cataract was removed, the visual power he had acquired was so small that he could not, by sight, tell a square from a circle, without previously directing his sight to the corners of the square figure as he did at first, and thus passing from corner to corner, and counting them one by one. It was noticed that the sight seemed to labour slowly onward from one point and angle to another, as if it were incapable of embracing the outline by a simultaneous and undivided movement. The process, however, became more and more easy and rapid, until the perception, which at first was obviously made up of distinct and successive acts, came to be in *appearance (and we must* suppose it was only in appearance) a concentrated and single one.

It was the same with Caspar Hauser. It is remarked by his biographer, that, whenever a person was introduced to him (this was probably soon after his release from his prison), he went up very close to him, regarded him with a sharp, staring look, and noticed particularly each distinct part of his face, such as the forehead, eyes, nose, mouth, and chin. He then collected and consolidated all the different parts of the countenance, which he had noticed separately and piece by piece, into one whole. And it was not till after this process that he seemed to have a knowledge of the countenance or face, in distinction from the parts of the face.

CHAPTER X.

MUSCULAR HABITS.

§ 111. Instances in proof of the existence of muscular habits.

From habits, considered as affecting the senses, the transition is easy to MUSCULAR HABITS. On this subject, therefore, we shall now offer a few remarks.—Of the fact that such habits exist, it is presumed no doubt can be generally entertained. Muscular habits may be detected in the gait and in the speech of men generally; they are found with specific characteristics in particular classes of men; every mechanic forms them, and they vary in their aspect with his particular business. Hence the enlarged and powerful neck of the porter, the strong and brawny arm of the blacksmith, and the particular habitudes of all their movements.

But we will not delay on this part of the subject any further than to point out one or two familiar instances.—Every man's handwriting is a striking instance and a proof of Muscular habit. In acquiring that art, the muscles have undergone a complete system of instruction. That instruction and training they practically and punctually regard ever afterward; so much so that we can tell a man's writing to which we are accustomed almost as readily as we recognise the man himself when we see him.—Again, walking is an instance and illustration of muscular habits. The process of walking is an easy one; but it is made so by a habit, founded upon a long and difficult training; and every man has his particular habit or method of walking. We see evidence that habit is involved in walking in children, who obviously do not walk by mere instinct, but learn to do it by repeated experiments made upon the muscles of motion. Not long since, a singular fact came to the knowledge of the writer, which confirms this remark. A man was accidentally thrown from his cart, and the wheel of the cart passed over his neck and injured his spine. For six weeks he was destitute of the power of sensation and motion. About that time his sensation was restored, and the various parts of the body were again subjected to the general control of the will. But he could not walk nor use his arms to any profitable purpose; not because he was destitute of the voluntary and muscular power, but because he unexpectedly found himself at a loss to determine what particular muscles to employ, in order to produce the desired result. If he wished, for example, to use an extensor muscle in the arm or leg, he was just as likely to use a flexor as the one he intended. In other words, he was about as likely to bend his arm, or to turn his leg in or out, as to straighten them, and it was only by repeated experiments he could ascertain the particular muscles which he wished to use. In everything relating to bodily action, he was thrown back into the condition of early childhood, and it was not till after a long and tedious process of experimenting on the numerous muscles of motion, that he was enabled to walk and to labour as he was accustomed to do before his injury. There are, then, muscular habits as well as habits of sensation and perception.—But the subject of these habits is introduced here, although the train of thought seemed naturally to lead to it, not so much for its own sake as in consequence of its connexion with volition.

§ 112. Muscular habits regarded by some writers as involuntary.

It seems to have been the opinion of some writers (among others of Drs. Reid and Hartley), that bodily or muscular habits operate in many cases without design and volition on the part of the person who has formed them; and that, as they are without any attendant thought, without any preceding mental operation, such bodily acts are to be considered as purely mechanical or automatic. They endeavour to explain and confirm their views by the instance of a person learning to play on the harpsichord. When a person first begins to learn, it is admitted by all that there is an express act of volition preceding every motion of the fingers. By degrees, the motions appear to cling to each other mechanically; we are no longer conscious of volitions preceding and governing them. In other words, there is nothing left but the motions; there is no act of the mind; the performance, admirable as it is, has the same character and the same merit with that of the action of a well-contrived machine.

§ 113. Objections to the doctrine of involuntry muscular habits.

In replying to these views, it may be safely admitted that, in playing the harpsichord and some other musical instruments, we have not always a distinct remembrance of volitions, and consequently the muscular effort has sometimes the appearance of being independent of the will. But this mere appearance is not sufficient to command our assent to the doctrine advanced by these writers until the four following objections be set aside.

(1.) The supposition that the acts in question are automatic is unnecessary.—If it be true, as there is so much reason to believe, that habit is a general law of our nature, then it may be regarded as applicable not only to the muscular efforts, but to the preceding *volitions* themselves. It is implied in this view (supposing it to be a correct one), that such volitions may be very rapid, so as scarcely to arrest our attention a moment. Now the natural result of such slight attention will be, that they will exist and pass away without being remembered. These considerations are sufficient to explain the mere appearance which is admitted to exist, but which Reid and Hartley attempt to explain by an utter denial of the putting forth of volitions at all. But, if this be the case, then the supposition that the acts in question are automatic and involuntary, is an unnecessary one.

(2.) The most rapid performers on musical instruments are able, when they please, to play so slowly that they can distinctly observe every act of the will in the various movements of the fingers. And when they have checked their motions so as to be able to observe the separate acts of volition, they can afterward so accelerate those motions, and, of course, so diminish the power (or, what may be regarded as the same thing, the time of attending to them), that they cannot recall the accompanying volitions. This is the rational and obvious supposition, that there is not an exclusion of volitions, but an inability to recollect them, on account of the slight degree of attention. Any other view necessarily implies an inexplicable jumble of voluntary and involuntary actions in the same performance.

(3.) If there be no volitions, the action must be strictly and truly automatic; that is, it must, from the nature of the case, be the motion of a machine. It must always go on invariably in the same track, without turning to the right hand or to the left. If this be the case in playing the harpsichord, which is by no means probable, it is certainly not in some other instances of habits. It must be supposed, that there is as much rapidity of volition put forth by the rope-dancer, the equilibrist, the equestrian actor of the circus, &c., as by the player on the harpsichord. Now if it be admitted that the ordinary steps of the singular and surprising feats they perform are familiar to them, still the process is evidently not an invariable one. It may be pronounced impossible for them to perform experiments which agree in every particular with preceding experiments. They are necessarily governed in their volitions and movements by a variety of circumstances, which arise on every particular occasion, and which could not be foreseen. Hence the muscular movements in these cases, being controlled by the will, are not mechanical; and as we have abundant reason to believe them often not less rapid in the performance than the muscular movements are in playing the harpsichord, why should we consider these last mechanical, and not voluntary?

(4.) And there is this additional consideration. If the physical action becomes strictly automatic, being impelled onward by its own law of movement, and at the same time placed beyond any volitional control, it does not appear how it is to stop at all. And besides, if the hypothesis of Reid and Hartley be true, then there is some general tendency or principle in our nature by which actions originally voluntary are converted into mechanical actions. Nor will it be easy to show why this principle should not extend further than mere bodily movements. It will be the result of this tendency to wrest all those powers which it reaches, whether bodily or mental, from the control of the will. In other words, when we consider the extent of its application, and its wonderful results, wherever it applies, we must conclude that this principle will infallibly make men machines, mere automatons, before they have lived out half their days.—Such are some of the objections to the doctrine that muscular habits are involuntary.

CHAPTER XI.

THE CONCEPTIVE POWER.—CONCEPTIONS.

§ 114. Conceptivity and characteristics of conceptions.

Having considered the Power of sensation or Sensationality, whose results, strictly considered, are wholly subjective or internal, and also the Power of perception or Perceptivity, by means of which the sensations are connected with their outward causes and thus give us a knowledge of the material world, and further considered the modification of their action by means of the auxiliary power of Habit, we proceed now to a third Cognitive power, namely, the Conceptive power or Conceptivity. By means of the first-named power alone, we should know nothing outside of ourselves; by means of the second we have a knowledge of outward things, but we are limited in our knowledge to the objects which are now before us. A little reflection, therefore, shows us that we need another power, which will enable us to keep our past knowledges in our possession, when the objects of knowledge have passed beyond the reach of our senses. The power which enables us to do this, and without which man would fall far below his present standard of intelligence and happiness, is the Conceptive power. Undoubtedly the basis of the existence and action of this faculty is found in the antecedent existence and action of sensation and perception; but it has its distinctive place and its appropriate laws and results. Some of the marks or characteristics of the mental states, which owe their origin to Conceptivity, and are therefore called Conceptions, are as follows.

(I.) As already intimated in what has been said of the necessity of the Conceptive power, conceptions differ in the first place from sensations and perceptions in this respect, that the external objects which are the foundation of them, and without which they never could have existed, are not present. When the rose, the honeysuckle, or other odoriferous body is presented to us, the effect which follows in the mind is termed a sensation. When we afterward think of that sensation (as we sometimes express it), when the sensation is recalled, even though very imperfectly, without the object which originally caused it being present, it then becomes, by the use of language, a CONCEPTION. And it is the same in instances of perception, considered as distinct from and additional to sensation. When, in strictness of speech, we are said to perceive anything, as a tree, a building, or a mountain, the objects of our perceptions are in all cases before us. But we may form conceptions of them; they may be recalled and exist in *the mind's eye*, however remote they may be in fact, both in time and place.

(II.) Conceptions differ also from remembrances or ideas of memory. We take no account of the period, the particular time, when those objects which laid the foundation of them were present; whereas in every act of the memory there is combined with the conception of the thing a notion also of the past time. It is true, that without conceptions there would be no possibility of the exercise of the power of memory; but remembrances, as we shall see when we come to the consideration of that subject, are something more. Conceptions, therefore, discriminated alike from what goes before and from what comes after, stand by themselves, with their appropriate origin and name. And in addition to what has been said there are some things further characteristic of them, which we will now proceed to notice.

§ 115. Of conceptions of objects of sight.

One of the striking facts in regard to our conceptions is, that we can far more easily conceive of the objects of some senses than of others. He who has beheld the pyramids of Egypt and the imposing remains of Grecian temples, or has visited among Nature's still greater works the towering heights of the Alps and the cataract of Niagara, will never afterward be at a loss in forming a vivid conception of those interesting objects. The visual perceptions are so easily and so distinctly recalled, that it is hardly too much to say of them that they seem to exist as permanent pictures in the mind. It is related of Carsten Niebuhr, a well-known traveller in the East, that, in extreme old age, after he had become blind, he entertained his visitors with interesting details of what he had seen many years before at Persepolis; describing the walls, on which the inscriptions and bas-reliefs of which he spoke were found, just as one would describe a building which he had recently visited. His son, who has given an account of his life, remarks, in connexion with this fact, "we could not conceal our astonishment. He said to us that, as he lay blind upon his bed, the images of all that he had seen in the East were ever present to his soul; and it was therefore no wonder that he should speak of them as of yesterday. In like manner, there was vividly reflected to him, in the hours of stillness, the nocturnal view of the deep Asiatic heavens, with their brilliant host of stars, which he had so often contemplated, or else their blue and lofty vault by day; and this was his greatest enjoyment."

There seems to be less vividness in the conceptions of sound, touch, taste, and smell, particularly the last three. Every one knows that it is difficult in ordinary cases to recall with much distinctness a particular pain which we have formerly experienced, or a particular taste or smell. The fact that the perceptions of sight are more easily and distinctly recalled than others may be thus partially explained.—Visible objects, or, rather, the outlines of them, are complex; that is, they are are made up of a great number of points or very small portions. Hence the conception which we form of such an object as a whole is aided by the principles of association. The reason is obvious. As every original perception of a visible object is a compound made up of many parts, whenever we subsequently have a conception of it, the process is the same; we have a conception of a part of the object, and the principles of association help us in conceiving of the other parts. Association connects the parts together; it presents them to the mind in their proper arrangement, and helps to sustain them there.

We are not equally aided by the laws of association in forming our conceptions of the objects of the other senses. In the latter case, the Associative power avails itself of the aid of the principle of contiguity in time merely; while in the former (that is to say, in the restoration of visual sensations and perceptions), it avails itself of the additional principle of contiguity in place. This will be better understood when we come to the subject of Association.

§ 116. Of the influence of habit on our conceptions.

It is another circumstance worthy of notice in regard to conceptions, that the power of forming them depends in some measure on HABIT.—A few instances will help to illustrate the statement, that what is termed Habit, and the auxiliary power involved in it, may extend to the susceptibility of conceptions as well as to sensations and perceptions; and the first to be given will be of conceptions of sound. Our conceptions of sounds are not, in general, remarkably distinct, as was intimated in the last section. It is nevertheless true, that a person may, by practice, acquire the power of amusing himself with merely reading written music. Having frequently associated the sounds with the notes, he has at last such a strong conception of the sounds, that he experiences by merely reading the notes a very sensible pleasure. It is for the same reason, viz., because our conceptions are strengthened by repetition or practice, that readers may enjoy the harmony of poetical numbers without at all articulating the words. In both cases they truly hear nothing; there is no actual sensation of sound, and yet there is a virtual enunciation and melody in the mind. It seems to be on this principle we are enabled to explain the fact, that Beethoven composed some of his most valued musical pieces after he had become entirely deaf; originating harmonic combinations so profound and exquisite as to require the nicest ear as a test, at the very time he was unable to hear anything himself.

§ 117. Influence of habit on conceptions of sight.

That our power of forming conceptions is strengthened by habit, is capable of being further illustrated from the sight. A person who has been accustomed to drawing retains a much more perfect notion of a building, landscape, or other visible object, than one who has not. A portrait painter, or any person who has been in the practice of drawing such sketches, can trace the outlines of the human form with very great ease; it requires hardly more effort from them than to write their names.—This point may also be illustrated by the difference which we sometimes notice in people in their conceptions of colours. Some are fully sensible of the difference between two colours when they are presented to them, but cannot with confidence give names to these colours when they see them apart, and may even confound the one with the other. Their original sensations and perceptions are supposed to be equally distinct with those of other persons; but their subsequent conception of the colours is far from being so. This defect arises partly at least from want of practice; that is to say, from the not having formed a habit. The persons who exhibit this weakness of conception have not been compelled by their situation, nor by mere inclination, to distinguish and to name colours so much as is common.

§ 118. Of the subserviency of our conceptions to description.

It is highly favourable to the talent for lively description when a person's conceptions are readily suggested and are distinct. Even such a one's common conversation differs from that of those whose conceptions arise more slowly and are more faint. One man, whether in conversation or in written description, seems to place the object which he wishes to describe directly before us; it is represented distinctly and to the life. Another, although not wanting in a command of language, is confused and embarrassed amid a multitude of particulars, which, in consequence of the feebleness of his conceptions, he finds himself but half acquainted with; and he therefore gives us but a very imperfect and confused notion of the thing which he desires to make known.

It has been by some supposed that a person might give a happier description of an edifice, of a landscape, or other object, from the conception than from the actual perception of it. The perfection of a description does not always consist in a minute specification of circumstances; in general, the description is better when there is a judicious selection of them. The best rule for making the selection is to attend to the particulars that make the deepest impression on our own minds, or, what is the same thing, that most readily and distinctly take a place in our conceptions. —When the object is actually before us, it is extremely difficult to compare the impressions which different circumstances produce. When we afterward conceive of the object, we possess merely the outline of it; but it is an outline made up of the most striking circumstances. Those circumstances, it is true, will not impress all persons alike, but will somewhat vary with the degree of their taste. But when, with a correct and delicate taste, any one combines lively conceptions, and gives a description from those conceptions, he can hardly fail to succeed in it. And, accordingly, we find here one great element of poetic power. It is the ability of forming vivid conceptions, which bodies forth

> "The forms of things unknown; the poet's pen
> Turns them to shapes, and gives to airy nothing
> A local habitation and a name."

§ 119. Of conceptions attended with a momentary belief.

Our conceptions are sometimes attended with belief; when they are very lively, we are apt to ascribe to them a real outward existence, or believe in them. We do not undertake to assert that the belief is permanent; but a number of facts strongly lead to the conclusion that it has a momentary existence.

(1.) A painter, in drawing the features and bodily form of an absent friend, may have so strong a conception, so vivid a mental picture, as to believe for a moment that his friend is before him. After carefully recalling his thoughts at such times, and reflecting upon them, almost every painter is ready to say that he has experienced some illusions of this kind. "We read," says Dr. Conolly, "that when Sir Joshua Reynolds, after being many hours occupied in painting, walked out into the street, the lamp-posts seemed to him to be trees, and the men and women moving shrubs." It is true, the illusion is, in these cases, very short, because the intensity of conception, which is the foundation of it, can never be kept up long when the mind is in a sound state. Such intense conceptions are unnatural. And, further, all the surrounding objects of perception, which no one can altogether disregard for any length of time, tend to check the illusion and terminate it.

(2.) When a blow is aimed at any one, although in sport, and he fully knows it to be so, he forms so vivid a conception of what might possibly be the effect, that his belief is for a moment controlled, and he unavoidably shrinks back from it. This is particularly the case if the blow approaches the eye. Who can help winking at such times? It is a proof of our belief being controlled under such circumstances, that we can move our own hands rapidly in the neighbourhood of the eye, either perpendicularly or horizontally, and, at the same time, easily keep our eyelids from motion. But when the motion is made by another, the conception becomes more vivid, and a belief of danger inevitably arises.—Again, place a person on the battlements of a high tower; his reason tells him he is in no danger; he knows he is in none. But, after all, he is unable to look down from the battlements without fear; his conceptions are so exceedingly vivid as to induce a momentary belief of danger, in opposition to all his reasonings.

(3.) When we are in pain from having struck our foot against a stone, or when pain is suddenly caused in us by any other inanimate object, we are apt to vent a momentary rage upon it. That is to say, our belief is so affected for an instant, that we ascribe to it an accountable existence, and would punish it accordingly. This is observed particularly in children and in savages. It is on the principle of our vivid conceptions being attended with belief that poets so often ascribe life, and agency, and intention to the rains and winds, to storms, and thunder, and lightning. How natural are the expressions of King Lear, overwhelmed with the ingratitude of his daughters, and standing with his old head bared to the pelting tempest!

> "Nor rain, wind, thunder, fire are my daughters;
> I tax not you, ye elements, with unkindness;
> I never gave you kingdoms, called you children."

(4.) There are persons who are entirely convinced of the folly of the popular belief of ghosts and other nightly apparitions, but who cannot be persuaded to sleep in a room alone, nor go alone into a room in the dark. Whenever they happen out at night, they are constantly looking on every side; their quickened perceptions behold images which never had any existence except in their own minds, and they are the subjects of continual disquiet and even terror.—"It was my misfortune," says Dr. Priestly, "to have the idea of darkness and the ideas of invisible, malignant spirits and apparitions very closely connected in my infancy, and to this day, notwithstanding I believe nothing of those invisible powers, and consequently of their connexion with darkness, or anything else, I cannot be perfectly easy in every kind of situation in the dark, though I am sensible I gain ground upon this prejudice continually."

In all such cases we see the influence of the prejudices of the nursery. Persons who are thus afflicted were taught in early childhood to form conceptions of ghosts, visible hobgoblins, and unearthly spirits, and the habit still continues. It is true, when they listen to their reasonings and philosophy, they may well say they do not believe in such things. But the effect of their philosophy is merely to check their belief; not in ten cases in a thousand is the belief entirely overcome. Every little while, in all solitary places, and especially in the dark, it returns, and, when banished, returns again; otherwise we cannot give an explanation of the conduct of these persons.

§ 120. Conceptions which are joined with perceptions.

The belief in our mere conceptions is the more evident and striking whenever they are at any time joined with our perceptions.—A person, for instance, is walking in a field in a foggy morning, and perceives something, no matter what it is; but he believes it to be a man, and does not doubt it. In other words, he truly perceives some object, and, in addition to that perception, has a mental conception of a man attended with belief. When he has advanced a few feet further, all at once he perceives that what he conceived to be a man is merely a stump with a few stones piled on its top. He perceived at first as plainly, or but little short of it, that it was a stump, as in a moment afterward; there were the whole time very nearly the same visible form and the same dimensions in his eye. But he had the conception of a man in his mind at the same moment, which overruled and annulled the natural effects of the visual perception; the conception being associated with a present visible object, acquired peculiar strength and permanency, so much so that he truly and firmly believed that a human being was before him. But the conception has departed, the present object of perception has taken its place, and it is now impossible for him to conjure up the phantom, the reality of which he but just now had no doubt of.

In his Voyage of Discovery to the Arctic Regions, Captain Ross mentions an incident illustrative of the power and fruitfulness of our conceptions, when upheld by the actual presence of objects. It will be recollected that the immense masses of ice which are found floating in the Polar Seas often display a variety of the most brilliant hues. Speaking of one of these icebergs, as they are called, which he early fell in with, and which was about forty feet high and a thousand feet long, "imagination," he says, "painted it in many grotesque figures; at one time it looked something like a white lion and horse rampant, which the quick fancy of sailors, in their harmless fondness for omens, naturally enough shaped into the lion and unicorn of the king's arms, and they were delighted accordingly with the good luck it seemed to augur."

One of the numerous characters whom Sir Walter Scott has sketched with so much truth to nature, speaks of himself as being banished on a certain occasion to one of the sandy keys of the West Indies, which was reputed to be inhabited by malignant demons. This person, after acknowledging he had his secret apprehensions upon their account, remarks, "in open daylight or in absolute darkness, I did not greatly apprehend their approach, but in the misty dawn of the morning, or when evening was about to fall, I saw, for the first week of my abode on the Key, many a dim and undefined spectre—now resembling a Spaniard with his capa wrapped around him, and his huge sombrera, as large as an umbrella, upon his head—now a Dutch sailor, with his rough cap and trunk hose—and now an Indian cacique, with his feathery crown and long lance of cane. I always approached them, but, whenever I drew near, the phantom changed into a bush, or a piece of driftwood, or a wreath of mist, or some such cause of deception."

But it is unnecessary to resort to books for illustrations of this topic. Multitudes of persons have a conceptive facility of creations, which is often troublesome and perplexing, especially in uncommon situations and in the night. And in all cases this tendency is greatly strengthened whenever it can lay hold of objects, the outlines of which it can pervert to its own purposes.—In instances of this kind, where the conceptions are upheld, as it were, by present objects of perception, and receive a sort of permanency from them, nothing is better known than that we often exercise a strong and unhesitating belief. These instances, therefore, can properly be considered as illustrating and confirming the views in the preceding section.

§ 121. **Conceptions as connected with fictitious representations.**

These observations suggest an explanation, at least in part, of the effects which are produced on the mind by exhibitions of fictitious distress. In the representation of tragedies, it must be admitted that there is a general conviction of the whole being but a fiction. But, although persons enter the theatre with this general conviction, it does not always remain with them the whole time. At certain peculiarly interesting passages in the poet, and at certain exhibitions of powerful and well-timed effort in the actor, this general impression that all is a fiction, fails. The feelings of the spectator may be said to rush into the scenes; he mingles in the events; carried away and lost, he for a moment believes all to be real, and the tears gush at the catastrophe which he witnesses. The explanation, therefore, of the emotions felt at the exhibition of a tragedy, such as indignation, pity, and abhorrence, is, that at certain parts of the exhibition we have a momentary belief in the reality of the events which are represented. And, after the illustrations which have been given, such a belief cannot be considered impossible.—The same explanation will apply to the emotions which follow our reading of tragedies when alone, or any other natural and affecting descriptions. In the world of conceptions which the genius of the writer conjures up, we are transported out of the world of real existence, and for a while fully believe in the reality of what is only an incantation.

The Conceptive power has a very close connexion with the Imagination; but the precise relation existing between the two will be more easily explained and understood, when we come in its proper place to the last-named power.

CHAPTER XII.

SIMPLICITY AND COMPLEXNESS OF MENTAL STATES.

§ 122. Origin of the distinction of simple and complex.

Before proceeding to the next cognitive power which comes in course, we delay here for the brief consideration of another subject, incidental to the proper and full knowledge of the mind, the importance of which can hardly fail to appear from a mere statement of it; a subject involving, not the origin of mental states, but their comparative value.

In looking at our thoughts and feelings as they continually pass under the review of our internal observation, we readily perceive that they are not of equal worth; we do not assign to them the same estimate; one state of mind is found to be expressive of one thing only, and that thing, whatever it is, is precise, and definite, and inseparable; while another state of mind is found to be expressive of, and virtually equal to, many others. And hence we are led, not only with the utmost propriety, but even by a sort of necessity, to make a division of the whole body of our mental affections into the two classes of simple and complex. Nature herself makes the division; it is one of those characteristics which gives to the mind, in part at least, its greatness; one of those elements of power without which the soul could not be what it is, and without a knowledge of which it is difficult to possess a full and correct understanding of it in other respects.

§ 123. Nature and characteristics of simple and mental states.

We shall first offer some remarks on those mental states, which are simple, and shall aim to give an understanding of their nature, so far as can be expected on a subject, the clearness of which depends more on a reference to our own personal consciousness than on the teaching of others.

Let it be noticed, then, in the first place, that a simple state of mind CANNOT BE SEPARATED INTO PARTS.—It is clearly implied in the very distinction between simplicity and complexity, considered in relation to the states of the mind, that there can be no such separation, no such division. It is emphatically true of our simple ideas, and emotions, and desires, and of all other simple states of mind, that they are one and indivisible. Whenever you can detect in them more than one element, they at once lose their character of simplicity, and are to be regarded as complex, however they may have previously appeared. Inseparableness consequently is their striking characteristic; and it may be added, that they are not only inseparable in themselves, but are separate from everything else. There is nothing which can stand as a substitute for them where they are, or represent them where they are not; they are independent unities, constituted exclusively by the mind itself, having a specific and positive character, but nevertheless known only in themselves.

§ 124. Simple mental states not susceptible of definition.

Let it be observed, in the second place, that simple mental states CANNOT BE DEFINED.—This view of them follows necessarily from what has been said of their oneness and inseparableness, compared with what is universally understood by defining. In respect to definitions, it is undoubtedly true, that we sometimes use synonymous words, and call such use a definition; but it is not properly such. In every legitimate definition, the idea which is to be defined is to be separated, as far as may be thought necessary, into its subordinate parts; and these parts are to be presented to the mind for its examination, instead of the original mental affection or state into which they entered. This process must be gone through in every instance of accurate defining; this is the general and authorized view of definition; and it is not easy to see in what else it can well consist.

But this process will not apply to our simple thoughts and feelings, because, if there be any such thing as simple mental states, they are characterized by inseparableness and oneness. And, furthermore, if we define ideas by employing other ideas, we must count upon meeting at last with such as shall be ultimate, and will reject all verbal explanation; otherwise we can never come to an end in the process. So that the simple mental affections are not only undefinable in themselves, but, if there were no such elementary states of mind, there could be no defining in any other case; it would be merely analysis upon analysis, a process without completion, and a labour without end; leaving the subject in as much darkness as when the process was begun.

When we speak of simple ideas and feelings, and a person, in consequence of our inability to define them, professes to be ignorant of the terms we use, we can frequently aid him in understanding them by a statement of the circumstances, as far as possible, under which the simple mental state exists. But, having done this, we can merely refer him to his own senses and consciousness, as the only teachers from which he can expect to receive satisfaction.

§ 125. Simple cognitive states representative of a reality.

The first two marks apply to all the mental states; the sentimentive and volitional as well as the intellective. A third mark or characteristic of those simple mental states, which appropriately belong to the intellect and may be spoken of as cognitive, is that they always stand for or REPRESENT A REALITY. In other words, no simple idea of this kind is, in its own nature, delusive or fictitious, but always has something precisely corresponding to it; we do not say in form or outline, but in the reality of existence. And this is true both of things mental and material. If the idea has relation to outward things, there is something answering to it; and if it has relation to mental things, it is the same.

It is not always so with complex ideas; these, as Mr. Locke justly gives us to understand, are sometimes CHIMERICAL. That is to say, the elements of which they are composed are so brought together and combined as to form something, of which nature presents no corresponding reality. If, for instance, a person had an idea of a body, yellow, or of some other colour, malleable, fixed, possessing, in a word, all the qualities of iron or of gold, with this difference only of its being lighter than water, it would be what Mr. Locke terms a CHIMERICAL idea; because the combination of the elements here exists only in the human mind, and not in nature; the thing has no outward or objective reality. The words CENTAUR, DRAGON, and HYPOGRIFF, which are the well-known names for imaginary beings possessing no actual existence, are expressive of chimerical complex ideas. These ideas have nothing corresponding to them. But it is not so with the simple states of mind, of the class which we are now considering. If it were otherwise, since in our inquiries after truth we naturally proceed from what is complex to what is simple, there would be no sure foundation of knowledge. Whenever, in our analysis of a subject, we arrive at truly simple ideas, we have firm footing; there is no mistake, no delusion. Nature, always faithful to her own character, gives utterance to the truth alone. But man, in combining together the elements which nature furnishes, does not always avoid mistakes.

§ 126. **Origin of complex notions and their relation to simple.**

Our simple cognitive states, which we have thus endeavoured to explain, were probably first in origin.

There are reasons for considering them as antecedent in point of time to mental states which are complex, although in many cases it may not be easy to trace the progress of the mind from the one to the other. The complex notions of external material objects embrace the separate and simple ideas and sensations of resistance, extension, hardness, colour, taste, and others. As these elementary cognitions, whatever may be the distinctive and appropriate name which attaches to them, evidently have their origin in distinct and separate senses, it is but reasonable to suppose that they possess a simple before they are combined together in a complex existence. Simple ideas, therefore, may justly be regarded as antecedent in point of time to those which are complex, and as laying the foundation of them.

Hence we see that it is sufficiently near the truth, and that it is not improper to speak of our complex ideas, as derived from, or made up of simple ideas. This is the well-known language of Mr. Locke on this subject; and when we consider how much foundation there is for it in the constitution and operations of the human mind, there is good reason for retaining it.— Although purely simple states of the mind are few in number, vast multitudes of a complex nature are formed from them. The ability which the mind possesses of originating complex thoughts and feelings from elementary ones, may be compared to our power of uniting together the letters of the alphabet in the formation of syllables and words.

§ 127. Supposed complexness without the antecedence of simple feelings.

It is possible, that some persons may object to the doctrine proposed in the last section, that complex mental states are subsequent in point of time to those which are simple; and may be inclined to adopt the opinion, that some at least of our complex notions are framed at once and immediately, whenever an occasion presents itself, and are not necessarily dependent on the prior existence of any other feelings. When the eye, for instance, opens on a wide and diversified landscape, they suppose the whole to be embraced in one complex mental state, the formation of which is not gradual and susceptible of measurement by time, but is truly instantaneous. When we direct our attention to objects of less extent, as a portrait, a landscape, or historical painting, they imagine it to be still more evident that the complexity of mind, corresponding to the complexity of the object, is a result without any antecedent process. Without doubt what has now been said is in some instances apparently the case; but this appearance (for we cannot speak of it as anything more than such) is susceptible of an obvious explanation, without an abandonment of the general principle which has been laid down. No one is ignorant that the mind often passes with exceeding rapidity along the successive objects of its contemplation. This rapidity may in some cases be so great, that no foundation will be laid for remembrance; and of course, in such cases, the complex feeling has the appearance of being formed without the antecedence of other simple feelings. Often the eye glances so rapidly over the distinct parts of the portrait, the historical painting, or even the wide landscape, that we are utterly unable in our recollection to detect the successive steps of its progress. There naturally seems, therefore, to be but one view, instead of distinct and successive glancings of the mind from hill to hill, from forest to forest, and from one verdant spot to another, prior to the supposed one and instantaneous comprehension of the whole. But there is much reason for saying that this oneness of comprehension is in seeming and appearance only, and not in fact. (See § 106–108.)

§ 128. The precise sense in which complexness is to be understood.

But while we distinctly assert the frequent complexness of the mental affections, it should be particularly kept in mind, that they are not to be regarded in the light of a material compound, where the parts, although it may sometimes appear to be otherwise, necessarily possess no higher unity than that of juxtaposition, and, of course, can be literally separated from each other, and then put together again. There is nothing of this kind; neither putting together nor taking asunder, in this literal and material sense.—But if our thoughts and feelings are not made up of others, and are not complex in the material sense of the expressions, what then constitutes their complexness? This inquiry gives occasion for the important remark, that complexness in relation to the mind is not literal, but virtual only. What we term a complex feeling, in itself considered and so far as its purely psychical nature is concerned, is truly simple; but, at the same time, it is equal to many others, and is complex only in that sense. Thought after thought, and emotion following emotion, passes through the mind; and, as they are called forth by the operation of the laws of association, many of them necessarily have relation to the same object. Then there follows a new state of mind, which is the result of those previous feelings, and is complex in the sense already explained. That is to say, it is felt by us to possess a virtual equality to those separate antecedent thoughts and emotions. Our simple feelings are like streams coming from different mountains, but meeting and mingling together at last in the common centre of some intermediate lake; the tributary fountains are no longer separable, but have disappeared, and become merged and confounded in the bosom of their common resting-place. Or they may be likened to the higher forms of coinage; the dimes and dollars, which are as much units, in themselves considered, as the tens and hundreds of the inferior coinage which they represent, and to which they are equal in value.

The language which expresses the composition and complexity of thought is, therefore, to be regarded as essentially metaphorical when applied to the mind, and is not to be taken in its literal meaning. We are under the necessity of employing in this case, as in others, language which has a material origin, but we shall not be led astray by it if we carefully attend to what has been said, and endeavour to aid our conception of it by a reference to our internal experience.

§ 129. Illustrations of analysis as applied to the mind.

The subject of the preceding section will be the better understood by the consideration of analysis as applicable to the mind. As we do not combine literally, so we do not untie or separate literally; as there is no literal complexness, so there is no literal resolution or analysis of it. Nevertheless, we have a meaning when we speak of analyzing our thoughts and feelings. And what is it? What are we to understand by the term analysis?

Although this subject is not without difficulty, both in the conception and in the expression of it, it is susceptible of some degree of illustration.—It will be remembered that there may be analysis of material bodies. The chemist analyzes when he takes a piece of glass, which appears to be one substance, and finds that it is not one, but is separable into silicious and alkaline matter. He takes other bodies, and separates them in like manner; and, whenever he does this, the process is rightly called analysis, which literally means taking apart.

Now we apply the same term to the mind; but the thing expressed by it, the process gone through, is not the same. All we can say is, there is something like this. We do not resolve and separate a complex thought as we do a piece of glass or other material body into its parts; we are utterly unable to do it, if we should seriously make the attempt; every mental state is in itself and in fact simple and indivisible, and is complex only virtually. Complex notions are the results rather than the compounds of former feelings; and, though not literally made up of parts, have the relation to them which any material whole has to the elements composing it, and in that particular sense may be said to comprehend or embrace the subordinate notions. Mental analysis accordingly concerns merely this relation. We perform such an analysis when, by means of our reflection and consciousness, aided by the power of abstraction, we are able to indicate those separate and subordinate feelings, to which, in our conception of it, the complex mental state is virtually equal.

The term GOVERNMENT, for instance, when used in reference to the mental perception of the thing thus named, expresses a complex state of the mind; we may make this mental state, which is in fact only one, although it is virtually more than one, a subject of contemplation; and we are said to analyze it when we are able to indicate those separate and more elementary notions, without the existence and antecedence of which it could not have been formed by the mind. We do not literally take the complex state in pieces, but we designate other states of mind, which every one's knowledge of the origin of thought convinces him must have preceded it, such as the ideas of power, right, obligation, command, and the relative notions of superior and inferior.

§ 130. Complex notions of external origin.

The doctrine of simplicity and complexness of mental states is applicable, in both its forms, to the Intellective and Sentimentive parts of our nature; in other words, there may be a complex affection or passion, as well as a complex perception. The acts of the Will, the other great division of the mental nature, are always simple. When we consider the subject in reference to the intellect alone, we may add further, that there is complexity of the Intellect, both in its internal and external action; and it seems proper, in this connexion, to say something in particular of COMPLEX NOTIONS OF EXTERNAL ORIGIN.

What we term our simple ideas are representative of the parts of objects only. The sensations of colour, such as red, white, yellow; the original intimations from the touch, such as resistance, extension, hardness, and softness, do not, in themselves considered, give us a knowledge of substances, but only of the parts, attributes, or elements of substances. Accordingly, the ideas which we have of the various objects of the external world are for the most part complex. We speak of a house, a tree, a flower, a plant, a mineral, an animal; and in none of these cases are the ideas which we have simple; but, on the contrary, embrace a considerable number of elements.

§ 131. Of objects contemplated as wholes.

In point of fact, the various external objects which come under our notice are presented to us as *wholes;* and, as such (whatever may have been the original process leading to that result), we very early contemplate them.—Take, for instance, a LOADSTONE. In their ordinary and common thoughts upon it (the result, probably, of some ancecedent and very early training), men undoubtedly contemplate it as a whole; the state of mind which has reference to it embraces it as such. This complex notion, like all others which are complex, is virtually equal to a number of others of a more elementary character.—Hence, when we are called upon to give an account of the loadstone, we can return no other answer than by an enumeration of its elements. It is something which has weight, colour, hardness, power to draw iron, and whatever else we discover in it.

We use the term GOLD. This is a complex term, and implies a complexity in the corresponding mental state. But if we use the word gold, or any other synonymous word, in the hearing of a man who has neither seen that substance nor had it explained to him, he will not understand what is meant to be conveyed. We must enter into an analysis, and show that it is a combination of the qualities of yellowness, great weight, fusibility, ductility, and whatever else it possesses. We look upward to the sun in the heavens.

But what should we know of that great aggregate, if we could not contemplate it in the elements of form and extension, of brightness and heat, of roundness and regularity of motion?—All the ideas, therefore, which we form of external objects considered as wholes, are complex; and all such complex notions are composed of those which are simple.

§ 132. Something more in external objects than mere attributes or qualities.

But it is to be anticipated that we shall expose ourselves here to be pressed by certain inquiries. It will be said, perhaps, that this makes the whole visible creation a mere aggregate (susceptible undoubtedly of being arranged into classes, but, after all, a mere aggregate) of attributes, qualities, or properties. What we behold yonder, it will perhaps be alleged as an illustration of the objection, is mere greenness, resistance, hardness, form, &c., but nothing more; it is not a TREE. In the firmament there is brightness, and heat, and roundness, and uniformity of motion, but that is all; we mistake when we suppose there is a reality, an actual SUN. In a word, this view of external objects brings us back to one of the doctrines ascribed in ancient times to Pyrrho, and in fact to that modern Idealism, which has already been noticed, that there is nothing external to us but certain uniform appearances, which are mistaken for existences and realities without being so.

It is, perhaps, enough to say in regard to this objection, that we reject the idea of its being rightfully applied to ourselves, because we do not hesitate to admit and assert the truth of an existence (however difficult it may be to the mind fully to conceive of it) independently of these qualities; in other words, that there is something more, in point of fact, than what is outwardly exhibited. On a careful examination of our feelings, we shall probably find it impossible even to conceive of a quality without a subject, or an attribute without some object to which it belongs. We believe (and we cannot help believing) that there must necessarily be some foundation, some basis, which is the support of such attributes and qualities. We may not be able to tell precisely what it is; we may not have it in our power to describe or define it; but still it exists. The quality, therefore, and the existence to which it belongs, the outward accessible presentation and the subjective nature or essence, are not, in the view of the mind, identical. (See § 93–96.)

It will, then, perhaps be asked, Why do we not direct our attention at once to the true subjective existence, to matter itself, and not delay upon its appendages? The answer is, we cannot; the mind has its limits. It might be asked, with the same reason, Why we do not look directly into the existence and essence of the Deity, instead of studying Him in his works and intermediate manifestations? It might be asked, Why we do not directly contemplate the existence and essence of the mind, instead of studying it in its attributes and operations? The answer in all these cases is the same, viz., that we are unable to do it. And yet we believe in the existence and reality of a God, although we know him only through his manifestations and attributes. We believe in the existence and reality of the human mind, although the direct subject of our knowledge is not the mind itself, but merely its attributes and operations. It is the same in regard to the material world. The qualities and properties of bodies are the signs or marks which are immediately presented to our notice. They form the occasion on which the mind, by its Suggestional or Intuitional power, to be considered hereafter in its appropriate place, assures us of something more than the signs which immediately fall under our notice. This something, which we cannot help regarding as an actual and independent reality, we call variously a material subject, material existence, or simply matter.

§ 133. Explanatory remarks on the true philosophical method.

And at this point in our inquiries we can perhaps

briefly state, with the hope of being better understood than at any earlier time, some of the characteristics of the mental method which we have proposed to pursue. And FIRST, in order to relieve this department of knowledge from some of the perplexities which have attended its progress, the distinction is to be carefully observed between mental philosophy and Ontology. Mental philosophy, conceding the existence of the mind and its inherent powers as an admitted fact, deals chiefly with the phenomena which the mind exhibits and the classification of them. Ontology, desirous of knowing what it is which lies back of phenomena, advances with greater boldness but with less success, and announces itself as the science of existence. The problems of existence, which are hidden in the Infinite or Absolute of things, belong to God, and can never be exhausted by any thing short of omniscience. The problems of phenomena, coming within the limits of the finite, can be dealt with by faculties which are adapted to them, and are brought within the reach of human cognitions, so far at least as it is necessary or best for us to know them.

(2.) Further, the most satisfactory method, in attempting to learn the history and character of the mind, is that which has been so successful in other departments of science, and which is known from its earliest and ablest expositor as the Baconian. A method which, commencing with the rejection of all prejudices, and having no interests but those of truth, proceeds with the careful observation and the equally careful classification of mental facts, as they are disclosed not only in the sphere of our own consciousness, but as they are revealed in the observation of the thoughts and feelings of others, and in the history of men in all ages. This method, in its application to the mind, includes all the facts and intimations, especially those relating to personality and the foundation of moral distinctions, which are suggested and affirmed by the Intuitional power, as well as the knowledge coming from other sources. The À PRIORI method, therefore, so far as it is legitimately based upon intuitional facts, and is kept true to the laws of our mental nature, is included within the sphere of the Baconian process, when the latter is understood and interpreted in its true spirit.

(3.) Again, such is the connexion between the mind and the body, that a true philosophy of the mind includes some knowledge of physical conditions. And although it would be an error to accept the extreme views of Cabanis, a well-known French physician and materialistic philosopher, who maintained that "all ideas, sentiments, and passions, goodness, and virtue, are derived from physical sensation," and of other writers of this class, the philosophic method will require the acceptance and study of certain departments of physiology and pathology, as helps in the interpretation of mental action. The distinction first drawn and demonstrated by Sir Charles Bell between the nervous filaments connected with sensation and those connected with motion may serve as an illustration of the importance of the study of the body, as an auxiliary means of understanding the action of the mind. Still more striking illustrations may be found in numerous able treatises on Insanity, which justly make great account, in their attempts to explain the disordered manifestations of the mind, of the physiology and functions of the brain and the nervous system.

(4.) It comes also within the sphere of mental philosophy to indicate its relation to the many and important departments of science, which, in their principles, if not in their applications, are based upon it, or are closely connected with it. The principles of morals, the laws of evidence, the doctrine of æsthetics, logic, language, axiomatic truths, artistic taste, the philosophy of eloquence, the philosophic relation of the sciences to each other, religion itself which connects the soul with God,—it is difficult to see how these and other great departments, involving thought and feeling, and truth and duty, can be rightly understood, except in the light which is communicated through a knowledge of the nature and operations of the human mind.

CHAPTER XIII.

ABSTRACTION.—THE ABSTRACTIVE POWER.

§ 134. Abstraction implied in the analysis of complex ideas.

THE remarks which have been made in the course of the foregoing chapter, on the analysis and examination of our Complex Intellectual states, naturally lead to the consideration of another subject, in some respects intimately connected with that topic. When we have once formed a complex notion (no matter at what period, in what way, or of what kind), it not unfrequently happens that we desire, for various reasons, to examine more particularly some of its parts. Very frequently this is absolutely necessary to the full understanding of it. Although undoubtedly its elementary parts once came under review, that time is now long past; it has become important to institute a new inspection, to take each simple notion involved in it, and examine it by itself. And this is done by means of the process of ABSTRACTION, and in no other way.

By the aid of that process, our complex notions, however comprehensive they may be, are susceptible, if one may be allowed so to speak, of being taken to pieces, and the elementary parts may be abstracted or separated from each other; that is, they are made subjects of consideration apart from other ideas, with which they are ordinarily found to be associated. And hence, whenever this is the case in respect to the states of the mind, they are sometimes called ABSTRACTIONS, and still more frequently are known by the name of ABSTRACT IDEAS.

For the purpose of distinctness in what we have to say, they may be divided into the two classes of Particular and General; that is to say, in some cases the abstraction relates only to a single idea or element; in others it includes more.—General Abstract Ideas (or the notions which we form of Genera and Species) will form a distinct subject of consideration.

§ 135. Instances of particular abstract ideas.

We shall proceed, therefore, to remark here on Particular abstractions. Of this class, the notions which we form of the different kinds of colours may be regarded as instances. For example, we hold in our hand a rose; it has extension, colour, form, fragrance. The mind is so deeply occupied with the colour as almost wholly to neglect the other qualities. This is a species of abstraction, although perhaps an imperfect one, because, when an object is before us, it is difficult, in our most attentive consideration of any particular quality or property, to withdraw the mind wholly from the others. When, on the contrary, any *absent* object of perception occurs to us, when we think of or form a conception of it, our thoughts will readily fix upon the colour of such object, and make that the subject of consideration, without particularly regarding its other qualities and attributes, such as weight, hardness, taste, extension, and form. We may also distinguish in any body (either when present or still more perfectly when absent) its solidity from its extension, or we may direct our attention to its weight, or its length, or breadth, or thickness, and make any one of these a distinct object in our thoughts.

And hence, as it is a well-known fact that the properties of any body may be separated in the view and examination of the mind, however closely they may be connected in their appropriate subjects, we may lay down this statement in respect to the states of the mind before us, viz.: When any quality or attribute of an object, which does not exist by itself, but in a state of combination, is detached by our minds from its customary associates, and is considered separately, the notion we form of it becomes a particular abstract idea.—The distinctive mark of this class is, that the abstraction is limited to one quality. It should, perhaps, be particularly added, that the abstraction or separation may exist mentally, when it cannot take place in the object itself. For instance, the length of a building, its breadth and color, and even its size and figure, may each of them be made subjects of separate mental consideration, although there can be no real or actual separation of these things in the building itself. If there be any one of these properties, there must necessarily be all.

§ 136. Names, and complexity in the power of abstraction.

The power by which this is done is variously called Abstraction, or the Abstractive power, and sometimes, without any violation of the recognised analogies of the language, by the appropriate term "Abstractment." A power of the mind always implies something to be effected; and if there is a definite susceptibility, either simple or complex, which is appropriate to the result, and which secures that result when nothing else can do it, it is entitled to be called a power. It stands as a distinct addition to the mental forces, and brings to our view a new element, without which man would fall short of that intellectual greatness which characterizes and illustrates his existence. And thus making, in this general Department of the mind, the Cognitive powers the special subjects of consideration, but introducing here and elsewhere, as it is most convenient, the Auxiliary powers which diversify and strengthen all other mental activities, we proceed, with a careful regard to the comparative position which nature has assigned them, from Sensation to Perception, from Perceptivity to the Conceptive power; and onward step by step to the important power of Abstraction, which, coming next in course, will be found to widen the sphere of mental activity, and to give a new element of dignity and strength.

(2.) We have already had occasion to say, in a former chapter, that some powers of the mind are simple, others complex; some, like the powers of Sensation and Intuition, securing their results, so far as we can judge, by a single movement; others, like the Reasoning power and the Imagination, fulfilling the objects for which they were given us by a complexity of action. It is generally conceded, I believe, that the abstractive or abstractional power aims at and secures the results which it holds under its control, not by a single act, but by a complexity of movement, consisting in a number of distinct mental operations, but all of them regulated and harmonized by appropriate relational adjustments and by unity of purpose. The statement may be illustrated thus. The process which is gone through in every case of abstraction, applies of course to those things and those states of mind which are complex; but which, though now consolidated in a complex form, are nevertheless made up of separate elements. Not only the object of thought, whether external or internal, sensuous or supersensuous, is a complexity; but the idea which corresponds to it, and which brings it within the reach of mental examination, is complex also. And accordingly, leaving the outward object, whether material or psychical, and limiting our examination to the corresponding idea, it will be found that the process under consideration presents, as the thing to be done by it, the separation of a particular abstract idea from those ideas with which it has been customarily associated.

(3.) And in doing this, it appears, in analyzing the complex activity of Abstractment, that there is, and must be, something of the nature of a mental determination or choice; in other words, an act of the will. And further, it is a necessity, that this act of the will shall concern the previous complex mental state, when viewed in one respect rather than another; or, what is the same thing, it will concern one part of the complex idea rather than another. So that we may truly and justly be said to have not only a desire, but a determination to consider or examine some part of the complex idea more particularly than the others. When the mind is in this manner directed to any particular part of a complex notion, we find it to be the fact, that the principle of association, or whatever principle it is, which keeps the other parts in their state of union with it, ceases in a greater or less degree to operate and to maintain that union; the other parts, ceasing to be kept together by the action of the power which had previously constituted their union, rapidly fall off and disappear, and the particular quality, towards which the mind is especially directed, remains the sole subject of consideration. That is to say, it is abstracted, and the mental state which interiorly corresponds to it becomes an abstract idea.—If, for example, we have in mind the complex notion of any object, a house, tree, plant, flower, and the like, but have a desire and determination to make the colour, which forms a part of this complex notion, a particular subject of attention, the consequence is, that, while the quality of colour occupies our chief regard, the other qualities will disappear and no more be thought of. If we determine to examine the weight or extension of an object, the result will be the same; in other words, the extension, weight, colour, and whatever else may be discriminated in its attributes, will become distinct and exclusive objects of attention, and will thus be mentally abstracted.

(4.) Such, in the formation of particular abstract ideas, seems, when we analyze it into its elementary steps, to be the process of the mind, viz.: The direction of an act of the will to a particular part of a complex notion, and the consequent detention of the part towards which the mental choice is directed, and the natural and necessary disappearance, under such circumstances, of the other parts. But the process, restricted by appropriate occasions and aiming at special objects, exhibits a unity of design and a certainty of result, which entitles it to be called a power.

§ 137. Of generalizations of particular abstract mental states.

The terms GENERALIZING and GENERALIZATION are often found applied to the states of mind under consideration. When we have made any quality of a body a distinct and separate subject of attention, we may further regard it as belonging to one or more objects, according as we find such to be the fact or otherwise. What is chiefly meant, therefore, when we speak of the generalizing of this class of abstract notions, is, that, in our experience of things, we observe them to be common to many subjects. We find whiteness to be a quality of snow, of chalk, of milk, and of other bodies; and whenever, with the simple abstract notion of whiteness, we connect in our thoughts the additional circumstance of its not being limited to one body, but the property of many, the term may be said to be generalized. And this seems to be all that can be properly understood by generalization when applied to the states of mind now before us.

§ 138. Of the importance and uses of abstraction.

The power of Abstraction is by no means an unimportant one, even when limited to the separation of the particular or simple elements of thought.—"A carpenter," says Kames,* speaking of the great utility of abstraction, "considers a log of wood with regard to hardness, firmness, colour, and texture; a philosopher, neglecting these properties, makes the log undergo a chemical analysis, and examines its taste, its smell, and component principles; the geometrician confines his reasoning to the figure, the length, breadth, and thickness; in general, every artist, abstracting from all other properties, confines his observations to those which have a more immediate connexion with his profession."

Besides its well-known uses in the various forms of reasoning (particularly demonstrative reasoning), abstraction is greatly subservient to the exertions of a creative imagination, as they appear in painting, archi-

* Elements of Criticism, vol. iii., Appendix.

tecture, poetry, and the other fine or liberal arts.—The poet and the painter are supplied with their materials from experience; without having received ideas from some source, they never could have practised their art. But, if they do not restrict themselves to mere imitation, they must combine and modify the ideas which they have, so as to be able to form new creations of their own. But every such exertion of their powers presupposes the exercise of abstraction in decomposing and separating actual conceptions, and in forming them anew. The power of abstraction, therefore, may justly be considered as a characteristic of the great masters in the liberal arts. From how many delightful forms in nature, and how many ideal temples, contemplated for a long time in the mind's eye, must the genius that planned the Parthenon have abstracted each form of beauty and excellence of proportion! From how many forests, both seen and imagined, and fields of bloom, and rivers and waterfalls, must the mind that conceived the Garden of Paradise Lost have drawn the sounds that delight the ear, and the colours that are pleasant to the sight!

CHAPTER XIV.

GENERAL ABSTRACT IDEAS.

§ 139. General abstract notions the same with genera and species.

WE proceed, in connexion with the remarks of the last chapter, to the consideration of GENERAL ABSTRACT ideas; a subject of so much interest that it deserves a separate notice; and which has frequently been thought to be attended with no small difficulty.

General Abstract notions are not only different, in consequence of embracing a greater number of elementary parts, from those which are particular, but are also susceptible of being distinguished from the great body of our other complex notions.—The idea, for example, which we form of any individual, of

John, Peter, or James, is evidently a complex one, but it is not necessarily a general one. The notion which we frame of a particular horse or of a particular tree, is likewise a complex idea, but not a general one. There will be found to be a clear distinction between them, although it may not be perfectly obvious at first. GENERAL ABSTRACT IDEAS are our notions of the classes of objects, that is, of Genera and Species. They are expressed by general names, without, in most cases, any defining or limitation, as when we use the words ANIMAL, MAN, HORSE, BIRD, SHEEP, FISH, TREE, not to express any one in particular of these various classes, but animals, men, horses, and trees in general.

§ 140. Process in classification, or the forming of genera and species.

Now if our general abstract ideas, as far as they relate to external objects, are truly notions of SPECIES and GENERA, it will aid us in the better understanding of them if we briefly consider how species and genera are formed. Men certainly find no great practical difficulty in forming these classifications, since we find that they do in fact make them in numberless instances, and at a very early period of life. They seem to be governed in the process by definite and uniform mental tendencies.—What, then, in point of fact, is the process in classification? It is obvious, in the first place, that no classification can be made without considering two or more objects together. A number of objects, therefore, are first presented to us for our observation and inquiry, which are to be examined first in themselves, and then in comparison with each other. We will take a familiar scene to illustrate what takes place.

We suppose ourselves to stand on the bank of a navigable river; we behold the flowing of its waters, the cliffs that overhang it, the trees that line its shore, the boats and boatmen on its bosom, the flocks and herds that press down to drink from its waves. With such a scene before us, it is to be expected that the mind will rapidly make each and all of these the subjects of its contemplation; nor does it pursue this contemplation and inquiry far, without perceiving certain relations of agreement or difference. Certain objects before it are felt to be essentially alike, and others to be essentially different; and hence they are not all arranged in one class, but a discrimination is made, and different classes are formed. The flocks and herds are formed into their respective classes. The tall and leafy bodies on the river's bank, although they differ from each other in some respects, are yet found to agree in so many others, that they are arranged together in another class, and called by the general name of TREE. The living, moving, and reasoning beings, that propel the boats on its waters, form another class, and are called MAN.—And there is the same process, and the same result, in respect to all other bodies coming within the range of our observation.

§ 141. Early classifications sometimes incorrect.

It has been intimated, that, in making these classifications, men are governed by definite and uniform mental tendencies; still it must be acknowledged that mistakes are sometimes committed, especially in the early periods of society, and in all cases where the opportunities of examination and comparison are imperfect. When man first opens his eyes on nature (and in the infancy of our race, he finds himself a novice wherever he goes), objects so numerous, so various in kind, so novel and interesting, crowd upon his attention, that, attempting to direct himself to all at the same time, he loses sight of their specifical differences, and blends them together more than a calm and accurate examination would justify. And hence it is not to be wondered at that our earliest classifications, the primitive genera and species, are sometimes incorrectly made.

Subsequently, when knowledge has been in some measure amassed, and reasoning and observation have been brought to a greater maturity, these errors are attended to; individuals are rejected from species where they do not properly belong, and species from genera. The most savage and ignorant tribes will in due season correct their mistakes and be led into the truth.

§ 142. Illustrations of our earliest classifications.

We are naturally led to introduce some circumstances here which throw light on this part of our subject. What we wish to illustrate is the simple fact, that men readily perceive the resemblances of objects, and exhibit a disposition to classify them in reference to such resemblance. The first case which we shall mention in illustration of this is that of Caspar Hauser. The principal objects which Caspar had to amuse himself with in his prison were two little wooden horses, which, in his entire ignorance, he believed to be possessed of life and sensibility. After the termination of his imprisonment, his biographer informs us, that to "every animal he met with, whether quadruped or biped, dog, cat, goose, or fowl, he gave the name of horse."

In the year 1814, Pitcairn's Island, a solitary spot in the Pacific Ocean, was visited by two English cruisers. Two of the young men that belonged on the island, and whose knowledge was, of course, exceedingly limited, came on board one of the vessels. "The youths," says the Narrative, "were greatly surprised at the sight of so many novel objects; the size of the ship, the guns, and everything around them. Observing a cow, they were at first alarmed, and expressed a doubt whether it was a huge goat or a horned hog, these being the only two species of quadrupeds they had ever seen."

The English navigator Cook, in going from New Zealand to the Friendly Islands, lighted on an island called Wateeoo.—"The inhabitants," he says, "were afraid to come near our cows and horses, nor did they form the least conception of their nature. But the sheep and goats did not surpass the limits of their ideas, for they gave us to understand they knew them to be *birds*."

Captain Cook informs us that these people were acquainted with only three sorts of animals, viz., dogs, hogs, and birds.—Of hogs and dogs they had probably never known more than one variety or class, and had never been led to suspect that there was, or could be, any other. But, having noticed a great variety of birds in their forests and waters, they had undoubtedly found it necessary, before this period, not only to give a general name expressive of all birds, but also to classify some of the subordinate varieties. This people, therefore, not unnaturally, although we we do not pretend to say with much discrimination, applied the term BIRDS to the sheep and goats of the English. They knew not but there might be some new class of birds which they had not hitherto noticed; and they saw no insuperable objection in the size of the sheep and goats to this disposition of them, whatever other objection they might, on a further examination, have subsequently found.

§ 143. Of the nature of general abstract ideas.

The notions which are thus formed in all cases of classification, are commonly known, in the Treatises having relation to these subjects, as General Abstract ideas. And they are no less numerous than the multiplied varieties of objects which are found to exist everywhere around us. It is thus that we form the general notions of animal and of all the subordinate species of animals; of tree and its numerous varieties; of earths and minerals, and whatever else is capable of being arranged into classes.

We may apply these views not only to natural objects, but to forms and relations of a very different character. The word Triangle is the name of a general abstract idea. Great exceptions, however, have been taken to certain incautious expressions of Mr. Locke on this point. He asserts that it requires some pains and skill to form the general idea of a triangle, and gives the following reason: "for it must neither be oblique nor rectangle, neither equilateral, equicrural, nor scalenon, but all and none of these at once." This language is undoubtedly open to some degree of criticism. The correct view seems to be this. The word TRIANGLE is not only the name of a class, but of a very general class; it is the name of a Genus, embracing all those figures which agree in the circumstance of being bounded by three straight lines meeting one another so as to form three angles. A figure having any other form (in other words, not exhibiting a resemblance or similarity in this respect), is excluded from the Genus; but it is still so extensive, taken in the sense just now mentioned, as to include all figures whatever of that name.—Now there are embraced within the genus, as in numerous other cases, subordinate classes, which are distinguished by their appropriate names, viz., the class of acute-angled triangles, that of right-angled triangles, of obtuse-angled triangles, &c.

But it is to be noticed, that the general idea, whatever objects it may be founded upon, does not embrace every particular which makes a part of such objects. When we look at a number of men, we find them all differing in some respects, in height, size, colour, tone of voice, and in other particulars. The mind fixes only upon those traits or properties with which it can combine the notion of resemblance; that is to say, those traits, qualities, or properties in which the individuals are perceived to be alike, or to resemble each other.—The complex mental state, which embraces these qualities and properties, and nothing more (with the exception of the superadded notion of other bodies having resembling qualities), is a General Abstract idea.

And hence the name. Such notions are called ABSTRACT, because, while embracing many individuals in certain respects, they detach and leave out altogether a variety of particulars in which those individuals disagree. If there were not this discrimination and leaving out of certain parts, we never could consider these notions, regarded as wholes, as otherwise than individual or particular.—They are called GENERAL, because, in consequence of the discrimination and selection which has just been mentioned, they embrace such qualities and properties as exist not in one merely, but in many.

The difference, therefore, between the complex notion which we form of any particular object, and the general complex feeling now under consideration, is truly this: the latter combines together fewer particulars, but unites with such as it does combine together the additional notion of resemblance, which implies as its basis the comparison of a number of objects, and is, perhaps, the distinguishing circumstance. If it should be asked, By virtue of what principle is this discovery of a resembling relation made? the answer is to be found in the fact, that there is in the mind an original tendency or susceptibility, by means of which, whenever we perceive different objects together, we are instantly, without the intervention of any other mental process, sensible of their relation in certain respects. This susceptibility, which deals with the relations of things, and which is known as the power of Relative Suggestion or Judgment, will be noticed in its appropriate place.

§ 144. Objection sometimes made to the existence of general notions.

It is proper briefly to notice an objection sometimes made, viz., that it is not possible for us to have such general notion at all, because there is nothing outward which the general notion or idea precisely corresponds to. This objection goes too far. It would seem even to lead to the conclusion that we can have no complex idea of any kind, neither particular nor general. It cannot be pretended that even our complex notions of particular objects correspond precisely to those objects. The ideas which we form of a particular house, tree, or plant, or any other individual object, are often erroneous in some respects, and probably always imperfect. But they are not, for that reason, to be regarded as false and chimerical, and to be rejected as having no foundation in nature.

We will suppose ourselves to have been acquainted in former years with a particular elm; we have looked upon it a thousand times, and it is familiar to us as any of our most cherished remembrances. At this great distance of time and place we form an idea, a conception, a notion of it, but it cannot be presumed to be a perfect or complete one. It cannot be pretended that we have a notion not only of the trunk, but of every leaf and of the form of every leaf, and of every branch and its intertwinings with every other branch; that it exists in our minds precisely, and in every respect, the same as it exists on the spot where it grows. If, therefore, general abstract ideas are to be rejected because they embrace only parts of those objects which are ranked under them, we must on the same grounds reject and deny also our complex notions of individual objects; but this probably no one is prepared to do.

§ 145. The power of general abstraction in connexion with numbers, &c.

The ability which the mind possesses of forming general abstract ideas is of much practical importance; but whether it be the characteristical attribute of a rational nature or not, as some have supposed, it is not necessary now to inquire. It is not easy to estimate the increase of power which is thus given to the action of the human mind, particularly in reasoning. By means of general abstract propositions, we are able to state volumes in a few sentences; that is to say, the truths, stated and illustrated in a few general propositions, would fill volumes in their particular applications. But it is enough here to refer to a single circumstance in illustration of the uses of this power.

Without the ability of forming general notions, we should not be able to *number*, even in the smallest degree. Before we can consider objects as forming a multitude, or are able to number them, it seems necessary to be able to apply to them a common name. This we cannot do until we have reduced them to a genus; and the formation of a genus implies and requires the exercise of the power of abstraction. Consequently, we should be unable, without such power, to number.—How great, then, is the practical importance of that intellectual process by which general abstractions are formed!—Without the ability to number, we should be at a loss in all investigations where this ability is required; without the power to classify, all our speculations must be limited to particulars, and we should be capable of no general reasoning.

§ 146. Of general abstract truths or principles.

There are not only general abstract ideas, but abstract truths or principles also of a general nature, which are deserving of some attention, especially in a practical point of view. Although enough has already been said to show the importance of abstraction, it may yet be desirable to have a more full view of its applications.

The process in forming general truths or principles of an abstract nature seems to be this. We must begin undoubtedly with the examination and study of particulars; with individual objects and characters, and with insulated events. We subsequently confirm the truth of whatever has been ascertained in such inquiry by an observation of other like objects and events. We proceed from one individual to another till no doubt remains.—Having in this way arrived at some general fact or principle, we thenceforward throw aside the consideration of the particular objects on which it is founded, and make it alone, exclusively and abstractly, the subject of our mental contemplations. We repeat this process again and again, till the mind, instead of being wholly taken up with a multitude of particulars, is stored with truths of a general kind. These truths it subsequently combines in trains of reasoning, compares together, and deduces from them others of still wider application.

§ 147. Of the speculations of philosophers and others.

What has been said leads us to observe, that there is a characteristical difference between the speculations of men of philosophic minds and those of the common mass of people which is worthy of some notice. The difference between the two is not so much, that philosophers are accustomed to carry on processes of reasoning to a greater extent, as this, that they are more in the habit of employing general abstract ideas and general terms, and that, consequently, the conclusions which they form are more comprehensive. Nor are their general reasonings, although the conclusions at which they arrive seem in their particular applications to indicate wonderful fertility of invention, so difficult in the performance as is apt to be supposed. They have so often and so long looked at general ideas and general propositions; have been so accustomed, as one may say, to contemplate the general nature of things, divested of all superfluous and all specific circumstances, that they have formed a *habit;* and the operation is performed without difficulty. It requires in such persons no greater intellectual effort than would be necessary in skilfully managing the details of ordinary business.

The speculations of the great bulk of mankind differ from those of philosophers in being, both in the subjects of them and in their results, particular. They discover an inability to enlarge their view to universal propositions, which embrace a great number of individuals. They may possess the power of mere argument, of comparing propositions together which concern particulars, and deducing inferences from them to a great degree; but when they attempt to contemplate general propositions, their minds are perplexed, and the conclusions which are drawn from them appear obscure, however clearly the previous process of reasoning may have been expressed.

§ 148. Of different opinions formerly prevailing.

The subject of general abstract ideas, of which we

have thus given a summary view, excited very considerable interest during the Scholastic ages; and different opinions have prevailed concerning them, not only at that period, but more or less down to the present time. It is perhaps not necessary in most cases and for most persons to plunge deeply into the history of philosophical opinions. The discordant views which are there found have a tendency to confuse and embarrass the young mind. A knowledge of the truth, when it is once found, is in general of far greater consequence than an acquaintance with the prolonged and conflicting discussions which led to it. The disputes, however, on the topic of general abstractions so widely prevailed, and excited so much interest and effort, that it seems to be necessary to give a short sketch of some of them. We propose, therefore, to refer briefly to two conflicting systems of thought and argument on this subject, Nominalism and Conceptualism.

§ 149. Of the opinions of the Nominalists.

About the commencement of the 12th century, Roscelinus, the instructor of Abelard, whose name occupies so conspicuous a place in the history of Scholastic learning, laid the foundations of Nominalism. Denying the existence of general abstract ideas, he maintained that nothing can be called general or universal but names, and that even to them universality can be ascribed only virtually, and not in the strict and literal sense of the term.—That is, the names are in the first instance given to individuals, but when any individuals are specified, the nature of the mind is such, that we naturally and immediately think of other individuals of the same kind. So that the names are in fact particular, although, owing to the operation of the principle of association, the practical effect is the same as if it were otherwise, and hence the epithets "general" and "universal" are applied to them. This opinion in respect to general ideas and names, or some doctrine essentially of this description, has found many advocates from the days of Roscelinus to those of Berkeley and Hume.

§ 150. Of the opinions of the Conceptualists.

Those who hold to the actual existence of general abstract ideas, a doctrine which is commonly and truly understood to imply the actual existence in some generic form of the objects which they represent, in other words an objective Realism, have generally been called Conceptualists. And of this number, among the celebrated men of earlier times, was Abelard, who seems to have had a deeper philosophical insight than his teacher Roscelinus. We have already given, with such distinctness as the obscurity and difficulty of the subject admitted, what we suppose to be the true mental process. Whether we are right, believing as we do that the mind itself is and must be its own interpreter, we leave to the testimony of each one's internal and external experience, subjected to the reflex process of a candid examination. But it is possible that some may be desirous of a single testimony from other sources.

Some of the objections to the doctrine of Roscelinus and those who have thought with him, are forcibly summed up in Dr. Thomas Brown's Philosophy of the Mind, Lectures 46 and 47. We quote the passages here, both on account of their intrinsic value, and for the purpose of recalling, as we have done in some other instances, the name and merits of an able writer.

"Of that rigid Nominalism, which involves truly no mixture of Conceptualism, or of the belief of those feelings of relation for which I have contended, but denies altogether the existence of that peculiar class of feelings or states of mind which have been denominated general notions or general ideas, asserting the existence only of individual objects perceived, and of general terms that comprehend these, without any peculiar mental state denoted by the general term, distinct from those separate sensations or perceptions which the particular objects comprehended under the term might individually excite, it seems to me that the very statement of the opinion itself is almost a sufficient confutation, since the very invention of the general term, and the extension of it to certain objects only, not to all objects, implies some reason for this limitation, some feeling of general agreement of the objects included in the class, to distinguish them from the objects not included in it, which is itself that very general notion professedly denied.* As long as some general notion of circumstances of resemblance is admitted, I see very clearly how a general term may be most accurately limited; but if this general notion be denied, I confess that I cannot discover any principles of limitation whatever. Why have certain objects been classed together, and not certain other objects, when all have been alike perceived by us; and all, therefore, if there be nothing more than mere perception in the process, are capable of receiving any denomination which we may please to bestow on them? Is it arbitrarily, and without any reason whatever, that we do not class a rose-bush with birds, or an elephant with fish? and if there be any reason for these exclusions, why will not the Nominalist tell us what that reason is—in what feeling it is found—and how it can be made accordant with his system?

* It is proper to remark, in introducing this passage from Dr. Brown, that this acute writer is to be considered as expressing himself too strongly when he asserts, in a sentence not here quoted, that the feeling of resemblance is *all* that the general name truly designates. Possibly he meant to convey by this assertion nothing more than this, that the feeling of resemblance is the prominent and distinguishing circumstance in the notions expressed by general names, since in another passage he speaks of general terms being "invented to express *all that multitude of objects* which agree in exciting one common feeling of relation, the relation of a certain similarity." If that were not his intention, then we are to consider his views as correct only so far as they go. The feeling of resemblance is a prominent circumstance; but there is something more than this. Whenever we form a complex notion, which is both general and abstract, we combine the feeling of resemblance, the existence of which Dr. Brown has so clearly demonstrated, with the notion of those properties which are found to be possessed in common.

Must it not be that the rose-bush and a sparrow, though equally perceived by us, do not excite that general notion of resemblance which the term *bird* is invented to express—do not seem to us to have those relations of a common nature, in certain respects, which lead us to class the sparrow and the ostrich, however different in other respects, as birds; or the petty natives of our brooks and rivulets with the mighty monsters of the deep, under one general and equal denomination? If this be the reason, there is more in every case than perception and the giving of a general name; for there is a peculiar state of mind—a general relative feeling—intervening between the perception and the invention of the term, which is the only reason that can be assigned for that very invention."

§ 151. Further remarks of Brown on general abstractions.

"Can the Nominalist then assert that there is no feeling of the resemblance of objects, in certain respects, which thus intervenes between the perception of them as separate objects, which is one stage of the process, and the comprehension of them under a single name, which is another stage of the process—or must he not rather confess that it is merely in consequence of this intervening feeling we give to the number of objects their general name, to the exclusion of the multitudes of objects to which we do not apply it, as it is in consequence of certain other feelings, excited by them individually, we give to each separate object its proper name, to the exclusion of every other object? To repeat the process, as already described to you, we perceive two or more objects—we are struck with their resemblance in certain respects. We invent a general name to denote this feeling of resemblance, and we class under this general name every particular object, the perception of which is followed by the same feeling of resemblance, and no object but these alone."

CHAPTER XV.

OF THE POWER OF ATTENTION.

§ 152. Names given it, and its result when in exercise.

We come now to another power, which does not directly and by virtue of its own activity originate knowledge, and therefore is not in strictness denominated and classed as one of the Cognitive faculties; but exceedingly important in its relations and influence, it is entitled to a leading place among those powers which we have found it necessary to notice and introduce from time to time as AUXILIARY powers. We refer to the power of Attention; the Attentional power; or simply and analogically, by adding the termination which indicates function or office, "Attentivement."

The result of the exercise of the power of attention is the realization in fact of that state of mind, which, in consequence of the imperfection of language, we call by the same name, attention; but which, considered as an effect, may easily be discriminated from its cause. We sometimes call it attentiveness. And it is this resulting experience which first claims our notice. When that state of mind exists, which is denominated attention, so that we can truly say of a person that he is attentive, it is found, that the mind is steadily directed, for a length of time, to some object of sense or intellect, exclusive of other objects. All other objects, for the time being, are shut out. In other words, the grasp, which the perceptive power fixes upon the object of its contemplations, is an undivided, an unbroken one.

§ 153. Of different degrees of attention.

In agreement with this view of the subject, we often speak of attention as great or small, as existing in a very high or a very slight degree. When the view of the mind is only momentary, and is unaccompanied, as it generally is at such times, with any force of emotion or energy of volitional action, then the attention is said to be slight. When, on the contrary, the mind directs itself to an object or series of objects with earnestness, and for a considerable length of time, and refuses to attend to anything else, then the attention is said to be intense.

We commonly judge at first of the degree of attention to a subject from the length of time during which the mind is occupied with it. But, when we look a little further, it will be found that the time will generally depend upon the strength and permanency of the attendant emotion of interest. And hence both the time and the degree of feeling are to be regarded in our estimate of the power of attention in any particular case; the former being the result, and, in some sense, a measure of the latter.

Of instances of people who are able to give but slight attention to any subject of thought, who cannot bring their minds to it with steadiness and power, we everywhere find multitudes, and there are some instances where this ability has been possessed in such a high degree as to be worthy of notice. There have been mathematicians who could investigate the most complicated problems amid every variety and character of disturbance. It was said of Julius Cæsar, that, while writing a despatch, he could at the same time dictate four others to his secretaries; and if he did not write himself, could dictate seven letters at once. The same thing is asserted also of the Emperor Napoleon, who had a wonderful capability of directing his whole mental energy to whatever came before him.*

The chess-player Philidor could direct three games of chess at the same time, of one of which only he required ocular inspection, the moves of the other two being announced to him by an assistant. The moves

* Segur's History of the Expedition to Russia, book vii., ch. 13.

of the chessmen formed the subject about which his thoughts were employed; and such was the intensity of interest and such the power of the will, that the mind found no difficulty in dwelling upon it to the entire exclusion of other subjects, and for a considerable length of time.

§ 154. Complexness of the power of attention.

The power, by means of which these remarkable results are experienced, is not simple, but complex. In its first aspect, it is purely intellectual. We see only the direction of the perceptive power to its appropriate object, which it holds firmly in its grasp, excluding the other objects which throng around it from the range of its contemplation. But if we look a little further, we shall find, that, back of the act of perceptivity, is an act of the will, directing, condensing, and confining the perception. And then, again, it is well understood, that the act of the will requires, in another part of our nature, but outside of the perceptive or intellectual, a feeling of desire or interest, which is antecedent to the volitional act, and which brings the will into action. Such is the analysis of the Attentional power, which of course implies its complexity; namely, an act of perception; the volitional control of the perceptive act, without which it would be unfixed and wandering; with the intermediate sentiment or feeling, which sometimes takes the form of a desire and sometimes of a sentiment of duty.

And at this point it is proper to add an explanatory remark. It is sometimes thought, that the powers or faculties of the mind which are complex, inasmuch as they are susceptible of being analyzed into their component elements, are for that reason not to be regarded as powers. We could not feel justified in assenting to such a view, because in settling the question of what are to be regarded as mental faculties and what are not, we are to take into consideration the objects had in view, and the combinations and relative adjustment of the component elements which constitute the complexness of such faculties, and also their modes and quickness of action, and the certainties of result. On the view that all the mental faculties are and must be simple, and that, if they are susceptible of being resolved by analytical processes into component parts or elements, they cease to be regarded as such, it logically follows, that the powers of perception and abstraction, of reasoning, imagination, and memory would be excluded from the list of mental faculties. A result, which would not only perplex the recognised facts and relations of the mind, but would violate the usages of language, and find itself at war with intuitive convictions.

§ 155. Dependence of memory on attention.

We are sometimes obliged, partially at least, to anticipate subjects. And on the supposition that we know something of the memory, an attribute of the mind which is to be particularly considered hereafter, we may refer here, in connexion with Attention, to the well-known fact, that memory depends on attention. That is to say, where attention is slight, remembrance is weak; and where attention is intense, remembrance continues longer.—There are many facts which confirm this statement.

(1.) In the course of a single day, persons who are in the habit of winking will close their eyelids perhaps thousands of times, and, as often as they close them, will place themselves in utter darkness. Probably they are conscious at the time both of closing their eyelids and of being in the dark; but, as their attention is chiefly taken up with other things, they have entirely forgotten it.—(2.) Let a person be much engaged in conversation, or occupied with any very interesting speculation, and the clock will strike in the room where he is, apparently without his having any knowledge of it. He hears the clock strike as much as at any other time, but, not attending to the perception of sound, and having his thoughts directed another way, he immediately forgets.—(3.) In the occupations of the day, when a multitude of cares are pressing us on every side, a thousand things escape our notice; they appear to be neither seen nor heard, nor to affect us in any way whatever. But at the stillness of evening, when anxieties and toils are quieted, and there is a general pause in nature, we seem to be endued with a new sense, and the slightest sound attracts our attention. Shakspeare has marked even this.

> "The crow doth sing as sweetly as the lark
> When neither is attended; and, I think,
> The nightingale, if she should sing by day,
> When every goose is cackling, would be thought
> No better a musician than the wren."

It is on the same principle that people dwelling in the vicinity of waterfalls do not appear to notice the sound. The residents in the neighbourhood even of the great cataract of Niagara are not seriously disturbed by it, although it is an unbroken, interminable thunder to all others.—The reason in all these cases is the same as has already been given. There is no attention and no remembrance, and, of course, virtually no perception.

(4.) Whenever we read a book, we do not observe the words merely as a whole, but every letter of which they are made up, and even the minute parts of these letters. But it is merely a glance; it does not for any length of time occupy our attention; we immediately forget, and with great difficulty persuade ourselves that we have truly perceived the letters of the word. The fact that every letter is in ordinary cases observed by us, may be proved by leaving out a letter of the word, or by substituting others of a similar form. We readily, in reading, detect such omissions or substitutions.

(5.) An expert accountant can sum up, almost with a single glance of the eye, a long column of figures. The operation is performed almost instantaneously, and yet he ascertains the sum of the whole with unerring certainty. It is impossible that he should learn the sum without noticing every figure in the whole column, and without allowing each its proper worth; but the attention to them was so very slight, that he is unable to remember this distinct notice.

Many facts of this kind evidently show, as we think, that memory depends upon attention, or, rather, upon a continuance of attention, and varies with that continuance.

§ 156. Of exercising attention in reading.

If attention, as we have seen, be requisite to memory, then we are furnished with a practical rule of considerable importance. The rule is, Not to give a hasty and careless reading of authors, but to read them with a suitable degree of deliberation and thought.—It is the fault of some persons that they are too quickly weary; that they skip from one author to another, and from one sort of knowledge to another. It is true, there are many things to be known; we would not have a person limit himself entirely to one science, but it is highly important that he should guard against that rapid and careless transition from subject to subject which has been mentioned.

If we are asked the reason of this direction, we find a good and satisfactory one in the fact referred to at the head of this section, that there cannot be memory without attention, or, rather, that the power of memory will vary with the degree of attention. By yielding to the desire of becoming acquainted with a greater variety of departments of knowledge than the understanding is able to master, and, as a necessary consequence, by bestowing upon each of them only a very slight attention, we remain essentially ignorant of the whole.

The person who pursues such a course finds himself unable to recall what he has been over; he has a great many half-formed notions floating in his mind, but these are so ill shaped and so little under his control as to be little better than actual ignorance. This is one evil result of reading authors and of going over sciences in the careless way which has been specified, that the knowledge thus acquired, if it can be called knowledge, is of very little practical benefit, in consequence of being so poorly digested and so little under control.

But there is another and, perhaps, more serious evil. This practice greatly disqualifies one for all intellectual pursuits. To store the mind with new ideas is only a part of education. It is at least a matter of equal importance to impart to all the mental powers a suitable discipline, to exercise those that are strong, to strengthen those that are weak, and to maintain among all of them a suitable balance. An attentive and thorough examination of subjects is a training of the mind in both these respects. It furnishes it with that species of knowledge which is most valuable, because it is not mixed up with errors; and, moreover, gives a strength and consistency to the whole structure of the intellect. Whereas, when the mind is long left at liberty to wander from object to object without being called to account and subjected to the rules of salutary discipline, it entirely loses at last the ability to dwell upon the subjects of its thoughts, and to examine them. And when this power is once lost, there is little ground to expect any solid attainments.

§ 157. Alleged inability to command the attention.

We are aware that those who, in accordance with these directions, are required to make a close and thorough examination of subjects, will sometimes complain that they find a great obstacle in their inability to fix their attention. They are not wanting in ability to comprehend, but find it difficult to retain the mind in one position so long as to enable them to connect together all the parts of a subject, and duly estimate their various bearings. When this intellectual defect exists, it becomes a new reason for that thorough examination of subjects which has been above recommended. It has probably been caused by a neglect of such strictness of examination, and by a too rapid and careless transition from one subject to another.

It will be recollected, that Attention, considered as a result in distinction from the Power of attention, expresses the state of the mind when it is steadily directed for some time, whether longer or shorter, to some object of sense or intellect, exclusive of other objects. All other objects are shut out; and, when this exclusion of everything else continues for some time, the attention is said to be intense.—Now it is well known that such an exclusive direction of the mind, or rather of the perceptive part of the mind, cannot exist for any long period without being accompanied with a feeling of desire or of duty. In the greatest intellectual exertions, not the mere powers of judging, of abstracting, and of reasoning are concerned; there will also be a greater or less movement of the feelings. And it will be found that no feeling so surely lays the foundation in cases of attention for that volitional action which gives a definite direction and pertinacity to the perceptions, as a love of the truth.

Mr. Locke thought that the person who should discover a remedy for wandering thoughts would do great service to the studious and contemplative part of mankind. We know of no other effective remedy than the one just mentioned, A LOVE OF THE TRUTH, a desire to know the nature and relations of things merely for the sake of knowledge. It is true that a conviction of duty will do much; ambition and interest may possibly do more; but when the mind is led to deep investigations by these views merely, without finding something beautiful and attractive in the aspect of knowledge itself, it is likely to prove a tiresome process.

There is a glory in the Truth, which it never imparts to another. Christ says of himself, that "he came into the world to bear witness to the truth." A desire to know the truth in morals, in religion, in science, in the arts, in government, and in all the various kinds and methods of thought and inquiry, furnishes the key to much that is great and ennobling in the history of the race. When the inspiration which lays the foundations of activity comes from God, it is always in this direction. It was the inspiration found in a love of the truth, far more than any aspirations and hopes of a personal nature, which gave strength and perseverance to Christopher Columbus in his multiplied disappointments and trials. It was such a desire as this, a desire to know the hidden forces and their applications which the God of nature had beneficently treasured up in the works of nature, that inspired and developed the mechanical genius of Fulton, and sustained him in his long and weary labours.

"I saw D'Alembert," says a recent writer, "congratulate a young man very coldly who brought him a solution of a problem. The young man said, 'I have done this in order to have a seat in the Academy.' 'Sir,' answered D'Alembert, 'with such dispositions you never will earn one. Science must be loved for its own sake, and not for the advantage to be derived. No other principle will enable a man to make progress in the sciences!'"*

CHAPTER XVI.

DREAMING AND SOMNAMBULISM.

§ 158. Definition of dreams and the prevalence of them.

Among numerous other subjects in mental philosophy which claim their share of attention, that of Dreaming is entitled to its place; nor can we be certain that any other will be found more appropriate to it than the present, especially when we consider how closely it is connected in all its forms with our sensations and conceptions. And what are Dreams? It

* Memoirs of Montlosier, vol. i., p. 59, as quoted in Mackintosh's Ethical Philosophy, sect. vii.

approaches perhaps sufficiently near to a correct general description to say, that they are our mental states and operations while we are asleep. But the particular views which are to be taken in the examination of this subject will not fail to throw light on this general statement.

The mental states and exercises which go under this name have ever excited much interest. It is undoubtedly one reason of the attention which the subject of our dreams have ever elicited among all classes of people, that they are so prevalent; it being very difficult, if not impossible, to find a person who has not had more or less of this experience. Mr. Locke, however, tells us of an individual who never dreamed till the twenty-sixth year of his age, when he happened to have a fever, and then dreamed for the first time. Plutarch also mentions one Cleon, a friend of his, who lived to an advanced age, and yet had never dreamed once in his life, and remarks that he had heard the same thing reported of Thrasymedes.

Undoubtedly these persons dreamed very seldom, as we find that some dream much more than others; but it is possible that they may have dreamed at some time and entirely forgotten it. So that it cannot with certainty be inferred, from such instances as these, that there are any who are entirely exempt from dreaming.

§ 159. Connexion of dreams with our waking thoughts.

In giving an explanation of dreams, our attention is first arrested by the circumstance that they have an intimate relationship with our waking thoughts. The great body of our waking experiences appear in the form of trains of associations; and these trains of associated ideas, in greater or less continuity, and with greater or less variation, continue when we are asleep. —Condorcet (a name famous in the history of France) told some one, that, while he was engaged in abstruse and profound calculations, he was frequently obliged to leave them in an unfinished state, in order to retire to rest; and that the remaining steps and the conclusion of his calculations have more than once presented themselves in his dreams.—Franklin also has made the remark, that the bearings and results of political events, which had caused him much trouble while awake, were not unfrequently unfolded to him in dreaming.—Mr. Coleridge says, that, as he was once reading in the Pilgrimage of Purchas an account of the palace and garden of the Khan Kubla, he fell into a sleep, and in that situation composed an entire poem of not less than two hundred lines, some of which he afterward committed to writing. The poem is entitled Kubla Khan, and begins as follows:

"In Xanadu did Kubla Khan
A stately pleasure-dome decree;
Where Alph, the sacred river, ran
Through caverns measureless to man
Down to a sunless sea."

It is evident, from such statements as these, which are confirmed by the experience of almost every person, that our dreams are fashioned from the materials of the thoughts and feelings which we have while awake; in other words, they will, in a great degree, be merely the repetition of our customary and prevailing associations. So well understood is this, that President Edwards, who was no less distinguished as a mental philosopher than as a theologian, thought it a good practice to take particular notice of his dreams, in order to ascertain from them what his predominant inclinations were.

§ 160. Dreams are often caused by our sensations.

But while we are to look for the materials of our dreams in thoughts which had previously existed, we further find that they are not beyond the influence of those slight bodily sensations, of which we are susceptible even in hours of sleep. These sensations, slight as they are, are the means of introducing one set of associations rather than another.—Dugald Stewart relates an incident which may be considered an evidence of this, that a person with whom he was acquainted had occasion, in consequence of an indisposition, to apply a bottle of hot water to his feet when he went to bed; and the consequence was, that he dreamed he was making a journey to the top of Mount Ætna, and that he found the heat of the ground almost insupportable. There was once a gentleman in the English army who was so susceptible of audible impressions while he was asleep, that his companions could make him dream of what they pleased. Once, in particular, they made him go through the whole process of a duel, from the preliminary arrangements to the firing of the pistol, which they put into his hand for that purpose, and which, when it exploded, waked him.

A cause of dreams closely allied to the above is the variety of sensations which we experience from the stomach, viscera, &c.—Persons, for instance, who have been for a long time deprived of food, or have received it only in small quantities, hardly enough to preserve life, will be likely to have dreams in some way or other directly relating to their condition. Baron Trenck relates, that, being almost dead with hunger when confined in his dungeon, his dreams every night presented to him the well-filled and luxurious tables of Berlin, from which, as they were presented before him, he imagined he was about to relieve his hunger. "The night had far advanced," says Irving, speaking of the voyage of Mendez to Hispaniola, "but those whose turn it was to take repose were unable to sleep from the intensity of their thirst; or, if they slept, it was to be tantalized with dreams of cool fountains and running brooks."

The state of health also has considerable influence, not only in producing dreams, but in giving them a particular character. The remark has been made by medical men, that acute diseases, particularly fevers, are often preceded and indicated by disagreeable and oppressive dreams.

§ 161. Explanation of the incoherency of dreams. (1st cause.)

There is frequently much of wildness, inconsistency, and contradiction in our dreams. The mind passes very rapidly from one object to another; strange and singular incidents occur. If our dreams be truly the repetition of our waking thoughts, it may well be inquired, How this wildness and inconsistency happen?

The explanation of this peculiarity resolves itself into two parts.—The FIRST ground or cause of it is, that our dreams are not subjected, like our waking thoughts, to the control and regulation of surrounding objects. While we are awake, our trains of thought are kept uniform and coherent by the influence of such objects, which continually remind us of our situation, character, and duties; and which keep in check any tendency to revery. But in sleep the senses are closed; the soul is accordingly, in a great measure, excluded from the material world, and is thus deprived of the salutary regulating influence from that source.

§ 162. Second cause of the incoherency of dreams.

In the second place, when we are asleep, our associated trains of thought are no longer under the control of the WILL. We do not mean to say that the operations of the will are suspended at such times, and that volitions have no existence. On the contrary, there is sufficient evidence of the continuance of these mental acts, in some degree at least, since volitions must have made a part of the original trains of thought, which are repeated in dreaming; and, furthermore, we are often as conscious of exercising or putting forth volitions when dreaming as of any other mental acts, for instance, imagining, remembering, assenting, or reasoning. When we dream that we are attacked by an enemy sword in hand, but happen, as we suppose in our dreaming experiences, to be furnished in self-defence with an instrument of the same kind, we dream that we *will* to exert it for our own safety and against our antagonist; and we as truly, in this case, put forth the mental exercise which we term *volition*, as in any other we exercise remembrance, or imagine, or reason in our sleep.

Admitting, however, that the will continues to act in sleep, it is quite evident that the volitions which are put forth by it have ceased to exercise their customary influence in respect to our mental operations. Ordinarily we are able, by means of an act of the will, to fix our attention upon some particular part of any general subject which has been suggested, or to transfer it to some other part of such subject, and thus to direct and to regulate the whole train of mental action. But, the moment we are soundly asleep, this influence ceases, and hence, in connexion with the other cause already mentioned, arise the wildness, incoherency, and contradictions which exist.

A person, while he is awake, has his thoughts under such government, and is able, by the direct and indirect influence of volitions, so to regulate them, as generally to bring them, in the end, to some conclusion which he foresees and wishes to arrive at. But in dreaming, as all directing and governing influence, both internal and external, is at an end, our thoughts and feelings seem to be driven forward, much like a ship at sea without a rudder, wherever it may happen.

§ 163. Apparent reality of dreams. (1st cause.)

When objects are presented to us in dreams, we look upon them as real; and events, and combinations and series of events, appear the same. We feel the same interest and resort to the same expedients as in the perplexities and enjoyments of real life. When persons are introduced as forming a part in the transactions of our dreams, we see them clearly in their living attitudes and stature; we converse with them, and hear them speak, and behold them move, as if actually present.

One reason of this greater vividness of our dreaming conceptions and of our firm belief in their reality seems to be this. The subjects upon which our thoughts are then employed occupy the mind *exclusively*. We can form a clearer conception of an object with our eyes shut than we can with them open, as any one will be convinced on making the experiment; and the liveliness of the conception will increase in proportion as we can suspend the exercise of the other senses. In sound sleep, not only the sight, but the other senses also, may be said to be closed; and the attention is not continually diverted by the multitude of objects which arrest the hearing and touch when we are awake.—It is, therefore, a most natural supposition, that our conceptions must at such times be extremely vivid and distinct. At § 119 we particularly remarked upon conceptions, or those ideas which we have of absent objects of perception, which possess this vividness of character. And it there appeared that they might be attended with a momentary belief even when we are awake. But, as conceptions exist in the mind when we are asleep in a much higher degree distinct and vivid, what was in the former case a momentary, becomes in the latter a permanent belief. Hence everything has the appearance of reality; and the mere thoughts of the mind are virtually transformed into persons, and varieties of situations, and events, which are regarded by us in precisely the same light as the persons, and situations, and events of our every-day's experience.

§ 164. Apparent reality of dreams. (2d cause.)

A second circumstance which goes to account for the fact that our dreaming conceptions have the appearance of reality is, that they are not susceptible of being controlled, either directly or indirectly, by mere volition.—We are so formed as almost invariably to associate reality with whatever objects of perception continue to produce in us the same effects. A hard or soft body, or any substance of a particular colour, taste, or smell, are always, when presented to our senses, followed by certain states of mind essentially the same; and we yield the most ready and firm belief in the existence of such objects. In a word, we are disposed, from our very constitution, to believe in the existence of objects of perception, the perceptions of which do not depend on the WILL, but which we find to be followed by certain states of the mind, whether we choose it or not.—But it is to be recollected that our dreaming thoughts are mere conceptions; our senses being closed and shut up, and external objects not being presented to them. This is true. But if we conclude in favour of the real existence of objects of perception because they produce in us sensations independently of our volitions, it is but natural to suppose that we shall believe in the reality of our conceptions also, whenever they are in like manner beyond our voluntary control. They are both merely states of the mind; and if belief always attends our perceptions wherever we find them to be independent of our choice, there is no reason why conceptions, which are ideas of absent objects of perception, should not be attended with a like belief under the same circumstances.—And essentially the same circumstances exist in dreaming; that is, a train of conceptions arise in the mind, and we are not conscious at such times of being able to exercise any direction or control whatever over them. They exist, whether we will it or not; and we regard them as real.

§ 165. Of our estimate of time in dreaming.

Our estimate of time in dreaming differs from that when awake. Events which would take whole days or a longer time in the performance, are dreamed in a few moments. So wonderful is this compression of a multitude of transactions into the very shortest period, that when we are accidentally awakened by the jarring of a door which is opened in the room where we are sleeping, we sometimes dream of depredations by thieves or destruction by fire in the very instant of our awaking.—"A friend of mine," says

Dr. Abercrombie, "dreamed that he crossed the Atlantic, and spent a fortnight in America. In embarking on his return he fell into the sea, and, having awoke with the fright, discovered that he had not been asleep above ten minutes." Count Lavallette, who some years since was condemned to death in France, relates a dream which occurred during his imprisonment as follows: "One night while I was asleep, the clock of the Palais de Justice struck twelve, and awoke me. I heard the gate open to relieve the sentry, but I fell asleep again immediately. In this sleep I dreamed that I was standing in the Rue St. Honoré, at the corner of the Rue de l'Echelle. A melancholy darkness spread around me; all was still; nevertheless, a low and uncertain sound soon arose. All of a sudden I perceived at the bottom of the street, and advancing towards me, a troop of cavalry, the men and horses, however, all flayed. This horrible troop continued passing in a rapid gallop, and casting frightful looks on me. Their march, I thought, continued for five hours, and they were followed by an immense number of artillery-wagons, full of bleeding corpses, whose limbs still quivered; a disgusting smell of blood and bitumen almost choked me. At length the iron gate of the prison, shutting with great force, awoke me again. I made my repeater strike; it was no more than midnight, so that the horrible phantasmagoria had lasted no more than two or three minutes, that is to say, the time necessary for relieving the sentry and shutting the gate. The cold was severe and the watchword short. The next day the turnkey confirmed my calculations."

Our dreams will not unfrequently go through all the particulars of some long journey, or of some military expedition, or of a circumnavigation of the globe, or of other long and perilous undertakings, in a less number of hours than it took weeks, or months, or even years in the actual performance of them. We go from land to land, and from city to city, and into desert places; we experience transitions from joy to sorrow, and from poverty to wealth; we are occupied in the scenes and transactions of many long months; and then our slumbers are scattered, and, behold, they are the doings of a fleeting watch of the night!

This striking circumstance in the history of our dreams is generally explained by supposing that our thoughts, as they successively occupy the mind, are more rapid than while we are awake. But their rapidity is at all times very great; so much so, that in a few moments crowds of ideas pass through the mind which it would take a long time to utter, and a far longer time would it take to perform all the transactions which they concern. This explanation, therefore, is not satisfactory, for our thoughts are oftentimes equally rapid in our waking moments.

The true reason, we apprehend, is to be found in those preceding sections, which took under examination the apparent reality of dreams. Our conceptions in dreaming are considered by us real; every thought is an action; every idea is an event; and successive states of mind are successive actions and successive events. He who in his sleep has the conception of all the particulars of a military expedition to Moscow or of a circumnavigation of the globe, seems to himself to have actually experienced all the various and multiplied fortunes of the one and the other. Hence what appears to be the real time in dreams, but is only the apparent time, will not be that which is sufficient for the mere thought, but that which is necessary for the successive actions.

"Something perfectly analogous to this may be remarked," says Mr. Stewart, "in the perceptions we obtain by the sight of sense.* When I look into a show-box, where the deception is imperfect, I see only a set of paltry daubings of a few inches in diameter; but if the representation be executed with so much skill as to convey to me the idea of a distant prospect, every object before me swells in its dimensions in proportion to the extent of space which I conceive it to

* Stewart's Elements, chapter on Dreaming.

occupy, and what seemed before to be shut within the limits of a small wooden frame, is magnified in my apprehension to an immense landscape of woods, rivers, and mountains."

§ 166. Of the senses sinking to sleep in succession.

It is true, as a general statement, that in sleep the mind ceases to retain its customary power over the muscular movements of the system; and all the senses are at such times locked up, and no longer perform their usual offices. The effect upon the senses is such that it seems to be proper to speak of them as individually going to sleep and awaking from sleep. It remains, therefore, to be observed, that there is considerable reason to suppose that the senses fall asleep in succession.—For a detailed explanation and proof of this singular fact, reference must be had to Cullen, and particularly to Cabanis, a French writer on subjects of this nature, whom we have already had occasion to mention; but the conclusion at which they arrive on this particular point may be here stated.*

The sight, in consequence of the protection of the eyelids, ceases to receive impressions first, while all the other senses preserve their sensibility entire, and may, therefore, be said to be first in falling asleep. The sense of taste, according to the above writers, is the next which loses its susceptibility of impressions, and then the sense of smelling. The hearing is the next in order, and last of all comes the sense of touch. —Furthermore, the senses are thought to sleep with different degrees of profoundness. The senses of taste and smelling awake the last; the sight with more difficulty than the hearing, and the touch the easiest of all. Sometimes a very considerable noise does not awake a person; but if the soles of the feet are tickled in the slightest degree, he starts up immediately.

Similar remarks are made by the writers above referred to on the muscles. Those which move the arms and legs cease to act when sleep is approaching

* Rapports du Physique et du Moral de l'Homme, Mem. x.

sooner than those which sustain the head; and the latter before those which support the back.—And here it is proper to notice an exception to the general statement at the commencement of this section, that the mind, in sleep, ceases to retain its power over the muscles. Some persons can sleep standing, or walking, or riding on horseback; with such we cannot well avoid the supposition, that the voluntary power over the muscles is in some way retained and exercised in sleep.—These statements are particularly important in connexion with the facts of somnambulism; only admit that the susceptibility of the senses and the power of the muscles may remain even in part while we are asleep, and we can account for them. We know that this is not the case in a vast majority of instances; but that it does sometimes happen is a point which seems at last to be sufficiently well established.

§ 167. General remarks on cases of somnambulism.

With the general subject of dreaming, that of Somnambulism is naturally and intimately connected. Somnambulists, as the term itself indicates, are persons who are capable of walking and of other voluntary actions while asleep.—Of such persons many instances are on record; and the facts which they present to our notice are both practically and psychologically matters of considerable interest and importance.

(I.) A number of things may be said in explanation of somnambulism. The somnambulist, in the first place, is in all cases dreaming, and we may suppose, in general, that the dream is one which greatly interests him. After he has awaked, the action he has passed through appears, in his recollection of it, to be merely a dream, and not a reality. "A young nobleman," says Dr. Abercrombie, "living in the citadel of Breslau, was observed by his brother, who occupied the same room, to rise in his sleep, wrap himself in a cloak, and escape by a window to the roof of the building. He there tore in pieces a magpie's nest, wrapped the young birds in his cloak, returned to his apartment, and went to bed. In the morning he mentioned the circumstances as having occurred in a dream, and could not be persuaded that there had been anything more than a dream, till he was shown the magpies in his cloak." And this is noticed to be commonly the fact. What has been done has the appearance of being a dream. And there is no doubt that the mind of the somnambulist is in that particular state which we denominate dreaming.

(II.) In the second place, those volitions which are a part of his dreams retain their power over the muscles, which is not the fact in the sleep and the dreaming of the great body of people.—Consequently, whatever the somnambulist dreams is not only real in the mind, as in the case of all other dreamers, but his ability to exercise his muscles enables him to give it a reality in action. Whether he dream of writing a letter, of visiting a neighbour's house, of cutting and piling wood, of thrashing his grain, or ploughing his field (acts which have at various times been ascribed to the somnambulist), his muscles are faithful to his vivid mental conceptions, which we may suppose in all cases closely connected with his customary labours and experiences, and frequently enable him to complete what he has undertaken, even when his senses are at the same time closed up.

But the inquiry arises here, How it happens, while in most cases both senses and muscles lose their power, in these, on the contrary, the muscles are active while the senses alone are asleep?—In reference to this inquiry, it must be acknowledged that it is involved at present in some uncertainty, although there is much reason to anticipate that it may hereafter receive light from further investigations and knowledge of the nervous system and functions. There is a set of nerves which are understood to be particularly connected with respiration, and which appear to have nothing to do with sensation and with muscular action. There is another set which are known to possess a direct and important connexion with sensation and the muscles. These last are separable into distinct filaments, having separate functions; some being connected with sensation merely, and others with volition and muscular action. In sensation, the impression made by some external body exists at first in the external part of the organ of sense, and is propagated along one class of filaments to the brain. In volition and voluntary muscular movement, the origin of action, as far as the body is concerned, seems to be the reverse, commencing in the brain, and being propagated along other and appropriate nervous filaments to the different parts of the system. Hence it sometimes happens, that, in diseases of the nervous system, the power of sensation is in a great measure lost, while that of motion fully remains; or, on the contrary, the power of motion is lost, while that of sensation remains. These views help to throw light on the subject of somnambulism. Causes at present unknown to us may operate, through their appropriate nervous filaments, to keep the muscles awake, without disturbing the repose and inactivity of the senses. A man may be asleep as to all the powers of external perception, and yet be awake in respect to the capabilities of muscular motion. And, aided by the trains of association which make a part of his dreams, may be able to walk about and to do many things without the aid of the sight and hearing.

§ 168. Further illustrations of somnambulism.

(III.) Further, we are not to forget here a remark on the sleep of the senses, a subject already briefly alluded to, and which is an exception to the general statement then made in regard to them. Both in somnambulism and in ordinary cases of dreaming the senses are not always entirely locked up; many observations clearly show that it is possible for the mind to be accessible through them, and that a new direction may be given in this way to a person's dreams without awaking him. Hence somnambulists may sometimes have very slight visual perceptions; they may in some slight measure be guided by sensations of touch; all the senses may be affected in a small degree by their appropriate objects, or this may be the case with some and not with others, without effectually disturbing their sleep.—These facts will be found to help in explaining any peculiar circumstances which may be thought not to come within the reach of the general explanation which has been given.

(IV.) But this is not all. There are some cases, which are not reached by the statements hitherto made. There are not only slight exceptions to the general fact, that somnambulists, like persons in ordinary sleep, are insensible to external impressions, but occasionally some of a marked and extraordinary character. There are a few cases (the recent instance of Jane Rider in this country is one) where persons in the condition of somnambulism have not only possessed slight visual power, but perceptions of sight increased much above the common degree. In the extraordinary narrative of Jane Rider, the author informs us that he took two large wads of cotton and placed them directly on the closed eyelids, and then bound them on with a black silk handkerchief. The cotton filled the cavity under the eyebrows, and reached down to the middle of the cheek, and various experiments were tried to ascertain whether she could see. In one of them a watch enclosed in a case was handed to her, and she was requested to tell what o'clock it was by it; upon which, after examining both sides of the watch, she opened the case, and then answered the question. She also read, without hesitation, the name of a gentleman, written in characters so fine that no one else could distinguish it at the usual distance from the eye. In another paroxysm, the lights were removed from her room, and the windows so secured that no object was discernible, and two books were presented to her, when she immediately told the titles of both, though one of them was a book which she had never before seen. In other experiments, while the room was so darkened that it was impossible, with the ordinary powers of vision, to distinguish the colours of the carpet, and her eyes were also bandaged, she pointed out the different colours in the hearth rug, took up and read several cards lying on the table, threaded a needle, and performed several other things, which could not have been done without the aid of vision.*—Of extraordinary cases of this kind, it would seem that no satisfactory explanation (at least no explanation which is unattended with difficulties) has as yet been given.

* As quoted in Dr. Oliver's Physiology, chap. 30.

DIVISION FIRST.

THE INTELLECT OR UNDERSTANDING.

INTELLECTIVE OR INTELLECTUAL STATES OF THE MIND.

PART SECOND.

THE INTERNAL OR SUPER-SENSUOUS INTELLECT.

INTELLECTUAL STATES OF INTERNAL ORIGIN.

CHAPTER I.

INTERNAL ORIGIN OF KNOWLEDGE.

§ 169. The soul has fountains of knowledge within.

IN tracing the history of the mind thus far, we have seen the beginnings of knowledge, and that the material world around us is the providentially appointed handmaid and nurse of the soul in the days of its infancy, and for that purpose is endued with form, fragrance, and colour. Material eyes were given to the soul (not made a part of its nature, but assigned to it as an instrumental and auxiliary agent), that it might see; and material hands, that it might handle; and hearing, that it might hear. By means of these and other senses we become acquainted with whatever is visible and tangible, and has outline and form. But there is not only a sensuous, but a super-sensuous experience; not only an EXTERNAL or SENSATIONAL intellect, but an INTERNAL or SUPER-SENSATIONAL intellect. And hence it happens, that the term Intellectualism, in distinction from Sensationalism, is often used as the name of a doctrine and method of philosophic inquiry which goes outside of and beyond the senses. The intellectualist accepts sensationalism as far as it goes, but he affirms that there is something beyond it. In other words, there are inward powers of perception, hidden fountains of knowledge, which open themselves and flow up in the interior and secret places of the soul. The soul finds knowledge in itself, which neither sight, nor touch, nor hearing, nor any other sense, nor any outward forms of matter could give.

"The natural progress of all true learning," says the author of Hermes, "is from sense to intellect." Having begun with the senses, and first considered the sensations and perceptions which we there receive, and other forms of knowledge, such as the conceptions, which are based immediately upon them, we are next to enter more exclusively into the mind itself, and to explore the fruitful sources of knowledge which are internal. And, in thus doing, it is a satisfaction to know that we are treading essentially in the steps of many distinguished writers, who maintain that a part of our knowledge only can be traced to the senses, and that the origin of other portions is to be sought wholly in the intellect itself.

§ 170. Declaration of Locke, that the soul has knowledge in itself.

After alluding to the senses as one great source of knowledge, "the other fountain," says Locke, "from which experience furnisheth the understanding with ideas, is the perception of the operations of our own minds within us, as it is employed about the ideas it has got; which operations, when the soul comes to reflect on and consider, do furnish the understanding with another set of ideas, which could not be had from things without, and such are perception, thinking, doubting, believing, reasoning, knowing, willing, and all the different actings of our own minds, which we, being conscious of, and observing in ourselves, do from these receive into our understandings ideas as distinct as we do from bodies affecting our senses. This source of ideas every man has wholly within himself. And though it be not sense, as having nothing to do with EXTERNAL objects, yet it is very like it, and might properly enough be called INTERNAL SENSE. But, as I call the other Sensation, so I call this Reflection; the ideas it affords being such only as the mind gets by reflecting on its own operations within itself."

It is, perhaps, necessary to remark here, that we introduce this passage from Mr. Locke merely in support of the general doctrine, without wishing to intimate a full approbation of the manner in which he has applied it in its details. It is probably true, that Mr. Locke, although he started upon a right track, failed very much in his attempts to carry out his own plan. But what we say now concerns the general question; and, in reference to that question, the passage just referred to is undoubtedly weighty in itself, as well as in consequence of the great reputation and acknowledged discernment of its author. It is undoubtedly the doctrine of Mr. Locke, that our knowledge begins with Sensation; in other words, that impressions made on the bodily system are the first occasions, so far as we are able to judge, of bringing the mind into action. But it does not follow from this (and the passage just quoted shows that Mr. Locke did not suppose it thus to follow), that sensation is the only source of knowledge. There is undeniably something distinct from sensation; thoughts, which have an interior origin, and cannot be accounted for by external objects alone; ideas, which are based upon the succession, relation, and infinite of things, and not upon what is fixed, tangible, and measurable; or which are the representatives and exponents of what is mental rather than of what is material.

§ 171. Opinions of Cudworth on the subject of internal knowledge.

We may properly introduce here a quotation or two from another great authority, nearly contemporaneous with Mr. Locke, that of Dr. Cudworth, a name which is acknowledged to rank deservedly high among those that are most closely associated with exalted wisdom and virtue. Let us, however, be again reminded, that our whole object here is to establish the general position, that there is knowledge of a purely internal, or, if the expression be preferred, of a super-sensuous origin, as well as of an external origin; and that, therefore, a reference to writers for that purpose does not necessarily involve an approbation of, or a responsibility for, their opinions any further than they relate to the particular object in view.—The posthumous work from which these extracts are made, is understood to have been written in reply to Mr. Hobbes, who held the opinion that all our thoughts, of whatever kind, are only either direct, or transformed and modified sensations. And, therefore, the statements made in it, being called forth under such circumstances, must be supposed to have been carefully meditated, and on that ground, among others, are entitled to much weight.

"That oftentimes," says Cudworth,* "there is more taken notice of and perceived by the mind, both in the sensible objects themselves and by occasion of them, than was impressed from them, or passively received by sense; which, therefore, must needs proceed from some inward active principle in that which perceives, I shall make it further appear by some other instances.

"For, first, let a brute and a man at the same time be made spectators of one and the same artificial statue, picture, or landscape; here the brute will passively receive all that is impressed from the outward object upon sense by local motion, as well as the man, all the several colours and figures of it; and yet the man will presently perceive something in this statue or picture which the brute takes no notice of at all, viz., beauty, and pulchritude, and symmetry, besides the liveliness of the effigies and portraiture. The eye of the brute being every jot as good a glass or mirror, and perhaps endued with a more perspicacious sense or power of passive perception than that of a man.

"Or, again, let both a man and a brute at the same time hear the same musical airs; the brute will only be sensible of noise and sounds, but the man will also perceive harmony in them, and be very much delighted with it, nay, even enthusiastically transported by it. Wherefore the brute perceiving all the sounds as well as the man, but nothing of the harmony, the difference must needs arise from some inward active principle or anticipation in the man, which the brute hath not."

§ 172. Further remarks of the same writer on this subject.

"But I shall yet further illustrate this business," says this learned writer near the conclusion of the same chapter, "that the mind may actively compre-

* Immutable Morality, book iv., chap. ii., § 14.

hend more in the outward objects of sense, and by occasion of them, than is passively received and impressed from them, by another instance. Suppose a learned written or printed volume held before the eye of a brute-creature or illiterate person; either of them will passively receive all that is impressed upon sense from those delineations, to whom there will be nothing but several scrawls of ink drawn upon white paper. But if a man that hath inward anticipations of learning in him look upon them, he will immediately have another comprehension of them than that of sense, and a strange scene of thoughts presently represented to his mind from them; he will see heaven, earth, sun, moon, and stars, comets, meteors, elements, in those inky delineations; he will read profound theorems of philosophy, geometry, astronomy in them, learn a great deal of new knowledge from them that he never understood before, and thereby justly admire the wisdom of the composer of them. Not that all this was passively stamped upon his soul by sense from those characters (for sense, as I said before, can perceive nothing here but inky scrawls, and the intelligent reader will many times correct his copy, finding *erratas* in it), but because his mind was before furnished with certain inward anticipations, that such characters signify the elements of certain sounds; those sounds, certain notions or cogitations of the mind; and because he hath an active power of exciting any such cogitations within himself, he reads in those sensible delineations the passive stamps or prints of another man's wisdom or knowledge upon them, and also learns knowledge and instruction from them, not as infused into his mind from those sensible characters, but, by reason of those hints and significations thereby proposed to it, accidentally kindled, awakened, and excited in it; for all but the phantasms of black, inky strokes and figures arises from the inward activity of his own mind. Wherefore this instance in itself shows how the activity of the mind may comprehend more in and from sensible objects than is passively imprinted by them upon sense."

There are other illustrations in this valuable writer. One is to this effect. We cast our eyes upon what he calls the book of nature, the sky, the earth, and the waters, with the multiplied forms which inhabit them. We see there many things addressed to the "outward mind," as he terms it (that is to say, the mind, or rather the intellective part of it, so far as it is connected with the external world and the senses), such as extension, and colour, and form, and whatever else is especially connected with the senses. The outward mind, operating, so to speak, through the outward eye of the mind, beholds whatever is in this way presented to it, and stops there. But to the inward mind, which has an inward vision, there is something more. To the inward or super-sensuous mind, availing itself of its intuitional suggestions, there are revelations, which in some respects are far more important, of causation and power, of space and time, of intelligence, design, and order, of unity and diversity, of goodness and wisdom.*

§ 173. Writers who have objected to the doctrine of an internal source of knowledge.

But it ought not to pass unnoticed, that there have been writers who have objected to the doctrine of an internal source of knowledge in distinction from that knowledge which is outward, and is dependent, not only for its occasion, but for its very nature, on the

* Many other writers, as Stewart, Degerando, Brown, Coleridge, Price, Jouffroy, and Cousin, advocate this general doctrine. Many German writers, with Leibnitz at their head, take the same view. Kant, in his Criticism of the Pure Reason, expresses himself thus: "Der Zeit nach geht also keine Erkenntniss in uns vor der Erfahrung vorher, und mit dieser fangt alle an. Wenn aber gleich alle unsere Erkenntniss mit der Erfahrung anhebt, so entspringt sie darum doch nicht eben alle aus der Erfahrung. Denn es könne wohl seyn, dass selbst unsere Erfahrungserkenntniss ein Zusammengesetztes aus dem sey, was wir durch Eindrücke empfangen, und dem, was unser eigenes Erkenntnissvermögen (durch sinnliche Eindrücke bloss veranlasst), aus sich selbst hergiebt, welchen Zusatz wir von jenem Grundstoffe nicht eher unterscheiden, als bis lange Uebung uns darauf aufmerksam, und zur Absonderung desselben geschikt gemacht hat."—*Kant's Critik der reinen Vernunft, Einleitung, I.*

senses. It was the opinion, among others, of Mr. Hobbes, who preceded Locke, and was not without merit as a metaphysician, that all our knowledge might be traced to the senses, and that, of course, no other origin of it need be sought. "The original of all thoughts," says that writer, Leviathan, ch. i., "is that which we call SENSE. There is no conception in a man's mind which hath not at first, totally or by parts, been begotten upon the organs of sense." This was the opinion also of his contemporary, Gassendi, who was his particular friend and correspondent, and, at a still later period, of Condillac. The latter supported his views at length and with much ingenuity, particularly in his Treatise on Sensations.

These writers appear to have maintained, as a general statement, that we have no simple ideas but such as exist in the mind directly by means of the senses. As they further maintained that those of a complex nature are composed, not merely virtually, but literally, of such as are simple, they consequently considered them in the light of combined and transformed sensations. Such appears to be the general outline of their doctrine, although it has its obscurities and perplexities, as might be expected, in consequence of being essentially ill-founded.—"If we consider," says Condillac, "that to remember, to compare, to judge, to distinguish, to imagine, to be astonished, to have abstract ideas, to have ideas of number and duration, to know truths, whether general or particular, are but so many modes of being attentive; that to have passions, to love, to hate, to hope, to fear, to will, are but so many different modes of desire; and that *attention* in the one case, and *desire* in the other case, of which all these feelings are modes, are themselves, in their origin, nothing more than modes of sensation, we cannot but conclude that SENSATION involves in itself all the faculties of the soul."*

This sentence, in its evident meaning, and as it is understood both by its author and his commentators,

* Traité des Sensations, pt. i., ch. 7, § 2.

is clearly at variance with the doctrine of Cudworth and of other advocates of the "super-sensuous" or transcendental philosophy, and entirely cuts off what has been variously termed the internal, reflex, or subjective source of our knowledge. According to the doctrine of Hobbes, Condillac, Helvetius, and other writers of the sensuous or material school, everything may be traced back to the senses, not merely as its occasion, but as its direct, or, at least, its essential cause; everything becomes tangible and material; we are utterly unable to form a conception even of the invisible and glorious Deity, except under such an appearance as the imagination, dealing with sensible images alone, can picture forth from the gross and limited materials of the earth. And in the same way, every other idea, however spiritual and whatever it may relate to, must be capable of being followed back to some archetype in outward material existences. The mind may separate, and modify, and combine sensible ideas or images, but can never get above them; there is a portion of earthliness in every possible thought.—It must, therefore, be obvious, that the tendency of this system is to lower the mind's position; not only to limit the range, but to depress the character of its powers, especially when we consider, that, as one of its legitimate results, it rejects the doctrine of a Moral Sense and of the Immutability of Moral Distinctions. It may be said, however, and perhaps with some degree of plausibility, that the propriety of receiving it does not depend so much upon its tendency, as upon the direct evidence which may be brought in its support, in which, nevertheless, it is found to be greatly deficient.

§ 174. **Knowledge begins in the senses, but has internal accessions.**

In order to have a clear understanding of the particular topic before us, let us briefly advert to certain general views, already more or less attended to, having a connexion with it. In making the human soul a subject of inquiry, it is an obvious consideration that a distinction may be drawn between the soul, contemplated in itself, and its acts, or states, or the knowledge which it possesses. The inquiry, therefore, naturally arises, Under what circumstances the acquisition of knowledge begins?

Now this is the very question which has already been considered; nor can it be deemed necessary to repeat here the considerations which have been brought up in reference to it. It is enough to express our continued reliance on the general experience and testimony of mankind, so far as it is possible to ascertain them on a subject of so much difficulty, that the beginnings of thought and knowledge are immediately subsequent to certain affections of those bodily organs which we call the SENSES. In other words, were it not for impressions on the senses, which may be traced to objects external to them, our mental capabilities, whatever they may be, would in all probability have remained folded up, and have never been redeemed from a state of fruitless inaction.

Hence the process, which is implied in the perception of external things, or what is commonly termed by Mr. Locke *sensation*, may justly be considered the OCCASION of the introductory step to all our knowledge. But it does not follow from this, nor is it by any means true, that the whole amount of it, in its ultimate progress, is to be ascribed directly to the same source. All that can be said with truth is, that the mind receives the earliest part of its ideas by means of the senses, and that, in consequence of having received these elementary cognitions, all its pow- become rapidly and fully operative.

And here we come to the SECOND great source of knowledge. The powers of the mind being thus fairly brought into exercise, its various operations then furnish us with another set of notions, which, by way of distinguishing them from those received through the direct mediation of the senses, may be called, in the language of Mr. Locke, ideas of reflection, or, to use a phraseology embracing all possible cases, ideas or knowledges of INTERNAL ORIGIN.

These two sources of human thought and knowledge, the Internal and External, however they may have been confounded by some writers, are easily distinguished from each other. The ideas which arise in the mind solely from the fact of the previous existence of certain mental operations, could not have been suggested by anything which takes place in the external world independently of those operations. Of this last class, some instances, with illustrations of the same, may properly be mentioned here.

§ 175. **Instances of notions which have an internal origin.**

Among other things which do not come within the limits of sensuous knowledge, but are to be ascribed to the second great source, are those mental experiences expressed by the terms THINKING, DOUBTING, BELIEVING, and CERTAINTY.—It is a matter of internal observation (that is, of consciousness or of inward reflection, which are synonymous with internal observation), that the mind does not, and cannot, for any length of time, remain inactive. Hence there is occasion for that specific experience which we denominate THINKING. There is both the process of thinking, which we express by the word thinking; and the additional idea founded upon that process, which we express by the word thought. But obviously the knowledge which we thus have, whether expressed by the word THINKING or the word THOUGHT, is of internal origin; it is not an object of touch, or taste, or sight; it is to be ascribed to the mind itself alone, and to its inherent activity, unaided by any immediate and direct action of the senses.

Again, in the examination of some topic which is proposed for discussion, a proposition is stated with little or no evidence attending it, and the mind, in reference to that proposition, is brought into a position to which we give the name of *doubting*. We have both the process of doubting, and the abstract idea founded upon it which we express by the word doubt. And here again, all we can say of this new form of experience is, that it has its origin within, and necessarily exists immediately subsequent, not to mere outward impressions, but to certain other mental states, of which we are conscious.

But then, in this very instance, if the evidence be considerably increased, the mental estimation which we form is altered in regard to it, and to this new state of the mind we give the name of *belief* or *believing*. And, in case the evidence of the proposition is of a higher and more decided character, then there arises another state of the mind, which we denominate *certainty*.

The ideas of right and wrong, of unity and number, of time and space, order, proportion, similitude, truth, wisdom, power, obligation, succession, cause, effect, and many others, have a like origin; at least there are none of them to be ascribed directly and exclusively to the senses.—It is cheerfully granted, that, in determining this point, it is proper to refer to the common experience of mankind, and to rely upon it. But it is believed in all these instances (certainly in the most of them), that such a reference will be amply decisive.

Let it, then, be left to the candid internal examination of each individual to determine, Whether a distinction be not rightly drawn between the origin of these ideas, and that of those forms of knowledge which we attribute to the senses, and which take their place as a part of our cognitions under the names of red, blue, sweet, fragrant, bitter, hard, smooth, loud, soft, &c.? On this question it is thought that, in general, there can be but one answer, although some writers, through the love of excessive simplification, have been betrayed into error in regard to it.

Hence it is distinctly to be kept in mind, that there are two sources of thought and knowledge. An affection of the senses by means of external objects is the immediate occasion of one portion; the constitution of the mind and its operations are the occasions or source of the other. Those notions which can be ascribed directly to any one of the senses as their specific source, and not merely as an indirect and general occasion of their origin, are External, while all others seem to be entitled to be called Internal. And yet it will be recollected that we have found it necessary to treat of some notions under the general head of External Knowledge, not precisely corresponding to the view now given. The mental states which we now have reference to, were found, however, to be so closely connected in their origin with the exercise of the senses, or with some other affection of the bodily system (such as the idea of externality, the uneasy feeling of hunger, thirst, &c.), as to come under consideration, in part or in whole, somewhat more naturally there than in any subsequent part of our inquiries.

§ 176. Imperfections attendant on classifications in mental philosophy.

The remarks just made naturally lead us to embrace this opportunity to suggest a caution applicable to the subject of Classification in mental philosophy in general. It will be recollected, that the first general arrangement of the states of the mind was into the great Divisions of Intellectual, Sentient or Sentimentive, and Volitional. Beginning with the INTELLECTUAL part of our nature, we found our intellections susceptible of being divided into those of an External and those of an Internal origin; and have hitherto directed our inquiries with a reference to this division. Now the remark we would make is, that the classifications just referred to, and all other general classifications in mental philosophy, although they may be theoretically and philosophically true, are nevertheless not always easy and satisfactory in their application. As the mind begins to operate in all its parts and in all its relations nearly simultaneously (and certainly at a very early period of life), the history of its multiplied acts and feelings becomes very much interwoven and perplexed. In the matter of Classification, therefore, nothing more is to be expected than a general outline, approximating as nearly as possible to an expression of what is conceived to be the truth; our inquiries are to be directed by such general outline so far as can be done consistently with the often involved and complicated nature of the mental operations; but, after all, the value of our investigations will depend essentially and chiefly on the accuracy of the details.

We make these remarks here, because some who assent to the general arrangement may perhaps imagine that they see reason for an alteration in the disposition of the subordinate parts. And we readily admit that cases are to be found where it is somewhat difficult to determine under what general head particular thoughts are to be placed, and particular mental exercises and associations are to be arranged. But if, as before intimated, the outlines of the system be generally correct or nearly so, and the details, although they may sometimes be wrongly placed relatively to such outlines, be given with accuracy, not much will be found which there will be occasion to object to.

CHAPTER II.

THE INTUITIONAL OR SUGGESTIONAL POWER.

§ 177. Place, general objects, and names of this power.

UNDER the head of the Internal or Super-sensuous intellect, there are four leading Cognitive principles, which are easily discriminated from all others, and are worthy of special notice: Intuition, Consciousness, Judgment, and Reasoning. The Intuitional or Suggestional power, which gives us a knowledge of things in the absolute; Consciousness, which gives us a knowledge of mental states and operations; Relative Suggestion or Judgment, by means of which we become acquainted with the immediate relations of objects; and Reasoning, which gives us a knowledge of relations that are more remote. The first of these which claims attention, and which seems to be first in the order of nature, inasmuch as it deals with those elementary truths which are fundamental to all others, is the Intuitional or Suggestional power. As discriminative and descriptive of this susceptibility, though imperfectly so, it may be enough to say now, that it is a power, which gives rise to knowledge, not secondarily by means of acts of comparison and deduction, but by means of its own original activity and vigor. Its appropriate objects must of course exist; and this important faculty, without asking aid of the senses on the one hand or of reasoning on the other, at once reveals them.

It is proper to say here, in justification in part of the arrangement of the mental powers which we have thought it necessary to make, that the powers of the mind are known and identified as such, not merely by the characteristics which discriminate the forms of their respective activities, but also in part by the objects with which they deal, and the ends or uses which they are intended to secure. The objects with which the Intuitional power deals are not merely mental, or those which transcend the function of the senses, but they are things in the absolute; and which, existing in the impersonalities of truth, are subjects of cognition, without being subjects of analysis. I think there are three marks or characteristics of them, although the marks are not laid down as exhaustive, but are meant rather as hints and helps than as exclusive and final affirmations. FIRST, they are necessary in their origin. Whatever and wherever they may be, they may be said to exist in the nature of things. The fact of their existence affirms itself, because the opposite of their existence is not a conceivable possibility. SECOND, they are essential and immutable. Space and duration, for instance, which are revealed to us by means of this power, are not only necessities in their origin, but they are necessities to every thing else; and they are immutable, because, as no reason can be given for their beginning, so none can be given for their termination. THIRD, as they are objects which are common to all, so, by means of the Intuitional or Suggestional power, they come within the knowledge of all.

The use of the term Suggestion, as applicable to the power under consideration, is proposed by Dr. Reid in his Inquiry into the Human Mind, chap. ii., § 7. He there speaks of certain notions or ideas, such as our ideas of existence, mind, and personality, as not gotten by comparing ideas and perceiving agreements and disagreements, but as the gifts of nature, and as immediately inspired by our mental constitution. And in a few paragraphs after, not knowing, as he says, any word more proper, he asks leave to make use of the term Suggestion as the name expressive of the faculty, to which we are indebted for notions of this kind. Mr. Stewart also, in his Philosophical Essays, speaks of certain mental phenomena, instancing among them our ideas of time and number, of existence, identity, and motion, as attendant upon the objects of our consciousness, and as SUGGESTED by them. The use of the term, in its philosophical application, is recognised also, among others who might be mentioned, by Dr. Thomas Brown and Sir William Hamilton. The term Intuition is frequently employed for the same purpose by other philosophical writers. And as there is sometimes an advantage in having more than one form of expression, we feel at liberty to accept both, and to use them as convertible.

§ 178. Ideas of existence, mind, self-existence, and personal identity.

It is a part of our plan, as we advance from one portion of the mind to another, not only to lay down its general divisions, and to indicate successively in their true place the powers or faculties coming under them, but also to mention specifically, so far as may be necessary for an illustration of the subject, some of the results of the exercise of those powers. Accordingly, we shall now proceed to give an account of some ideas which have an intuitional origin, without undertaking to give a complete enumeration of them. (I.) Of the idea of Existence. Among the various notions, the origin of which naturally requires to be considered under the head of Suggestion or Intuition, is that of Existence. What existence is in itself (that is to say, independently of any existent being), it would be useless to inquire. Using the phrase idea of existence as expressive of a mental state, by means of which that which we call existence is made known to us, it is the name of a purely simple idea, and cannot be defined. The history of its rise is briefly this: Such is our nature that we cannot exist without having the notion of existence. So that the origin of the idea of existence is inseparable from the mere fact that we have a percipient and sentient nature. An insentient being, if such a supposition be possible, may exist without having any such idea. But man, being constituted with powers of perception and feeling, cannot help perceiving that he is what he is. If we think, then there is something which has this capability of thought; if we feel, then there is not only the mere act of feeling, but something also which puts forth the act.

(II.) The idea of MIND. The origin of the notion of Mind is similar to that of existence. Neither of them can be strictly and properly referred to the senses. We do not see the mind, nor is it an object of touch, or of taste, or of any other sense. Nor, on the other hand, is the notion of mind a direct object of the memory, or of reasoning, or of imagination. The notion arises naturally, or is SUGGESTED or INTUITIONED, from the mere fact that the mind actually exists, and is susceptible of various feelings and operations.—The same may be said of all the distinct powers of the mind, such as the power of perception, of memory, of association, of imagination, of the will; not of the *acts* or *exercises* of these powers, it will be noticed, but of the powers themselves. That is to say, they are made known to us, considered abstractly and as distinct subjects of thought, not by *direct* perception, either inward or outward, but by spontaneity or suggestion. We say not by *direct* perception, because there is something intermediate between the power and the knowledge of it, viz., the act or exercise of the power, which is the *occasion* of the knowledge of the power itself. The Suggestional or Intuitional Power, availing itself of this occasion, gives us a knowledge of the distinct susceptibilities of the mind, just as it does of the mind as a whole.

(III.) Similar remarks, as far as spontaneity is concerned, will apply to the notions (whether we consider them as simple or complex) of SELF-EXISTENCE and PERSONAL IDENTITY. At the very earliest period they flow out, as it were, from the mind itself; not resulting from any prolonged and laborious process, but freely and spontaneously suggested or intuitioned by it. This is so true, that no one is able to designate either the precise time, or the precise circumstances under which they originate; for they spring into being under all circumstances. We cannot look, or touch, or breathe, or move, or think without them. These are products of our mental nature too essential and important to be withheld, or to be given only on rare and doubtful occasions; but are brought into existence in all times and places, and under all the varieties of action and feeling.—(See, in connexion with this section, § 4, 5, 6.)

§ 179. Origin of the idea of externality.

In giving an account of the origin of ideas, it is proper, in this connexion, to refer to the notion of outwardness or externality. Outwardness, although it is involved in everything which the senses have a connexion with, is, nevertheless, not a direct subject of the senses. As in other cases of ideas of internal origin, we do not, in strictness of speech, smell it, or taste it, or see it, or hear it, or touch it; and yet there is nothing which we see, taste, hear, or touch, of which externality is not predicable. The simple fact is, that the senses (or, rather, in this case one of them, that of TOUCH) furnish the *occasion* (not the thing itself, but simply the *occasion*) on which the Intellect, in virtue of its own spontaneity of action, gives us a knowledge of it. We have already had opportunity (§ 70) to speak of this idea as a most important one; as the connecting thought, which introduces us to a new manifestation of existence, different from that interior existence, which we variously call by the names spirit, mind, or soul. It is evident, if we could not form the idea of externality, everything which is the subject of mental experience would seem to be wholly internal, mere modifications of the inward or mental being. It is this idea, taken in connexion with the circumstances of its origin, which solves what has sometimes been considered a great mystery. The question is often asked, How is it possible that the mind should pass over from the circle of its own existence, the limits of its own actual personality, into the region and the knowledge of things wholly different from itself? In other words, using forms of expression which certain German philosophers have made familiar, from the EGO to the NON-EGO? If we will interrogate nature, and rest satisfied with her responses, the matter is simple. It is the power that gives us a knowledge of Mind, and uniting mind with its operations gives us the idea of Personality, and combining the present with the past originates the idea and the conviction of Personal Identity, which assures us also of outwardness, of an externality inconsistent with the assumption of all things into our own nature; the power, overlooked too often, and still more frequently estimated too lightly, which is known under the names of Suggestion and Intuition. Nature has implanted within us this spontaneity of thought, this intuitive directness of perception, and thus taken care to furnish important elements of knowledge, which could be possessed in no other way.

§ 180. Idea of matter or material existence.

It is here also that we find the basis of our conception of MATTER or material existence, when considered in distinction from the mere outward presentations or attributes of matter. The connexion which we have with the material world by means of the senses, makes us acquainted with whatever is strictly appropriate to those senses, such as colour, taste, hardness or softness, and extension. When, for instance, we look on a piece of wood or any other of those material bodies by which we are surrounded, an impression is made on the organ of vision, and we have the sensation, or, as we sometimes express it, the idea of colour. By applying the hand to the wood, we learn the penetrability or impenetrability, the softness or hardness of the mass which we hold. By moving the hand from one point to another in the mass, we are informed of the continuity or extension of its parts. But it does not appear that we are able, by means of the senses alone, to carry our inquiries beneath the surface of the body in such a way or to such a degree as to become directly acquainted with that interior something, whatever it is, which is the basis or support of these qualities. The external or sensuous Intellect (that is, the intellect operating by means of the senses) furnishes simply the *occasion* of the idea of matter or material existence;. while the internal or pure Intellect (that is, the intellect independent of the senses), acting upon that occasion, and availing itself of its power of Suggestion, brings into existence and realizes the idea itself.—This is the simple statement of the fact; but it appears to be abundantly authenticated by the common experience of men. That which is outward and operates upon the senses, that which we taste, and see, and handle, is presented to us (in other words, we regard it) in the light of an attribute or quality rather than of substance. But the very idea of a quality or attribute implies as the antecedent condition of its own existence, an object or subject to which it belongs. The idea of such a subject or object is, under these circumstances (that is to say, when anything presents itself to our notice in the aspect of an attribute or quality), not only naturally and necessarily suggested to us, but it obviously compels our belief. As we have already had occasion to remark (§ 132), we believe, and we cannot help believing, that there is some basis, some foundation, which is the support of the various attributes and qualities which are presented to our senses; just as we have the idea and believe in the existence of a God, although we know nothing of his interior essence or nature, but only of his manifestations, attributes, or operations; or as we have the idea of mind suggested to us, and fully believe in the existence of mind, although mind is entirely inaccessible in itself, and is made known wholly by those various acts of which we are conscious, such as perceiving, remembering, reasoning, willing, and the like.

§ 181. Origin of the idea of motion.

The idea of Motion, one of those with which we are most early and familiarly acqainted, is of internal and suggestional origin. Motion does not appear to be addressed directly to the senses. We can see things *in* motion, but not motion itself; we can touch things *in* motion, but motion itself is not accessible and knowable by that sense, nor by any other. When bodies move from each other, this new state of things is always indicated by a change in the appearance of the respective bodies, such as increased dimness of colour, diminished size, and obscurity in the outline. The relation of things, considered in regard to mere *position*, is disturbed and altered also. Under these circumstances, the idea of motion is naturally and necessarily suggested. And it exists with all that degree of definiteness and distinctness which is necessary for our present purposes.

§ 182. Of the nature of unity and the origin of that notion.

Another important notion, properly entitled to a consideration here, is that of UNITY. We shall decline attempting to explain the nature of unity, for the simple reason that nothing is more easy to be understood; every child knows what is meant by *one*. And how can we explain it if we would? We can explain a hundred by resolving it into parts; we can explain fifty or a score by making a like separation of the whole number into the subordinate portions of which it is made up; but when we arrive at unity, we must stop, and can go no further.

It is true, attempts have been made to define it, but, like many other such attempts, they have proved futile. Unity has been called *a thing indivisible in itself, and divided from everything else.* But this makes us no wiser. Is it anything more than to say that the unity of an object is its indivisibility? Or, in other words, that its unity is its unity?

As the idea of unity is one of the simplest, so it is one of the earliest notions which men have. It originates in the same way, and very nearly at the same time, with the notions of existence, self-existence, personal identity, and the like. When a man has a notion of himself, he evidently does not think of himself as two, three, or a dozen men, but as *one.* As soon as he is able to think of himself as distinct from his neighbour, as soon as he is in no danger of mingling and confounding his own identity with that of the multitude around him, so soon does he form the notion of unity. It exists as distinct in his mind as the idea of his own existence does; and arises there immediately successive to that idea, because it is impossible, in the nature of things, that he should have a notion of himself as a twofold or divided person.

Unity is the fundamental element of all enumeration. By the repetition or adding of this element, we are able to form numbers to any extent. These numbers may be combined among themselves, and employed merely as expressive of mutual relations, or we may apply them, if we choose, to all external objects whatever, to which we are able to give a common name.—(See § 145.)

§ 183. Nature of succession, and origin of the idea of succession.

Another of those conceptions which naturally offer themselves to our notice here is that of SUCCESSION. This term (when we inquire what succession is in itself) is one of general application, expressive of a mode of existence rather than of existence itself; and in its application to mind in particular, expressive of a condition of the mind's action, but not of the action itself, which that condition regulates. It is certainly a fact too well known to require comment, that our minds exist at different periods in successive states; that our thoughts and feelings, in obedience to a permanent law, follow each other in a train. This is the simple fact. And the fact of such succession, whenever it takes place, forms the occasion on which the notion or idea of succession is SUGGESTED or INTUITIONED to the mind. Being a simple mental state, it is not susceptible of definition; yet every man possesses it, and every one is rightly supposed to understand its nature.

Accordingly, it is not necessary to refer the origin of this idea to anything external. It is certain that the sense of smell cannot directly give us the idea of succession, nor the sense of taste, nor of touch. And we well know that the deaf and dumb possess it not less than others. The blind also, who have never seen the face of heaven, nor beheld that sun and moon which measure out for us days, and months, and years, have the notion of succession. They feel, they think, they reason, at least in some small degree, like other men; and it is impossible that they should be without it. The origin, therefore, of this notion is within; it is the unfailing result of the inward operation to call it forth, however true it may be that it is subsequently applied to outward objects and events.

§ 184. Origin of the notion of duration.

There is usually understood to be a distinction between the idea of succession and that of duration, though neither can be defined. The idea of succession is supposed to be antecedent in point of time to that of duration (we speak now of succession and duration relatively to our conception of them, and not in themselves considered). Duration must be supposed to exist antecedently to succession in the order of nature; but succession is the form in which it is made to apply to men, and is, therefore, naturally the occasion on which the idea of it arises in men's minds. Having the notion of succession, and that of personal or self-existence, a foundation is laid for the additional conception of permanency or duration; in other words, the idea of duration naturally arises in the mind, or is suggested, under these circumstances.

As we cannot, according to this view of its origin, have the notion of duration without succession, hence it happens that we know nothing of duration when we are perfectly asleep, because we are not then conscious of those intellectual changes which are involved in succession. If a person could sleep with a perfect suspension of all his mental operations from this time until the period spoken of as the resurrection, the whole of that period would appear to him as nothing. Ten thousand years passed under such circumstances would be less than a few days, or even hours.

That the notion of succession (we do not say succession itself, but only our *notion* or *idea* of it) is antecedent to, and is essential to that of duration, is in some measure proved by various facts. There are on record a number of cases of remarkable somnolency, in which persons have slept for weeks and even months. One of the most striking is that of Samuel Chilton, a labourer of Tinsbury, near Bath, in England. On one occasion, in the year 1696, he slept from the ninth of April to the seventh of August, about seventeen weeks, being kept alive by small quantities of wine poured down his throat. He then awoke, dressed himself, and walked about the room, "being perfectly unconscious that he had slept more than one night. Nothing, indeed, could make him believe that he had slept so long, till, upon going to the fields, he saw crops of barley and oats ready for the sickle, which he remembered were only sown when he last visited them."*

The result is similar when the suspension of the mental action is caused in any other way. It is related, for instance, of a British captain at the battle of the Nile, that he was giving an order from the quarter-deck of his vessel, when a shot struck him in the head, depriving him instantaneously of sense and speech. Living, however, he was taken home, and remained in this condition for the period of fifteen months in the Greenwich Hospital. At the end of that period, during which he had exhibited no signs of intelligence, an operation was performed on him by a skilful surgeon, that restored him at once to the exercise of his mental faculties. And it is stated, as the first result of this mental restoration, that he immediately rose in his bed, and completed the order which had been so abruptly interrupted so many months before.

In the Proceedings of the French Royal Academy of Sciences in 1719, there is also a statement illustrative of the subject under consideration, to the following effect.—There was in Lausanne a nobleman, who, as he was giving orders to a servant, suddenly lost his speech and all his senses. Different remedies were tried, but, for a very considerable time, without effect. For six months he appeared to be in a deep sleep, unconscious of everything. At the end of that period, however, resort having been had to certain surgical operations, he was suddenly restored to his speech and the exercise of his understanding. When he recovered, the servant to whom he had been giving orders happening to be in the room, he asked him if he had done what he had ordered him to, not being sensible that any interval, except perhaps a very short one, had elapsed during his illness.†

* The publication from which this statement is taken, and which contains others of similar import, refers to Frazer's Magazine as its authority.

† The Academy received this statement from Crousaz, Mathematical Professor at Lausanne, and author of a Treatise on Logic, &c.—

§ 185. Of time and its measurements, and of eternity.

When duration is estimated or measured, we then call it Time. Such measurements, as every one is aware, are made by means of certain natural or artificial motions. The annual revolution of the sun (using language in accordance with the common apprehensions on the subject) marks off the portion of duration which we call a YEAR; the revolution of the moon marks off another portion, which we call a MONTH; the diurnal revolution of the sun gives us the period of a DAY; the movements of the hands over the face of a clock or watch give the diminished durations of hours and minutes. This is TIME, which differs from duration only in the circumstance of its being measured.

What we call Eternity is only a modified or imperfect time; or, rather, time not completed. We look back over the months, and days, and years of our former existence; we look forward and onward, and behold ages crowding on ages, and time springing from time. And in this way we are forcibly led to think of time unfinished, of time progressive but never completed; and to this complex notion, or rather to this notion arising under this combination of circumstances, we give the name of Eternity.

§ 186. Marks or characteristics of time.

To this notice of the origin of the notion of time, it will not be improper to add, as it is one of great importance, some of its marks or characteristics.—(1.) Time (meaning by the term duration as existing in succession, and as susceptible of being measured) is strictly and properly predicable only of finite beings, and not of the Supreme Being. It is evident that, in its application to the human mind, time becomes a law or fixed condition of the mental action, a restriction

Persons suddenly attacked by delirium and afterward restored, exhibit the same unconsciousness and ignorance of the intermediate lapse of time.—See Abercrombie's Intellectual Philosophy, Section on Insanity.

placed upon it, a sort of veil, which would hide knowledge from us, were it not that it is drawn up gradually, and lets it in by degrees. But it is equally evident that there can be no law of this nature restricting the Divine Mind. Those multiplied facts and events, which are brought one after another before the minds of men, in consequence of their limited mental constitution, are spread out at once before the Divine Mind, as on a map. Whether past, present, or future, they are embraced and comprehended in a single glance. In this respect there is not the slightest analogy between the Supreme Mind and the minds of men.—(2.) Time is not susceptible of any visible or outward representation, as might be expected if its origin had been external instead of internal. It is true, we apply language to time, which wonld imply, if strictly interpreted, that it has extension or length. We speak of a *long* or *short* time, as if it were actually susceptible of material measurement. But this is owing partly to certain casual associations, and partly to the imperfection of language, and not to anything in the nature of time itself. (See the chapter on Casual Associations.)

(3.) Time, as it exists in our mental apprehension and in its relation to the intellect, is inseparable from events. Whatever event has taken place, whether it be some act of men or some occurrence in nature, although we are ignorant of the hour, the day, or the month, we cannot possibly conceive of it independently of time. This is a fixed, immutable, and ultimate condition of all our perceptions, so far as they regard events. That is to say, we cannot think of them, we cannot conceive of them as existing or taking place out of time.—(4.) Time, in its specific and appropriate nature, is indestructible, while the human soul remains the same it now does. It is not within the limits of human capability to contemplate events as the Supreme Being does, at once and simultaneously; but it can be done in succession alone; nor have we reason to suppose that it will ever be otherwise. It is true, the Angel shall at last appear, standing on the land and the sea, and shall swear that time shall be no longer; yet the time which the angel of the Apocalypse is destined thus to abolish, is only that which is measured by these stars, this moon, and the revolutions of this earth. As long as the human soul exists, in whatever part of the universe, there must at least be, not only duration, but duration as existing in succession, unless the nature of the soul be fundamentally changed.

§ 187. The idea of space not of external origin.

Another of those notions, the origin of which we propose to consider under the head of the Suggestional or Intuitional Power, is the idea of SPACE.—Perhaps it will be asked why we have disregarded in this instance the authority and example of Mr. Locke, who has ranked it with the notions of External origin, or, in his own phraseology, with those which come into the mind by the way of *sensation*. And certainly it might be expected that we should assent to that arrangement, if it could be definitely shown to us which of the senses it is to be ascribed to. But it is obvious that this cannot easily be done.

If it were of external origin, if it could properly be said to come into the mind by the way of sensation, we should be able to make such a reference of it. But let us inquire. It will evidently not be pretended that the notion of space is to be ascribed to the senses of taste, of smell, or of hearing. And can it be ascribed to the sense of touch? Is it a matter of feeling? A single consideration will suggest a satisfactory answer. It will certainly be acknowledged that we can have no knowledge by the sense of touch (with the single exception perhaps of the ideas of heat and cold, which are sometimes ascribed to it) of anything which does not present some resistance. The degree of resistance may greatly vary, but there will be always some. But no one will undertake to say that resistance is a quality of space, or enters in any way into his notion of it.

Nor are there less obvious objections to regarding it as a direct object of sight. The sense of sight gives us no direct knowledge of anything but of colours; all other visual perceptions are original in the sense of touch, and are made the property of the sight by transference. No one certainly ever speaks of space as red, or white, or of any other colour, or conceives of it as such.

There is another consideration, adverse to ascribing the idea of space to the senses, applicable equally to the sight and the touch. Everything coming within the cognizance of those two senses (with the exception already alluded to) has form, limits, bounds, and place. But the idea to which we are now attending is utterly exclusive of everything of this nature; it is not susceptible of circumscription and figure. So far from it, when we escape beyond the succession of circumscribed and insulated objects, we have but just entered within its empire. If we let the mind range forth beyond the forms immediately surrounding us, beyond the world itself, beyond all the systems of worlds in the universe; if we stand in our conception on the verge of the remotest star, and look downward and upward, it is then the idea of space rushes upon the mind with a power before unknown.—These considerations clearly lead to the conclusion that the notion of space is not susceptible of being ascribed directly to sensation in any of its forms, and is not, in the proper sense of the terms, of external origin. It may perhaps be maintained, that we shall find an adequate account of its origin if we combine the aid of abstraction with sensation. It is admitted, that by the sense of touch we have a knowledge of the extension of bodies, which includes, when it is contemplated under different views, length, breadth, and height. But still it does not appear how abstraction, applied to extension, or anything included in extension, can give us space. It is evident that the abstract notion which we form of the length of a body is different from the one in question. And if we abstract height or breadth, these also come short of giving us space. If we could abstract height, length, and breadth at once, and then combine them together, we should not even then have space, but, on the contrary, a solid body.

§ 188. The idea of space has its origin in suggestion.

What then shall we say of the origin of the notion of space? When pressed on this point we have but one answer to give; it is the natural offspring of the mind; it is a creation of the soul, wholly inseparable from its elementary constitution and action; an intimation, coming from an interior and original impulse. The opinion of Cousin (not to mention that of others of a like import) closely approximates to this statement. After criticising upon Locke, as Mr. Stewart has done before him, and asserting the futility of pretending to derive this notion directly from the senses, he adds as follows: "*Au contraire l'ideé d'espace nous est donneé, à l'occasion de l'ideé de corps, par la penseé, l'entendement, l'esprit, la raison, enfin par une puissance autre que la sensation.*"*

It remains to be added, that, while we cannot directly refer the notion in question to the senses, we cannot even state with certainty any particular occasion on which it arises, for we have the notion at a period further back than we can remember. On this point, however, it is undoubtedly true, that we may advance opinions more or less probable.—It is, for instance, a supposition not altogether worthless, that motion may have been the original occasion of the rise of this idea. At an early period we moved the hand, either to grasp something removed at a little distance, or in the mere playful exercise of the muscles, or perhaps we transferred the whole body from one position to another; and it is at least no impossibility, that on such an occasion the idea of space may have been called forth in the soul.

But there is another supposition still more entitled to notice, the one referred to in the above quotation

* L'Histoire de la Philosophie, tome ii., Dix-septieme Leçon.

from Cousin. Our acquaintance with external bodies by means of the senses may have been the *occasion* of its rise, although the senses themselves are not its direct source. It is certain that we cannot contemplate any body whatever, an apple, a rose, a tree, a house, without always finding the idea of space a ready and necessary concomitant. We cannot conceive of a body which is *nowhere.* So that we may at least date the origin of the idea of space as early as our acquaintance with any external body whatever. In other words, it is a gift of the mind, made simultaneously with its earliest external perceptions.

§ 189. Characteristic marks of the notion of space.

What has been said has prepared the way for the better understanding of the characteristic marks of space, as it exists in the mind's view of it. Of these marks there are four which will help to distinguish it. —(1.) Like duration or time, space is not capable of being visibly represented. The remarks which have already been made clearly evince this. Nothing can be visibly represented which does not come within the direct range and cognizance of the senses, as space does not.—(2.) It has no form nor limits. This might, perhaps, be considered as naturally resulting from the characteristic first mentioned. And, besides, we may safely appeal here to general experience, and assert without hesitation that no man limits space in his conception of it, nor is it even in his power so to do.—(3.) It is absolute and necessary. We speak of a thing as absolute which is not dependent on another, and is unalterable. This is not the case with anything whatever which we become acquainted with by means of the direct agency of the senses. All such bodies are constantly changing, and there is no difficulty in the supposition that they may all be struck out of existence. But it is impossible for us to associate the idea of non-existence with space. It is unalterably the same. But there is evidently nothing unalterable which is not naturally and necessarily so.

It is on this ground, therefore, that we assign to space the characteristic of being absolute and necessary.—(4.) A fourth characteristic is, that it is the condition of the existence of all bodies; that is to say, it is impossible for us to conceive of a body without associating the notion of space with it. We are so constituted that what we understand by space is utterly inseparable from everything outward which has outlines and form. So that we may truly say of space that it is the condition of the existence of all bodies, at least relatively to ourselves.

And hence, as it is internally conceived of, it becomes a great law of the mind, modifying and limiting all its outward perceptions. We cannot conceive of objects out of space any more than we can conceive of events out of time. It is true, the poet Gray represents Milton as having, in his Paradise Lost, scaled the limits which time and space impose on human conceptions; the *flaming bounds*, as he calls them. But this is only the license and fiction of a poet. If that should ever happen which he has so sublimely imagined, and men should ever break through those great and unalterable barriers which God has erected between himself and inferior intelligences, we might well anticipate the result which the same glowing fancy has indicated:

> "They saw, but, blasted with excess of light,
> Closed their eyes in endless night."

§ 190. Of the origin of the idea of power.

Under the head of the Intuitional or Suggestional faculty, the idea of POWER properly belongs. Every man has this notion; every one feels, too, that there is a corresponding reality; in other words, power is not only a mere subject of thought, but has, in some important sense, a real existence. And we may add that every one knows, although there is somewhere a great original fountain of power, independent of all created beings, that he has a portion (small indeed it may be, but yet a portion) of the element of power in his own mind and in his own person. There is indeed a Power, unexplored and invisible, which has reared the mountains, which rolls the ocean, and which propels the sun in his course; but it is nevertheless true, that man, humble as he is in the scale of rational and accountable beings, possesses, as an attribute of his own nature, an amount of real efficiency suited to the limited sphere which Providence has allotted him. This is a simple statement of the fact. Power goes hand in hand with existence, intelligence, and accountability. There is no existence, either intelligent or unintelligent, without power, either in the thing itself, or in something else which sustains it. There is no *accountable* existence without power, existing in and participating in such existence, and constituting the basis of its accountability.

But the principal question here is, not what power is in itself, nor whether man possesses power in fact, but under what circumstances the notion or idea of power arises in the human mind. The occasions of the origin of this idea, so far as we are able to judge, appear to be threefold.—(1.) All cases of antecedence and sequence in the natural world. We are so constituted that, in connexion with such cases of antecedence and sequence, we are led, at a very early period of life, to frame the proposition and to receive it as an undeniable truth, that there can be no beginning or change of existence without a cause. This proposition involves the idea of efficiency or power.—(2.) The control of the will over the muscular action. We are so constituted that, whenever we will to put a part of the body in motion, and the motion follows the volition, we have the idea of power.—(3.) The control of the will over the other mental powers. Within certain limits and to a certain extent there seems to be ground for supposing that the will is capable of exercising a directing control over the mental as well as over the bodily powers. And whenever we are conscious of such control being exercised, whether it be greater or less, occasion is furnished for the origin of this idea. It is then called forth or SUGGESTED. It is not seen by the material eye, nor reached by the sense of touch; but, emerging of itself from the mind, like a star from the depths of the firmament, it reveals itself distinctly and brightly to the intellectual vision.

§ 191. Origin of the idea of the first or primitive.

The mind, satisfied with nothing short of the elements and foundations of knowledge, seeks, in its inquiry into the origin and causation of things, not only for the element of Power, but also for the FIRST cause, the antecedent which has no other antecedent, the PRIMITIVE. Whenever we see a thing, we are naturally led to think of, and to inquire for the *beginning* of that thing. There is a sort of natural consanguinity of events, an unalterable tie, which binds the present with the past, and the past with that which is still further back in the depths of time. The thing, the event, the fact (whatever exists or takes place), calls for that to which it is related, the antecedent and basis of its own existence, in the language of Scripture, as "deep calls to deep." Hence the idea of the Primitive.—This important notion (which we variously express by the words FIRST, ORIGINAL, BEGINNING, and the like) originates in the Intellect rather than in Sense, and in that particular form of intellectual activity which we denominate Suggestion. It is obvious, while we can see, or hear, or touch anything which is an object of the outward senses, we cannot, with strict propriety and truth of speech, be said to touch or see its antecedence or primitiveness. In fact, there is only one object, and that no other than the Supreme Being himself, to whom this idea, with absolute truth or strictness, will apply at all. We look at the works of man and the works of nature; everything which has form or activity; the sun, the moon, the stars, the ocean, the forests. But the mind, not satisfied with the perception of the thing, looks still further for its cause, its effective antecedent, the foundation of its existence. It inquires, who reared the forest, who rolls the ocean, who made the sun? The mind itself, therefore, suggests the notion of something which goes before, of PRIORITY; and, advancing under the impulses of its own nature, it proceeds from step to step, from star to star, from existence to existence, till it finds the absolute Primitive in that great Being, who involves in the fact of his Supremacy not only the subordination, but the subsequence of all things else. And it is to be kept in mind, that it is found there, not as a matter of outward, but of inward perception; revealed, not to the understanding, perceiving through the restricted instrumentality of the senses, but to the understanding, perceiving in the intuitive light of its own spontaneous action.

§ 192. Of the ideas of right and wrong.

Right and Wrong also are conceptions of the pure Understanding; that is, of the Understanding operating in virtue of its own interior nature, and not as dependent on the senses. We are constituted intellectually in such a manner, that, whenever occasions of actual right or wrong occur, whenever objects fitted to excite a moral approval or disapproval are presented to our notice, the ideas of RIGHT and WRONG naturally and necessarily arise within us. In respect to these ideas or *intellections* (if we choose to employ an expressive term partially fallen into disuse), Cudworth, Stewart, Cousin, and other writers of acknowledged discernment and weight, appear to agree in placing the origin of them here. And this arrangement of them is understood to be important in connexion with the theory of Morals. If these ideas originate in the pure intellect, and are simple, as they obviously are, then each of them necessarily has its distinctive nature; each of them is an entity by itself; and it is impossible to conceive of them as identical or interchangeable with each other. They are as truly unlike as our conceptions of *unity* and *time*, or of *space* and *power*. And if this is true of our *ideas* of right and wrong, it is not less so of right and wrong themselves. In other words, right can never become wrong, nor wrong right; they are placed forever apart, each occupying its own sphere; and thus we have a foundation laid for the important doctrine of the immutability of moral distinctions.—"The distinction between right and wrong," says Cousin (Psychology, chap. 5), "may be incorrectly applied, may vary in regard to particular objects, and may become clearer and more correct in time, without ceasing to be with all men the same thing at the bottom. It is a universal conception of Reason, and hence it is found in all languages, those products and faithful images of the mind.—Not only is this distinction universal, but it is a necessary conception. In vain does the reason, after having once received, attempt to deny it, or call in question its truth. It cannot. One cannot at will regard the same action as just and unjust. These two ideas baffle every attempt to commute them, the one for the other. Their objects may change, but never their nature."

§ 193. Origin of the ideas of moral merit and demerit.

Closely connected with the ideas of right and wrong are the ideas of moral MERIT and DEMERIT. In the order of nature (what is sometimes called the *logical* order), the ideas of right and wrong come first. Without possessing the antecedent notions of right and wrong, it would be impossible for us to frame the ideas of moral merit and demerit. For what merit can we possibly attach to him in whom we discover no rectitude; or what demerit in him in whom we discover no want of it! Merit always implies virtue as its antecedent and necessary condition, while demerit as certainly implies the want of it or vice. Although the ideas of merit and demerit, in consequence of being simple, are undefinable, there can be no doubt of their existence, and of their being entirely clear to our mental perception; and that they furnish a well-founded and satisfactory basis for many of our judgments in respect to the moral character and conduct of mankind.

§ 194. Of other elements of knowledge developed in suggestion.

In giving an account of the ideas from this source, we have preferred, as designative of their origin, the term SUGGESTION, proposed and employed by Reid and Stewart, or as interchangeable and synonymous with it, the word INTUITION, which has equally good authority in its favour, to the word REASON, proposed by Kant, and adopted by Cousin and some other writers, as, on the whole, more conformable to the prevalent usage of the English language. In common parlance, and by the established usage of the language, the word REASON is expressive of the rationative or inductive rather than of the suggestive or intuitional faculty; and if we annul or perplex the present use of that word by a novel application of it, we must introduce a new word to express the process of reasoning.

In bringing this interesting topic to a close, we would not be understood to intimate that the notions of existence, mind, personal identity, unity, succession, motion, duration, power, and the others which have been mentioned, are all which Suggestion furnishes. It might not be easy to make a complete enumeration; but, in giving an account of the genesis of human knowledge, may we not ascribe the ideas of truth, freedom, design or intelligence, necessity, fitness or congruity, reality, order, plurality, totality, immensity, possibility, infinity, happiness, reward, punishment, and perhaps many others, to this source? In particular, may we not assign here (such is the doctrine, and one of the excellences of the system of Kant) the abstract conceptions of Beauty and Deformity? It is true that we *feel* the Beautiful and its opposite by the inward Sensibilities, as we shall have occasion to notice and explain when we come to that interesting view of the mind. But is it not true also, availing ourselves of the occasion furnished by our sentimentive experience, that we can abstractly *conceive* or have an idea of it by means of the intuitional intellect? We may not be able to tell what the BEAUTIFUL is, but does not the intellect, by a spontaneous and effective intimation, assure us of the fact of its existence? And if there is a Beautiful, is there not also a Deformed, and, of course, a fixed and immutable distinction between them? Could we have a distinct idea of the Beautiful without an idea of the Deformed, any more than we could have an idea of Right without an idea of Wrong? Our opinions as to what is in fact beautiful may vary in a given case; but that does not prove the absence of the reality, nor alter the essentialities of its nature. It is a common remark that religion is practically no religion to those who have no *faith* in it; so the Beautiful is practically annihilated to those who have not the power of perceiving it; but, independent of the circumstance of its being perceived or not, it is the Beautiful still; like the sweet song of the bird in the desert, the same in itself, though there is no one to hear it and rejoice in it. So that we cannot but assent to those who assert that the foundations of Æsthetics (that is, the science of the Beautiful as applied to nature and the arts) are firm; not depending upon variable circumstances, but substantiated by the permanency of nature. And hence it has happened, that what was beautiful and pleasing to mankind four thousand years ago, is beautiful and pleasing still, simply because Beauty in nature, like Rectitude in morals, is, in the element and substance of its constitution, indestructible and invariable. The idea of the Beautiful, as thus explained, and as discriminated from the emotive or sentimentive experience of the Beautiful, is made known by Suggestion.

§ 195. Suggestion a source of principles as well as of ideas.

The power, which we variously call Intuitional or Suggestional, is not only the source of ideas (and particularly of ideas fundamental and unalterable), but also of *principles.* The reasoning faculty, which in its nature is essentially comparative and inductive, must have something to rest upon back of itself, and of still higher authority than itself, with which, as a first link in the chain, the process of induction begins. It is the suggestive intellect which is the basis of the action of the comparing and inductive intellect. Of those elementary or transcendental propositions, which are generally acknowledged to be prerequisites and conditions of the exercise of the reasoning faculty, there are four particularly worthy of notice.—(1.) There is no beginning or change of existence without a cause.—(2.) Matter and mind have uniform and permanent laws.—(3.) Every quality supposes a subject, a real existence, of which it is a quality.—(4.) Means, conspiring together to produce a certain end, imply intelligence.—The first of these propositions is the basis of all those reasonings which are employed to prove the existence of God from the light of nature, besides having other important applications in regard to anything and everything that is past. The second is essential to the continuance of our existence and our activity, inasmuch as it lays the foundation of all foresight into the future, and of the important consequences dependent upon such foresight. The third gives us a knowledge of mind and matter, the mental and material world, in distinction from their mere attributes and operations; assuring us of a substance or actuality of existence, as well as of the manifestations or signs of existence. By means of the fourth we are enabled to conduct the difficult and important process of separating the two great domains of matter and mind, detecting indications of intelligence under material forms, and assigning both to mind and matter their appropriate sphere and responsibilities.—These great truths, some of which are more particularly remarked upon in the chapter on Primary Truths, are made known, not by induction nor by direct experience, but by a spontaneous and original intimation of the Suggestional Intellect. As they are not the creations of a process of reasoning, so they are not destructible by such a process. In their interior or subjective revelation, they stand imbedded, as it were, in the mind's structure, and cannot be overthrown without a subversion of the essential elements of our mental nature.

ADDITIONAL PRACTICAL REMARK.

A single remark further. It has relation to inspirational influences. The susceptibility of inspiration from higher sources is not merely, as some may perhaps suppose, a theological dogmatism, but is one of the great and precious facts of humanity. God never ignores the sublime truth of his universal Fatherhood, and has never released his connexion with any of the tribes of men. He utters his voice everywhere. Homer, Plato, Euripides, Cicero, Livy, and Plutarch, as well as the long record of those whose inspirational history has given lustre and power to the unequalled pages of the Bible, have recognised the fact, that man, in the weaknesses and ignorance incidental to his finite nature, is susceptible of strength and guidance from the Infinite.

But these results are reached through law. The conditions of inspirational receptivity, at least those which are leading and indispensable, are three. (1.) Faith in this great fact, that there is thus an open door of communication between God and man; (2.) a sincere desire that God, who never violates our freedom, will by means of his inspirational influences come into communication with us; and, (3.) a freedom from all biases and prejudices of self-will—in other words, unselfishness. Under such circumstances, the human mind, in virtue of the unchangeable laws of its being, is susceptible of being reached, instructed, and guided. Nothing is more important to man than such guidance. And the mental susceptibility (not exclusively, but much more than some other of our mental powers), which is open to divine influences, and which turns to catch the inspirational suggestions of God, is the Intuitional power.

CHAPTER III.

CONSCIOUSNESS.

§ 196. Consciousness the 2d source of internal knowledge; its nature.

As we proceed in the investigation of the mind, we discover what may be termed separate spheres of knowledge; each having its place, and all in their own place and way contributing something to the great sum of our cognitions. The cognitive powers, which are External in their origin, give us a knowledge of external objects. The intuitional power, which is the first of those that are Internal or Supersensuous, gives us a knowledge of things in the absolute or unconditional. The second source of internal knowledge, with its separate and appropriate sphere of activity, is Consciousness. By the common usage of the language, the term Consciousness is appropriated to express the way or method in which we obtain the knowledge of those objects which belong to the mind itself, and which do not, and cannot, exist independently of some mind. It is a sort of affirmation of the soul itself by means of a reflex act based upon its own experiences, not only of the existence and nature of mental operations, but of the fact that they are *its own* operations. Definite and fixed in its modes of action, and adapted to secure definite cognitive results, it is entitled to be regarded as a distinct mental susceptibility.

Every act of consciousness, when analyzed, will be found to embrace in itself the three following distinct notions and feelings, viz., (1.) The idea of self or of personal existence, which we possess, not by direct consciousness, but by means of intuition or suggestion, expressed in English by the words SELF, MYSELF, and the personal pronoun I; (2.) some quality, state, or operation of the mind, whatever it may be; and, (3.)

a relative perception, perhaps instinctive in its action, of possession, appropriation, or belonging to. For instance, a person says, I AM CONSCIOUS OF LOVE, OR OF ANGER, OR OF PENITENCE. Here the idea of SELF or of personal existence is expressed by the pronoun I; there is a different mental state, and expressed by its appropriate term, that of the affection of ANGER; the phrase CONSCIOUS OF, expresses the feeling of relation, which instantaneously and necessarily recognises the passion of anger as the attribute or property of the subject of the proposition. And in this case, as in all others where we apply the term under consideration, consciousness does not properly extend to anything which has an existence extraneous to the conscious subject or soul itself.

It may be added further, that Consciousness seems to sustain the same relation to the various attributes of the mind which Sensation, or perhaps, more properly, Perception, does to those of matter. In both cases, viz., in Consciousness and in External Perception, we may be said, with a great deal of propriety, to have direct knowledge; that is to say, knowledge without the intervention of a series of intermediate facts. In the case of Perception, we have a new state of mind; and by means of it (or perhaps we may say, as involved in it) we immediately and necessarily have a knowledge of the corresponding external object. And so in Consciousness, whenever a new state of mind exists, we recognise its existence at once, and as an attribute of our own minds. We cannot help doing it. And this recognition, being itself a new mental state and necessarily existing, constitutes, through the fixed relation of effects and causes, the fact and consciousness of a distinct causative and cognitive power.

§ 197. Further remarks on the proper objects of consciousness.

As there are some things to which Consciousness relates, and others to which it does not, it is proper to consider it in this respect more fully.—In the first place, as to those thoughts which may have arisen, or those emotions which may have agitated us in times past, we cannot with propriety be said to be conscious of them at the present moment, although we may be conscious of that present state of mind which we term the *recollection* of them.

Again, Consciousness has no direct connexion with such objects, whether material or immaterial, as exist at the present time, but are external to the mind, or, in other words, have an existence independent of it. For instance, we are not, strictly speaking, conscious of any material existence whatever; of the earth which we tread, of the food which nourishes us, of the clothes that protect us, or of anything else of the like nature with which we are conversant; but are conscious merely of the effects they produce within us, of the sensations of taste, of heat and cold, of resistance, of hardness and softness, and the like.

This view holds also in respect to immaterial things, even the mind itself. We are not directly conscious, using the term in the manner which has been explained, of the existence even of our own mind, but merely of its qualities and operations, and of that firm belief or knowledge of its existence necessarily attendant on those operations. "According to the common doctrine," says Mr. Stewart (Philos. Essays, i., ch. i.), "of our best philosophers, it is by the evidence of *consciousness* we are assured that we ourselves exist. The proposition, however, when thus stated, is not accurately true; for our own existence is not a direct or immediate object of consciousness, in the strict and logical meaning of that term. We are conscious of sensation, thought, desire, volition, but we are not conscious of the existence of mind itself; nor would it be possible for us to arrive at the knowledge of it (supposing us to be created in the full possession of all the intellectual *capacities* that belong to human nature) if no impression were ever to be made on our external senses. The moment that, in consequence of such an impression, a sensation is excited, we learn two facts at once; the existence of the sensation, and our own existence as sentient beings; in other words, the very first exercise of my consciousness necessarily implies a belief, not only of the present existence of what is felt, but of the present existence of *that* which feels and thinks, or (to employ plainer language) the present existence of that being which I denote by the words *I* and *myself*. Of these facts, however, it is the former alone of which we can properly be said to be conscious, agreeably to the rigorous interpretation of the expression. The latter is made known to us by a suggestion of the understanding *consequent* on the sensation, but so intimately *connected* with it that it is not surprising that our belief of both should be generally referred to the same origin."

§ 198. Consciousness a ground or law of belief.

Consciousness, as was remarked in the introduction to this work, is a ground or law of belief; and the belief attendant on the exercise of it, like that which accompanies the exercise of the Suggestional or Intuitional power, is of the highest kind. It appears to be utterly out of our power to avoid believing beyond a doubt that the mind experiences certain sensations, or has certain thoughts, or puts forth particular intellectual operations, whenever, in point of fact, that is the case. We may be asked for the reason of this belief, but we have none to give, except that it is the result of an ultimate and controlling principle of our nature; and hence that nothing can ever prevent the convictions resulting from this source, and nothing can divest us of them.

Nor has the history of the human mind made known any instances that have even the appearance of being at variance with this view, except a few cases of undoubted insanity. A man may reason against Consciousness as a ground and law of belief, either for the sake of amusing himself or of perplexing others; but when he not only reasons against it as such, but seriously and sincerely rejects it, it becomes quite another concern; and such a one has, by common consent, broken loose from the authority of his nature, and is truly and emphatically beside himself. It will be impossible to find a resting-place where such a mind can fix itself and repose; the best established truths and the wildest and most extravagant notions will stand nearly an equal chance of being either rejected or received; fancy and fact will be confounded and mingled together, and the whole mind will exhibit a scene of chaotic and irretrievable confusion.

§ 199. Instances of knowledge developed in consciousness.

It would be no easy task to point out the numerous states of mind, the ideas, and emotions, and desires, and volitions, which come within the range and cognizance of Consciousness; nor is there any special reason, connected with any object we have in view at present, why such a full enumeration should be attempted. A few instances will suffice to show how fruitful a source of experience and of knowledge this is.

(I.) All the various degrees of belief are matters of Consciousness. We are so constituted that the mind necessarily yields its assent, in a greater or less degree, when evidence is presented. These degrees of assent are exceedingly various and multiplied, although only a few of them are expressed by select and appropriate names; nor does it appear to be necessary for the ends of society, or for any other purpose, that it should be otherwise. Some of them are as follows: doubting, assenting, presumption, believing, disbelieving, probability, certainty.

(II.) The names of all other intellectual acts and operations (not the names of the intellectual Powers, which, like the mind itself, are made known to us by Intuition or Suggestion, and are expressed by a different class of terms, but simply of *acts* and *operations*) are expressive of the subjects of our Consciousness; among others, the terms perceiving, thinking, attending, conceiving, remembering, comparing, judging, abstracting, reasoning, imagining.

(III.) Consciousness, considered as a source of knowledge of mental acts and operations belonging to ourselves, includes likewise all our emotions and desires (everything, in fact, which really and directly comes within the range of the SENTIMENTIVE or SENTIENT part of our nature), as the emotions of the beautiful, the grand, the sublime, the ludicrous; the feelings of pleasure, and pain, and aversion; of hope and joy, of despondency and sadness, and a multitude of others.

(IV.) Here also originates our acquaintance, in such a manner as to affirm them as our own, with the complex emotions or passions. A man bestows a benefit upon us, and we are conscious of a new complex feeling, which we call GRATITUDE. Another person does us an injury, and we are conscious of another and distinct feeling, which we call ANGER. In other words, we feel, we know that the passion exists, and that it belongs to ourselves; and it is the same of jealousy, hatred, revenge, friendship, sympathy, love, and the various forms of the filial and parental affection.

(V.) All the moral and religious emotions and affections, regarded as subjects of internal knowledge and as sustaining a personal relation, belong here, such as approval, disapproval, remorse, humility, repentance, religious faith, forgiveness, benevolence, the sense of dependence, adoration.—When we consider that the mind is constantly in action; that, in all our intercourse with our fellow-beings, friends, family, countrymen, and enemies, new and diversified feelings are called forth; that every new scene in nature and every new combination of events have their appropriate results in the mind, it will be readily conjectured that this enumeration might be carried to a much greater extent. What has been said will serve to indicate some of the prominent sources for self-inquiry on this subject.

EXPLANATORY REMARKS.

As explanatory and in confirmation of what has been said in this chapter, it should be remembered that the states of the mind are one thing, and the knowledge of them as our own mental states is another; and I cannot well see that the latter is less important than the former. Thoughts, emotions, desires, and volitions may be supposed to exist; but without that distinct cognitive susceptibility, generally known under the name of Consciousness, which recognises and affirms them as the attributes of the intuitioned Self or Personality, they would not be available as the constituents of an intellectual and moral nature. Without consciousness, even admitting the fact of their existence, we could not know them as OUR OWN, which, in any true philosophical analysis of the matter, would be practically the same as not knowing them at all. Consciousness, for instance, does not, properly speaking, create an original thought, emotion, or desire; but it creates or originates the accessory thought or intellectual affirmation, not only that such antecedent thought, emotion, or desire exists, but that they are all the attributes of the same personal Self. So that consciousness is not only a distinct cognitive power, but one of the greatest importance; first, because by its own additional or accessory act it recognises the fact of the existence of all mental states arising from other sources; second, because in doing this it necessarily discriminates between one mental state and another, so far as they differ in their specific or generic nature, and thus affirms not only their existence, but their differences; and, third, because it harmonizes and consolidates the mental action, so that we can now say, in direct and positive terms, *I* think, *I* feel, *I* will; inasmuch as it follows, as the result of the act of consciousness, a result which would not be possible without such act, that we now have a knowledge of the act of thinking, not as an independent entity, but as *our own* thinking, of the act of feeling as *our own* feeling, of the act of willing or volition as *our own* volition.

CHAPTER IV.

RELATIVE SUGGESTION OR JUDGMENT.

§ 200. Of the susceptibility of perceiving or feeling relations.

In proceeding to the consideration of the third of the cognitive powers, which come within the limits of the department of the Internal or Super-sensuous intellect, we are led to remark, in the first place, the important fact, hitherto unnoticed by us, that the mind has the power of bringing its thoughts together, and of placing them side by side, and comparing them. Such are nearly the expressions of Mr. Locke, who speaks of the mind bringing one thing *to* and setting it *by* another, and carrying its view from one to the other. And such is the imperfect nature of all arbitrary signs, that this phraseology will probably continue to be employed, although without some attention it will be likely to lead into error. Such expressions are evidently of material origin, and cannot be rightly interpreted, in their application to the mind, without taking that circumstance into consideration. When it is said that our thoughts are brought together, that they are placed side by side, and the like, the meaning, when the terms are translated from their material to their mental or spiritual import, seems to be, in the first place, that they are immediately successive to each other. And when it is further said that we compare them, the meaning is, that we perceive or feel their relation to each other in certain respects.

The mind, therefore, has an original susceptibility or power corresponding to the last-named result; in other words, by which this result is brought about; which is sometimes known as its power of RELATIVE SUGGESTION, and at other times the same thing is expressed by the term JUDGMENT, although the latter term is sometimes employed with other shades of meaning. It is also otherwise known as the relational power and "relationment."—"With the susceptibility of Relative Suggestion," says Dr. Brown, lect. 51, "the faculty of *judgment*, as that term is commonly employed, may be considered as nearly synonymous, and I have accordingly used it as synonymous in treating of the different relations that have come under our review." Degerando, in his treatise on the Origin of Human Knowledge, pt. ii., chap. ii., has a remark nearly to the same effect: "*Le judgment* nous fournit de nombreux secours; combien *d'idées de relation* n'avons nous pas? *Le judgment* seul peut, en comparant les objets, nous en faire decouvrir *les rapports.*"

We arrive here, therefore, at an ultimate fact in our mental nature; in other words, we reach a principle so thoroughly elementary that it cannot be resolved into any other. The human intellect is so made, so constituted, that, when it perceives different objects together, or has immediately successive conceptions of any absent objects of perception, their mutual relations are immediately felt by it. It considers them as equal or unequal, like or unlike, as being the same or different in respect to place and time, as having the same or different causes and ends, and in various other respects. And this is another and additional source of its power.

§ 201. Occasions on which feelings of relation may arise.

The occasions on which feelings of relation may arise, and which, in their origin, are to be ascribed to the relational power, are almost innumerable. It would certainly be no easy task to specify them all. Any of the ideas which the mind is able to frame may either directly or indirectly lay the foundation of other ideas of relation, since they may in general be compared together; or, if they cannot themselves be readily placed side by side, may be made the means of bringing others into comparison. But those ideas which are of an external origin are representative of objects and their qualities; and hence we may speak of the relations of things no less than of the relations of thought. And such relations are everywhere discoverable.

We behold the flowers of the field, and one is fairer than another; we hear many voices, and one is louder or softer than another; we taste the fruits of the earth, and one flavour is more pleasant than another. But these differences of sound, and brightness, and taste could never be known to us without the power of perceiving relations.—Again, we see a fellow-being, and, as we make him the subject of our thoughts, we at first think of him only as a man. But then he may at the same time be a father, a brother, a son, a citizen, a legislator; these terms express ideas of relation.

§ 202. Of the use of correlative terms.

Correlative terms are such terms as are used to express corresponding ideas of relation. They suggest the relations with great readiness, and by means of them the mind can be more steadily, and longer, and with less pain, fixed upon the ideas of which they are expressive. The words father and son, legislator and constituent, brother and sister, husband and wife, and others of this class, as soon as they are named, at once carry our thoughts beyond the persons who are the subjects of these relations to the relations themselves. Wherever, therefore, there are correlative terms, the relations may be expected to be clear to the mind.

The word CITIZEN is a relative term; but there being no correlative word expressing a precisely corresponding relation, we find it more difficult to form a ready conception of the thing signified than of SUBJECT, which has the correlatives ruler and governor.—It is hardly necessary to remind any one that the relation is something different from the things related. The relations are often changing, while the subjects of them remain the same. A person may sustain the relation and the name of a father to-day, but the inroads of death may on the morrow deprive him of his offspring, and thus terminate that character which the relative term father expresses.

§ 203. Of the great number of our ideas of relation.

Mr. Locke has somewhere made a remark to this effect, that it would make a volume to describe all sorts of relations, and with good reason, since they are as numerous as that almost endless variety of respects in which all our ideas, and all other subjects of knowledge, may be compared together. With the single idea of man, how many others are connected in consequence of the various relations which he sustains.—He may, at one and the same time, be a father, brother, son, brother-in-law, son-in-law, husband, friend, enemy, subject, general, judge, patron, townsman, servant, master, possessor, superior, inferior, greater, smaller, older, younger, wiser, contemporary, like, unlike, together with sustaining a variety of other relations too numerous to be mentioned.

Such is the number of relations, that it is found difficult to reduce them to classes; and probably no classification of them which has been hitherto proposed, exhausts them in their full extent. The most of those which it will be necessary to notice may be brought into the seven classes of relations of IDENTITY and DIVERSITY, of DEGREE, of PROPORTION, of PLACE, of TIME, of POSSESSION, and of CAUSE and EFFECT.

§ 204. Of relations of identity and diversity.

The first class of ideas of relation which we shall proceed to consider are those of IDENTITY and DIVERSITY.—Such is the nature of our minds, that no two objects can be placed before us essentially unlike without our having a perception of this difference. When, on the other hand, there is an actual sameness in objects contemplated by us, the mind perceives or is sensible of their identity. It is not meant by this that we are never liable to mistake; that the mind never confounds what is different, nor separates what is the same; our object here is merely to state the general fact.

Two pieces of paper, for instance, are placed before us, the one white and the other red; and we at once perceive, without the delay of resorting to other objects and bringing them into comparison, that the colours are not the same. We immediately and necessarily perceive a difference between a square and a circle, between a triangle and a parallelogram, between the river and the rude cliff that overhangs it, the flower and the turf from which it springs, the house and the neighbouring hill, the horse and his rider.

Whatever may be the appearance of this elementary perception at first sight, it is undoubtedly one of great practical importance. It has its place in all forms of reasoning, as the train of argument proceeds from step to step; and in Demonstrative reasoning in particular, it is evident that, without it, we should be unable to combine together the plainest propositions.

§ 205. Of axioms in connexion with relations of identity and diversity.

The remark at the close of the last section will be better understood on a little further explanation. The statement was, that without the relative perceptions or suggestions of IDENTITY and DIVERSITY (otherwise denominated perceptions of AGREEMENT and DISAGREEMENT) we should be incapable of demonstrative reasoning. Such reasoning, as is well known, is carried on by the help of axioms. And, accordingly, we generally find a number of axioms placed at the head of geometrical treatises, and of other treatises involving geometrical principles, such as the following: Things equal to the same are equal to one another; If equals be added to equals, the wholes are equal; The whole is greater than a part; Things which are double of the same are equal to one another; Things which are halves of the same are equal to one another; Magnitudes which coincide with one another (that is, which exactly fill the same space) are equal to one another.

It will be admitted (and we shall see it perhaps more clearly when we again have occasion to revert to this subject) that demonstrative reasoning implies a constant reference to such axioms; that its advancement through the successive series of propositions is by means of their aid. But it is too evident to require remark, that these axioms are nothing more than particular instances of the relative suggestion of identity and diversity, expressed in words. It is the perceptions of agreement and disagreement, actually arising in the mind, and not the mere verbal expression of them, which form the true cement and bond of the successive links, and impart consistency and strength to the whole chain.

§ 206. (II.) Relations of degree, and names expressive of them.

Another class of those intellectual perceptions, which are to be ascribed to the Judgment, or what we term more explicitly the power of RELATIVE SUGGESTION, may properly enough be named perceptions of relations of Degree. Such perceptions of relation are found to exist in respect to all such objects as are capable of being considered as composed of parts, and as susceptible, in some respects, of different degrees.—We look, for instance, at two men; they are both tall; but we at once perceive and assert that one is taller than the other. We taste two apples; they are both sweet; but we say that one is sweeter than another. That is to say, we discover, in addition to the mere perception of the man and the apple, a relation, a difference in the objects in certain respects.

There are terms in all languages employed in the expression of such relations. In English, a reference to the particular relation is often combined in the same term which expresses the quality. All the words of the comparative and superlative degrees, formed by merely altering the termination of the positive, are of this description, as whiter, sweeter, wiser, larger, smaller, nobler, kinder, truest, falsest, holiest, and a multitude of others. In other cases (and probably the greater number), the epithet expressive of the quality is combined with the adverbs *more* and *most*, *less* and *least*. But certainly we should not use such terms if we were not possessed of the power of relative suggestion. We should ever be unable to say of one apple that it is sweeter than another, or of one man that he is taller than another, without considering them in certain definite respects, and without perceiving certain relations. So that, if we had no knowledge of any other than relations of Degree, we should abundantly see the importance of the mental susceptibility under review, considered as a source of words, and of grammatical forms in language.

It will be noticed, as we proceed from one part of the mind to another, that we are able to indicate not only cognitive results, but results in language also, as well as in knowledge. New terms and words, constituting the elements of language, are the necessary results of new thoughts and feelings; and it will be found further, that their relations to each other are the basis, in whole or in part, of grammatical forms; so that, in certain important respects, the philosophy of language may be regarded as having its foundation in the philosophy of mind.

§ 207. Relations of degree in adjectives of the positive form.

Although relations of degree are discoverable more frequently in comparative and superlative adjectives than anywhere else, they may sometimes be detected also in abstract terms which have the appearance of being entirely positive, and not unfrequently in adjectives of the positive form.—Let it be considered, as one instance among many others, what we mean when we say of a person, He is an AGED man. Although the epithet has the positive form, we always tacitly compare the age of the subject of it with that of others, of people in general, and place the particular number of years to which he may have attained by the side of that period which we are in the habit of regarding as the ordinary term of man's pilgrimage.—It is the same when we say of any person that he is YOUNG. He is then, by a tacit mental reference, considered as falling far short of an assumed period, an approximation to which gives to another person the reputation of age.

Buffier, whose remarks are generally entitled to great weight, illustrates this subject as follows.*—"If we should, for example, never have seen or heard of any hill or mountain of greater height than a quarter of a mile, as might happen to some of the inhabitants of the Low Countries, a mountain a mile high would appear a considerable one to such people; but this mountain would be looked upon as inconsiderable and trifling to the people of the Alps, who are accustomed to see mountains of much greater height." And again he says, "What has been here said of greatness is manifestly applicable to all the other qualities of *long*, *broad*, *happy*, *unhappy*, *convenient*, *inconvenient*, *easy*, *difficult*, *rich*, *poor*, *good*, *bad*, *excellent*, and many others of a similar nature, that have no determinate sense, but by a relation founded on an arbitrary and accidental idea formed within our own minds. A man thought himself miserable in having a slight headache: being afterward seized with a giddiness and violent swimming in the head, the first reflection that occurred to him was, *how happy he was when he had only his first headache.* We here see that the arbitrary idea on which the comparison and relation are founded changes the signification, and, in a manner, the nature of the qualities of *happy* and *miserable*."

§ 208. (III.) Of relations of proportion.

Among other relations which are discovered to us by the power of judgment or relative suggestion are those of PROPORTION; a class of relations which are peculiar in this, that they are felt only on the presence of three or more objects of thought. They are

* First Truths of Pere Buffier, part ii., chap. xxviii.

discoverable particularly in the comparison of numbers, as no one proceeds far in numerical combinations without a knowledge of them. On examining the numbers two, three, four, twenty, twenty-seven, thirty-two, nine, five, eight, and sixteen, we feel certain relations existing among them; they assume a new aspect, a new power in the mental view. We perceive (and we can *assert*, in reference to that perception) that three is to nine as nine to twenty-seven; that two is to eight as eight to thirty-two; that four is to five as sixteen to twenty.

And when we have once felt or perceived such relation actually existing between any one number and others, we ever afterward regard it as a property inseparable from that number, although the property had remained unknown to us until we had compared it with others. We attach to numbers, under such circumstances, a new attribute, a new power; the same as we do, under similar circumstances, to all the other subjects of our knowledge. There are many properties, for instance, of external bodies which were not known to us at first, but, as soon as they are discovered, they are, of course, embraced in the general notion which we form of such bodies, and are considered as making a part of it. And pursuing the same course in respect to numbers, if, on comparing them with each other, we perceive certain relations never discovered before, the circumstance of their sustaining those relations ever afterward enters into our conception of them.

§ 209. (IV.) Of relations of place or position.

Other feelings or perceptions of relation arise when we contemplate the place or position of objects. Our minds are so constituted, that such perceptions are the necessary results of our contemplations of the outward objects by which we are surrounded. Perhaps we are asked, What we mean by position or place? Without professing to give a confident answer, since it is undoubtedly difficult, by any mere form of words, fully to explain it, we have good grounds for saying that we cannot conceive of any body as having place without comparing it with some other bodies. If, therefore, having two bodies fixed, or which maintain the same relative position, we can compare a third body with them, the third body can then be said to have place or position.

This may be illustrated by the chessmen placed on the chessboard. We say the men are in the same place, although the board may have been removed from one room to another. We use this language, because we consider the men only in relation to each other and the parts of the board, and not in relation to the room or parts of the room.—Again, a portrait is suspended in the cabin of a ship; the captain points to it, and says to a by-stander that it has been precisely in the same place this seven years. Whereas, in point of fact, it has passed from Europe to Africa, from Africa to America, and perhaps round the whole world. Still the speaker uttered no falsehood, because he spoke of the portrait (and was so understood to speak of it) in relation to the ship, and particularly the cabin, and not in relation to the parts of the world which the ship had visited.—Such instances show that place is relative.

Hence we may clearly have an idea of the place or position of all the different parts of the universe, considered separately, because they may be compared with other parts, although we are unable to form any idea of the place or position of the universe considered as a whole, because we have then no other body with which we can compare it. If it were possible for us to know all worlds and things at once, to comprehend the universe with a glance, we could not assert, with all our knowledge of it, that it is here, or there, or yonder, or tell where it would be.

But if place express a relative notion, then it follows that all words which involve or imply the place or position of an object are of a similar character. Such are the words high and low, superior and inferior (when used in respect to the position of objects), near and distant, above and beneath, further, nearer, hither, yonder, here, there, where, beyond, within, around, without, and the like.

§ 210. (V.) Of relations of time.

Another source of relative perceptions or judgments is TIME. Time holds nearly the same relation to duration as position does to space. The position or place of objects is but space marked out and limited; time, in like manner, is duration set off into distinct periods; and as our notions of the place of bodies are relative, so also are our conceptions of events considered as happening in time. It is true that the notions of duration and space are in themselves original and absolute; they are made known to us by Intuition rather than by Relative Suggestion; but when they are in any way limited, and events are thereby contemplated in reference to them under the new forms of place and time, certain new conceptions arise which are relative.

All time is contemplated under the aspect of past, present, or future. We are able, chiefly in consequence of the revolution of the heavenly bodies, to form a distinct notion of portions of time, a day, a month, a year, &c.; we can contemplate events, not only as existing at present, but as future or past. But always when we think or speak of events in time (in other words, when we speak of the *date* of events), there is a comparison and a perception of relation.

What, therefore, is the import of our language, when we say the independence of the North American colonies was declared July 4th, 1776?—The meaning of these expressions may be thus illustrated. We assume the present year, whatever it may be, as a given period, and reckon back to the year *one*, which coincides with the birth of our Saviour; then the year 1776 expresses the distance between these two extremes, viz., the year one, and the year of the present time. This seems to be what we learn, and apparently all that we learn, when we say the Independence of the United States was declared at the period above mentioned.—Again, we obviously mean the same thing, and convey the same idea, whether, in accordance with the commonly received chronology, we say that the Saviour was born in the year ONE of the Christian era, or in the year 4004 from the creation of the world. But, in the last case, the year 4004 expresses the distance between these two extremes, viz., the beginning of the world and the present time; while, in the first instance, the event itself forms the beginning of the series.—So that all dates, considered as the names of corresponding mental states and as including those states, appear to be properly classed under the head of ideas of relation; and also all names whatever, which are in any way expressive of the time of events, as a second, a minute, day, week, hour, month, year, cycle, yesterday, to-morrow, to-day, and others.

§ 211. (VI.) Of relations of possession.

Another class of relations may be called relations of POSSESSION.—Every one knows that not unfrequently, in his examination of objects, there arises a new feeling, which is distinct from, and independent of the mere conceptions of the objects themselves; and which, as it differs from other feelings of relation, may be termed the relation of possession, or belonging to. This is one of the earliest feelings which human beings exercise. When we see the small child grasping its top and rattle with joy, and disputing the claims of another to a share in them, we may know that he has formed the notion of possession. It is not only formed in early life, but experience fully shows that it loses neither activity nor strength by the lapse of years.

The application of the Judgment, or that power by which we perceive the relation of things, is frequent in this particular form; and we find here a fruitful source of words. The whole class of possessive pronouns, which are to be found in all languages, have their origin here, such as MINE, THINE, YOUR, HIS, HER. The relation of possession is imbodied also in the Genitive case of the Greeks, Latins, Germans, and whatever other languages express relations in the same way; in the construct state of nouns in the Hebrew and the other cognate dialects; and in the preposition OF, which is the substitute for the genitive termination in English, and the articles DE, DU, DE'L, and DE LA in French.

The verbs TO BE in English, ESSE in Latin, ÊTRE in French (and the same may undoubtedly be said of the corresponding verb of existence in many other languages), are often employed to express the relation of possession or belonging to. To say that the rose is red or the orange yellow, is as much as to say that the qualities of yellowness and redness are the possession of, or belong to the rose and orange. But it will be observed that the relation is not indicated by the name of the subject, nor by the epithet expressive of its quality, but by the verb which connects the subject and predicate. And similar remarks will apply to some other verbs.

This class of relations is involved in many complex terms, which imply definite qualities and affections of mind, as friend, enemy, lover, hater, adorer, worshipper. These terms not only indicate certain individuals, to whom they are applied, but assert the existence of certain mental affections as their characteristics, and as belonging to them.

§ 212. (VII.) Of relations of cause and effect.

There are relations also of Cause and Effect. We will not delay here to explain the origin of the notions of cause and effect any further than to say, that the notion of cause, as it first exists in the mind, presents itself in the form, and apparently includes nothing more than invariable antecedence. When the antecedence to the event, or the sequence of any kind, is our own volition (and probably in one or two other cases, see § 190), we have the new idea of POWER. The idea of invariable antecedence, therefore, which of course supposes some sequence when it is combined with that of Power, constitutes, for our present purpose, and in explanation of this class of relations, the full notion of CAUSE. When the sequence is found invariably to follow, and its existence cannot be ascribed to anything else, it is called the EFFECT. Accordingly, men usually give the name of *events*, of *occurrences*, or *facts*, to those things which from time to time fall under their notice, when they are considered in themselves. They are the *mere* facts, the mere events, and nothing more. But when, in the course of their further experience, such events are found to have certain invariable forerunners, they cease to apply these terms, and call them, in reference to their antecedents, EFFECTS. And, in like manner, the antecedents are called CAUSES, not in themselves considered, but in reference to what invariably comes after.

Cause and effect, therefore, have certainly a relation to each other; it is thus that they exist in the view of the mind and in the nature of things, however true it may be that men are unable to trace any *physical* connexion between them. We cannot conceive of a cause, if we exclude from the list of our ideas the correlative notion of effect, nor, on the other hand, do we call anything an effect without a reference to some antecedent. These two notions, therefore, involve or imply the existence of each other; that is, are relative.

§ 213. Of complex terms involving the relation of cause and effect.

The suggestion of the relation of Cause and Effect exists on occasions almost innumerable, and in all languages gives a character to a multitude of words. This relation is imbodied, for instance, in a multitude of names which are expressive of complex objects, such as printer, farmer, sculptor, warrior, writer, poet, manufacturer, painter.

This may be thus illustrated: When we look at any interesting piece of statuary, the sight of it naturally suggests its author. But when our mind is thus directed from the statue to the sculptor, it is evident we do not think of him as we do of a thousand others, but we combine with the conception of the individual a reference to what he has done. We unite with the mere complex notion of man that of a cause, and this combination evidently alters its character, making it relative instead of absolute.—In like manner, when we look at a fine portrait or historical painting, we are naturally reminded of the artist, whose ingenuity has been displayed in its proportions and colouring. But the word painter, which we apply to him, expresses not merely the man, but comprises the additional notion of the relation of cause which he holds to the interesting picture before us.

§ 214. Remarks on instituted or conventional relations.

Perhaps we may be thought not to have completed this subject without remarking that there are certain complex terms, expressive of what Mr. Locke calls INSTITUTED or CONVENTIONAL relations. As the epithets indicate which are applied to them, they are not permanent, but are dependent on the will, agreement, or appointment of men; such as citizen or burgher, governor, judge, senator, general, legislator. Accordingly, a CITIZEN is one who has a right to the privileges of civil society in a certain place; that is to say, is the subject of some government, to the principles of whose organization and authority he is supposed to have consented, in the expectation of receiving its protection. A GENERAL is one who has the power to command an army, with the various powers incidental to it; the right being delegated to him by the choice and consent of the government of the country.

But it is obviously unnecessary to stop for the purpose of considering the innumerable and constantly changing relations of this kind. They assume the most multiplied shapes; not taking their character from any one fixed and definite principle of the mind, but embracing a complication of qualities both absolute and relative.—There are other complex names, involving various relations which chiefly differ from the conventional relations in being natural and more permanent, such as father, son, brother, sister, nephew.

§ 215. Connexion of relative suggestion or judgment with reasoning.

Such is the power, definite in its position, and definite in its results, and discriminated also in its modes of action, and therefore like Intuition and Consciousness and for similar reasons entitled to be regarded as a separate cognitive power, which is known as Relative Suggestion or Judgment, and sometimes as the relational power or "relationment." And it remains only to be added that this distinct and indispensable susceptibility has a close connexion with the Reasoning or inductive power which is hereafter to be considered. The suggestions of relation (or elementary judgments, as they may, perhaps, properly be called) are, in some respects, to a train of reasoning, what parts are to the whole. They evidently do not of themselves include all the parts in a train of reasoning, and are distinguished by this peculiarity, that their office in a great measure is to connect together other subordinate parts in the train. In the combination of numbers, and in the various applications of demonstrative reasoning, the relations of PROPORTION and the relations of IDENTITY and DIVERSITY (otherwise called of AGREEMENT and DISAGREEMENT) find a conspicuous place. Moral reasoning embraces all kinds of relations, those of degree, time, place, possession, and cause and effect, as well as of agreement and disagreement, and of proportion. Relative feelings, sometimes of one kind and sometimes of another, continually unfold themselves as the mind advances in argument. So that, although there are elements in reasoning besides perceptions of relation, it is evident that it cannot advance independently of their aid. Facts may be accumulated having close and decisive relations to the points to be proved, but those facts can never be so bound together as to result in any decisive conclusion without a perception and knowledge of the relations.

CHAPTER V.

ASSOCIATION. (I.) PRIMARY LAWS.

§ 216. Reasons for considering this subject here.

IN giving an account of the internal origin of knowledge, we might be expected to proceed directly from Relative Suggestion to a consideration of the Reasoning power, which is one of the most effective and fruitful sources of intellectual perception. By means of this power, which we have already spoken of as one of the cognitive powers coming under the head of the Internal or Super-sensational Intellect, we are enabled to combine and compare the ample materials furnished by SUGGESTION, CONSCIOUSNESS, and RELATIVE SUGGESTION, and thus to develope in the mind new elements of thought, and to cast light on the darkened places in the field of truth by the external powers, and also by those just considered. But there are powers of the mind, subordinate to the reasoning power and essential to its action, which may with propriety be first considered, particularly Association and Memory. Other persons, perhaps, in examining the various parts of the mind, would propose for the consideration of these powers some other place; but we see no valid objection to considering them here. On the contrary, they have comparatively so little to do with what has gone before, and so much to do with what comes after, and, in particular, are so essential to every process of ratiocination, that this seems to be their appropriate position. As Association is presupposed and involved in memory as well as in reasoning, we naturally begin with that principle first. Association is one of the most interesting of that class of powers which we have spoken of as Auxiliary powers, and which are introduced to our notice, not in consecutive order, but wherever a favourable opportunity presents.

§ 217. Meaning of association and illustrations.

Our first explanatory remark, in examining the subject of association, is, that our thoughts and feelings follow each other in a regular train. Of this statement no one needs any other proof than his individual experience. We all know, not only that our minds are susceptible of new states, but, what is more, that this capability of new states is not fortuitous, but has its laws. Therefore we not only say that our thoughts and feelings succeed each other, but that this antecedence and sequence is in a *regular* train. To this regular and established consecution of the states of the mind we give the name of MENTAL ASSOCIATION.

Illustrations of this important principle, which exerts an influence over the emotions and desires as well as over the thoughts, are without number. Mr. Hobbes relates, in his political treatise of the Leviathan, that he was once in company where the conversation turned on the English Civil War. A person abruptly asked, in the course of the conversation, What was the value of a Roman denarius? Such a question, so remote from the general direction of the conversation, had the appearance not only of great abruptness, but of impertinence. Mr. Hobbes says that, on a little reflection, he was able to trace the train of thought which suggested the question. The original subject of discourse naturally introduced the history of King Charles; the king naturally suggested the treachery of those who surrendered him up to his enemies; the treachery of these persons readily introduced to the mind the treachery of Judas Iscariot; the conduct of Judas was associated with the thirty pieces of silver; and as the Romans occupied Judea at the time of the crucifixion of the Saviour, the pieces of silver were associated with the Roman denarii.

"When I was travelling through the wilds of America," says the eloquent Chateaubriand, "I was not a little surprised to hear that I had a countryman established as a resident at some distance in the woods. I visited him with eagerness, and found him employed in pointing some stakes at the door of his hut. He cast a look towards me, which was cold enough, and continued his work; but, the moment I addressed him in French, he started at the recollection of his country, and the big tear stood in his eye. These well-known accents suddenly roused in the heart of the old man all the sensations of his infancy."*

The Emperor Napoleon, whose present cares might be supposed to have greatly weakened the chain of thought and feeling that bound him to the past, is said to have once expressed himself thus: "Last Sunday evening, in the general silence of nature, I was walking in these grounds [of *Malmaison*]. The sound of the church-bell of Ruel fell upon my ear, and renewed all the impressions of my youth. I was profoundly affected, such is the power of early associations."†—Such illustrations, which appeal to every one's consciousness in confirmation of their truth, show what association is.

§ 218. Of the general laws of association.

In regard to Association, all that we know is the fact that our thoughts and feelings, under certain circumstances, appear together and keep each other company. We do not undertake to explain *why* it is that association, in the circumstances appropriate to its manifestation, has an existence. We know the simple fact; and if it be an ultimate principle in our mental constitution, as we have no reason to doubt that it is, we can know nothing more.

Association, as thus understood, has its laws. By the Laws of association, we mean no other than the general designation of those circumstances under which the regular consecution of mental states which has been mentioned occurs. The following may be named as among the Primary or more important of those laws, although it is not necessary to take upon us to assert either that the enumeration is complete, or that

* Chateaubriand's Recollections of Italy, England, and America.
† Scott's Life of Napoleon, vol. iii., chap. xxxiv.

some better arrangement of them might not be proposed, viz., RESEMBLANCE, CONTRAST, CONTIGUITY in time and place, and CAUSE and EFFECT.

§ 219. Resemblance the first general law of association.

New trains of ideas and new emotions are occasioned by Resemblance; but when we say that they are occasioned in this way, all that is meant is, that there is a new state of mind immediately subsequent to the perception of the resembling object. Of the efficient cause of this new state of mind under these circumstances, we can only say, the Creator of the soul has seen fit to appoint this connexion in its operations, without our being able, or deeming it necessary, to give any further explanation. A traveller, wandering in a foreign land, finds himself, in the course of his sojournings, in the midst of aspects of nature not unlike those where he has formerly resided, and the fact of this resemblance becomes the antecedent to new states of mind. There is distinctly brought before him the scenery which he has left, his own woods, his waters, and his home.—The enterprising Lander, in giving an account of one of his excursions in Africa, expresses himself thus: "The foliage exhibited every variety and tint of green, from the sombre shade of the melancholy yew to the lively verdure of the poplar and young oak. For myself, I was delighted with the agreeable ramble, and imagined that I could distinguish among the notes of the songsters of the grove, the swelling strains of the English skylark and thrush, and the more gentle warbling of the finch and linnet. It was, indeed, a brilliant morning, teeming with life and beauty, and recalled to my memory a thousand affecting associations of sanguine boyhood, when I was thoughtless and happy."

The result is the same in any other case, whenever there is a resemblance between what we now experience and what we have previously experienced. We have been acquainted, for instance, at some former period with a person whose features appeared to us to possess some peculiarity, a breadth and openness of the forehead, an uncommon expression of the eye, or some other striking mark; to-day we meet a stranger in the crowd by which we are surrounded whose features are of a somewhat similar cast, and the resemblance at once vividly suggests the likeness of our old acquaintance.

Nor is the association which is based upon resemblance limited to objects of sight. Objects which are addressed to the sense of hearing are recalled in the same way.

> "How soft the music of those village bells,
> Falling at intervals upon the ear.
> With easy force it opens all the cells
> Where memory slept. Wherever I have heard
> A kindred melody, the scene recurs,
> And with it all its pleasures and its pains."

§ 220. Resemblance in every particular not necessary.

It is not necessary that the RESEMBLANCE should be complete in every particular in order to its being a principle or law of association. It so happens (to use an illustration of Brown*) that we see a painted portrait of a female countenance which is adorned with a ruff of a peculiar breadth and display, and we are, in consequence, immediately reminded of Queen Elizabeth. Not because there is any resemblance between the features before us and those of the English sovereign, but because, in all the painted representations which we have seen of her, she is uniformly set off with this peculiarity of dress, with a ruff like that which we now see. Here the resemblance between the suggesting thing and that which is suggested is not a complete resemblance, does not exist in all the particulars in which they may be compared together, but is limited to a part of the dress.

That a single resembling circumstance (and perhaps one of no great importance) should so readily suggest the complete conception of another object or scene, which is made up of a great variety of parts,

* Brown's Philosophy of the Human Mind, lect. xxxv.

seems to admit of some explanation in this way. We take, for example, an individual; the idea which we form of the individual is a complex one, made up of the forehead, eyes, lips, hair, general figure, dress. These separate subordinate ideas, when combined together and viewed as a whole, have a near analogy to any of our ideas, which are compounded, and are capable of being resolved into elements more simple. When, therefore, we witness a ruff of a size and decoration more than ordinary, we are at once reminded of that ornament in the habiliments of the British queen; and this on the ground of Resemblance. But this article in the decorations of her person is the foundation of only one part of a very complex state of mind, which embraces the features and the general appearance. As there has been a long-continued coexistence of those separate parts which make up this complex state, the recurrence to the mind of one part or of one idea is necessarily attended with the recurrence of all the others.

§ 221. Of resemblance in the effects produced.

Resemblance operates, as an associating principle, not only where there is a likeness or similarity in the things themselves, but also when there is a resemblance in the *effects* which are produced upon the mind.—The ocean, for instance, when greatly agitated by the winds, and threatening every moment to overwhelm us, produces in the mind an emotion similar to that which is caused by the presence of an angry man who is able to do us harm. And, in consequence of this similarity in the effects produced, it is sometimes the case that they reciprocally bring each other to our recollection.

Dark woods hanging over the brow of a mountain cause in us a feeling of awe and wonder, like that which we feel when we behold approaching us some aged person, whose form is venerable for his years, and whose name is renowned for wisdom and justice. It is in reference to this view of the principle on which we are remarking, that the following comparison is introduced in Akenside's Pleasures of the Imagination:

> "Mark the sable woods,
> That shade sublime yon mountain's nodding brow;
> With what religious awe the solemn scene
> Commands your steps! As if the reverend form
> Of Minos or of Numa should forsake
> The Elysian seats, and down the embowering glade
> Move to your pausing eye."

As we are so constituted that all nature produces in us certain effects, causes certain emotions similar to those which are caused in us in our intercourse with our fellow-beings, it so happens that, in virtue of this fact, the natural world becomes living, animated, operative. The ocean is in *anger;* the sky *smiles;* the cliff *frowns;* the aged woods are *venerable;* the earth and its productions are no longer a dead mass, but have an existence, a soul, an agency.—We see here the foundation of metaphorical language; and it is here that we are to look for the principles by which we are to determine the propriety or impropriety of its use.

§ 222. Contrast the second general or primary law.

CONTRAST is another law or principle by which our successive mental states are suggested; or, in other terms, when there are two objects, or events, or situations of a character precisely opposite, the idea or conception of one is immediately followed by that of the other. When the discourse is of the *palace* of the king, how often are we reminded, in the same breath, of the *cottage* of the peasant! And thus it is, that wealth and poverty, the cradle and the grave, and hope and despair, are found, in public speeches and in writings, so frequently going together and keeping each other company. The truth is, they are connected together in our thoughts by a distinct and operative principle; they accompany each other, certainly not because there is any resemblance in the things thus associated, but in consequence of their very marked contrariety. Darkness reminds of light, heat of cold, friendship of enmity; the sight of the conqueror is associated with the memory of the conquered, and, when beholding men of deformed and dwarfish appearance, we are at once led to think of those of erect figure or of Patagonian size. Contrast, then, is no less a principle or law of association than resemblance itself.

Count Lemaistre's touching story, entitled, from the scene of its incidents, THE LEPER OF AOST, illustrates the effects of the principle of association now under consideration. Like all persons infected with the leprosy, the subject of the disease is represented as an object of dread no less than of pity to others; and while he is an outcast from the society of men, he is a loathsome spectacle even to himself. But what is the condition of his mind? What are the subjects of his thoughts? The tendencies of his intellectual nature prevent his thinking of wretchedness alone. His extreme misery aggravates itself by suggesting scenes of ideal happiness, and his mind revels in a paradise of delights, merely to give a greater intensity to his actual woes by contrasting them with imaginary bliss. —"I represent to myself continually," says the Leper, "societies of sincere and virtuous friends; families blessed with health, fortune, and harmony. I imagine I see them walk in groves greener and fresher than these, the shade of which makes my poor happiness, brightened by a sun more brilliant than that which sheds its beams on me; and their destiny seems to me as much more worthy of envy in proportion as my own is the more miserable."

Association by CONTRAST is the foundation of the rhetorical figure of Antithesis. In one of the tragedies of Southern we find the following antithetic expressions:

"Could I forget
What I have been, I might the better bear
What I am destined to. I am not the first
That have been wretched: but to think how much
I have been happier."

Here the present is placed in opposition with the past, and happiness is contrasted with misery; not by a cold and strained artifice, as one might be led to suppose, but by the natural impulses of the mind, which is led to associate together things that are the reverse of each other.

§ 223. Contiguity the third general or primary law.

Those thoughts and feelings which have been connected together by nearness of time and place are readily suggested by each other, and, consequently, contiguity in those respects is rightly reckoned as another and third primary law of our mental associations. When we think of Palestine, for instance, we very readily and naturally think of the Jewish nation, of the patriarchs, of the prophets, of the Saviour, and of the apostles, because Palestine was their place of residence and the theatre of their actions. So that this is evidently an instance where the suggestions are chiefly regulated by proximity of place. When a variety of acts and events have happened nearly at the same period, whether in the same place or not, one is not thought of without the other being closely associated with it, owing to proximity of time. If, therefore, the particular event of the crucifixion of the Saviour be mentioned, we are necessarily led to think of various other events which occurred about the same period, such as the treacherous conspiracy of Judas, the denial of Peter, the conduct of the Roman soldiery, the rending of the veil of the temple, and the temporary obscuration of the sun.

The mention of Egypt suggests the Nile, the Pyramids, the monuments of the Thebais, the follies and misfortunes of Cleopatra, the battle of Aboukir. The mention of Greece is associated with Thermopylæ and Salamis, the Hill of Mars and the Vale of Tempe, Ilissus, the steeps of Delphi, Lyceum, and the "olive shades of Academus." These, it will be noticed, are associations on the principle of contiguity in PLACE. But if a particular event of great interest is mentioned, other events and renowned names, which attracted notice at the same period, will eagerly cluster around it.

The naming of the AMERICAN REVOLUTION, for instance, immediately fills the mind with recollections of Washington, Franklin, Morris, Greene, Jay, and many of their associates, whose fortune it was to enlist their exertions in the support of constitutional rights, not merely in the same country (for that circumstance alone might not have been sufficient to recall them), but *at the same period of time.*

It is generally supposed, and not without reason for it, that the third primary law of mental association is more extensive in its influence than any others. It has been remarked, with truth, that proximity in time and place forms the basis of the whole calendar of the great mass of mankind. They pay but little attention to the arbitrary eras of chronology, but date events by each other, and speak of what happened at the time of some dark day, of some destructive overflow of waters, of some great eclipse, of some period of drought and famine, of some war or revolution.

§ 224. Cause and effect the fourth primary law.

There are certain facts or events which hold to each other the relation of invariable antecedence and sequence. That fact or event, to which some other one sustains the relation of constant antecedence, is in general called *an effect;* and that fact or event, to which some other one holds the relation of invariable sequence, has in general the name of a *cause.* Now there may be no resemblance in the things which reciprocally bear this relation, there may be no contrariety, and it is by no means necessary that there should be contiguity in time or place, as the meaning of the term contiguity is commonly understood. There may be CAUSE and EFFECT without any one or all of these circumstances. But it is a fact, which is known to every one's experience, that, when we think of the cause in any particular instance, we naturally think of the effect, and, on the contrary, the knowledge or recollection of the effect brings to mind the cause.—And, in view of this well-known and general experience, there is good reason for reckoning CAUSE and EFFECT among the primary principles of our mental associations. What we here understand by principles or laws will be recollected, viz., The general designation of those circumstances under which the regular consecution of mental states occurs.

It is on the principle of Cause and Effect that, when we see a surgical instrument, or any engine of torture, we have a conception of the pain which they are fitted to occasion. And, on the contrary, the sight of a wound, inflicted however long before, suggests to us the idea of the instrument by which it was made. Mr. Locke relates an incident, which illustrates the statements made here, of a man who was restored from a state of insanity by means of a harsh and exceedingly painful operation. "The gentleman who was thus recovered, with great sense of gratitude and acknowledgment, owned the cure all his life after as the greatest obligation he could have received; but, whatever gratitude and reason suggested to him, he could never bear the sight of the operator; that image brought back with it the idea of that agony which he suffered from his hands, which was too mighty and intolerable for him to endure."—The operation of the law of Cause and Effect, in the production of new associations, seems to be involved in the following characteristic passage of Shakspeare, Henry IV., 2d part, act i.

> "Yet the first bringer of unwelcome news
> Hath but a losing office; and his tongue
> Sounds ever after as a sullen bell,
> Remember'd knolling a departed friend."

CHAPTER VI.

ASSOCIATION. (II.) SECONDARY LAWS.

§ 225. Secondary laws and their connexion with the primary.

THE subject of Association is not exhausted in the enumeration and explanation of its Laws which has thus far been given. Besides the PRIMARY LAWS which have fallen under our consideration, there are certain marked and prominent circumstances, which are found to exert, in a greater or less degree, a modifying and controlling influence over the more general principles. As this influence is of a permanent character, and not merely accidental and temporary, the grounds or sources of it are called, by way of distinction, SECONDARY LAWS.

These, which we are now to consider, will probably appear at first sight to be more numerous than they are in fact. It is undoubtedly somewhat difficult to make out a just and unalterable designation of them. Nevertheless, it is believed that, on a careful examination, their multiplicity will be lessened, and that they will be found to be but four in number, viz., lapse of Time, degree of coexistent Feeling, repetition or Habit, and original or constitutional Difference in character.

It must at once be obvious, that these principles, although holding a subordinate rank, give an increased range and power to the PRIMARY laws. It is not to be inferred, from the epithet by which they are distinguished, that they are, therefore, of a very minor and inconsiderable importance. On the contrary, human nature without them, as far as we are capable of judging, would have assumed a sort of fixed and inflexible form, instead of presenting those pleasing and almost endless diversities it now does.—The primary laws are the great national roads along which the mind holds its course; the secondary are those cross-roads that intersect them from time to time, and thus afford an entrance into, and a communication with the surrounding country; and yet all have a connexion with each other, and, with all their turnings and intersections, concur at last in the ultimate destination.

§ 226. Of the influence of lapse of time.

The first of the four secondary laws which we shall consider is LAPSE OF TIME. Stated more particularly, the law is this: Our trains of thought and emotion are more or less strongly connected and likely to be restored, according as the lapse of time has been greater or less.

Perhaps no lapse of time, however great, will utterly break the chain of human thought, and cause an entire inability of restoring our former experiences; but it appears evident from observation, as much so as observation renders evident in almost any case, that every additional moment of intervening time weakens, if it do not break and sunder, the bond that connects the present with the past, and diminishes the probability of such a restoration. We remember many incidents, even of a trifling nature, which occurred today or the present week, while those of yesterday or of last week are forgotten. But if the increased period of months and years throws itself between the present time and the date of our past experiences, our ancient joys, regrets, and sufferings, then how unfrequent is their recurrence, and how weak and shadowy they appear! Increase the lapse of time a little further, and a dark cloud rests on that portion of our history; less substantial than a dream, it utterly eludes our search, and becomes to us as if it never had been.

There is, however, an apparent exception to this law which should be mentioned. The associated feelings of old men, which were formed in their youth and the early part of manhood, are more readily revived than those of later origin.—On this state of things in old men, two remarks are to be made. The FIRST is, that the law under consideration fully and unfailingly maintains itself in the case of aged persons, whenever the time is not extended far back. Events which happened but a few hours before are remembered, while there is an utter forgetfulness of those which happened a few weeks or even days before. So far as this, the law operates in old men precisely as in others. The SECOND remark is, that the failure of its operation in respect to the events of youth is caused, not by an actual inability in the secondary law before us to blot out and diminish here as in other cases, but by the greater power of the combined action of the two other laws, viz., Coexistent feeling, and Repetition or habit. Our early life, as a general statement, was the most deeply interesting, and is the most frequently recurred to; and in this way its recollections become so incorporated with the mind as to hold a sort of precedence over our more recent experiences, and thrust them from their proper place.

§ 227. Secondary law of repetition or habit.

Another secondary law is REPETITION; in other words, successions of thought are the more readily suggested in proportion as they are the more frequently renewed. If we experience a feeling once, and only once, we find it difficult to recall it after it has gone from us, but repeated experience increases the probability of its recurring. Every schoolboy who is required to commit to memory, puts this law to the test, and proves it. Having read a sentence a number of times, he finds himself able to repeat it out of book, which he could not do with merely reading it once.

The operation of this law is seen constantly in particular arts and professions. If men be especially trained up to certain trades, arts, or sciences, their associations on those particular subjects, and on everything connected with them, are found to be prompt and decisive. We can but seldom detect any hesitancy or mistake within the circle where their minds have been accustomed to operate, because every thought and process have been recalled and repeated thousands of times. With almost everything they see or hear, there is a train of reflection, connecting it with their peculiar calling, and bringing it within the beaten and consecrated circle. Every hour, unless they guard against it, hastens the process which threatens to cut them off, and insulate them from the great interests of humanity, and to make them wholly professional.

"Still o'er those scenes their memory wakes,
And fondly broods with miser care;

Time but the impression stronger makes,
As streams their channels deeper wear."

§ 228. Of the secondary law of coexistent emotion.

A third secondary law is coexistent emotion.—It may be stated in other words as follows: The probability that our mental states will be recalled by the general laws will in part depend on the depth of feeling, the degree of interest, which accompanied the original experience of them.

Why are bright objects more readily recalled than faint or obscure? It is not merely because they occupied more distinctly our perception, but because they more engaged our attention and interested us, the natural consequence of that greater distinctness. Why do those events in our personal history which were accompanied with great joys and sorrows, stand out like pyramids in our past life, distinct to the eye and immoveable in their position, while others have been swept away and cannot be found? Merely because there were joy and sorrow in the one case, and not at all, or only in a slight degree, in the other; because the sentimentive part of our nature combined itself with the intellectual; the heart gave activity to the operations of the understanding.

We learn from the Bible that the Jews, in their state of exile, could not forget Jerusalem, the beloved and beautiful City. And why not? How did it happen that in their Captivity they sat down by the rivers of Babylon, wept when they remembered Zion, and hung their harps on the willows? It was because Jerusalem was not only an object of thought, but of feeling. They had not only known her gates and fountains, her pleasant dwelling-places and temples, but had loved them. The Holy City was not a lifeless abstraction of the head, but a sacred and delightful image engraven in the heart. And hence it was that, in their solitude and sorrow, she arose and shone before them so distinctly, "the morning star of memory."

§ 229. Original difference in the mental constitution.

The fourth and last secondary law of association is ORIGINAL DIFFERENCE IN THE MENTAL CONSTITUTION.—This Law, it will be noticed, is expressed in the most general terms, and is to be considered, therefore, as applicable both to the Intellectual and the Sentimentive part of man. It requires, accordingly, to be contemplated in two distinct points of view.

The law of original difference in the mental constitution is applicable, in the FIRST place, to the Intellect, properly and distinctively so called; in other words, to the perceiving, comparing, judging, and reasoning part of the soul. That there are differences in men intellectually, it is presumed will hardly be doubted, although this difference is perceptible in different degrees, and in some cases hardly perceptible at all. And these original or constitutional peculiarities reach and affect the associating principle, as well as other departments of intellectual action. The associations of the great mass of mankind (perhaps it may be entirely owing, in some cases, to the accidental circumstance of a want of education and intellectual development) appear to run exclusively in the channel of Contiguity in time and place. They contemplate objects in their nearness and distance, in their familiar and outward exhibitions, without examining closely into analogies and differences, or considering them in the important relation of cause and effect. But not unfrequently we find persons whose minds are differently constructed, who exhibit a higher order of perception. But even in these cases we sometimes detect a striking difference in the application of their intellectual powers. One person, for instance, has from childhood exhibited a remarkable command of the relations and combinations of numbers; another exhibits in like manner an uncommon perception of uses, adaptations, and powers, as they are brought together, and set to work in the mechanic arts; another has the power of generalizing in an uncommon degree, and, having obtained possession of a principle in a particular case, which may appear to others perfectly and irretrievably insulated, he at once extends it to hundreds and thousands of other cases. In no one of these instances does the Associating power operate in precisely the same way, but exhibits in each a new aspect or phasis of action.

It is, perhaps, unnecessary to delay here for the purpose of confirming what has now been said by a reference to the history of individuals. A slight acquaintance with literary history will show that diversities of intellect, such as have been alluded to, and founded, too, in a great degree on peculiarities of the associating principle, have been frequent. How often had the husbandman seen the apple fall to the ground without even asking for the cause? But when Newton saw the fall of an apple, he not only asked for the cause, but, having conjectured it, he at once perceived its applicability to everything in like circumstances around him, to all the descending bodies on the earth's surface. And this was not all. Immediately expanding the operations of the principle which he had detected, from the surface of the earth to the stars of heaven, he showed its universality, and proved that the most distant planet is controlled by the same great law which regulates the particles of dust beneath our feet.—Here was a mind, not merely great by toil, but constitutionally great and inventive; a mind which was regulated in its action, not by the law of mere contiguity in time and place, but by the more effective associating principles of Analogy, and of Cause and Effect.

§ 230. The foregoing law as applicable to the sensibilities.

The law under consideration holds good, in the SECOND place, in respect to original differences of emotion and passion, or, as it is more commonly expressed, of disposition. It will help to make us understood if we allude briefly, in this part of the subject, to two different classes of persons. One of the descriptions of men which we have now in view is composed of those, for such are sometimes found, who are constitutionally of a pensive and melancholy turn. From their earliest life they have shown a fondness for seclusion, in order that they might either commune with the secrets of their own hearts, or hold intercourse, undisturbed by others, with whatever of impressiveness and sublimity is to be found in the works of nature. The other class are naturally of a lively and cheerful temperament. If they delight in nature, it is not in solitude, but in the company of others. While they seldom throw open their hearts for the admission of troubled thoughts, they oppose no obstacle to the entrance of the sweet beams of peace, and joy, and hope.

Now it is beyond question that the primary laws of association are influenced by the constitutional tendencies manifest in these two classes of persons; that is to say, in the minds of two individuals, the one of a cheerful, the other of a melancholy or gloomy disposition, the trains of thought will be very different. This difference is finely illustrated in two beautiful poems of Milton. Prompted by his recollections of Italy, where he had resided in earlier life, and by his admiration of her literature and arts, he gave them the Italian names of L'Allegro and Il Penseroso. L'Allegro, or the cheerful man, finds pleasure and cheerfulness in every object which he beholds; the great sun puts on his amber light, the mower whets his scythe, the milkmaid sings,

> "And every shepherd tells his tale
> Under the hawthorn in the dale."

But the man of a melancholy disposition, Il Penseroso, chooses the evening for his walk, as most suitable to the temper of his mind; he listens from some lonely hillock to the distant curfew, and loves to hear the song of that "sweet bird,

> That shunn'st the noise of folly,
> Most musical, most melancholy."

Further: Our trains of suggested thoughts will be

modified by those temporary feelings which may be regarded as exceptions to the more general character of our dispositions. The cheerful man is not always cheerful, nor is the melancholy man at all times equally sober and contemplative. They are known to exchange characters for short periods, sometimes in consequence of good or ill health, or of happy or adverse fortune, and sometimes for causes which cannot be easily explained. So that our mental states will be found to follow each other with a succession, varying not only with the general character of our temper and dispositions, but with the transitory emotions of the day or hour.

All the laws of association may properly be given here in a condensed view. The PRIMARY or general laws are RESEMBLANCE, CONTRAST, CONTIGUITY in time and place, and CAUSE and EFFECT. Those circumstances which are found particularly to modify and control the action of these are termed SECONDARY laws, and are as follows: Lapse of time, Repetition or habit, Coexistent feeling, and Constitutional difference in mental character.

§ 231. Of associations caused by present objects of perception.

There remains another point of view in which it seems proper that the subject of association should be contemplated before we leave it.—Associated thoughts and emotions, when made to pass through the mind by some sound which the ear has caught, by some object which has met the eye, or any present object of perception whatever, are peculiarly vivid and strong. Associations which do not admit any of our present perceptions as a part of the associated train, cannot but impress us as being in some measure airy and unsubstantial, however distinct. We deeply feel that they are part of the experiences of departed days, and which, in departing from us, have become almost as if they had never been. But let them partake of our present experience, of what we now feel and know to exist, and they seem to gain new strength; the remembrances are not only distinct, but what was airy and unsubstantial fades away, and they have life, and power, and form.

How often, in the wanderings of life, are we led, by some apparently accidental train of thought, to the recollection of the residence of our early years and of the incidents which then occurred! The associations are interesting, but we find it difficult to make them permanent, and they are comparatively faint. But let there be connected with the train of thought the present sound of some musical instrument which we then used to hear, and of our favourite tune, and it will be found that the reality of the tune blends itself with the airy conceptions of the mind, and, while we kindle with an illusive rapture, the whole seems to be real. Some illustrations may tend to make these statements more clear, and to confirm them.

It is related in one of the published Lectures of Dr. Rush, that an old native African was permitted by his master, a number of years since, to go from home in order to see a lion that was conducted as a show through the State of New-Jersey. He no sooner saw him, than he was so transported with joy as to express his emotions by jumping, dancing, and loud acclamations, notwithstanding the torpid habits of mind and body superinduced by half a century of slavery. He had known that animal when a boy in his native country, and the sight of him suddenly revived the memory of his early enjoyments, his native land, his associates, and his freedom.

There is in the same writer another interesting instance of the power of association, in which he himself had a part, and which will be given in his own words.—"During the time I passed at a country-school in Cecil county, in Maryland, I often went on a holyday with my schoolmates to see an eagle's nest, upon the summit of a dead tree in the neighbourhood of the school, during the time of the incubation of that bird. The daughter of the farmer in whose field this tree stood, and with whom I became acquainted, married, and settled in this city about forty years ago. In our occasional interviews, we now and then spoke of the innocent haunts and rural pleasures of our youth, and, among other things, of the eagle's nest in her father's field. A few years ago I was called to visit this woman when she was in the lowest stage of a typhus fever. Upon entering her room, I caught her eye, and, with a cheerful tone of voice, said only, '*The eagle's nest.*' She seized my hand, without being able to speak, and discovered strong emotions of pleasure in her countenance, probably from a sudden association of all her early domestic connexions and enjoyment with the words I had uttered.* From that time she began to recover. She is now living, and seldom fails, when we meet, to salute me with the echo of the 'eagle's nest.'"

§ 232. Causes of increased vividness in these instances.

From such illustrations it would seem to be sufficiently clear that, whenever associated thoughts and emotions are connected with any present perceptions, they are peculiarly strong and vivid. They steal into all the secret chambers of the soul, and, seemingly by some magic power, impart a deep intensity to its feelings, and give to the fleeting world of memory the stability of real existence. There are two causes why such associated feelings should possess more than ordinary strength and vividness.

(1.) The particular train of thought and feeling which is excited in the mind continues longer than in other cases, in consequence of the greater permanency and fixedness of the present objects of perception, which either suggested the train or make a part of it. So long as the lion was permitted to remain in the sight of the aged African, so long without interruption was the series of delightful thoughts kept up within him. The bright images which threw him into such raptures, and awoke stupidity itself, were not fleeting away with every breath, but remained per-

* Rush's Introductory Lectures, lect. xi.

manent.—The sick lady of Philadelphia saw the physician with whom she had been acquainted in the early part of life. By the mention of the eagle's nest he vividly recalled the scenes of those young days. But it was the presence of the person, whose observation had given rise to the train of association, which contributed chiefly to keep it so long in her thoughts. Had it occurred merely from some accidental direction of her own mind, without any present object which had made a part of it, no doubt her sufferings or other circumstances would soon have banished it.

(2.) The second cause of the increased vividness of associations, suggested by a present object of perception or combined with it, is this, viz.: The reality of the thing perceived (we do not profess to assert precisely in what manner it is done) is communicated, in the illusions of the moment, to the thing suggested.—The trees of the desert were the hiding-place of the lion when the African saw him in early life; and now, after the lapse of so many years, he imagines that, in the quickened eye of his mind, he beholds the forests of his native soil, because he has before him the proud and powerful animal that crouched under their shade. And the presence of the monarch of the forest gives a reality not only to woods and deserts, but, by a communication of that which exists to that which is merely suggested, the whole group of his early experiences, of whatever kind, so far as they are recalled, virtually acquire a like truth and reality.

CHAPTER VII.

CASUAL ASSOCIATIONS. (I.) INTELLECTUAL.

§ 233. Association sometimes misleads our judgments.

It seems to be important, in this portion of the history of the mind, to illustrate still further the operations of the great principle of Association. There are some cases where the power of association so misleads us that we cannot easily form a correct judgment of the true nature of things. Every object of thought, in order to be fully understood, ought to be so much in our power that we may examine it separately from all other objects. Whenever, therefore, it happens, from any circumstances, that the power of association so combines one object of thought with another that the object cannot readily be looked at and examined by itself, it so far has the effect to perplex and hinder correct judgment.

It will be found, when we look into our minds, that there exist a few associations or combinations of thought of this kind which are obstinate and almost invincible. To explain the origin, and to correct the erroneous tendencies of all such connexions of thought, although the number of such as we have now in view cannot be large, would occupy us too long. The examination of a few somewhat striking instances will not only throw light on the philosophy of the mind in general, but will be of some practical benefit.—Other instances of CASUAL ASSOCIATION, which have a more intimate connexion with the Sensibilities than with the Intellect, will be more appropriately considered under that head.

§ 234. Casual association in respect to the place of sensation.

One of the casual associations of that extreme kind which we have now especial reference to, concerns the place, or, rather, the supposed place of sensation.—All sensation, it will not be forgotten, is in the mind. Whatever is inanimate or material can of course have no feeling. Nevertheless, if a wound be inflicted on the hand or foot, we seem to experience the sensation of pain in that particular place. When we merely bring the hand in contact with a warm or cold body, we even then assign a local habitation to the subsequent feeling, and it clearly seems to be not in the mind, but in the hand.

This reference of the sensation to the outward organ and place, instead of thinking of it as existing in the soul, is the result of an early and strong association. As the wound in the hand, for instance, is the cause of the painful feeling, the consequence is, that the sensation, and the place whence it arose, constantly go together in our thoughts. The result of this connexion, which has been repeated and continued from our youth up, is, that we find it extremely difficult in later life to separate them, even with the greatest effort. So difficult is it, that a soldier whose arm or leg has been amputated still speaks of feeling pain in those limbs, though they are now, perhaps, buried in the earth or the depths of the sea.—Count Segur, in giving an account of the great battle of Borodino, observes of a certain wounded soldier that he complained of suffering in the limbs which he no longer possessed. And he immediately adds (and there is no question probably as to the fact), that this is a common case with mutilated persons.

Although we are liable in these cases to be led into a mistake, if we do not guard against it with care, it is, perhaps, an obvious remark, that the foundation of this liability to error is laid in our constitution for beneficent ends. It is not ordinarily so important in a practical point of view that we should attend to the internal feeling, as to the external part which is affected. An injury in the external senses, the muscles, or the limbs, if it be not attended to, soon affects other parts of the body, and even life itself. Hence Providence has put us in the way to form this strong and almost unconquerable mental habit, in order to secure protection where it seems to be most urgently and frequently needed.

§ 235. Connexion of our ideas of extension and time.

If we examine carefully our notions of Time, we shall find here also a CASUAL ASSOCIATION of long continuance and of great strength. It is believed to be the fact, that Time, as it exists in the apprehensions of most persons, is regarded as something *extended.* It is not necessary to delay here to undertake a definition of time, to show what it is in the abstract, or to give a history of the notion which we form of it. Taking it for granted that every one knows what is meant when we use that term, we merely assert here, that for some cause or other it is exceedingly difficult to think of it except in the light of a modification of EXTENSION. The correctness of this remark may not, perhaps, appear perfectly obvious at first; but the expressions which we apply to intervals of duration are an evidence of its truth.

We say *before* such a time or *after* such a time, the same as before or after any material object; we speak of a *long* or *short* time with no more hesitation than of a long or short distance, of a long or short bridge, or railway, or any other object of extension. We utter ourselves precisely in the same way we should do if we were certain of having detected some real analogy between the two, between length and shortness in material substances, and what are called length and shortness in time. But it is not too much to say that there is no such analogy, no such similitude; nor is it worth while to anticipate that we shall ever be able to detect such analogy or similitude until we can in practice apply the measures of feet, ells, roods, &c., to hours, and days, and weeks. How then can it be accounted for, that we apply terms nearly in the same way as if this were the case, and as if such measurements could be made?

To this inquiry we are not prepared to return an answer which we can assert to be entirely satisfactory. It is probably only another instance of that early and strong habit which we have all formed, of transferring in our thoughts the material to the immaterial, and of contemplating what is abstract and invisible in the light of what is seen and tangible. Mr. Stewart, however, is more definite in his explanation. He suggests that the strong association of these ideas has most probably arisen in this manner, viz., from our constantly measuring one of these quantities by the other. It is the common method, as is well known, to measure time by motion, and motion is measured by extension. In an hour the hand of a clock moves over a certain space; in two hours over double the space, and so on. And in this way he supposes we may have been gradually led to associate so strongly with the idea of time a conception analogous to that of visible and material length.

No doubt it is convenient to apply the terms "long" and "short," "before" and "after," and others similar, to Time. We could not well dispense with them. But it ought to be remembered, if we would have a right notion of things, that the application of those expressions has arisen either from the mode in which we measure time, or from some other accidental grounds of association; and that time and extension are essentially distinct in their nature.

§ 236. Of high and low notes in music.

We speak of high and low in reference to notes in music, the same as of the high or low position of material bodies. There is supposed to be some analogy between the relation which the notes in the scale of music bear to each other, and the relation of superiority and inferiority in the position of bodies of matter. But it is impossible to prove the existence of such analogy, however generally it may have been supposed; and the supposition itself of its existence has no doubt arisen from a casual association of ideas, which has acquired strength by lapse of time and by repetition.

A proof of this association of ideas being purely accidental is, that an association the very reverse of this was once prevalent.—It is remarked in the preface to Gregory's edition of Euclid's works, that the more ancient Greek writers considered the grave sounds as high, and the acute ones as low. The present mode of speaking on the subject is of more recent origin; but at what time and in what way it was introduced cannot be asserted with confidence. In the preface just referred to, it is, however, observed, that the ancient Greek custom of looking upon the grave sounds as high and the acute as low, precisely the reverse of what is now common, continued down until the time of Boethius. It has been conjectured with some ingenuity, that this connexion or association of thought among the Greeks and Romans, for it was equally prevalent among both, might have been owing to the construction of their musical instruments. The string which sounded the grave, or what we call the low tone, it has been supposed, was placed highest, and that which gave the shrill or acute had the lowest place. If this conjecture could be ascertained to be well founded, it would strikingly show from what very slight causes strong and permanent associations often arise. It is hardly necessary to observe, that it is important to examine the origin and progress of such associations, in order that we may correct those erroneous and illusive notions which will be found to be built upon them.*

§ 237. Connexion of the ideas of extension and colour.

There is no necessary connexion between colour, as the term is commonly employed by philosophers, and extension. The word COLOUR, in its interior or psychical application, properly denotes a sensation in the mind; the word EXTENSION, the quality of an external, material object. There is, therefore, no more natural connexion, and no more analogy between the two, than there is between pain and solidity. And yet it so happens that we never have the sensation or idea of colour without at the same time associating extension with it; we find them, however different they may be in their nature, inseparable in our thoughts. This

* It is not necessary, for any purpose we have in view, here to trace the origin of the association; but it is undoubtedly the fact, that we almost invariably attribute the notion of highness or loftiness to those who excel, or are particularly favored in any respects. We can hardly think of a nobleman, prince, or king, without creating for them an imaginary orbit somewhere in the upper sky, where they revolve far above the heads of ordinary mortals. Hence the expressions High rank, High birth, Elevated genius, Superior talents, &c., and their opposites, Low rank, Inferior genius, and the like.—(See Stewart's Essays, ii., ch. iii. Kames's Criticism, part vii., ch. iv.)

strong association is formed in consequence of our always perceiving extension at the very time in which the sensation of colour is excited in the mind. The perception of the one and the sensation of the other have been so long simultaneous, that we have been gradually drawn into the belief that, on the one hand, all colour has extension, and on the other, all extension has colour. But what we call colour being, in its subjective experience, merely a state of the mind, it is not possible that it should with propriety be predicated of any external, material substances. Nor is it less evident, if colour be merely a sensation or state of the mind, that matter can exist and does exist without it.

But what has been said will not satisfy all the queries which may be started on this point, unless we remark also on the ambiguity in the word COLOUR. The view which has been taken of the connexion between colour and extension is founded on the supposition that color denotes a sensation of the mind, and that merely. It is maintained by some writers, and not without some reason for their opinion, that the word colour has two meanings, and that it is thus generally understood: (1.) It denotes that disposition, or arrangement, or whatever it may be, in the particles of matter, which not only cause the rays of light to be reflected, but to be reflected in different ways; (2.) It denotes that mental sensation which follows when the rays have reached the retina of the eye. When people use the term with this diversity of signification, they can say with truth that external bodies have colour, and also that colour is a sensation of the mind. It may be said also, in the first sense of the term which has been mentioned, that colour has extension, because particles of matter have extension.

§ 238. Tendency of the mind to pass from the sign to the thing signified.

Mr. Stewart gives a reason for our inattention to the internal sensation of colour (or colour considered as an affection of the mind), which is worthy of some notice. The principle, it will be observed, is a general one, applicable to other cases as well as this.—"It is well known," he says, "to be a general law of our constitution, when one thing is destined, either by nature or by convention, to be *the sign* of another, that the mind has a disposition to pass on as rapidly as possible to the thing signified, without dwelling on *the sign* as an object worthy of its attention. The most remarkable of all examples of this occurs in the acquired perceptions of sight, where our estimates of distance are frequently the result of an intellectual process, comparing a variety of different *signs* together, without a possibility on our part, the moment afterward, of recalling one single step of the process to our recollection. Our inattention to the sensations of colour, considered as affections of the Mind or as modifications of our own being, appears to me to be a fact of precisely the same description; for all these sensations were plainly intended by nature to perform the offices of *signs*, indicating to us the figures and distances of things external. Of their essential importance in this point of view, an idea may be formed by supposing for a moment the whole face of nature to exhibit only one uniform colour, without the slightest variety even of light and shade. Is it not self-evident, that, on this supposition, the organ of sight would be entirely useless, inasmuch as it is by the *varieties* of colour alone that the outlines or visible figures of bodies are so defined as to be distinguishable one from another? Nor could the eye in this case give us any information concerning diversities of *distance;* for all the various signs of it enumerated by optical writers presuppose the antecedent recognition of the bodies around us as separate objects of perception. It is not, therefore, surprising, that *signs* so indispensably subservient to the exercise of our noblest sense should cease in early infancy to attract notice as the subjects of our consciousness, and that afterward they should present themselves to the Imagination rather as qualities of Matter than as attributes of Mind."*

§ 239. Whether there be heat in fire, &c.

The questions, whether there be heat in fire, coldness in snow, sweetness in sugar, and the like, seem well suited to the inquisitive and nicely discriminating spirit of the Scholastic ages. Although well adapted to exercise the ingenuity of the Schools, they are far from being without some importance in the more practical philosophy of later times. If these questions concern merely the matter of fact; if the inquiry be, What do people think on these points? it admits of different answers. But this is of less consequence to be known, than to know what is the true view of this subject.

The following, there is much reason to think, is the view which should be taken: If by heat, cold, and taste in bodies we merely mean that there is this or that disposition, or motion, or attraction in the particles, then it must clearly be granted that fire is hot, that snow is cold, and sugar is sweet. But if by heat is understood what one feels on the application of fire to the limbs, or if by sweetness is understood the sensation of taste when a sapid body is applied to the tongue, &c., then fire has no heat, sugar no sweetness, and snow is not cold. These states of the mind can never be transformed into anything material and external. The heat or the cold which I feel, and the different kinds of taste, are sensations in the soul, and nothing else.

§ 240. Whether there be meaning in words.

We say in our common discourse that there is meaning in words, that there is meaning in the printed page of an author; and the language is perhaps sufficiently correct for those occasions on which it is ordinarily employed. We do not deem it necessary to object to the common mode of speaking in this

* Stewart's Historical Dissertation, pt. i., sect. ii., ch. ii.

particular instance, nor to undertake to propose anything better. But there is here an association of ideas similar, both in its nature and its effects, to that existing between extension and colour already remarked upon.

When objects external to us are presented to the sense of sight, there is immediately the sensation of some colour. This sensation we have been so long in the habit of referring to the external object, that we speak and act as if the colour were truly in that object and not in ourselves; in the language of D'Alembert, as if the sensation were transported out of the mind, and spread over the material substance. And it is not until we take some time to reflect, and until we institute a careful examination, that we become satisfied of our error.

In the same way, when we look upon the page of an author, we say it has meaning, or that it is full of thought; whereas, in truth, in consequence of a long-continued and obstinate association, of which we are hardly sensible ourselves, we transport the meaning or thought out of ourselves, and spread it upon that page. The thought or meaning is in ourselves, but is placed by us, through the means of a casual but very strong association, in the written marks which are before us. All the power which the words have results from convention, or, what is the same thing, exists in consequence of certain intellectual habits formed in reference to those words. It is these habits, formed in reference to them, it is this mental correspondence, which gives these characters all their value; and without the mind, which answers to and which interprets them, they could be considered as nothing more than mere black strokes drawn upon white paper, and essentially differing in nothing from the zigzag and unmeaning delineations of a schoolboy on the sand. As all the beautiful varieties of colour do not and cannot have an existence without the mind, which has sensations of them or perceives them, so words are useless, are unmeaning, are nothing without the interpretations of an intellect that has been trained up so as to correspond to them. If it were otherwise, there would be meaning in the unknown inscriptions on the bricks and other fragments of antiquity which are occasionally brought from the banks of the Euphrates; there would be meaning in those hieroglyphic figures on the monuments of Egypt, which have hitherto, or, at least, until a very recent period, eluded the efforts to interpret them; in neither case would they stare upon us with that unintelligent vacancy which has so long characterized them. They are now to a considerable extent without meaning, without life and intelligence, for this reason, and this only, that the minds which once corresponded to them, and which gave them life and intelligence, are no more. By association, therefore, we refer the meaning to the written characters or words, when, in truth, it is in the mind, and there alone.

§ 241. **Benefit of examining such connexions of thought.**

It is of great importance to us to be able to separate ideas which our situation and habits may have intimately combined together. To a person who has this power in a considerable degree, we readily give the credit of possessing a clear and discriminating judgment. And this mental characteristic is of great consequence, not only in pursuing the study of mental philosophy, but in the conduct of life. It is, in particular, directly subservient to the power of reasoning, since all processes of reasoning are made up of successive propositions, the comparison of which implies the exercise of judgment. The associations of thought which have been mentioned in this chapter are so intimate, or, rather, almost indissoluble, that they try and discipline the mind in this respect; they teach it to discriminate. They are worthy to be examined, therefore, and to be understood, not only for the immediate pleasure which they afford in the discovery of our errors, but also because they have the effect of training up one's powers to some good purpose. Let a person be accustomed to making such discriminations as are implied in fully understanding the instances in this chapter, and he acquires a readiness which is not easily outwitted; he trains himself to such a quickness of perception in finding out what truly belongs to an object and what does not, as will not allow him to be imposed upon by that confusion of ideas which in so many cases distorts the judgments of the multitude.

§ 242. Power of the will over mental associations.

In view of what has been said in this and the former chapters, the interesting inquiry naturally arises, What is the degree of influence which we are able to exercise by mere volition or will over associated trains of mental states? In reply to this inquiry, an obvious remark is, that we cannot, by a mere *direct* and positive act of the will, call up or create such associated trains. What has already been said on the subject of laws of association, involves that their appearance and departure depend on other causes than a mere unconditional order or command. Furthermore, such is the nature of the votional faculty, that we evidently can never will the existence of anything without knowing what it is which we will or choose. This, viz., that the act of volition necessarily implies a perceived or known object of volition, requires no further proof than is contained in the proposition itself. Therefore the expressions, to will to have a certain thought or train of thought, clearly imply the present existence of that thought or train; and, consequently, there can be no such thing as calling up or originating thoughts by immediate volition.

To this view of the inefficiency of direct voluntary power in the origination of our associated ideas and feelings, and to the argument in support of it, those mental efforts which we term Recollection or intentional memory have been brought up as an answer. In cases of intentional memory it will be said, an object or event is remembered, or, in other words, an idea or train of ideas is called up, by mere direct volition or choice. To this objection may we not satisfactorily propose this reply? It is evident, before we attempt or make a formal effort to remember the particular circumstances of an event, that the event itself, in general, must have been the object of our attention. There is some particular thing in all cases of intentional remembrance which we wish to call to mind, although we are totally unable to state what it is; but we know that it is somehow connected with some general event which we already have in memory. Now, by revolving in mind the great facts or outlines of that event, it so happens that the particular circumstance which we were in search of is called up. But certainly no one can say that this is done by a direct volition; so far from it, nothing more is wanted to explain it than the common principles of association. This statement is illustrated whenever, in reciting an extract which we had committed to memory, we are at a loss for the beginning of a particular sentence. In such a case we naturally repeat a number of times the concluding words of the preceding sentence, and very soon we recall the sentence which was lost; not, however, by direct volition, but by association.

§ 243. Association controlled by indirect voluntary power.

But we would not be understood to say that the will possesses no influence whatever in the origination and control of trains of thought; its influence is very considerable, although it is not, as far as the *origination* of them is concerned, immediate and direct.—(1.) We have, in the first place, the power of checking or delaying the succession of mental states. This power is always found to exist when the direction of the mind towards a particular subject is attended with those feelings of desire or sentiments of duty which are understood to be prerequisite as a basis or foundation for the acts of the will. We are not, indeed, enabled by our power in this respect either directly to call up or to banish any one or any number of our thoughts. But the consequence is, a variety of trains of thought are suggested, which would not have been suggested had it not been for the circumstance of the original train being delayed.

Thus, in the course of our mental associations, the name of Sir Isaac Newton occurs; we experience a strong emotion of interest; we voluntarily check the current of our thoughts at that name, and we feel and are conscious that we have within us the ability to do so. While we delay upon it, a variety of series of ideas occurs. At one moment we think of eminent mathematicians and astronomers, for he himself was one; at another, we think of those contemporaries who were his particular friends, whatever their rank in science, because they lived at the same time; a moment after, our minds dwell upon some striking incidents in his life, or some marked features in his social or intellectual character; and again, we may be led to think, almost in the same instant, of some proposition or demonstration which had once exercised his patience and skill. In consequence of delaying a few moments on the name, or, rather, on the general idea of the man, these different trains of thought are presented. And this is not all. When these various trains of thought are brought before the mind, we can evidently fix our meditations upon one of them, if we have a desire to do it and choose to do it, in such a way and with such intensity as to result in the dismission and absence of others.—This is one way in which, by an act of volition, we are able to exercise a considerable indirect power in calling up associations, besides a power in regard to them, both direct and indirect, when they are thus brought into existence.

§ 244. Further illustrations of indirect voluntary power.

(2.) We acquire, in the second place, great power over our associations by HABIT; and as no man ordinarily forms such habit without choosing and determining to form it, we have here another instance of the indirect power of volition. By the term Habit, when it is applied to our mental operations, we mean, in particular, that facility or readiness which they acquire by being frequently repeated. The consequence of repetition or frequent practice is, that certain associations are soon very much strengthened, or that a facility in them is acquired. (See § 98.)

Striking instances of the effect of habit have been given in the course of this chapter, although it might perhaps be said, in respect to the results involved in these cases, that they were forced upon us by our particular situation rather than brought about by positive desire and choice. But there are other instances to which this remark is not equally applicable. It is a well-known fact, that almost any person may become a punster or rhymer by taking the pains to form a habit, that is, by increasing the facility of certain associations by frequent repetition. If a person, for instance, makes it a practice to recall words which have a similar sound, this particular form of association will by degrees be so strengthened, that in the end it will be by no means difficult to secure the recurrence of such words. This is the true explanation of the power of rhyming. It is well known that most persons, whether they possess poetical genius or not, may acquire this power by continuing for a length of time their search after words of a like termination.—Again, if a public speaker has taken the pains to fix in his mind certain permanent principles, which are to guide him in the division and subdivision of his discourse, he acquires by practice a great readiness in respect to them, and immediately applies them to every subject of debate. By means of the habit which he has formed, he is not only enabled to resolve a subject into suitable parts, but to pass without hesitation or danger of mistake from one part of it to another; whereas a person who has not formed this habit is perpetually at a loss; he advances and retreats, goes over the ground again and again, and involves himself in inextricable confusion.

These are instances, among many others, of power acquired by Habit; and these habits are formed in obedience to an act of the Will; in other words, in conformity with a purely voluntary determination.—(See, in connexion with this subject, Stewart's Elements, vol. i., ch. vi., pt. 2; Historical Dissertation, pt. i., § ii., ch. 2; Brown's Lectures, xli., xlii., xlix.)

CHAPTER VIII.

MEMORY.

§ 245. Remarks on the general nature of memory.

In the further prosecution of the analysis of the mind, we naturally proceed from association to the examination of the Memory, inasmuch as the latter necessarily implies the antecedent existence of the former, and in its very nature is closely allied to it. In reference to the great question of the Origin of human Knowledge, the Memory, as has already been intimated, is to be considered a source of knowledge rather in its connexion with other mental susceptibilities than *in itself*. It does not appear how we could form any abstract ideas, based upon a knowledge of objects and classes of objects, without the aid of memory; and it is well known that its presence and action is essentially involved in all the exercises of the reasoning power and of the imagination. Without delaying, however, on its connexion with the origin of knowledge, and merely adding that, like association, it may properly be ranked as one of the Auxiliary powers, we shall proceed at once to consider the susceptibility itself, both in its general nature and in some of its peculiarities.

Memory is that power or susceptibility of the mind, by which those conceptions are originated which are modified by a perception of the relation of past time. Such is its definition; and accordingly it is not a simple, but complex power, implying, (1.) a conception of the object, (2.) a perception of the relation of priority in its existence. That is, we not only have a conception of the object, but this conception is attended with the conviction that it underwent the examination of our senses, or was in some way perceived by us at some former period.

When we imagine that we stand in the midst of a forest or on the top of a mountain, but remain safe all the while at our own fireside, these pleasing ideas of woods and of skies painted over us, and of plains under our feet, are mere conceptions. But when with these insulated conceptions we connect the relation of time, and they gleam upon our souls as the woods, plains, and mountains of our youthful days, then those intellectual states, which were before mere conceptions, become REMEMBRANCES. And the power which the mind possesses of originating these latter complex states, standing in the relation of cause to effect, appropriately bears the name of the power or faculty of MEMORY.

§ 246. Of memory as a ground or law of belief.

Memory, as explained in the preceding section, is a ground or law of Belief. So far as we have no particular reason to doubt that the sensations and perceptions in any given case are correctly reported in the remembrance, the latter controls our belief and actions not less than those antecedent states of mind on which it is founded. Such is the constitution of the human mind. (See § 26.)—It will be noticed that, in asserting the natural dependence of belief on memory, we guard it by an express limitation. It is only when we have no reason to doubt of our antecedent experiences being correctly reported in the remembrances, that our reliance on them is of the highest kind. It is the same here as in respect to the Senses and Testimony; we confidently rely on the memory, but are not exempt from some degree of exposure to error from it, although, as in those cases, it is an exposure which we are able to guard against with suitable care and pains. (See § 27, 89.)

In what way and in what particulars this caution and pains are to be exerted, it is not necessary minutely to detail here. One thing, however, seems to be in general certain, that we are not led into error by means of the memory ignorantly, and without the ability to guard against it. Every man knows, from a species of internal feeling, whether there be grounds for doubting his memory in any particular case or not; for the same Consciousness which gives him a knowledge of the *fact* of memory, gives him a knowledge of the *degree* also in which it exists; viz., whether in a high degree or low, whether distinct or obscure. If it be the fact that he finds reason for suspecting its reports, his reliance will either be diminished in proportion to this suspicion, or he will take means, if he be able to, to remove the grounds of such suspicion.

It cannot reasonably be anticipated that any objection will be made to the doctrine of a reliance on memory, with the limitation which has now been mentioned. Without such reliance, our situation would be no better at least than if we had been framed with an utter inability to rely on the Senses or on Testimony; we could hardly sustain an existence; we certainly could not derive anything in aid of that existence from the experience of the past.

§ 247. Of differences in the strength of memory.

The ability to remember is the common privilege of all, and, generally speaking, it is possessed in nearly equal degrees. To each one there is given a sufficient readiness in this respect; his power of remembrance is such as to answer all the ordinary purposes of life. But, although there is in general a nearly equal distribution of this power, we find a few instances of great weakness, and other instances of great strength of memory.

It is related by Seneca of the Roman orator Hortensius, that, after sitting a whole day at a public sale, he gave an account from memory, in the evening, of all things sold, with the prices and the names of the purchasers; and this account, when compared with what had been taken in writing by a notary, was found to be exact in every particular.

The following is an instance of strength of memory somewhat remarkable: An Englishman, at a certain time, came to Frederic the Great of Prussia for the express purpose of giving him an exhibition of his power of recollection. Frederic sent for Voltaire, who read to the king a pretty long poem which he had just finished. The Englishman was present, and was in such a position that he could hear every word of the poem, but was concealed from Voltaire's notice. After the reading of the poem was finished, Frederic observed to the author that the production could not be an original one, as there was a foreign gentleman present who could recite every word of it. Voltaire listened with amazement to the stranger, as he repeated word for word the poem which he had been at so much pains in composing; and, giving way to a momentary freak of passion, he tore the manuscript in pieces. A statement was then made to him of the circumstances under which the Englishman became acquainted with his poem, which had the effect to mitigate his anger, and he was very willing to do penance for the suddenness of his passion by copying down the work from a second repetition of it by the stranger, who was able to go through with it as before.

A considerable number of instances of this description are found in the recorded accounts of various individuals, but they must be considered as exceptions to the general features of the human mind, the existence of which it is difficult to explain on any known principles. They are probably original and constitutional traits; and, if such be the case, they necessarily preclude any explanation further than what is involved in the mere statement of that fact. There are, however, some diversities and peculiarities of memory, less striking, perhaps, than those just referred to, which admit a more detailed notice.

§ 248. Of circumstantial memory, or that species of memory which is based on the relations of contiguity in time and place.

There is a species of memory more than usually obvious and outward in its character, which is based essentially upon the relations of Contiguity in time and place.—In the explanation of this form or species of memory, it may be proper to recur a moment to the explanations on the general nature of memory which have already been given. It will be kept in mind that our remembrances, considered as results of the exercise of the power of memory, are merely conceptions, modified by a perception of the relation of past time. Removing, then, the modification of past time, and the remaining element of our remembrances will be conceptions merely. Our conceptions, it will be recollected, cannot be called up by a mere voluntary effort, because to will the existence of a conception necessarily implies the actual existence of the conception already in the mind. They arise in the mind, therefore, in obedience to the influence of some of those principles of ASSOCIATION which have already been considered. And Memory, accordingly, will assume a peculiarity of aspect corresponding to the associating principle which predominates. If it be based, for instance, on the law of Contiguity, as it will deal chiefly with mere facts, and their outward incidents and circumstances, without entering deeply into their interior nature, it will be what may be described, not merely as an obvious and practical, but, in particular, as a *circumstantial* memory. If it be based chiefly on the other principles, it may be expected to exhibit a less easy and flexible, a less minute and specific, but a more philosophical character.

That species of memory which is founded chiefly on the law of contiguity, and which is distinguished by its specificalness or circumstantiality, will be found to prevail especially among uneducated people, not merely artisans and other labouring classes, but among all those, in whatever situation of life, who have either not possessed, or, possessing, have not employed, the means of intellectual culture. Every one must have recollected instances of the great readiness exhibited by these persons in their recollection of facts, places, times, names, specific arrangements in dress and in buildings, traditions, and local incidents. In their narrations, for instance, of what has come within their knowledge, they will, in general, be bound to specify the time of events; not merely an indefinite or approximated time, but the identical year, and month, and day, and hour. In their description of persons and places, and in their account of the dress and equipage of persons, and of the localities and incidents of places, they are found to be no less particular.—When we assert, however, that this species of memory, which, from the peculiar aspect it exhibits, may conveniently be designated as CIRCUMSTANTIAL memory, is based upon the principle of Contiguity, we do not mean to intimate that its possessors are naturally destitute of the other associating principles, or that they necessarily possess them in a much lower degree than others. As compared with the principle of Contiguity, the principles of Resemblance or Analogy, of Contrast, and of Cause and Effect, appear to be more remote and inward, and less accessible by familiar and outward influences. Accordingly, as a general statement, they imply, in their exercise, a greater degree of mental developement. And hence it naturally happens, that those persons who have not possessed or have not employed the means of this developement, even if they are possessed of the principles themselves, avail themselves of those more obvious and easy helps to memory which nature has placed within their reach. In other words, it is almost invariably the case, that they aim to strengthen their recollections of facts and events, by associating them with those things which happened at the same time, or were proximate in position. And having, by almost constant exercise, greatly strengthened the tendency to those associations which exist in consequence of mere contiguity, they can readily tell you not only the precise *place* where anything has happened, but almost everything which has happened in the immediate neighbourhood; not only the *time* when the event occurred, but many other things which occurred about the same period; not only the *person*, but numberless particularities of dress, form, and position.

§ 249. Illustrations of specific or circumstantial memory.

The great masters of human nature (Shakspeare among others) have occasionally indicated their knowledge of this species of memory. Mrs. Quickly, in reminding Falstaff of his promise of marriage, discovers her readiness of recollection in the specification of the great variety of circumstances under which the promise was made. Her recollection in the case was not a mere general remembrance of the solitary fact, but was, in the manner of a witness in a court of justice, circumstantial.—"Thou didst swear to me on a parcel-gilt goblet, sitting in my Dolphin chamber, at the round table, by a sea-coal fire, on Wednesday in Whitsun week, when the prince broke thy head for likening him to a singing man of Windsor."—The coachman in Cornelius Scriblerus gives an account of what he had seen in Bear Garden: "Two men fought for a prize; one was a fair man, a sergeant in the Guards; the other black, a butcher; the sergeant had red trousers, the butcher blue; they fought upon a stage about four o'clock, and the sergeant wounded the butcher in the leg."

"In a certain village of Estremadura," says the humble squire of the Knight of La Mancha, "there lived a certain goat-shepherd. I mean one that keeps goats; and this shepherd or goatherd, as the story goes, was called Lope Ruyz; and it came to pass that this Lope Ruyz fell in love with a shepherdess, whose name was Torralva; which shepherdess, whose name was Torralva, was the daughter of a rich herdsman; and this rich herdsman," &c. Don Quixote took exception to Sancho's telling the story with so much particularity; but he frankly and honestly replied, that all the people in his country told stories in that manner, and he must tell it so, or not tell it at all.

§ 250. Of philosophic memory, or that species of memory which is based on other relations than those of contiguity.

There is another species of memory, clearly distinguishable from the CIRCUMSTANTIAL memory, which may be described as the Philosophic. This form of memory, relying but seldom on the aids of mere Contiguity, is sustained chiefly by the relations of Resemblance, Contrast, and Cause and Effect. The circumstantial memory, which deals almost exclusively with minute particulars, and especially with those which are accessible by the outward senses, admirably answers the purpose of those persons in whom it is commonly found. But mere contiguity in time and place, which is almost the sole principle that binds together facts and events in the recollection of those whose powers are but imperfectly developed, possesses comparatively little value in the estimation of the philosopher. He looks more deeply into the nature of things. Bestowing but slight attention on what is purely outward and incidental, he detects with a discriminating eye the analogies and oppositions, the causes and consequences of events. It would seem that the celebrated Montaigne was destitute, perhaps in a more than common degree, of that form of reminiscence which we have proposed to designate as the circumstantial memory. He says on a certain occasion of himself, "I am forced to call my servants by the names of their employments, or of the countries where they were born, for I can hardly remember their proper names; and, if I should live long, I question whether I should remember my own name." But it does not appear, notwithstanding his inability to remember names and insulated facts, especially if they related to the occurrences of common life, that he had much reason to complain of an absolute want of memory. His writings indicate his cast of mind, that he was reflective and speculative; and he expressly gives us to understand, that he was much more interested in the study of the principles of human nature than of outward objects. Accordingly, the result was such as might be expected, that his memory was rather philosophical than circumstantial, and more tenacious of general principles than of specific facts.

A man, whose perceptions are naturally philosophic, and whose remembrances consequently take the same turn, may not be able to make so rapid and striking advances in all branches of knowledge as a person of different intellectual bias. Almost every department of science presents itself to the student's notice under two forms, the practical and theoretical; its facts and its rules of proceeding on the one hand, and its principles on the other. The circumstantial memory rapidly embraces the practical part, seizing its facts and enunciating its rules with a promptness of movement and a show of power which throws the philosophic memory quite into the shade. But it is otherwise when they advance into the less obvious and showy, but more fertile region of analogies, classification, and principles.—On this topic Mr. Stewart has some pertinent remarks. "A man destitute of genius [that is to say, in this connexion, of a naturally philosophic turn of mind], may, with little effort, treasure up in his memory a number of particulars in chemistry or natural history, which he refers to no principle, and from which he deduces no conclusion; and from his facility in acquiring this stock of information, may flatter himself with the belief that he possesses a natural taste for these branches of knowledge. But they who are really destined to extend the boundaries of science, when they first enter on new pursuits, feel their attention distracted and their memory overloaded with facts, among which they can trace no relation, and are sometimes apt to despair entirely of their future progress. In due time, however, their superiority appears, and arises in part from that very dissatisfaction which they at first experienced, and which does not cease to stimulate their inquiries, till they are enabled to trace, amid a chaos of apparently unconnected materials, that simplicity and beauty which always characterize the operations of nature."

§ 251. Further illustrations of philosophic memory.

Mr. Stewart pursues this train of remark further, maintaining, as a general thing, that a man of genius has his knowledge less at command than those who are possessed of an inferior degree of originality, and particularly in respect to those subjects on which he has found his originality and invention most fertile. And in this connexion he mentions the case of Sir Isaac Newton in terms as follows: "Sir Isaac Newton (as we are told by Dr. Pemberton) was often at a loss when the conversation turned on his own discoveries. It is probable that they made but a slight impression on his mind, and that a consciousness of his inventive powers prevented him from taking much pains to treasure them up in his memory.—Men of little ingenuity seldom forget the ideas they acquire, because they know that, when an occasion occurs for applying their knowledge to use, they must trust to memory and not to invention. Explain an arithmetical rule to a person of common understanding who is unacquainted with the principles of the science; he will soon get the rule by heart, and become dexterous in the application of it. Another, of more ingenuity, will examine the principle of the rule before he applies it to use, and will scarcely take the trouble to commit to memory a process which he knows he can at any time, with a little reflection, recover. The consequence will be, that, in the practice of calculation, he will appear more slow and hesitating than if he followed the received rules of arithmetic without reflection or reasoning.

"Something of the same kind happens every day in conversation. By far the greater part of the opinions we announce in it are not the immediate result of reasoning on the spot, but have been previously formed in the closet, or, perhaps, have been adopted implicitly on the authority of others. The promptitude, therefore, with which a man decides in ordinary discourse, is not a certain test of the quickness of his apprehension, as it may perhaps arise from those uncommon efforts to furnish the memory with acquired knowledge, by which men of slow parts endeavour to compensate for their want of invention; while, on the other hand, it is possible that a consciousness of originality may give rise to a manner apparently embarrassed, by leading the person who feels it to trust too much to extempore exertions."

§ 252. Of that species of memory called intentional recollection.

There is a species of exercise of the memory, known as INTENTIONAL RECOLLECTION, the explanation of which renders it proper briefly to recur again to the nature of memory in general.—The definition of MEMORY which has been given is, that it is the power or susceptibility of the mind by which those conceptions are originated, which are modified by the perception of the relation of past time. This definition closely connects memory with Association; at least, without association memory could not exist. And we have here a good illustration of what has already been intimated, that in the study of the mind it is of great importance to arrange and consider its separate powers in their natural place and order, because they thus mutually illustrate and explain each other. Now it will be recollected that our trains of associated thought are not, in the strict sense, voluntary; that is, are not *directly* under the control of the WILL. They come and depart (we speak now exclusively of their *origination*) without its being possible for us to exercise anything more than an INDIRECT power over them. (See § 242.) It follows, from these facts, that our remembrances also, which may be regarded in part as merely associated trains, are not, in the strict sense, voluntary; or, in other words, it is impossible for us to remember in consequence of merely choosing to remember. To will or to choose to remember anything implies that the thing in question is already in the mind; and hence there is not only an impossibility resulting from the nature of the mind, but also an absurdity in the idea of calling up thought by a mere direct volition. Our chief power, therefore, in quickening and strengthening the memory, will be found to consist in our skill in applying and modifying the various principles or laws of association. And this brings us to an explanation of what is called INTENTIONAL MEMORY or RECOLLECTION; a subject which was partly illustrated in the section above referred to.

Whenever we put forth an exercise of intentional memory, or make a formal attempt to remember some circumstance, it is evident that the event in general, of which the circumstance, when recalled, will be found to be a part, must have previously been an object of attention. That is, we remember the great outlines of some story, but cannot, in the first instance, give a complete account of it, which we wish to do. We make an effort to recall the circumstances not remembered in two ways.—We may, in the *first* place, form different suppositions, and see which agrees best with the general outlines; the general features or outlines of the subject being detained before us, with a considerable degree of permanency, by means of some feeling of desire or interest. This method of restoring thoughts is rather an inference of reasoning than a genuine exercise of memory.

We may, in the *second* place, merely delay upon those thoughts which we already hold possession of, and revolve them in our minds, until, aided by some principle of association, we are able to lay hold of the particular ideas for which we were searching. Thus, when we endeavour to recite what we had previously committed to memory, but are at a loss for a particular passage, we repeat a number of times the concluding words of the preceding sentence. In this way the sentence which was forgotten is very frequently recalled.

§ 253. Instance illustrative of the preceding.

The subject of the preceding section will perhaps be more distinctly understood in connexion with the following illustration: Dr. Beattie informs us that he was himself acquainted with a clergyman, who, on being attacked with a fit of apoplexy, was found to have forgotten all the transactions of the four years immediately preceding the attack. And yet he remembered as well as ever what had happened before that period. The newspapers which were printed during the period mentioned were read with interest, and afforded him a great deal of amusement, being entirely new to him. It is further stated, that this individual recovered by degrees all he had lost; so as, after a while, to have nearly or quite as full a remembrance of that period as others. In this instance the power of the principles of association appears to have been at first completely prostrated by the disease, without any prospect of their being again brought into action, except by some assistance afforded them. This assistance, no doubt, was conversation, the renewed notice of various external objects addressed to the senses, and reading. By reading old newspapers, and by conversation in particular, he occasionally fell upon ideas which he had not only been possessed of before, but which had been associated with other ideas, forming originally distinct and condensed trains of thought. And thus whole series were restored.—Other series, again, were recovered by applying the methods of INTENTIONAL RECOLLECTION; that is, by forming suppositions and comparing them with the ideas already recovered, or by voluntarily delaying upon and revolving in mind such trains as were restored, and thus rousing up others. Such we can hardly doubt to have been, in the main, the process by which the person of whom we are speaking recovered the knowledge he had lost.

These views, in addition to what has now been said, may be illustrated also by what we sometimes observe in old men. Question them as to the events of early life, and at times they will be unable to give any answer whatever. But, whenever you mention some prominent incident of their young days, or perhaps some friend on whom many associations have gathered, it will often be found that their memory revives, and that they are able to state many things, in respect to which they were previously silent.

§ 254. Remarks on the memory of the aged.

In noticing the interesting aspects which the memory presents to our consideration, it may be proper to delay a moment on the memory of the aged. And here the leading remark is, that a weakness of memory, a slowness and inability of recollection, exists in such persons. This weakness of remembrance, which is so frequently observed in men of advanced age, appears to be owing to two causes, viz., the impaired state of the organs of perception, and a defect of attention.

(1.) Their organs of external perception are impaired.—We find it difficult, in consequence of the failure of their sense of hearing, to converse with people advanced in years, and it requires a great effort, both on our part and theirs, to make them understand what we say. The most conclusive arguments, and flashes of wit, and rich strains of music, have in a great measure ceased to attract their notice. —There is a like failure of the sense of seeing also. They no longer take pleasure in the delightful aspects of creation. The waving forest, the blooming field, the gay beams of the sun, all the charming varieties of nature, although they have not ceased to have charms for others, have but little or none for them. The natural and necessary consequence of this state of things is, that the ideas, which are let in by the senses, make but a very feeble impression, and are almost immediately erased from the mind.

(2.) The second cause of the weakness of memory, of which old people complain, is a defect in attention. —That mental state to which we give the name of Attention, always implies, in a greater or less degree, an emotion of interest; and, without some feeling of this kind, it does not well appear how it could exist. But the world (including in the term what is beautiful in nature, and what is important in the duties and callings of life) has at last ceased to excite the emotions which it formerly awakened. The aged are like the prisoner, released in the period of the French Revolution from the Bastile; they find themselves, as it were, in a new creation, which passes before them with great indistinctness, and with which they feel but little sympathy. As their organs of external perception have failed them, and as there has also been a defect of attention, the memory, as a natural consequence, has become broken and powerless.

It should, however, be remarked here, that, notwithstanding what has been said, aged people often recall, with great readiness and precision, the feelings and the incidents of their youth. The explanation of this striking trait in the memory of the aged, which we have already had occasion to notice in one of the chapters on Association, seems to be this.—As a general statement, our early feelings and associations are the *strongest.* That they should be so is not strange, since we have then entered on a state of things which, in its essential features, is new, and which, in all its diversities of duty, and pleasure, and danger, attracts and excites us by continual novelty. Who can forget the plains where he wandered in early life? Who can erase from his recollection the associates of those days of wonder, activity, and hope? Who can obliterate from his heart his youthful toils, his sufferings, and his joys?—These things remain, while others vanish. Such feelings, so deeply fixed in the mind, and bound together and made permanent by the strength of a mutual association, are frequently recalled; they recur to the soul in the activity and bustle of life, and in those more favoured moments when it is given up to silent and solemn meditations. The effect of this frequent recurrence can easily be imagined. The early impressions which are the subjects of such recurrence, become in time, if one may be allowed the expression, a part of the mind itself; they seem to be woven into its existence. Hence old men, who have no eye and no hearing for the events that are passing around them, repeat, with the greatest animation, the stories of scenes, and actions, and friendships of fifty years ago.

§ 255. On the compatibility of strong memory and good judgment.

It has sometimes been a question of considerable interest, whether the possession of a remarkably strong memory is not inconsistent with entire soundness of judgment. This question has perhaps been suggested by the fact that, in some instances, idiots, and other persons not much above the condition of idiocy, have been remarkable for memory.—"I knew a fool," says a recent writer, "who was placed under the charge of a clergyman in the country, as being utterly incapable of conducting himself in ordinary matters (he was a young man of fortune, and did not need to work, except for his amusement), and yet he could repeat every word of the clergyman's sermon, tell how many people were in the church, how any one that sat in a pew named to him was dressed, and who did or did not contribute to the poor. He could do that for any Sunday if you gave him any hint of it; last week or last year was all the same to him. His memory was, in short, as perfect as memory could be; but then he had no judgment in the using of it; and so, when in company, it often made him seem, and not unfrequently made other people feel, very ridiculous."*

Throwing out of the question cases of original malformation, such as idiocies, which properly have no place in it, it may be said without any hesitation that the connexion between a strong memory and a weak judgment is not necessary, but merely accidental; that is, is not the constitution of nature, but, in general, the result of circumstances. As it is an incidental state

* Mudie's Popular Guide, sect. 1.

of things, and not anything essential and permanent in our mental structure, we must look for its appropriate cause in erroneous mental discipline.—It may well be supposed that those who possess strong memories are not insensible of their superiority in this respect; and the approbation which they have received in consequence of it, encourages them to treasure up a dry collection of all facts which will in any way bear repetition. Dates, names, genealogies, places, local incidents, traditional anecdotes, are all seized and retained with peculiar avidity. But, too much intent upon outward incidents, the mere dates, names, and forms of things, such persons fail to inquire into their true nature; they neglect other and more important forms of mental discipline, and thus justly sustain the reputation of possessing a showy rather than discriminating and sound knowledge. In instances of this description, the relations by which the suggested trains of thought are associated are the more slight and obvious ones, such as of time and place. But there are some exceptions to this unwise course; individuals may be found, who, with astonishing ability to recall the most unimportant incidents of daily occurrence, as well as the dry details of historical facts, combine the far more enviable ability of discriminating the true differences of things, of combining means for the attainment of ends, and of rightly estimating evidence in its various applications; traits of mind which are certainly to be included among the characteristics of sound judgment.

§ 256. Marks of a good memory.

The great purpose to which the faculty of memory is subservient is to enable us to retain the knowledge which we have from our experiences for future use. The prominent marks of a good memory, therefore, are these two, viz., tenacity in retaining ideas, and readiness in bringing them forward on necessary occasions.

First: of tenacity or power of retaining ideas.—

The impressions which are made on some minds are durable. They are like channels worn away in stone, and names engraven in monumental marble, which defy the operation of the ordinary causes of decay, and withstand even the defacing touch of time. But other memories, which at first seemed to grasp as much, are destitute of this power of retention. The inscriptions made upon them are like characters written on the sand, which the first breath of wind covers over, or like figures on a bank of snow, which the sun shines upon and melts. The inferiority of the latter description of memory to the former must be obvious; so much so as to require no comment. A memory whose power of retaining is greatly diminished, of course loses a great part of its value.

SECOND: of readiness or facility in bringing forward what is remembered.—Some persons who cannot be supposed to be deficient in tenacity of remembrance, appear to fail in a confident and prompt command of what they remember. Some mistake has been committed in the arrangement of their knowledge; there has been some defect in the mental discipline; or for some other cause, whatever it may be, they often discover perplexity, and remember slowly and indistinctly. This is a great practical evil, which not only ought to be, but which can, in a great degree, be guarded against.

It is true that so great readiness of memory cannot rationally be expected in men of philosophic minds as others, for the reason that they pay but little or no attention to particular facts, except for the purpose of deducing from them general principles. But it is no less true, that when this want of readiness is such as to cause a considerable degree of perplexity, it must be regarded a great mental defect. And, for the same reason, a prompt command of knowledge is to be regarded a mental excellence.

§ 257. Directions or rules for the improvement of the memory.

In whatever point of view the memory may be contemplated, it must be admitted that it is a faculty always securing to us inestimable benefits. For the purpose of securing the most efficient action of this valuable faculty, and particularly that tenacity and readiness which have been spoken of, the following directions may be found worthy of attention.

(I.) *Never be satisfied with a partial or half acquaintance with things.*—There is no less a tendency to intellectual than to bodily inactivity; students, in order to avoid intellectual toil, are too much inclined to pass on in a hurried and careless manner. This is injurious to the memory. "Nothing," says Dugald Stewart, "has such a tendency to weaken, not only the powers of invention, but the intellectual powers in general, as a habit of extensive and various reading without reflection." Always make it a rule fully to understand what is gone over. Those who are determined to grapple with the subject in hand, whatever may be its nature, and to become master of it, soon feel a great interest; truths which were at first obscure, become clear and familiar. The consequence of this increased clearness and interest is an increase of attention; and the natural result of this is, that the truths are very strongly fixed in the memory.

(II.) *We are to refer our knowledge as much as possible to general principles.*—To refer our knowledge to general principles is to classify it; and this is perhaps the best mode of classification. If a lawyer or merchant were to throw all their papers together promiscuously, they could not calculate on much readiness in finding what they might at any time want. If a man of letters were to record in a commonplace book all the ideas and facts which occurred to him, without any method, he would experience the greatest difficulty in applying them to use. It is the same with a memory where there is no classification. Whoever fixes upon some general principle, whether political, literary, or philosophical, and collects facts in illustration of it, will find no difficulty in remembering them, however numerous; when, without such general principles, the recollection of them would have been extremely burdensome.

(III.) *Consider the nature of the study, and make use of those helps which are thus afforded.*—This rule may be illustrated by the mention of some departments of science. Thus, in acquiring a knowledge of geography, the study is to be pursued, as much as possible, with the aid of good globes, charts, and maps. It requires a great effort of memory, and generally an unsuccessful one, to recollect the relative extent and situation of places, the numerous physical and political divisions of the earth, from the book. The advantages of studying geography with maps, globes, &c., are two. (1.) The form, relative situation, and extent of countries become in this case ideas, or, rather, conceptions of *sight;* such conceptions (§ 115) are very vivid, and are more easily recalled to remembrance than others.

(2.) Our remembrances are assisted by the law of contiguity in place (§ 223), which is known to be one of the most efficient aids. When we have once, from having a map or globe before us, formed an acquaintance with the general visible appearance of an island, a gulf, an ocean, or a continent, nothing is more easy than to remember the subordinate divisions or parts. Whenever we have examined and fixed in our minds the general appearance or outlines of a particular country, we do not easily forget the situation of those countries which are contiguous.

We find another illustration of this rule in the reading of history.—There is such a multitude of facts in historical writings, that to endeavour to remember them all is fruitless; and if it could be done, would be of very small advantage. Hence, in reading the history of any country, fix upon two or three of the most interesting epochs; make them the subject of particular attention; learn the spirit of the age, and the private life and fortunes of prominent individuals; in a word, study these periods not only as annalists, but as philosophers. When they are thus studied, the mind can hardly fail to retain them; they will be a sort of landmarks; and all the other events in the history of the country, before and afterward, will naturally arrange themselves in reference to them. The memory will strongly seize the prominent periods, in consequence of the great interest felt in them; and the less important parts of the history of the country will be likely to be retained, so far as is necessary, by the aid of the principle of contiguity, and without giving them great attention.—Further, historical charts or genealogical trees of history are of some assistance for a similar reason that maps and globes are in geography.

This rule for strengthening the memory will apply also to the more abstract sciences.—"In every science," says Stewart (Elements, ch. vi., § 3), "the ideas, about which it is peculiarly conversant are connected together by some associating principle; in one science, for instance, by associations founded on the relation of cause and effect; in another, by the associations founded on the necessary relations of mathematical truths."

§ 258. Further directions for the improvement of the memory.

(IV.) *The order in which things are laid up in the memory should be the order of nature.*—In nature everything has its appropriate place, connexions, and relations. Nothing is insulated, and wholly cut off, as it were, from everything else; but whatever exists or takes place falls naturally into its allotted position within the great sphere of creation and events. Hence the rule, that knowledge, as far forth as possible, should exist mentally or subjectively in the same order as the corresponding objective reality exists. The laws of the mind will be found in their operation to act in harmony with the laws of external nature. They are, in some sense, the counterparts of each other. We might illustrate the benefits of the application of this rule by referring to almost any well-digested scientific article, or historical narration, or poem. But perhaps its full import will be more readily understood by an instance of its utter violation.

A person was one day boasting, in the presence of Foote the comedian, of the wonderful facility with which he could commit anything to memory, when the modern Aristophanes said he would write down a dozen lines in prose which he could not commit to memory in as many minutes. The man of great memory accepted the challenge; a wager was laid, and Foote produced the following.—"So she went into the garden to cut a cabbage-leaf to make an apple pie; and at the same time a great she-bear coming up the street, pops its head into the shop. What, no soap? So he died, and she very imprudently married the barber; and there were present the Picininnies, and the Joblillies, and the Garyulies, and the grand Panjandrum himself, with the little round button at the top; and they all fell to playing catch as catch can, till the gunpowder ran out of the heels of their boots."—The story adds that Foote won the wager. And it is very evident that statements of this description, utterly disregarding the order of nature and events, must defy, if carried to any great length, the strongest memory.

(V.) *The memory may be strengthened by exercise.*—Our minds, when left to sloth and inactivity, lose their vigour; but when they are kept in exercise, and, after performing what was before them, are tasked with new requisitions, it is not easy to assign limits to their ability. This seems to be a general and ultimate law of our nature. It is applicable equally to every original susceptibility, and to every combination of mental action. In repeated instances we have had occasion to refer to its results, both on the body and the mind. The power of perception is found to acquire strength and acuteness by exercise. There are habits of conception and of association, as well as of perception; and we shall be able to detect the existence and operation of the same great principle when we come to speak of reasoning and imagination. As this principle applies equally to the memory, we are able to secure its beneficial results by practising that repetition or exercise on which it is founded.

§ 259. Of observance of the truth in connexion with memory.

Another help to the memory, which has seldom been noticed, and certainly not so much as its importance demands, is the conscientious and strict observance of the truth.—It will be found, on inquiry, that those who are scrupulous in this respect will be more prompt and exact in their recollections, within the sphere of what they undertake to remember, than others. A man of this description may possibly not remember so *much* as others; for the same conscientiousness which is the basis of his veracity, would instinctively teach him to reject from his intellectual storehouse a great deal of worthless trash. But within the limits which, for good reasons, undoubtedly, he sets to his recollections, he will be much more exact, much more to be relied on, provided there is no original or constitutional ground of difference. It has been suggested in regard to Dr. Johnson, that his rigid attention to veracity, his conscientious determination to be exact in his statements, was the reason, in a considerable degree, that his memory was so remarkably tenacious and minute. And the suggestion is based in sound philosophy. If a man's deep and conscientious regard for the truth be such that he cannot, consistently with the requisitions of his moral nature, repeat to others mere vagueness and uncertainties, he will naturally give such strict and serious attention to the present objects of inquiry and knowledge, that they will remain in his memory afterward with remarkable distinctness and permanency.

§ 260. Of committing to writing as a means of aiding memory.

Among other means of aiding the memory, it is often recommended to commit to writing the knowledge which we acquire. This practice, if not carried too far, so as greatly to supersede the direct exercise of the memory, is attended with certain advantages, which justify an occasional resorting to it.—(1.) Often, in the course of a person's opportunities of reading and of intercourse with the world, he becomes acquainted with facts with which he is unwilling to burden his memory, and which he is equally unwilling to lose. Here it is proper to resort to this method, which at the same time leaves the memory free for other subjects, and retains what may be found at some future period important.—(2.) In the progress of a person's experience and investigations, he arrives at certain important conclusions; for in literature, and in the departments of science, and in the philosophy of human conduct, there are certain principles to be ascertained, which hold a first rank, and exert their influence on all collateral inquiries. The means or process by which he arrived at them is permitted to fade away from the mind, because he has no desire to remember it. But it may often be found desirable to call in the aid of writing, in order to prevent the possibility of a like result with those important principles which he has established with no small labour. These occasional records will not only secure the great truths he has gained, but will furnish landmarks of the gradual developement of the mind, and profitable intimations concerning the laws by which it is governed.

§ 261. Of mnemonics or systems of artificial memory.

We shall conclude these suggestions on the subject of aiding and improving the memory, by a remark or two on the method or system of MNEMONICS.—By a system of mnemonics or of artificial memory is meant "a method of connecting in the mind things difficult to be remembered with things easily remembered, so as to enable it to retain and recollect the former by means of the latter."—The things easy to be remembered are short and simple verses, or the walls and compartments of a room, or grotesque pictures, and the like. Important facts are to be connected with these, in the expectation that the former will be remembered because the latter are.

It is no doubt possible to give a temporary aid to the memory by such arbitrary arrangements; by associating our ideas with a set of sounds, places, and images. Such assistance may occasionally be of some advantage to public speakers, and to persons who are called to remember a large number of insulated facts. But there is reason to fear that the benefit is more than counterbalanced by burdening and distracting the memory with what is allowedly frivolous and perhaps ridiculous. However this may be, it is generally admitted to be the fact, that those systems that are proposed for use at the present time are too complicated for plans which profess to render the acquisition of knowledge more easy. They can never be adopted into general use unless they are rendered more simple; nor do we apprehend that a person who follows the rules for strengthening and applying the memory, which have been laid down in this chapter, will stand greatly in need of any other helps in recollecting most things that will be useful and important.

CHAPTER IX.

DURATION OF MEMORY.

§ 262. Restoration of thoughts and feelings supposed to be forgotten.

Before quitting the subject of Memory, there is another point of view, not wholly wanting in interest, in which it is susceptible of being considered; and that is the permanency or duration of its power to call up its past experiences. It is said to have been an opinion of Lord Bacon, that no thoughts are lost, that they continue virtually to exist, and that the soul possesses within itself laws which, whenever fully brought into action, will be found capable of producing the prompt and perfect restoration of the collected acts and feelings of its whole past existence.

This opinion, which other able writers have fallen

in with, is clearly worthy of examination, especially when we consider that it has a practical bearing, and involves important moral and religious consequences. Some one will perhaps inquire, is it possible, is it in the nature of things, that we should be able to recall the million of little acts and feelings which have transpired in the whole course of our lives? Let such an inquirer be induced to consider, in the first place, that the memory has its fixed laws, in virtue of which the mental exercises are recalled; and that there can be found no direct and satisfactory proof of such laws ever wholly ceasing to exist. That the operation of those laws appears to be weakened, and is in fact weakened, by lapse of time, is admitted; but, while the frequency, promptness, and strength of their action may be diminished in any assignable degree, the laws themselves yet remain. This is the view of the subject which at first obviously and plainly presents itself, and, we may venture to add, is recommended by common experience.

It is known to every one that thoughts and feelings sometimes unexpectedly recur which had slumbered in forgetfulness for years. Days, and months, and years have rolled on; new scenes and situations occupy us; and all we felt, and saw, and experienced in those former days and years appears to be clothed in impenetrable darkness. But suddenly some unexpected event, the sight of a waterfall, of a forest, of a house, a peculiarly pleasant or gloomy day, a mere change of countenance, a word, almost anything we can imagine, arouses the soul, and gives a new and vigorous turn to its meditations. At such a moment we are astonished at the novel revelations which are made, the recollections which are called forth, the resurrections of withered hopes and perished sorrows, of scenes and companionships, that seemed to be utterly lost.

> "Lulled in the countless chambers of the brain,
> Our thoughts are linked by many a hidden chain.
> Awake but one, and lo, what myriads rise!
> Each stamps its image as the other flies."

This is, perhaps, a faint exhibition of that perfect restoration of thought which Bacon and other philosophic minds have supposed to be possible. But, if the statement be correct, it is undoubtedly one circumstance among others in support of that sentiment, although of subordinate weight.

§ 263. Mental action quickened by influence on the physical system.

The ability of the mind to restore its past experiences depends in some degree on the state of the physical system. It is well known that there is a connexion existing between the mind and the body, and that a reciprocal influence is exercised. It is undoubtedly true that the mental action is ordinarily increased or diminished, according as the body is more or less affected. And may not the exercise of the laws of memory be quickened, as well as the action of other powers? While it is admitted that an influence on the body exerts an influence on the mind, may it not be true that this general influence sometimes takes the particular shape of exciting the recollection, and of restoring long-past events.

There are various facts, having a bearing on this inquiry, and which seem to show that such suggestions are not wholly destitute of foundation.—It appears, for instance, from the statements of persons who have been on the point of drowning, but have been rescued from that situation, that the operations of their minds were peculiarly quickened. In this wonderful activity of the mental principle, the whole past life, with its thousand minute incidents, has almost simultaneously passed before them, and been viewed as in a mirror. Scenes and situations long gone by, and associates not seen for years, and perhaps buried and dissolved in the grave, came rushing in upon the field of intellectual vision, in all the activity and distinctness of real existence.

If such be the general experience in cases of this kind, it confirms a number of important views; placing beyond doubt that there is a connexion between the mind and body; that the mental operation is susceptible of being quickened; and that such increase of action may be attributable, in part at least, to an influence on the body. The proximate cause of the great acceleration of the intellectual acts, in cases of drowning, appears to be (as will be found to be the fact in many other similar cases) an affection of the brain. That is to say, in consequence of the suspension of respiration, the blood is prevented from readily circulating through the lungs, and hence becomes accumulated in the brain. It would seem that the blood is never thrown into the brain in unusual quantities without being attended with unusual mental affections.

§ 264. Other instances of quickened mental action and of a restoration of thoughts.

The doctrine which has been proposed, that the mental action may be quickened, and that there may be a restoration or remembrance of all former thoughts and feelings, is undoubtedly to be received or rejected in view of facts. The only question in this case, as in others, is, What is truth? And how are we to arrive at the truth?

If the facts which have been referred to be not enough to enable one to form an opinion, there are others of a like tendency and in a less uncertain form. A powerful disease, while at some times it prostrates the mind, at others imparts to it a more intense action. The following passage from a recent work (although the cause of the mental excitement, in the instance mentioned in it, is not stated) may properly be appealed to in this connexion.—"Past feelings, even should they be those of our earliest moments of infancy, never cease to be under the influence of the law of association, and they are constantly liable to be renovated, even to the latest period of life, although they may be in so faint a state as not to be the object of consciousness.

It is evident, then, that a cause of mental excitement may so act upon a sequence of extremely faint feelings as to render ideas, of which the mind had long been previously unconscious, vivid objects of consciousness. Thus it is recorded of a female in France, that while she was subjected to such an influence, the memory of the Armorican language, which she had lost since she was a child, suddenly returned."*

§ 265. Effect on the memory of a severe attack of fever.

We may here add the following account of the mental affections of an intelligent American traveller. He was travelling in the State of Illinois, and suffered the common lot of visitants from other climates in being taken down with a bilious fever.—"As very few live," he remarks, "to record the issue of a sickness like mine, and as you have requested me, and as I have promised to be particular, I will relate some of the circumstances of this disease. And it is in my view desirable, in the bitter agony of such diseases, that more of the symptoms, sensations, and sufferings should be recorded than have been; and that others, in similar predicaments, may know that some before them have had sufferings like theirs, and have survived them.

"I had had a fever before, and had risen and been dressed every day. But in this, with the first day, I was prostrated to infantile weakness, and felt, with its first attack, that it was a thing very different from what I had yet experienced. Paroxysms of derangement occurred the third day, and this was to me a new state of mind. That state of disease in which partial derangement is mixed with a consciousness generally sound, and a sensibility preternaturally excited, I should suppose the most distressing of all its forms. At the same time that I was unable to recognise my friends, I was informed *that my memory was more than ordinarily exact and retentive, and that I repeated whole passages in the different languages which I knew with entire accuracy. I recited*, with-

* Hibbert's Philosophy of Apparitions, pt. iv., ch. v.

out losing or misplacing a word, a passage of poetry which I could not so repeat after I had recovered my health," &c.*

§ 266. Approval and illustrations of these views from Coleridge.

An opinion favourable to the doctrine of the durability of memory, and the ultimate restoration of thought and feeling, is expressed in the BIOGRAPHIA LITERARIA of Coleridge, in an article on the Laws of Association. In confirmation of it, the writer introduces a statement of certain facts which became known to him in a tour in Germany in 1798, to the following effect.

In a Catholic town of Germany, a young woman of four or five-and-twenty, who could neither read nor write, was seized with a nervous fever, during which she was incessantly talking Greek, Latin, and Hebrew, with much pomp and distinctness of enunciation. The case attracted much attention, and many sentences which she uttered, being taken down by some learned persons present, were found to be coherent and intelligible, each for itself, but with little or no connexion with each other. Of the Hebrew, only a small portion could be traced to the Bible; the remainder was that form of Hebrew which is usually called Rabbinic. Ignorant, and simple, and harmless as this young woman was known to be, no one suspected any deception; and no explanation could for a long time be given, although inquiries were made for that purpose in different families where she had resided as a servant.

Through the zeal, however, and philosophical spirit of a young physician, all the necessary information was in the end obtained. The woman was of poor parents, and at nine years of age had been kindly taken to be brought up by an old Protestant minister, who lived at some distance. He was a very learned man, being not only a great Hebraist, but acquainted also with Rabbinical writings, and with the Greek and

* Flint's Recollections of the Valley of the Mississippi, Letter xiv.

Latin Fathers. The passages which had been taken down in the delirious ravings of the young woman were found by the physician precisely to agree with passages in some books of those languages which had formerly belonged to him. But these facts were not a full explanation of the case. It appeared, on further inquiry, that the patriarchal Protestant had been in the habit for many years of walking up and down a passage of his house, into which the kitchen door opened, and to read to himself with a loud voice out of his favourite books. This attracted the notice of the poor and ignorant domestic whom he had taken into his family; the passages made an impression on her memory; and although probably for a long time beyond the reach of her recollection when in health, they were at last vividly restored, and were uttered in the way above mentioned, in consequence of the feverish state of the physical system, particularly of the brain.

From this instance, and from several others of the same kind which Mr. Coleridge asserts can be brought up, he is inclined to educe the following positions or inferences—(1.) Our thoughts may, for an indefinite time, exist in the same order in which they existed originally, and in a latent or imperceptible state.—(2.) As a feverish state of the brain (and, of course, any other peculiarity in the bodily condition) cannot create thought itself, nor make any approximation to it, but can only operate as an excitement or quickener to the intellectual principle, it is therefore probable that all thoughts are in themselves imperishable.—(3.) In order greatly to increase the power of the intellect, he supposes it would require only a different organization of its material accompaniment. —(4.) And, therefore, he concludes the book of final judgment, which, the Scriptures inform us, will at the last day be presented before the individuals of the human race, may be no other than the investment of the soul with a *celestial* instead of a *terrestrial* body; and that this may be sufficient to restore the perfect record of the multitude of its past experiences. He supposes it may be altogether consistent with the nature of a living spirit, that heaven and earth should sooner pass away, than that a single act or thought should be loosened and effectually struck off from the great chain of its operations.—In giving these conclusions, the exact language of the writer has not been followed, but the statement made will be found to give what clearly seems to have been his meaning.

§ 267. Application of the principles of this chapter to education.

Whether the considerations which have been brought forward lead satisfactorily to the conclusion of the duration of memory and of the possible restoration of all mental exercises, must of course be submitted to each one's private judgment. But on the supposition that they do, it must occur to every one that certain practical applications closely connect themselves with this subject.—The principle in question has, among other things, a bearing on the education of the young, furnishing a new reason for the utmost circumspection in conducting it. The term EDUCATION, in application to the human mind, is very extensive; it includes the example and advice of parents, and the influence of associates, as well as more direct and formal instruction. Now, if the doctrine under consideration be true, it follows, that a single remark of a profligate and injurious tendency, made by a parent or some other person in the presence of a child, though forgotten and neglected at the time, may be suddenly and vividly recalled some twenty, thirty, or even forty years after. It may be restored to the mind by a multitude of unforeseen circumstances, and even those of the most trifling kind; and even at the late period when the voice that uttered it is silent in the grave, may exert a most pernicious influence. It may lead to unkindness; it may be seized and cherished as a justification of secret moral and religious delinquencies; it may prompt to a violation of public laws, and in a multitude of ways conduct to sin, to ignominy, and wretchedness. Great care, therefore, ought to be taken not to utter unadvised, false, and evil sentiments in the hearing of the young, in the vain expectation that they will do no hurt, because they will be speedily and irrecoverably lost.

And for the same reason, great care and pains should be taken to introduce truth into the mind, and all correct moral and religious principles. Suitably impress on the mind of a child the existence of a God and his parental authority; teach the pure and benevolent outlines of the Redeemer's character, and the great truths and hopes of the Gospel; and these instructions form essential links in the grand chain of memory, which no change of circumstances, nor lapse of time, nor combination of power can ever wholly strike out. They have their place assigned them; and, though they may be concealed, they cannot be obliterated. They may perhaps cease to exercise their appropriate influence, and not be recalled for years; the pressure of the business and of the cares of life may have driven them out from every prominent position, and buried them for a time. But the period of their resurrection is always at hand, although it may not be possible for the limited knowledge of man to detect the signs of it. Perhaps, in the hour of temptation to crime, they come forth like forms and voices from the dead, and with more than their original freshness and power; perhaps, in the hour of misfortune, in the prison-house, or in the land of banishment, they pay their visitations, and impart a consolation which nothing else could have supplied; they come with the angel-tones of parental reproof and love, and preserve the purity, and check the despondency of the soul.

§ 268. Connexion of this doctrine with the final judgment and a future life.

There remains one remark more of a practical nature to be made.—The views which have been proposed in respect to the ultimate restoration of all mental experiences may be regarded as in accordance with the Divine Word. It may be safely affirmed, that no mental principle, which, on a fair interpretation, is laid down in that sacred book, will be found to be at variance with the common experience of mankind. The doctrine of the Bible, in respect to a future judgment, may well be supposed to involve considerations relative to man's intellectual and moral condition. In various passages, the Scriptures plainly and explicitly teach that the Saviour in the last day shall judge the world, and that all shall be judged according to the deeds done in the body, whether they be good or whether they be evil. But an objection has sometimes been raised of this sort, that we can never feel the justice of that decision without a knowledge of our whole past life, on which it is founded, and that this is impossible. It was probably this objection that Mr. Coleridge had in view when he proposed the opinion, that the clothing of the soul with a celestial instead of a terrestrial body would be sufficient to restore the perfect record of its past experiences.

In reference to this objection to the scriptural doctrine of a future judgment, the remark naturally presents itself, that it seems to derive its plausibility chiefly from an imperfect view of the constitution of the human mind. It is thought that we cannot be conscious of our whole past life, because it is utterly forgotten, and is, therefore, wholly irrecoverable. But the truth seems to be, that nothing is *wholly* forgotten; the probability that we shall be able to recall our past thoughts may be greatly diminished, but it does not become wholly extinct. The power of reminiscence slumbers, but does not die. At the Judgment-day, whenever and wherever it may come, we are entirely at liberty to suppose, from what we know of the mind, that it will awake to the recollection of itself—that it will summon up thought and feeling from its hidden recesses, and will clearly present before us the perfect form and representation of the past.

"Each fainter trace, that memory holds
So darkly of departed years,
In one broad glance the soul beholds,
And all that was at once appears."

CHAPTER X.

REASONING.

§ 269. Reasoning a source of ideas and knowledge.

Thus passing in review, under the head of the Internal Intellect, the susceptibilities of Intuition or Suggestion, of Consciousness, and of relative Suggestion or Judgment, with such notices as we were able to give of the great Auxiliary powers of Association and Memory, we come now to the fourth internal Cognitive power, not less interesting and important than the others, that of Reasoning. In Stirling's Commentary on the Hegelian System, entitled the "Secret of Hegel," vol. i., page 134, it is stated that Hegel invariably designates this power by the French term RAISONNEMENT, which the commentator translates into English in the appropriate and convenient expression "reasonment." This term, in its formation and in its import, is analogous to the word relationment, which has sometimes been applied to the relational power or relative suggestion.

For our knowledge of the operations of the reasoning faculty we are indebted, as was seen in a former chapter, to Consciousness, which gives us our direct knowledge of all other mental acts. But it will be remarked, that Reasoning is not identical with, or involved in Consciousness. If consciousness gives us a knowledge of the act of reasoning, the reasoning power, operating within its own limits and in its own right, gives us a knowledge of other things. It stands by itself; not exclusive of important relations with other powers, but still in its own place and with its own results. It is a source of perceptions and knowledge which we could not possibly possess in any other way.

Without the aid of Suggestion, it does not appear

how we could have a knowledge of our existence; without Consciousness we should not have a knowledge of our mental operations; without Relative Suggestion or Judgment, which is also a distinct source of knowledge, there would be no Reasoning; and, unassisted by Reasoning, we could have no knowledge of the relations of those things which cannot be compared without the aid of intermediate propositions. The reasoning power, accordingly, is to be regarded as a new and distinct fountain of thought, which, as compared with the other sources of knowledge just mentioned, opens itself still further in the recesses of the Internal Intellect; and as it is later in its develompement, so it comes forth with no less and probably with greater efficiency. Accordingly, Degerando, in his instructive treatise on the beginnings and early history of knowledge, entitled DE LA GENERATION DES CONNOISSANCES, expressly and very justly remarks, after having spoken of judgment or Relative Suggestion as a distinct source of knowledge, "The Reasoning faculty also serves to enrich us with ideas; for there are many relations so complicated or remote, that one act of judgment is not sufficient to discover them. A series of judgments or process of reasoning is therefore necessary."—But we would not be understood to limit the results of reasoning, considered as a distinct source of knowledge, to a few simple conceptions, such as the discovery, in a given case, of the mere relation of agreement or disagreement. It sustains the higher office of bringing to light the great principles and hidden truths of nature; it reveals to the inquisitive and delighted mind a multitude of fruitful and comprehensive views, which could not otherwise be obtained; and invests men, and nature, and events with a new character.

§ 270. Illustrations of the value of the reasoning power.

The suggestions at the close of the last section are worthy of being considered in some particulars. It may be remarked, therefore, that the value of the Reasoning power is particularly observable in two things, viz., in its flexibility, and in its growth or expansion.

(1.) When we speak of the flexibility of the reasoning power, we mean to intimate the facility and perfect fitness with which it can apply itself to the numerous and almost infinitely varied subjects of our knowledge. This remark is perhaps susceptible of illustration, by a slight reference to the instincts of the lower animals. Such instincts, according to the usual understanding of their nature, imply an original and invariable tendency to do certain things, without previous forethought and deliberation. Accordingly, it has been observed, that a bird which has always been confined in a cage will build, when suitable materials are furnished it, a nest precisely similar to those of its own kind in the woods. It places with the greatest ingenuity the sticks, leaves, and clay of its frail dwelling, without going through a long process of previous training, and without incurring a debt to others for their assistance. But the instinct in this and other analogous cases is limited to its one definite object; it discovers an utter inflexibility, neither varying the mode of its action, nor extending its range so as to include other objects.

But the reasoning faculty, altogether different in this particular, applies itself to almost everything. It is not easy to designate and limit the vast number of objects in nature, in events, and individual conduct, where it furnishes its aid, and secures the most beneficial results. It is an instrument equally fitted to investigate things that are most diverse; the mysteries of the mechanical arts, and the problems of political philosophy; the growth of a plant or flower, and the obscurities of the human intellect.

(2.) The excellency of the reasoning power is seen also in its expansion and growth.—Instinct appears to be full and perfect at the very first opportunity of its exercise; but there are no such restricted bounds to reasoning. Though weak at first, it is endlessly progressive. It is seen distinctly at work in the child, that frames his miniature house of small sticks and blocks; and in the architect, whose scientific views and exquisite labours have resulted in forming edifices that attract a nation's admiration. It is discovered, in its incipient efforts, in the regulation of the sports of childhood; but, without changing the elements of its nature, it gradually enlarges itself to the capability of administering the affairs of an empire.

§ 271. Definition of reasoning, and of propositions.

Reasoning may be defined the mental process or operation whereby we deduce or develope conclusions from two or more propositions premised.—A train of reasoning may be regarded, therefore, as a *whole;* and, as such, it is made up of separate and subordinate parts. These elementary parts are usually termed PROPOSITIONS; and before we can proceed with advantage in the further consideration of reasoning, it is necessary to go into a brief explanation of them.

A PROPOSITION has been defined to be a verbal representation of some perception, act, or affection of the mind.—Accordingly, when we speak of a Proposition, we are usually understood to mean some mental perception or combination of perceptions, expressed and laid out before us in words. Although such seems to be the ordinary meaning of the term, we may admit the possibility of propositions existing wholly in the mind without being expressed in words. Mr. Locke expressly speaks of mental propositions, or those states of mind where two or more ideas are combined together previous to their being imbodied and set forth in the forms of language.

The parts of the proposition are, (1.) The SUBJECT, or that concerning which something is either asserted or denied, commanded or inquired; (2.) The PREDICATE, or that which is asserted, denied, commanded, or inquired concerning the subject; (3.) The COPULA, by which the two other parts are connected.—In these two propositions,

Cæsar was brave,
Men are fallible,

Men and *Cæsar* are the subjects; *fallible* and *brave* are the predicates; *are* and *was* are the copulas.

Propositions have been divided, (1.) Into SIMPLE, or those whose subject and predicate are composed of single words, as in this,

Benevolence is commendable;

(2.) Into COMPLEX, or those where the subject and predicate consist of a number of words, as in this,

Faithfulness in religion is followed by peace of mind;

(3.) Into modal, where the copula is qualified by some word or words, representing the manner or possibility of the agreement or discrepance between the subject and predicate, as in these,

Men of learning *can* exert an influence;
Wars *may* sometimes be just.

PROPOSITIONS, more or less involved, are necessary parts in every process of reasoning. They may be compared to the separate and disjointed blocks of marble, which are destined to enter into the formation of some edifice; the completed process of reasoning is the edifice; the propositions are the materials.

§ 272. Process of the mind in all cases of reasoning.

Leaving the consideration of its subordinate parts or elements, we are further to consider the general nature of reasoning; in other words, we are to examine the character of the complex mental process involved in that term. The definition given of reasoning, it will be remembered, was, That it is the mental process by which we deduce conclusions from two or more propositions premised. Hence there will be in every such process a succession of propositions, never less than two, and often a much greater number. The propositions often follow each other with much regularity; and hence, not unfrequently, we consider the arrangement of them as entirely arbitrary. But this is a mistaken supposition. It is true, when a number of ideas or propositions are presented nearly at the same time, the mind puts forth a volition, or exercises choice, in selecting one idea or proposition in preference to another. But the ideas or propositions from which the choice is made, and without the presence of which it could not be made, are not brought into existence by a direct volition, and, therefore, mere arbitrary creations, but are suggested by the laws of association.

As an illustration, we will suppose an argument on the justice and expediency of capital punishments in ordinary cases. The disputant first denies in general terms the right which social combinations have assumed of capitally punishing offences of a slight nature. But, before considering the cases he has particularly in view, he remarks on the right of capital punishment for murder; and admits, we will suppose, that the principle of self-defence gives such a right. He then takes up the case of stealing, and contends that we have no right to punish the thief with death, because no such right is given by the laws of nature; for, before the formation of the civil compact, the institution of property, as a matter of civil and judicial regulation, was not known. He then considers the nature of civil society, and contends that, in the formation of the social compact, no such extraordinary power as that of putting to death for stealing, or other crimes of similar aggravation, could have been implied in that compact, because it never was possessed by those who formed it, &c.

Here is an argument made up of a number of propositions, and carried on, as may be supposed, to a very considerable length. And in this argument, as in all others, every proposition is in the first instance suggested by the laws of association; it is not at all a matter of arbitrary volition. The disputant first states the inquiry in general terms; he then considers the particular case of murder; the crime of theft is next considered; and this is examined, first, in reference to natural law, and afterward in reference to civil law. — And this consecution of propositions takes place in essentially the same way as when the sight of a stranger in the crowd suggests the image of an old friend, and the friend suggests the village of his residence, and the village suggests an ancient ruin in its neighbourhood, and the ruin suggests warriors and battles of other days.—It is true that other propositions may have been suggested at the same time, and the disputant may have had his choice between them, but this was all the direct voluntary power which he possessed.

§ 273. Grounds of the selection of propositions.

A number of propositions are presented to the mind by the principles of association; the person who carries on the process of reasoning makes his selection among them. But it is reasonable to inquire, How it happens that there is such a suitableness or agreement in the propositions, as they are successively adopted into the train of reasoning? And this seems to be no other than to inquire into the circumstances under which the choice of them is made, or the grounds of the selection.

Let it be considered, then, that in all arguments, whether moral or demonstrative, there is some general subject on which the evidence is made to bear; there is some point in particular to be examined. In reference to these general outlines, we have a prevailing and permanent desire. This desire is not only a great help in giving quickness and strength to the laws of association, but exercises also a very considerable indirect influence in giving an appropriate character to the thoughts which are suggested by those laws. Hence the great body of the propositions which are at such times brought up will be found to have a greater or less reference to the general subject. These are all very rapidly compared by the mind with those outlines, in regard to which its feelings of desire are exercised, or with what we usually term *the point to be proved*.—Here the mind, in the exercise of that susceptibility of feelings of relation which we have already seen it to possess, immediately discovers the suitableness or want of suitableness, the agreement or want of agreement of the propositions presented to it, to the general subject. This perception of agreement or disagreement, which is one of those relative feelings of which the mind is from its very nature held to be susceptible, exists as an ultimate fact in our mental constitution. All that can profitably be said in relation to it is the mere statement of the fact, and of the circumstances under which it is found to exist. —Those propositions which are judged by the mind, in the exercise of that capacity which its Creator has given it, to possess a congruity or agreement with the general subject or point to be proved, are permitted by it to enter in, as continuous parts of the argument. And in this way a series of propositions rises up, all having reference to one ultimate purpose, regular, appropriate, and in their issue laying the foundation of the different degrees of assent.—This explanation will apply not only to the supposed argument in the last section, which is an instance of moral reasoning, but will hold good essentially of all other instances of whatever kind. The difference in the various kinds of reasoning *consists less in the mental process than in the nature of the subjects compared together, and in the conditions attending them.*

§ 274. Reasoning implies the existence of antecedent or assumed propositions.

In attempting to give some explanation of the reasoning power, it is to be remarked further, that reasoning, both in its inception and its prosecution, has this characteristic, that it necessarily proceeds, in a great degree, upon assumptions. As every process of the reasoning faculty implies a comparison of propositions, there must, of course, be some propositions given, by the aid of which the comparison is prosecuted. There must be something assumed as known, by means of which to find out what is unknown. Accordingly, assumed propositions (either those which are known to be true, or, for the purposes of argument, are regarded as such) are always found at the commencement of the series; and they are also introduced frequently in its progress, particularly in Moral reasoning. But the propositions which are assumed are not always expressed; especially those which, from the circumstance of their being representative of elementary convictions of the understanding, are denominated PRIMARY TRUTHS. (See chap. i. of the Introduction.)—"In every process of reasoning," says Abercrombie, "we proceed by founding one step upon another which has gone before it; and when we trace such a process backward, we must arrive at certain truths which are recognised as fundamental, requiring no proof and admitting of none."

But when we say that reasoning proceeds upon assumptions, it does not necessarily follow that it proceeds upon propositions which are unknown or doubtful. The propositions which the referred to are *assumed in reference to the reasoning power*, and not in reference to other sources of knowledge, which the understanding possesses besides reasoning; such as perception, suggestion or intuition, consciousness, and relative suggestion.

A remark further remains to be made here on the general nature of reasoning, viz.: that there is what may be called INTUITIONAL reasoning, in distinction from INDUCTIVE reasoning. It consists in an arrangement of propositions, the truth of which is intuitively perceived, with a view to develope (not strictly to deduce, but to *develope*) some remote intuitional truth which could not otherwise be reached. If this view be accepted as a correct one, it necessarily implies a modification of the common definition of reasoning, making it the process whereby we deduce or DEVELOPE conclusions from two or more propositions premised. The successful exercise of intuitional reasoning, such as we see in some of the orations and speeches of Edmund Burke and of the distinguished American orator, Daniel Webster, implies the possession of great intuitional power—a power which affirms by its own intuitional grasp, and which, by adding affirmation to affirmation, opens in a corresponding degree the intuitional power of the hearer.

§ 275. Of reasoning À PRIORI.

There are various methods of conducting ratiocination. One method of reasoning, for instance, is termed À PRIORI. À PRIORI reasoning is that whereby an effect is proved from a cause, whether that cause be directly proximate or be remote. For instance, a nation is possessed of a well-ordered government and wise rulers. And we infer, À PRIORI, that justice will be carefully administered, and that there will be a high degree of harmony, security, and prosperity among the people.

Under the results of this form of reasoning may be embraced also any conclusion which is ascertained and proved by something previously existing, whether such antecedent be a cause in the proper sense of the term, or possess merely an accidental priority. It embraces also those cases where, in view of the correspondence and adaptation of things which we so generally witness in the universe, we are impelled, by the consideration of the nature of one thing, to believe in the existence of something else corresponding to it.—One of the various arguments which has a bearing on the existence of God is of this description. It is to this effect. We are so constituted that we naturally and necessarily form certain ideas, such as the ideas of space, time, and infinity; and by the aid of these we frame the additional ideas of unlimited space and unlimited time, or IMMENSITY and ETERNITY. These conceptions are Absolute or Unconditioned; in other words, we cannot possibly conceive of the opposite; we cannot conceive of a state of things where time and space are not; so that, in view of the human intellect, there are, and necessarily must be, both an eternity of duration and illimitability of space; which, however, we commonly express by the single terms ETERNITY and IMMENSITY. Nor are we at liberty to suppose that the human intellect is deceived as to the results involved in the formation of these conceptions; in other words, we are not at liberty to suppose that it is led by its very constitution to form conceptions of what does not exist, and to which there is nothing corresponding. So that we may regard ourselves as fully and legitimately possessed of the fact or reality of eternity, and also of immensity or boundless space. It is obvious that in this way we possess the knowledge of a state of things which is adapted, and adapted exclusively, to the nature of God. We naturally inquire, why should there be ETERNITY without an Eternal Being of whom eternity is predicable? Why should there be immensity of space without an Omnipresent Being who may occupy it? If there be no God, but nothing but limited finite beings, then there is, comparatively speaking, an infinity of time and of space, which is unoccupied and unavailable. But, as this is inconsistent with that harmony and adaptation of things which we witness in every other case, we are led to infer, À PRIORI, that there is, and must be, a God.

À PRIORI reasoning is more frequently made use of, than anywhere else, in the mathematics, and in all cases of demonstration. The definitions which are given embrace general truths, from which other truths are evolved or brought out by a successive comparison of propositions. We say, for instance, that a square is a figure, which has all its sides equal, and all its angles right angles. In this definition there is not only involved equality of sides, but equality of angles. And it is evident, that if the definitions were altered, and were so restricted as to exclude the notion of equality of angles, many properties which are now demonstrated of the square would be unsusceptible of proof. In other words (and it is the same of other analogous cases), such properties are deduced by an À PRIORI process from the general notions involved in the definition of a square.

§ 276. Of reasoning À POSTERIORI.

Another method of reasoning is termed À POSTERIORI. À POSTERIORI reasoning is that by which either a cause is proved from an effect; or, in more general terms, by which a conclusion is proved by something posterior in time, whether it be properly an effect or not. For instance (reversing one of the illustrations in the last section), if justice is not properly administered among the people, and if discord and insecurity prevail, we infer, À POSTERIORI, that there is a deficiency in the constitution of the country, or in the rulers, or in both.—It is narrated of Aristippus the Cyreniac, that he was once shipwrecked on an unknown coast. As he was there wandering about on the desert shore, he discovered some geometrical diagrams traced in the sand. He immediately called out to his companions to be of good courage, as he saw the traces and evidences of human beings. In other words, reasoning À POSTERIORI, or from effects to causes, and combining with that process the general principle that a combination of means conspiring to a particular end indicates design, he did not hesitate to infer, from what he had discovered, that the country either was or had been inhabited.

The À PRIORI process, as we have already had occasion to see, is sometimes employed in proving the existence of God; but still more frequently, and probably to better effect, the method of reasoning À POSTERIORI. The idea of God is not simple, but complex; embracing, in particular, the two great elements of intelligence and power. Accordingly, in endeavouring to prove his existence from the works of nature, we assume, on the ground of their being original and necessary suggestions of the human intellect, the following propositions: (1.) That there is no beginning or change of existence without a cause; and, (2.) That means conspiring to a particular end indicate design or intelligence. With these two propositions given, we look at the multiplied works of nature, we contemplate them in their progress, harmony, and results;

and thus, reasoning À POSTERIORI, from the consequent to the antecedent, from the effect to the cause, we infer the existence of God.

§ 277. Of reasoning À FORTIORI.

Another process of ratiocination is denominated reasoning À FORTIORI. This consists in deducing a proposition as true from another known or admitted proposition, the truth of which is less obvious or less probable. Hence the application of the term À FORTIORI, which indicates that the conclusion is clearer or stronger. Thus, if a man who merely robs on the highway is worthy of death, then, A FORTIORI, the murderer is deserving of the same punishment. Again, if he who murders his enemy is worthy of death, still more is he who commits parricide.—We have an instance of this species of reasoning in the passage of the Apostle Paul, where he shows that the Almighty will not fail to bestow upon good men the necessaries of life. "He that spared not his own Son, how shall he not with him freely give us all things." If he gave us the greater blessing of his Son, À FORTIORI he will give us such other inferior things as may be necessary for us.

§ 278. Of differences in the power of reasoning.

The faculty of reasoning, or "reasonment," as it is appropriately proposed to be called, exists in different individuals in very different degrees. There is the same diversity here which is found to exist in respect to every other mental susceptibility and mental process. In some persons it is not even powerful enough to meet the ordinary exigences of life, and hardly rescues its possessor from the imputation of idiocy; in others it elevates human nature, and bestows extraordinary grasp and penetration. And between the extremes of extraordinary expansion and marked imbecility, there are multitudes of distinct grades, almost every possible variety.

This difference depends on various causes.—(1.) It

will depend, in the first place, on the amount of knowledge which the reasoner possesses. No man can permanently sustain the reputation of great ability in argument without having previously secured a large fund of knowledge as its basis. And we may add, that no man can reason well on any given subject unless he has especially prepared himself in reference to that subject. All reasoning implies a comparison of ideas; or, more properly, a comparison of propositions, or of facts stated in propositions. Of course, where there is no knowledge on any given subject, where there is no accumulation of facts, there can be no possibility of reasoning; and where the knowledge is much limited, the plausibility and power of the argument will be proportionally diminished.

That many persons speak on subjects which are proposed to them without having made any preparation, cannot be denied; but there is a vast difference between noisy, incoherent declamation, and a well-wrought argument, made up of suitable propositions, following each other with a direct and satisfactory reference to the conclusion. In every case of reasoning, the mind passes successively along the various topics involved in the argument; and, in so doing, is governed by the principles of association, as we have already had occasion to notice. But what opportunity can there possibly be for the operation of these principles, when the mind is called to fasten itself upon a subject, and to decide upon that subject, without any knowledge of those circumstances which may be directly embraced in it, or of its relations and tendencies?

(2.) The power of reasoning will depend, in the second place, on the powers of attention and memory. There are some persons who seem to have no command of the ATTENTION, as we commonly express it; that is, no persistency of thought, no fixedness of intellective perception. Everything interests them slightly, and nothing in a high degree. They are animated by no strong feeling, and enter into no subject, requiring long-continued and abstract investigation, with a suitable intensity of ardour. A defective remembrance of the numerous facts and propositions which come under review is the natural consequence of this. And this necessarily implies a perplexed and diminished power of ratiocination.

(3.) A third ground of difference is diversity in the susceptibility of feeling relations. The remark has already been made (§ 215), that facts may be accumulated having close and decisive relations to the points to be proved, but that they can never be so bound together as to result in any conclusion, without a perception or feeling of those relations. But it is well known, whatever it may be owing to, that the relations of objects are much more readily and clearly perceived by some than by others. As, therefore, every train of reasoning implies a succession or series of relative perceptions, a defect in the power of relative suggestion necessarily implies a defect in the reasoning power. And, on the other hand, a great quickness and clearness in the perception of relations is necessarily attended (other things being equal) with an augmented efficiency of reasoning.

§ 279. Of habits of reasoning.

But, whatever may be the mental traits that render, in particular cases, the reasoning power more or less efficient, its efficacy will undoubtedly depend in a great degree on Habit.—The effect of frequent practice, resulting in what is termed a HABIT, is often witnessed in those who follow any mechanic calling, where we find that what was once done with difficulty comes in time to be done with great ease and readiness. The muscles of such persons seem to move with a kind of instinctive facility and accuracy in the performance of those works to which they have been for a long time addicted.

There is a similar effect of frequent practice in the increase of quickness and facility in our mental operations; and certainly as much so in those which are implied in reasoning as in any others. If, for instance, a person has never been in the habit of going through geometrical demonstrations, he finds his mind very slowly and with difficulty advancing from one step to another; while, on the other hand, a person who has so often practised this species of argumentation as to have formed a habit, advances forward from one part of the train of reasoning to another with great rapidity and delight. And the result is the same in any process of moral reasoning. In the prosecution of any argument of a moral nature, there is necessarily a mental perception of the congruity of its several parts, or of the agreement of the succeeding proposition with that which went before. The degree of readiness in bringing together propositions, and in putting forth such perceptions, will greatly depend on the degree of practice.

§ 280. **Of reasoning in connexion with language or expression.**

Language is the great instrument of reasoning. There may indeed be a deductive process, which is purely mental; but, in point of fact, this is seldom the case. In the use of language, it is worthy of notice, that there is often a want of correspondence between the purely mental process in reasoning and the outward verbal expression of it. When persons are called upon to state their arguments suddenly and in public debate, they often commit errors which are at variance with the prevalent opinion of their good sense and mental ability. This is particularly true of men who are chiefly engaged in the ordinary business of life, or are in any situation where there is a constant call for action. The conclusions at which such persons arrive may be supposed to be generally correct, but they frequently find themselves unable to state clearly and correctly to others the process of reasoning by which they arrived at them.—Oliver Cromwell, the famous English Protector, is said to have been a person to whom this statement would well apply. The complicated incidents of his life, and the perplexities of his situation, and his great success, sufficiently evince that he possessed a clear insight into events, and was in no respect deficient in understanding; but when he attempted to express his opinions in the presence of others, and to explain himself on questions of policy, he was confused and obscure. His mind readily insinuated itself into the intricacies of a subject; and while he could assert with confidence that he had arrived at a satisfactory conclusion, he could not so readily describe either the direction he had taken or the involutions of the journey.—"All accounts," says Mr. Hume, "agree in ascribing to Cromwell a tiresome, dark, unintelligible elocution, even when he had no intention to disguise his meaning; yet no man's actions were ever, in such a variety of difficult cases, more decisive and judicious."

Such instances are not unfrequent. Mr. Stewart somewhere mentions the case of an English officer, a friend of Lord Mansfield, who had been appointed to the government of Jamaica. The officer expressed some doubts of his competency to preside in the court of chancery. Mansfield assured him that he would not find the difficulty so great as he imagined.—"Trust," said he, "to your own good sense in forming your opinions, but beware of stating the grounds of your judgments. The judgments will probably be right, the arguments will infallibly be wrong."

The perplexity which is so often experienced by men engaged in active life, in giving a prompt and correct verbal expression to the internal trains of thought, is probably owing, in part, to a want of practice of that kind, and in part to certain mental habits, which they have been led, from their situation, to form and strengthen. In a thousand emergencies they have been obliged to act with quickness, and, at the same time, with caution; in other words, to examine subjects, and to do it with expedition. In this way they have acquired exceeding readiness in all their mental acts. The consequence of this is, that the numerous minute circumstances, involved more or less in all subjects of difficult inquiry, are passed in review with such rapidity, and are made in so very small a degree the objects of separate attention, that they vanish and are forgotten. Hence these persons, although the conclusion to which they have come be satisfactory, are unable to state to others all the subordinate steps in the argument. Everything has once been distinctly and fairly before their own minds, although with that great rapidity which is always implied in a HABIT; but their argument, as stated in words, owing to their inability to arrest and embody all the evanescent processes of thought, appears to others defective and confused.

CHAPTER XI.

DEMONSTRATIVE REASONING.

§ 281. **Of the subjects of demonstrative reasoning.**

IN the remarks which have hitherto been made, the subject of reasoning has been taken up in the most general point of view. The considerations that have been proposed are applicable, in the main, to reasoning in all its forms. But it is necessary, in order to possess a more full and satisfactory conception of this subject, to examine it under the two prominent heads of Moral and Demonstrative.

There are various particulars in which moral and demonstrative reasoning differ from each other, the consideration of which will suggest more fully their distinctive nature. Among other things, DEMONSTRATIVE reasoning differs from any other species of reasoning in the subjects about which it is employed. The subjects are abstract ideas, and the necessary relations among them. Those ideas or thoughts are called abstract which are representative of such qualities and properties in objects as can be distinctly examined by the mind separate from other qualities and properties with which they are commonly united. And there may be reckoned, as coming within this class of subjects, the properties of numbers and of geometrical figures; also extension, duration, weight, velocity, and forces, so far as they are susceptible of being accurately expressed by numbers or other mathematical signs. But the subjects of moral reasoning, upon which we are to remark hereafter, more particularly, are matters of fact, including their connexion with other facts, whether constant or variable, and all attendant circumstances.—That the exterior angle of a triangle is equal to both the interior and opposite angles, is a truth which comes within the province of demonstration. That Homer was the author of the Iliad, that Xerxes invaded Greece, that Columbus first discovered America, are facts or alleged facts, which involve inquiries that belong to moral reasoning.

§ 282. Use of definitions and axioms in demonstrative reasoning.

In every process of reasoning there must be at the commencement of it something to be proved; there must also be some things either known, or taken for granted as such, with which the comparison of the propositions begins. The preliminary truths in demonstrative reasonings are involved in such definitions as are found in all mathematical treatises. It is impossible to give a demonstration of the properties of a circle, parabola, ellipse, or other mathematical figure, without first having given a definition of them. DEFINITIONS, therefore, are the facts assumed, the FIRST PRINCIPLES in demonstrative reasoning, from which, by means of the subsequent steps, the conclusion is derived.—We find something entirely similar in respect to subjects which admit of the application of a different form of reasoning. Thus, in Natural Philosophy, the general facts in relation to the gravity and elasticity of the air may be considered as first principles. From these principles in Physics are deduced, as consequences, the suspension of the mercury in the barometer, and its fall when carried up to an eminence.

We must not forget here the use of axioms in the

demonstrations of mathematics. Axioms are certain self-evident propositions, or propositions the truth of which is discovered by intuition, such as the following: "Things equal to the same are equal to one another;" "From equals take away equals, and equals remain." We generally find a number of them prefixed to treatises of geometry, and other treatises involving geometrical principles; and it has been a mistaken supposition, which has long prevailed, that they are at the foundation of geometrical, and of all other demonstrative reasoning. But axioms, taken by themselves, lead to no conclusions. With their assistance alone, it cannot be denied, that the truth, involved in propositions susceptible of demonstration, would have been beyond our reach. (See § 205.)

But axioms are by no means without their use, although their nature may have been misunderstood. They are properly and originally intuitive perceptions of the truth; and whether they be expressed in words, as we generally find them, or not, is of but little consequence, except as a matter of convenience to beginners, and in giving instruction. But those intuitive perceptions which are always implied in them are essential helps; and if by their aid alone we should be unable to complete a demonstration, we should be equally unable without them. We begin with definitions; we compare together successively a number of propositions; and these intuitive perceptions of their agreement or disagreement, to which, when expressed in words, we give the name of axioms, attend us at every step.

§ 283. The opposites of demonstrative reasonings absurd.

In demonstrations we consider only one side of a question; it is not necessary to do anything more than this. The first principles in the reasoning are given; they are not only supposed to be certain, but they are assumed as such; these are followed by a number of propositions in succession, all of which are compared together; if the conclusion be a demonstrative one, then there has been a clear perception of certainty at every step in the train. Whatever may be urged against an argument thus conducted is of no consequence; the opposite of it will always imply some fallacy. Thus the proposition that the three angles of a triangle are *not* equal to two right angles, and other propositions, which are the opposite of what has been demonstrated, will always be found to be false, and also to involve an absurdity; that is, are inconsistent with, and contradictory to themselves.

But it is not so in Moral Reasoning. And here, therefore, we find a marked distinction between the two great forms of ratiocination. We may arrive at a conclusion on a moral subject with a great degree of certainty; not a doubt may be left in the mind; and yet the opposite of that conclusion may be altogether within the limits of possibility. We have, for instance, the most satisfactory evidence that the sun rose to-day, but the opposite *might* have been true without any inconsistency or contradiction, viz., That the sun did not rise. Again, we have no doubt of the great law in physics, that heavy bodies descend to the earth in a line directed towards its centre. But we can conceive of the opposite of this without involving any contradiction or absurdity. In other words, they might have been subjected, if the Creator had so determined, to the influence of a law requiring them to move in a different direction. But, on a thorough examination of a demonstrative process, we shall find ourselves unable to admit even the *possibility* of the opposite.

§ 284. **Demonstrations do not admit of different degrees of belief.**

When our thoughts are employed upon subjects which come within the province of moral reasoning, we yield different degrees of assent; we form opinions more or less probable. Sometimes our belief is of the lowest kind; nothing more than mere presumption. New evidence gives it new strength; and it may go on, from one degree of strength to another, till all doubt is excluded, and all possibility of mistake shut out.—It is different in demonstrations; the assent which we yield is at all times of the highest kind, and is never susceptible of being regarded as more or less. This results, as must be obvious on the slightest examination, from the nature of demonstrative reasoning.

In demonstrative reasonings we always begin with certain first principles or truths, either known or taken for granted; and these hold the first place, or are the foundation of that series of propositions over which the mind successively passes, until it rests in the conclusion. In mathematics, the first principles, of which we here speak, are the definitions.

We begin, therefore, with what is acknowledged by all to be true or certain. At every step there is an intuitive perception of the agreement or disagreement of the propositions which are compared together. Consequently, however far we may advance in the comparison of them, there is no possibility of falling short of that degree of assent with which it is acknowledged that the series commenced.—So that demonstrative certainty may be judged to amount to this. Whenever we arrive at the last step or the conclusion of a series of propositions, the mind, in effect, intuitively perceives the relation, whether it be the agreement or disagreement, coincidence or want of coincidence, between the last step or the conclusion, and the conditions involved in the propositions at the commencement of the series; and, therefore, demonstrative certainty is virtually the same as the certainty of intuition. Although it arises on a different occasion, and is, therefore, entitled to a separate consideration, there is no difference in the degree of belief.

§ 285. Of the use of diagrams in demonstrations.

In conducting a demonstrative process, it is frequently the case that we make use of various kinds of figures or diagrams.—The proper use of diagrams, of a square, circle, triangle, or other figure, which we delineate before us, is to assist the mind in keeping its ideas distinct, and to help in comparing them together with readiness and correctness. They are a sort of auxiliaries, brought in to the help of our intellectual infirmities, but are not absolutely necessary, since demonstrative reasoning, wherever it may be found, resembles any other kind of reasoning in this most important respect, viz., in being a comparison of our ideas.

In proof that artificial diagrams are only auxiliaries, and are not essentially necessary in demonstrations, it may be remarked, that they are necessarily all of them imperfect. It is not within the capability of the wit and power of man to frame a perfect circle, or a perfect triangle, or any other figure which is perfect. We might argue this from our general knowledge of the imperfection of the senses; and we may almost regard it as a matter determined by experiments of the senses themselves, aided by optical instruments. "There never was," says Cudworth, "a straight line, triangle, or circle, that we saw in all our lives, that was mathematically exact, but even sense itself, at least by the help of microscopes, might plainly discover much unevenness, ruggedness, flexuosity, angulosity, irregularity, and deformity in them."*

Our reasonings, therefore, and our conclusions will not apply to the figures before us, but merely to an imagined perfect figure. The mind can not only originate a figure internally and subjectively, but can ascribe to it the attribute of perfection. And a verbal statement of the properties of this imagined perfect figure is what we understand by a DEFINITION, the use of which, in this kind of reasoning in particular, has already been mentioned.

§ 286. **Of signs in general as connected with reasoning.**

The statements in the last section will appear the less exceptionable when it is recollected that in all cases reasoning is purely a mental process. From be-

* Treatise concerning Immutable Morality, book iv., ch. iii.

ginning to end, it is a succession of perceptions. Neither mathematical signs nor words constitute the process, but are only its attendants and auxiliaries. We can reason without diagrams or other signs employed in mathematics, the same as an infant reasons before it has learned artificial language.

When the infant has once put his finger in the fire, he avoids the repetition of the experiment, reasoning in this way, that there is a resemblance between one flame and another, and that what has once caused him pain, will be likely, under the same circumstances, to cause the same sensation. When the infant sees before him some glittering toy, he reaches his hand towards it, and is evidently induced to do so by a thought of this kind, that the acquisition of the object will soon follow the effort of the hand, as it has a similar effort previously made.—Here is reasoning without words; it is purely internal; nevertheless, no one will presume to say that words are not great helps in reasoning. And thus in demonstrative reasoning, although diagrams, and numerical and algebraic signs are assistances, they do not constitute the process; nor can it be even said that they are indispensably essential to it.

"Some geometricians," says Buffier (First Truths, pt. i., ch. vi.), "are led into a palpable error in imagining that things demonstrated by Geometry exist, out of their thought, exactly similar to the demonstration formed of them in their mind. They must be quickly sensible of their mistake, if they will but reflect a moment on the perfect globe, the imaginary properties of which are demonstrated in Geometry, though the thing itself has no real existence in nature. Geometry shows nothing of the existence of things, but only what they are, supposing them to exist really such as they are conceived by the mind. And, indeed, were all created things existing annihilated, geometry would not lose a single point of its demonstrations; the circle would still remain a round figure, of which all the points of the circumference would be equally distant from the centre."

§ 287. Of the influence of demonstrative reasoning on the mental character.

A considerable skill in demonstrative reasoning is on a number of accounts desirable, although it cannot be denied that very frequent practice and great readiness in it are not always favourable; so that it seems proper briefly to mention some of the effects, both propitious and unpropitious, on the mental character.

(I.) A frequency of practice in demonstrative reasoning greatly aids in giving one a ready command of his attention. And this is said for two reasons. First, because the subjects of such reasoning are not objects of the senses, but immaterial; are conceptions rather than existences; the abstractions of things rather than things themselves; and, consequently, are not distinctly comprehensible without considerable effort. And, second, because, in this species of reasoning, the propositions follow each other in such regular order and so closely, and so great is the importance of perceiving the agreement or disagreement of each succeeding one with that which goes before, that a careless, unfixed, and dissipated state of the mind seems to be utterly inconsistent with carrying on such a process with any sort of success to the conclusion. As, therefore, the strictest attention is here so highly necessary, the more a person subjects himself to this discipline, the more ready and efficient will be the particular application of the mind to which we give that name. And we often find distinguished individuals in political life and in the practice of the law who are desirous of holding their mental powers in the most prompt and systematic obedience, imposing on themselves exercises in geometry and algebra for this purpose.

(II.) This mode of reasoning accustoms one to care and discrimination in the examination of subjects.—In all discussions where the object is to find out the truth, it is necessary to take asunder all the parts having relation to the general subject, and bestow upon them a share of our consideration. And, in general, we find no people more disposed to do this than mathematicians; they are not fond of reasoning, as Mr. Locke expresses it, in the lump, but are for going into particulars, for allowing everything its due weight and nothing more, and for resolutely throwing out of the estimate all propositions which are not directly and fully to the point.—It must further be said, as a general remark closely connected with what has just been observed, that those departments of science which require demonstrative reasoning are promotive of a characteristic of great value—a love of the truth..

(III.) Demonstrative reasoning, although this beneficial result is not exclusively appropriate to this mode of reasoning, gives to the mind an increased grasp or comprehension. This result, it is true, will not be experienced in the case of those who have merely exercised themselves in the study of a few select demonstrations; it implies a familiarity of the mind with long and complicated trains of deductions. A thorough mathematician, who has made it a business to exercise himself in this method of reasoning, can hardly have been otherwise than sensible of that intellectual comprehension, or length and breadth of survey, which we have in view; since one demonstration is often connected with another, much in the same way as the subordinate parts of separate demonstrations are connected with each other; and he therefore finds it necessary, if he would go on with satisfaction and pleasure, to gather up and retain, in the grasp of his mind, all the general and subordinate propositions of a long treatise.

§ 288. Further considerations on the influence of demonstrative reasoning.

But, on the other hand, there are some results of a very great attention to sciences, which require the exclusive application of demonstrative reasoning, of a less favourable kind.—(I.) An exclusive culture of demonstrative reasoning unfavourably affects the operations of the susceptibility of belief on all subjects out of the circle of the mathematical; or perhaps we may say, in direct terms, that out of that circle it positively diminishes the power of belief. The exclusive mathematician has been accustomed to yield his assent to demonstration only; and it is but natural that he should find some difficulty in being satisfied with any lower degree of evidence. This disposition to doubt will be in some measure experienced, even in the transition from pure to mixed mathematics; at least there will be an absence of that full and delighted satisfaction which had hitherto been enjoyed. Still more will it be felt when he is called upon to judge of events, and duties, and actions of common life, which do not admit of the application of demonstration.—In a word, it has been supposed to unfit the mind in a considerable degree for accurate discriminations as to moral evidence on all subjects whatever, where that species of evidence is alone admissible; and also for fair and correct judgment in matters of taste.

(II.) Again, it has been thought, among other things, that this form of reasoning, when carried to a great length, has a tendency to render the mind mechanical. That is, while it increases its ability of acting in a given way, it diminishes the power of invention, and prevents its striking out into a new path, different from that which it has been in the habit of going over. And hence it is that men of the strictest virtue and the most powerful intellect have sometimes discovered an unexpected weakness and made extraordinary mistakes when placed in certain new situations.—We may illustrate our meaning by one or two instances. The celebrated Turgot, who combined the purest moral sentiments with the rarest intellectual endowments, was what may be termed a mathematical politician. History has recorded the result. When the King of France called him to direct the political concerns of the French empire, he decidedly failed, where half the talents and integrity had firmly held the helm amid political tempests. When called from the abstractions of science to deal with the realities of life, with the interests, and prejudices, and passions of mankind, mathematician and philosopher as he was, he found, too late, that we cannot estimate the intellect as we can estimate the arc of a circle, and that the calculus which can measure the motions of the stars may not succeed in ascertaining the momentum and the obliquities of human nature.—But La Place, a far higher name on the list of eminent mathematicians, is an instance still more to our purpose. After the accession of Napoleon to the first Consulship in France, La Place was appointed Minister of the Interior; an office which he held six weeks, and was then dismissed. "A geometrician of the first rank," says Napoleon, "he did not reach mediocrity as a statesman. From the first, the Consuls became sensible that they had made a mistake in his appointment. He never viewed any subject in its true light; he was always occupied with subtilties; his notions were all problematic, and he carried the spirit of the *infinitely small* into the administration."

Such, on the whole, being the result of an exclusive attention to sciences which admit of demonstration alone, it is obvious, when pursuing studies of that kind, that we should avail ourselves of the benefit resulting from other modes of mental discipline. Those who aim at a perfect education will not "canton out to themselves a little Goshen in the intellectual world," which is to receive all their labours, and leave the rest of the vast field of the mind to neglect, but will bestow a suitable share of culture on every part of it.

CHAPTER XII.

MORAL REASONING.

§ 289. Of the subjects and importance of moral reasoning.

MORAL REASONING, which is the second great division or kind of reasoning, concerns opinions, actions, and events; embracing, in general, those subjects which do not come within the province of demonstrative reasoning. The subjects to which it relates are often briefly expressed by saying that they are *matters of fact;* nor would this somewhat indefinite statement, concise as it is, be likely to give an erroneous idea of them.

Skill in this kind of reasoning is of great use in the formation of opinions concerning the duties and the general conduct of life. Some may be apt to think that those who have been most practised in demonstrative reasoning can find no difficulty in adapting their intellectual habits to matters of mere probability. This opinion is not altogether well-founded, as we have seen in the preceding chapter. Although that species of reasoning has a favourable result in giving persons a command over the attention, and, in some other respects, whenever exclusively employed, it has the effect in some degree to disqualify them for a correct judgment on those various subjects which properly belong to moral reasoning.—The last, therefore, which has its distinctive name from the primary signification of the Latin MORES, viz., *manners and customs*, but which in the extension of its meaning applies to the great sum of man's acts and habits, requires a separate consideration.

§ 290. Of the nature of moral certainty.

Moral reasoning causes in us different degrees of assent, and in this respect differs from demonstrative. In demonstration there is not only an immediate perception of the relation of the propositions compared together, but, in consequence of their abstract and determinate nature, there is also a knowledge or absolute certainty of their agreement or disagreement. In moral reasoning the case is somewhat different.—In both kinds we begin with certain propositions, which are either known or regarded as such. In both there is a series of propositions successively compared. But in moral reasoning, in consequence of the propositions not being abstract and fixed, and, therefore, often uncertain, the agreement or disagreement among them is in general not said to be known, but *presumed;* and this presumption may be more or less, admitting a great variety of degrees. While, therefore, one mode of reasoning is attended with knowledge, the other can properly be said to produce in most cases only judgment or opinion.—But the probability of such judgment or opinion may sometimes arise so high as to exclude all reasonable doubt; and hence we then speak as if we possessed certainty in respect to subjects which admit merely of the application of moral reasoning. Although it is possible that there may be some difference between the belief attendant on demonstration and that produced by the highest probability, the effect on our feelings is at any rate essentially the same. A man who should doubt the existence of the cities of London and Pekin, although he has no other evidence of it than that of the testimony of other persons and of the deductions drawn from such testimony, would be considered hardly less singular and unreasonable than one who might take it into his head to doubt of the propositions of Euclid. —It is this very high degree of probability which we term *moral certainty.*

§ 291. Of reasoning from analogy.

MORAL REASONING admits of some subordinate divisions; and of these, the first to be mentioned is reasoning from *analogy.*—The word analogy is used with some vagueness, but in general denotes a resemblance, either greater or less.—Having observed a consistency and uniformity in the operations of the physical world, we are naturally led to presume that things of the same nature will be affected in the same way, and will produce the same effects; and also that the same or similar effects are to be attributed to like causes. ANALOGICAL REASONING, therefore, is that mental process by which unknown truths or conclusions are inferred from the resemblance of things.

The argument by which Sir Isaac Newton establishes the truth of universal gravitation is of this sort. He proves that the planets in their revolutions are deflected towards the sun in a manner precisely similar to the deflection of the earth towards the same luminary; and also that there is a similar deflection of the moon towards the earth, and of a body projected obliquely at the earth's surface towards the earth's centre. Hence he infers by analogy, inasmuch as the effects are similar, that all these deflections originate from a similar or resembling cause, and are governed by one and the same law, viz., *the power of gravitation.*

This method of reasoning is applicable to the inquiry, Whether the planets are inhabited? and furnishes the principal, if not the sole ground for the indulgence of such a supposition. We observe a resemblance in certain respects between Mars, Jupiter, Saturn, and other planets, and the Earth. They all revolve around the sun as the Earth does, and all derive light from that source. Several of them are ascertained to revolve on their axis, and, consequently, must have a succession of day and night. Some of them have moons, and all are subject to the law of gravitation. From these various similitudes we draw the conclusion by analogy, that those planets must be inhabited like the Earth.

There are a variety of subjects, both speculative and practical, in respect to which we may reason in this way, and sometimes with considerable satisfaction. And, among others, this method of reasoning finds a place in the arguments of persons in the practice of the law. An attorney, for instance, advocates a case which does not fall within the provisions of existing statutes, and for which he finds in his authorities no exact precedent. He is therefore under the necessity of ascertaining, as far as possible, the analogy or resemblance between this case and others which have been made the subject of judicial decisions; and this analogy he makes the basis of his argument.

§ 292. Caution to be used in reasoning from analogy.

The remark remains to be made, that much care is necessary in arguments drawn from this source, especially in scientific investigations; and they are in all cases to be received with some degree of distrust. The ancient anatomists are an instance of precipitate reasoning from analogy. Being hindered by certain superstitions from dissecting the bodies of men, they endeavoured to obtain the information they wanted by the dissection of those animals whose internal structure was supposed to come nearest to that of the human body. In this way they were led into a variety of mistakes, which have been detected by later anatomists. It does not follow, because things resemble each other in a multitude of particulars, that this resemblance will be found in all others; and we are, therefore, always to consider ourselves in danger of pushing the supposition of similitude too far.

The proper use of analogical reasoning seems to be, in all scientific inquiries, merely to illustrate and confirm truths which are susceptible of proof from other sources of evidence, either by casting a direct additional light or by answering objections. A happy instance of this use of it is the work of Bishop Butler, entitled, "The Analogy of Religion, natural and revealed, to the Constitution and Course of nature."— It is not the object of the writer to prove the truth of religion, but to answer some objections which may be brought against its practical details and its principles by those who, while they object to the Bible, still maintain the existence of a God. And this he does by proving that the same objections exist to the providence of God in the natural world. There is an Analogy or resemblance in the two, viz., between the administration of God as made known in the Bible and in natural religion, and his administration of things as made known in the constitution and course of the natural world; and if the objections which are brought forward will reject him from the authorship of what we term Religion, they will dethrone him also, for the same reason, from all authorship and direction in the ordinary economy of nature.

§ 293. Of reasoning by induction.

We now come to another method of moral reasoning, viz., by induction. *Inductive reasoning* is the inferring of general truths from particular facts that have fallen under our observation. Our experience in the past teaches us that nature has been governed in all past periods by uniform laws; and we have a firm expectation, so clear and decided that it verifies itself as intuitional in its origin, and takes its place in the category of Primary Truths, that events will happen in future, as we have seen them happen in times past. With the great truth of the uniformity of nature conceded, we are prepared to deduce inferences by induction.

When a property has been found in a number of subjects of the same kind, and nothing of a contradictory nature appears, we have the strongest expectation of finding the same property in all the individuals of the same class; in other words, we come to the conclusion that the property is a general one. Accordingly, we apply a magnet to several pieces of iron; we find in every instance a strong attraction taking place; and we conclude, although we have made the experiment with only a small number of the masses of iron actually in existence, that it is a property of iron to be thus affected by that substance, or that all iron is susceptible of magnetical attraction. This is a conclusion drawn by induction.

The belief which attends a well-conducted process of inductive reasoning bears a decided character; it is moral probability of the highest kind, or what is sometimes termed moral certainty; and is at least found to be sufficient for all practical purposes. We obtain all the general truths relating to the properties and laws of material objects in this way.

And we thus not only acquire a knowledge of material objects, but apply the same inductive process also in the investigation of laws which govern the operations of the mind. It is by experience, or observing what takes place in a number of individuals, that we are able to infer the general law of association, viz., when two or more ideas have existed in the mind in immediate succession, they are afterward found to be mutually suggested by each other. It is the same in ascertaining other general laws of the mind.

§ 294. Of the caution necessary in inductive processes.

Reasoning in this method requires the exercise of caution no less than by analogy. It is especially liable to prove fallacious, whenever our investigations have been marked with impatience, and our judgments are formed on a very small number of facts.

When the number of examined instances is large, and the results are uniform, the conclusion amounts to moral certainty. But when the number of such instances is small, and the results are not altogether uniform, the judgments formed will possess a greater or less degree of probability, varying with circumstances.—And especially is the mind left in a state of vacillation and uncertainty, when results have repeatedly occurred under such circumstances as to leave us at liberty to ascribe them to a diversity of causes. In such cases we find ourselves reduced to the necessity of resorting to what writers on this subject have termed INSTANTIÆ CRUCIS.—The important and decisive method in Inductive Reasoning of INSTANTIÆ CRUCIS was first laid down in the Novum Organum of Bacon, and has recently been happily illustrated in Playfair's View of the Progress of Mathematical and Physical Science in the following terms.

§ 295. Of instances or experiments in inductive reasoning termed instantiæ crucis.

"When the understanding is placed in *equilibrio*, as it were, between two or more causes, each of which accounts equally well for the appearances, as far as they are known, nothing remains to be done but to look out for a fact which can be explained by one of these causes and not by the other; if such a one can be found, the uncertainty is removed, and the true cause is determined. Such facts perform the office of a cross, erected at the separation of two roads, to direct the traveller which he is to take, and on this account Bacon gave them the name of *instantiæ crucis.*

"Suppose that the subject inquired into were the motion of the planets, and that the phenomena which first present themselves, or the motion of these bodies in longitude, could be explained equally on the Ptolemaic and the Copernican system, that is, either on the system which makes the Earth, or that which makes the Sun, the centre of the planetary motions, a cautious philosopher would hesitate about which of the two he should adopt; and, notwithstanding that one of them was recommended by its superior simplicity, he might not think himself authorized to give to it a decided preference above the other. If, however, he consider the motion of these bodies in latitude, that is to say, their digressions from the plane of the ecliptic, he will find a set of phenomena which cannot be reconciled with the supposition that the Earth is the centre of the planetary motions, but which receive the most simple and satisfactory explanation from supposing that the Sun is at rest, and is the centre of those motions. The latter phenomena would therefore serve as *instantiæ crucis*, by which the superior credibility of the Copernican system was fully evinced."*

§ 296. Of combined or accumulated arguments.

When a proposition in geometry is given to be demonstrated, it sometimes happens that two or more solutions may be offered leading to the same end. The theorem or the problem is one and the same, as also the conclusion; but there may be more than one train of reasoning, more than one series of intermediate steps, connecting the proposition which is to be inves-

* See Works of John Playfair, Esq., Edinburgh edition, vol. ii., p. 105.

tigated with the result. But as the conclusion in each of these different cases is certain, it does not strengthen it, although it may gratify curiosity to resort to a different and additional process.

It is not thus in moral reasoning. The great difference between the two kinds of reasoning, as before observed, is not so much in the mental process as in the subjects about which they are employed. Now as the subjects in moral reasoning are not of a purely abstract nature, and are, therefore, often attended with uncertainty, our belief, when we arrive at the conclusion, is not always of the highest kind. More frequently it is some inferior degree of probability. Hence, in any moral inquiry, the more numerous the series of arguments which terminates in a particular conclusion, the stronger will be our belief in the truth of that conclusion.

Thus we may suppose a question to arise, Whether the Romans occupied the island of Great Britain at some period previous to the Saxon conquest? In reference to this inquiry a number of independent arguments may be brought forward: (1.) The testimony of the Roman historians; (2.) The remains of buildings, roads, and encampments, which indicate a Roman origin; (3.) The coins, urns, &c., which have been discovered. Although these arguments are independent of each other, they all bear upon the same conclusion; and, being combined together, they very essentially increase the strength of our belief.

It ought, however, to be further added, that the mental powers are often exercised, and the discovery of truth promoted, by what may be called the Criticism of argument. Take the cumulative argument just mentioned. The testimony of Roman historians is undoubtedly appropriate to the question under consideration. But in subjecting it to the right of an opponent to exercise his powers of criticism upon it, the question may well be asked by the adverse party, what is the comparative weight and authority of the historical writer or writers who are appealed to; and again, whether the alleged historical statement in this particular case is well authenticated or otherwise; and whether there are not some doubts expressed or countervailing statements made in other historians, which are entitled to consideration. The interests of truth often require the exercise of critical sagacity in this way, and the power of a master of argument is advantageously seen in it.

CHAPTER XIII.

PRACTICAL DIRECTIONS IN REASONING.

§ 297. Logic, and rules relating to the practice of reasoning.

IT may be expected that, in connexion with the analysis which has thus far been given of the reasoning power, we shall make some reference to systems of LOGIC. The object of Logic, using the term in its most general and unobjectionable sense, is to secure the more prompt, accurate, and efficient use of the reasoning power. In a more limited sense it means the syllogistic method of Aristotle, which for a long period prescribed the formulas of rationative action; with favourable results in the view of some, but with great injury in the view of others, to the true progress of the human race. It is thought by many, while conceding the great ability of its reputed author, and of those who both before and since his time have aided in framing and expanding its fundamental principles, that the syllogistic method, taken as a whole, compresses and restrains the mental action, and that its supposed beneficial applications are more than counterbalanced by its evil results. Is there not some ground for saying that the Syllogistic method, expanded as it is to nearly an hundred specific forms, sustains the same or nearly the same relation to the true doctrine of reasoning, which the doctrine of Mnemonics sustains to the true doctrine of the memory?

It was a remark of a distinguished American scholar and orator, who was an acknowledged master of reasoning (we refer to the late Rufus Choate, of Massachusetts), that the mind, when left to itself, reasons of itself; meaning that, if we will free it from the obstructions of prejudice, and furnish it with the facts appropriate to the case before it, it will not be necessary to resort to the Aristotelian method, or any other method separate from its own laws of action, in order to secure a true result. And in this matter he seems to have thought with Locke, who says, in a chapter on Reason, where he enters at some length into the value of syllogistic arguments, "If we will observe the actings of our own minds, we shall find that we reason best and clearest when we only observe the connection of the proof, without reducing our thoughts to any rule of syllogism." But Logic in a broader sense, such as finds an illustration in the truly valuable system known as the Port Royal Logic, proposes, as we have attempted briefly to do in the preceding chapters, to define the nature, kinds, and applications of reasoning, including what remains to be done, a notice of such auxiliary dialectical suggestions and rules as may be of special value in securing its free and energetic movement. The directions or rules which we shall now proceed to mention have, of course, a more intimate connexion with Moral than with Demonstrative reasoning; but this is a circumstance which enhances rather than diminishes their worth. The occasions which admit and require the application of moral reasoning, being inseparable from the most common occurrences and exigences of life, are much more numerous than those of demonstrative reasoning.

§ 298. Of being influenced in reasoning by a love of the truth.

(I.) The first direction in relation to reasoning which will be given, concerns the feelings with which it is proper to be animated. It is this: In all questions which admit of discussion, and on which we find ourselves at variance with the opinions of others, *we are to make truth our object.* There is no topic in the NOVUM ORGANON of Bacon more interesting and important than this. In describing the different IDOLA or prejudices to which the human mind is subject, and in illustrating the importance of removing them, he harmonizes, under a different form of expression, with what is here said of making the truth the paramount object of search. Prejudices cannot live in the presence and in connexion with such a state of mind.

The opposite of this indispensable state of mind is a wish to decide the subject of dispute in one way or another, independently of a just consideration of the evidence. The foundation of such a preference of one result to another is in general the prejudices of interest and passion; and these are the great enemies of truth. Whenever we are under their influence, we form a different estimation of testimony and of other sources of evidence from what we should do under other circumstances; and at such times they can hardly fail to lead us to false results. The dialectical rule, which makes the truth the first and paramount object of search, is important on all occasions of reasoning whatever, but particularly in public debate; because at such times the presence of others and the love of victory combine with other unpropitious influences to induce men to forget or to disregard the claims which truth is always entitled to enforce.

§ 299. Care to be used in correctly stating the subject of discussion.

(II.) Another rule in the prosecution of an argument is, that the question under debate is to be fairly and correctly stated. The matter in controversy may be stated in such a way as to include, in the very enunciation of it, something taken for granted, which must necessarily lead to a decision in favour of one of the opponents. But this amounts to begging the question, a species of fallacy or sophism upon which we shall again have occasion to remark.—Sometimes the subject of discussion is stated so carelessly, that the true point at issue is wholly left out. It may be proper, therefore, in many cases to adopt the practice of special pleaders, and first to ascertain all the points in which the opponents agree, and those in which they differ. And then they can hardly fail of directing their arguments to what is truly the subject of contention.

In order that there may not be a possibility of misunderstanding here, dialecticians should aim to have clear ideas of everything stated in the question which has an intimate connexion with the point at issue. Subordinate parts of the question, and even particular words, are to be examined. If, for instance, the statement affirm or deny anything in regard to the qualities or properties of material bodies, it is incumbent upon us to possess as clear ideas as possible both of the object in general and of those properties or qualities in particular. Similar remarks will apply to other subjects of inquiry of whatever kind.

§ 300. Consider the kind of evidence applicable to the subject.

(III.) As one subject clearly admits of the application of one species of evidence, while another as clearly requires evidence of a different kind, we are thence enabled to lay down this rule, viz., We are to consider what kind of evidence is appropriate to the question under discussion.

When the inquiry is one of a purely abstract nature, and all the propositions involved in the reasoning are of the same kind, then we have the evidence of Intuition or intuitive perception; and the conclusion, for reasons already mentioned, is certain.—In the examination of the properties of material bodies, we depend originally on the evidence of the Senses, which gives a character and strength to our belief according to the circumstances under which the objects are presented to them.—In judging of those facts in events and in the conduct of men which have not come under our own observation, we rely on Testimony. This source of belief causes probability in a greater or less degree, according as the testimony is from one or more, given by a person who understands the subject to which it relates, or not, &c.—And again some subjects admit of the evidence of Induction, and in respect to others we have no other aids than the less authoritative reasonings from Analogy. In other cases, the evidence is wholly made up of various incidental circumstances which are found to have relation to the subject in hand, and which affect the belief in different degrees and for various causes.

And hence, as the sources of belief, as well as the belief itself, have an intimate connexion with the subject before us, they ought to be taken into consideration. The evidence should be appropriate to the question. But if the question admit of more than one kind of evidence, then all are entitled to their due weight.

§ 301. Reject the aid of false arguments or sophisms.

(IV.) There is a species of false reasoning which we call a SOPHISM. A sophism is an argument which contains some secret fallacy under the general appearance of correctness. The aid of such arguments, which are calculated to deceive, and are, in general, inconsistent with a love of the truth, should be rejected.

(1.) IGNORATIO ELENCHI, or misapprehension of the question, is one instance of sophism. It exists when, from some misunderstanding of the terms and phrases that are employed, the arguments advanced do not truly apply to the point in debate. It was a doctrine, for instance, of some of the early philosophic teachers of Greece, that there is but *one principle of things.* Aristotle, understanding by the word principle what we commonly express by the word ELEMENT, attempted to show the contrary, viz., that the elements are not one, but many, thus incurring the imputation of IGNORATIO ELENCHI; for those who held the doctrine which was thus subjected to his animadversion, had reference, not to the form, but the *cause* of things; not to any doctrine of elementary material particles, but to the intellectual origin, the creative mind, the Supreme Being, whom, as the PRINCIPLE (that is, as the beginning and the support of things), they maintained to be one.*

(2.) Petitio principii, or begging of the question, is another instance of sophism. This sophism is found whenever the disputant offers in proof of a proposition, the proposition itself in other words. The following has been given as an instance of this fallacy in reasoning: A person attempts to prove that God is eternal by maintaining that his existence is without beginning and without end. Here the proof which is offered, and the proposition itself which is to be proved, are essentially the same.—When we are told that opium causes sleep because it has a soporific quality, or that grass grows by means of its vegetative power, the same thing is repeated in other terms.—This fallacy is very frequently practised; and a little care in detecting it would spoil many a fine saying, as well as deface many an elaborate argument. What is called *arguing in a circle* is a species of sophism very nearly related to the above. It consists in making two propositions reciprocally prove each other.

(3.) Non causa pro causa, or the assignation of a false cause.—People are unwilling to be thought ignorant; rather than be thought so, they will impose on the credulity of their fellow-men, and sometimes on themselves, by assigning false causes of events. Nothing is more common than this sophism among illiterate people; pride is not diminished by deficiency of learning, and such people, therefore, must gratify it by assigning such causes of events as they find nearest at hand. Hence, when the appearance of a comet is followed by a famine or a war, they are disposed to consider it as the cause of those calamities. If a person have committed some flagrant crime, and shortly after suffer some heavy distress, it is no uncommon thing to hear the former assigned as the direct and the sole cause of the latter.—This was the fallacy which historians have ascribed to the Indians of Paraguay, who supposed the baptismal ceremony

* La Logique ou l'Art de Penser (Port Royale), pt. iii., chap. xix.

to be the cause of death, because the Jesuit missionaries, whenever opportunity afforded, administered it to dying infants, and to adults in the last stage of disease.

(4.) Another species of sophistry is called FALLACIA ACCIDENTIS.—We fall into this kind of false reasoning whenever we give an opinion concerning the general nature of a thing from some accidental or incidental circumstance, not essentially connected with the thing. Thus, the Christian religion has been made the pretext for persecutions, and has, in consequence, been the source of much suffering; but it is a sophism to conclude that it is, on the whole, not a great good to the human race, because it has been attended with this perversion. Again, if a medicine has operated in a particular case unfavourably, or in another case has operated very favourably, the universal rejection or reception of it, in consequence of the favourable or unfavourable result in a particular instance, would be a hasty and fallacious induction of essentially the same sort. That is, the general nature of the thing is estimated from a circumstance which may be wholly accidental.

§ 302. Fallacia equivocationis, or the use of equivocal terms and phrases.

(V.) It is a further direction of much practical importance, that the reasoner should be careful, in the use of language, to express everything with plainness and precision; and especially never attempt to prejudice the cause of truth, and snatch a surreptitious victory by the use of an equivocal phraseology. No man of an enlarged and cultivated mind can be ignorant that multitudes of words in every language admit of diversities of signification. There are found also in all languages many words, which sometimes agree with each other, and sometimes differ in signification, according to the connexion in which they appear, and their particular application. There is, therefore, undoubtedly an opportunity, if any should be disposed to embrace it, of employing equivocal terms, equivocal phrases, and perplexed and mysterious combinations of speech, and thus hiding themselves from the penetrating light of truth, under cover of a mist of their own raising.

No man, whose sole object is truth and justice, will resort to such a discreditable subterfuge. If in reasoning he finds himself inadvertently employing words of an equivocal signification, it will be a first care with him to guard against the misapprehensions likely to result from that source. He will explain so precisely the sense in which he uses the doubtful terms as to leave no probability of cavilling and mistake.

And besides the invaluable reputation of a man of honor and justice, he will in this way realize results in respect to his own intellectual character of the most beneficial nature. The practice of verbal criticism, as it has been called (that is, of discriminating readily and accurately the meaning of words), will result in a HABIT, giving to the dialectician a vast power over his opponent, who has not been trained to the making of such nice discriminations. There will be a keenness of intellectual perception which, while it helps to untie the perplexities of language, at the same time resolves the perplexities of thought; separating meaning from meaning, and dividing truth from falsehood in those cases where at first sight it appeared to be impossible. But it is a power which cannot be possessed without a laborious acquaintance with the purest writers and the ablest reasoners in a language, together with a systematic and philosophic study of its origin, idioms, and general forms. And while it may be employed to the most beneficial purposes, it is far too formidable to be intrusted in the management of any one who is not under the influence of that moral rectitude and that love of the truth which have been so repeatedly insisted on.

§ 303. On the sophism of estimating actions and character from the circumstance of success merely.

(VI.) The foregoing are some of the fallacies in reasoning which have found a place in writers on Logic. To these might be added the fallacy or sophism to which men are obviously so prone, of judging favourably of the characters and the deeds of others from the mere circumstance of success. Those actions which have a decidedly successful termination are almost always applauded, and are looked upon as the result of great intellectual forecast; while, not less frequently, actions that have an unsuccessful issue are not only stigmatized as evil in themselves, but as indicating in their projector a flighty and ill-balanced mind.—The fallacy, however, does not consist in taking the issues or results into consideration, which are undoubtedly entitled to their due place in estimating the actions and characters of men, but in too much limiting our view of things, and forming a favourable or unfavourable judgment from the mere circumstance of good or ill success alone.

While there is no SOPHISM more calculated to lead astray and perplex, there is none more common than this; so much so, that it has almost passed into a proverb, that a hero must not only be brave, but *fortunate*. Hence it is that Alexander is called Great, because he gained victories and overran kingdoms; while Charles XII. of Sweden, who the most nearly resembles him in the characteristics of bravery, perseverance, and chimerical ambition, but had his projects cut short at the fatal battle of Pultowa, is called a madman.

"Machiavel has justly animadverted," says Dr. Johnson, "on the different notice taken by all succeeding times of the two great projectors, Catiline and Cæsar. Both formed the same project, and intended to raise themselves to power by subverting the commonwealth. They pursued their design, perhaps, with equal abilities and equal virtue; but Catiline perished in the field, and Cæsar returned from Pharsalia with unlimited authority; and from that time, every monarch of the earth has thought himself honoured by a comparison with Cæsar; and Catiline has never been mentioned but that his name might be applied to traitors and incendiaries."

In the same Essay* he happily illustrates this subject by a reference to the discovery of America, in the following terms: "When Columbus had engaged King Ferdinand in the discovery of the other hemisphere, the sailors with whom he embarked in the expedition had so little confidence in their commander, that, after having been long at sea looking for coasts which they never expected to find, they raised a general mutiny and demanded to return. He found means to soothe them into a permission to continue in the same course three days longer, and on the evening of the third day descried land. Had the impatience of his crew denied him a few hours of the time requested, what had been his fate but to have come back with the infamy of a vain projector, who had betrayed the king's credulity to useless expenses, and risked his life in seeking countries that had no existence? How would those that had rejected his proposals have triumphed in their acuteness! and when would his name have been mentioned but with the makers of potable gold and malleable glass!"

§ 304. Of adherence to our opinions.

Whenever the rules laid down have been followed, and conclusions have been formed with a careful and candid regard to the evidence presented, those opinions are to be asserted and maintained with a due degree of confidence. It would evince an unjustifiable weakness to be driven from our honest convictions by the effrontery, or even by the upright, though misguided zeal of an opponent. Not that a person is to set himself up for infallible, and to suppose that new accessions of evidence are impossible, or that it is an impossibility for him to have new views of the evidence already examined. But a suitable degree of

* See the Adventurer, No. 99.

stability is necessary in order to be respected and useful; and, in the case supposed, such stability can be exhibited without incurring the charge which is sometimes thrown out, of doggedness and intolerance.

It is further to be observed, that we are not always to relinquish judgments which have been formed in the way pointed out, when objections are afterward raised which we cannot immediately answer. The person thus attacked can, with good reason, argue in this way: I have once examined the subject carefully and candidly; the evidence, both in its particulars and in its multitude of bearings, has had its weight; many minute and evanescent circumstances were taken into view by the mind, which have now vanished from my recollection; I therefore do not feel at liberty to alter an opinion thus formed, in consequence of an objection now brought up, which I am unable to answer, but choose to adhere to my present judgment until the whole subject, including this objection, can be re-examined.—This reasoning would in most cases be correct, and would be entirely consistent with that love of truth and openness to conviction which ought ever to be maintained.

§ 305. **Effects on the mind of debating for victory instead of truth.**

By way of supporting the remarks under the first rule, we here introduce the subject of contending for victory merely. He who contends with this object takes every advantage of his opponent which can subserve his own purpose. For instance, he will demand a species of proof or a degree of proof which the subject in dispute does not admit; he gives, if possible, a false sense to the words and statements employed by the other side; he questions facts, which he himself fully believes and everybody else, in the expectation that the opposite party is not furnished with direct and positive evidence of them. In a word, wherever an opening presents, he takes the utmost advantage of his opponent, however much against his own internal convictions of right and justice.

Such a course, to say nothing of its moral turpitude, effectually unsettles that part of our mental economy which concerns the grounds and laws of belief. The practice of inventing cunningly-devised objections against arguments known to be sound, necessarily impairs the influence which such arguments ought ever to exert over us. Hence the remark has been made with justice, that persons who addict themselves to this practice frequently end in becoming skeptics. They have so often perplexed, and apparently overthrown what they felt to be true, they at last question the existence of any fixed grounds of belief in the human constitution, and begin to doubt of everything.

This effect, even when there is an undoubted regard for the truth, will be found to follow from habits of ardent disputation, unless there be a frequent recurrence to the original principles of the mind which relate to the nature and laws of belief. The learned Chillingworth is an instance. The consequences to which the training up of his vast powers to the sole art of disputation finally led, are stated by Clarendon: "Mr. Chillingworth had spent all his younger time in disputations, and had arrived at so great a mastery, that he was inferior to no man in those skirmishes; but he had, with his notable perfection in this exercise, contracted such an irresolution and habit of doubting, that, by degrees, he grew confident of nothing. Neither the books of his adversaries nor any of their persons, though he was acquainted with the best of both, had ever made great impression on him. All his doubts grew out of himself, when he assisted his scruples with all the strength of his own reason, and was then too hard for himself."

CHAPTER XIV.

IMAGINATION.

§ 306. Imagination an intellectual process closely related to reasoning.

Leaving the subject of reasoning, we next proceed to the consideration of the Imagination; which, as well as the reasoning power, obviously comes under the general head of the Intellect rather than of the Sensibilities. It is true, we are apt to associate the exercises of the heart with those of the imagination, and undoubtedly we have some reason for doing so; but in doing this we are liable not merely to associate, but to identify and confound them. But they are, in fact, essentially different. An exercise of the Imagination, *in itself considered*, is purely an intellectual process. The process may, indeed, be stimulated and accelerated by a movement of the sensibilities; there may be various extraneous influences operating either to increase or to diminish its vivacity and energy; but the process itself, considered separately from contingent circumstances, is wholly intellectual. So that he who possesses a creative and well-sustained imagination may be said, with no small degree of truth, to possess a powerful intellect, at least in this respect, whatever feebleness of action may characterize the affections.

The imagination is not only entitled to be ranked under the general head of the Intellect, in distinction from the Sensibilities, but it is to be remarked further, which may, perhaps, have escaped the notice of some, that it possesses, especially in the process or mode of its action, a close affinity with the reasoning power. It is a remark ascribed to D'Alembert, whose great skill in mathematics would seem to justify his giving an opinion on such a subject, that the imagination is brought into exercise in geometrical processes; which is probably true, so far as some of the mental acts involved in imagination, such as association and the perception of relations, are concerned; and also in another respect, which he probably had in view, namely, in forming hypotheses or conjectural problems, which are subject to subsequent disproof or verification. And, in illustration of his views, he intimates, in the same connexion, that Archimedes the geometrician, of all the great men of antiquity, is best entitled to be placed by the side of Homer.* Certain it is, that, in some important respects, there is an intimate relationship between the powers in question, the rationative and imaginative. They both imply the antecedent exercise of the power of abstraction; they are both occupied in framing new combinations of thought from the elements already in possession; they both put in requisition, and in precisely the same way, the powers of association and relative suggestion. But, at the same time, they are separated from each other and characterized by the two circumstances, that their objects are different, and that they operate, in part, on different materials. Reasoning, as it aims to give us a knowledge of the truth, deals exclusively with facts more or less probable. Imagination, as it aims chiefly to give pleasure, is at liberty to transcend the limits of the world of reality, and, consequently, often deals with the mere conceptions of the mind, whether they correspond to reality or not. Accordingly, the one ascertains what is true, the other what is possible; the office of the one is to inquire, of the other to create; reasoning is exercised within the limits of what is known and actual, while the appropriate empire of the imagination is the region of the conjectural and conceivable.

§ 307. Definition of the power of imagination.

Without delaying longer upon the subject, which, however, is not without its importance, of the place which imagination ought to occupy in a philosophical

* Stewart's Historical Dissertation, Prefatory Remarks.

classification of the mental powers, we next proceed to consider more particularly what imagination is, and in what manner it operates.—Imagination, in its definition, is a complex mental power, *by means of which various conceptions are combined together so as to form new wholes.* The conceptions have properly enough been regarded as the materials from which the new creations are made; but it is not until after the existence of those mental acts, which are employed in every process of imagination, that they are fixed upon, detained, and brought out from their state of singleness into happy and beautiful combinations.

Our conceptions have sometimes been compared to shapeless stones as they exist in the quarry. These rude stones are the materials which the builder makes use of, and which subsequently appear in houses and palaces. That rude and little more than mechanic effort, which converts them into common dwellings, may justly be considered, when divested of its metaphorical aspect, a correct representation of the imagination, as it exists among the great mass of mankind; while the architectural genius which creates palaces and temples is the well-furnished and sublime imagination of poets, painters, and orators.

We speak of imagination as a complex mental operation, because it implies, in particular, the exercise of the power of association in furnishing those conceptions which are combined together; also the exercise of the power of relative suggestion, by means of which the combination is effected.

§ 308. Process of the mind in the creations of the imagination.

It may assist us in more fully understanding the nature of imagination if we endeavour to examine the intellectual operations of one who makes a formal effort at writing, whether the production he has in view be poetical or of some other kind.—A person cannot ordinarily be supposed to sit down to write on any occasion whatever, whether it involve a higher or less degree of the exercise of the imagination, without having some general idea of the subject to be written upon already in the mind. The general idea, or the subject in its *outlines*, must be supposed to be already present. He accordingly commences the task before him with the expectation and the desire of developing the subject more or less fully, of giving to it not only a greater continuity and a better arrangement, but an increased interest in every respect. As he feels interested in the topic which he proposes to write upon, he can, of course, by a mere act of the will, although he might not have been able, in the first instance, to have originated it by such an act, detain it before him for a length of time.

Various conceptions continue, in the mean while, to arise in the mind, on the common principles of association; but, as the general outline of the subject remains fixed, they all have a greater or less relation to it. And partaking, in some measure, of the permanency of the outline to which they have relation, the writer has an opportunity to approve some and to reject others, according as they impress him as being suitable or unsuitable to the nature of the subject. Those which affect him with emotions of pleasure, on account of their perceived fitness for the subject, are retained and committed to writing; while others, which do not thus affect and interest him, soon fade away altogether.—Whoever carefully notices the operations of his own mind when he makes an effort at composition, will probably be well satisfied that this account of the intellectual process is very near the truth.

§ 309. Further remarks on the same subject.

The process, therefore, stated in the most simple and concise terms, is as follows. We first think of some subject. With the original thought or design of the subject, there is a coexistent desire to investigate it, to adorn it, to present it to the examination of others. The effect of this desire, followed and aided as it naturally is at such times by an act of the will, is to keep the general subject in mind; and, as the natural consequence of the exercise of association, various conceptions arise, in some way or other related to the general subject. Of some of these conceptions we approve in consequence of their perceived fitness to the end in view, while we reject others on account of the absence of this requisite quality of agreeableness or fitness.

For the sake of convenience and brevity, we give the name of IMAGINATION to this complex state or series of states of the mind. It is important to possess a single term expressive of the complex intellectual process; otherwise, as we so frequently have occasion to refer to it in common conversation, we should be subjected, if not properly to a circumlocution, at least to an unnecessary multiplication of words. But, while we find it so much for our convenience to employ a single term, we should be careful to remember that it is the name, not of a simple, but a complex faculty; which, while it has its appropriate position, and is one in its general objects and nature, secures its results, nevertheless, by a number of successive steps.

§ 310. Illustration from the writings of Dr. Reid.

Dr. Reid (Essay iv., ch. iv.) gives the following graphical statement of the selection which is made by the writer from the variety of his constantly arising and departing conceptions: "We seem to treat the thoughts, that present themselves to the fancy in crowds, as a great man treats those [courtiers] that attend his levee. They are all ambitious of his attention. He goes round the circle, bestowing a bow upon one, a smile upon another; asks a short question of a third, while a fourth is honoured with a particular conference; and the greater part have no particular mark of attention, but go as they came. It is true, he can give no mark of his attention to those who were *not there*, but he has a sufficient number for making a choice and distinction."

§ 311. Grounds of the preference of one conception to another.

A question after all arises, On what principle is the mind enabled to ascertain that congruity or incongruity, fitness or unfitness, agreeably to which it makes the selection from its various conceptions? The fact is admitted, that the intellectual principle is successively in a series of different states, or, in other words, that there are successive conceptions or images; but the inquiry still remains, Why is one image in the group thought or known to be more worthy than any other image, or why are any two images combined together in preference to any two others?

The answer is, It is owing to no secondary law, but to an instantaneous and original suggestion of fitness or unfitness. Those conceptions which, by means of this original power of perceiving the relations of things, are found to be suitable to the general outlines of the subject, are detained. Those images which are perceived to possess a peculiar congruity and fitness for each other are united together, forming new and more beautiful compounds. While others, although no directly voluntary power appears to be exercised over either class, are neglected, and soon become extinct. The power which originates this rapid perception of the mutual congruity of the images for each other, and also for the general conception of the subject, is the relational power or relationment, which has been considered in a former chapter.

§ 312. Illustration of the subject from Milton.

What has been said can perhaps be made plainer by considering in what way Milton must have proceeded in forming his happy description of the garden of Eden. He had formed, in the first place, some general outlines of the subject; and as it was one which greatly interested his feelings, the interest which was felt tended to keep the outlines steadily before him. If the feeling of interest was not sufficient to keep the general subject before the mind, he could hardly fail to detain it there by adding the influence of a direct and decisive act of the will. Then the principles of association, which are ever at work, brought up a great variety of conceptions, having a relation of some kind to those general features, such as conceptions of rocks, and woods, and rivers, and green leaves, and golden fruit.

The next step was the exercise of that power which we have of perceiving relations, which we sometimes denominate the Judgment, but more appropriately the susceptibility or power of Relative Suggestion. By means of this he was at once able to determine whether the conceptions which were suggested were suitable to the general design of the description and to each other, and whether they would have, when combined together to form one picture, a pleasing effect. Accordingly, those which were judged most suitable were combined together as parts of the imaginary creation, and were detained and fixed by means of that feeling of interest and those acts of the will which were at first exercised towards the more prominent outlines merely; while others speedily disappeared from the mind. And thus arose an imaginary landscape, glowing with a greater variety and richness of beauty, more interesting and perfect in every respect, than we can ever expect to find realized in nature.

§ 313. The creations of imagination not entirely voluntary.

From the explanation which has been given of the operations of the power under consideration, it will be seen that in its action it is subject to limitations and restrictions. The opinion that even persons of the most ready and fruitful imagination can form new imaginary creations whenever they choose by a mere volition, however widely it may have prevailed, does not appear to be well founded. In accordance with what may be regarded as the common opinion, we will suppose, as an illustration of what we mean, that a person wills to imagine a sea of melted brass, or an immense body of liquid matter which has that appearance. The very expressions, it will be noticed, are nugatory and without meaning, since the sea of brass which the person wills to conceive of or imagine is, by the very terms of the proposition, already present to his thoughts. Whatever a person wills, or, rather, professes to will to imagine, he has, in fact, already imagined; and, consequently, there can be no such thing as imaginations which are exclusively the result of a direct act of the will. So that the powers of invention, although the influence of the indirect and subordinate action of the will may be considerable, must be aroused and quickened to their highest efforts in some other way.

And this view admits of some practical applications. Men of the greatest minds (great, we mean, in the walks of literature) are kept in check by the principles which are involved in the exercise of imagination. Genius, whatever capabilities we may attribute to it, has its laws. And it is true, in regard to every standard work of the imagination, that it is the result, not of an arbitrary and unexplainable exercise of that power, but of a multitude of circumstances prompting and regulating its action; such as the situation in life, early education, domestic habits, associates, reading, scenery, religion, and the influence of local superstitions and traditionary incidents. These are like the rain and sunshine to the earth, without which it necessarily remains in its original barrenness, giving no signs of vivification and beauty. In the matter of creative power Bunyan will bear a comparison undoubtedly with Walter Scott; but Scott, in the situation in which he was placed, and with the habits of thought and feeling which he cherished, could not have written the Pilgrim's Progress, nor could Bunyan, on the other hand, have written the Heart of Mid Lothian; not because either of them was destitute of the requisite degree of imagination, but because the creations of the imagination always have a relation to circumstances, and are not the result of a purely arbitrary act of the will.

§ 314. Illustration of the statements of the preceding section.

It would be an easy matter, and not without interest, to illustrate this fact in the operations of the mind by a reference to the private history of those individuals from whom the great works of literature have originated. But, as this does not come within our plan, we will refer merely to a single instance.—Moore relates, in his life of Lord Byron, that on a certain occasion he found him occupied with the history of Agathon, a romance by Wieland. And, from some remarks made at the time, he seems to be of opinion that Byron was reading the work in question as a means of furnishing suggestions to, and of quickening his own imaginative powers. He then adds: "I am inclined to think it was his practice, when engaged in the composition of any work, to excite his vein by the perusal of others on the same subject or plan, from which the slightest hint caught by his imagination as he read was sufficient to kindle there such a train of thought as but for that spark had never been awakened."

This is said of a distinguished poet. Painting is an art kindred with poetry, and both are based on the imagination. Accordingly, the remarks which have been made apply also to painting, and, indeed, to every other art which depends essentially on the imaginative power. "Invention," says Sir Joshua Reynolds, "is one of the great marks of genius; but, if we consult experience, we shall find that it is by being conversant with the inventions of others that we learn to invent, as by reading the thoughts of others we learn to think. It is in vain for painters or poets to endeavour to invent without materials on which the mind may work, and from which invention must originate. Nothing can come of nothing. Homer is supposed to have been possessed of all the learning of his time; and we are certain that Michael Angelo and Raffaelle were equally possessed of all the knowledge in the art which had been discovered in the works of their predecessors."*

* Discourses before the Royal Academy, VI.

§ 315. On the utility of the faculty of the imagination.

We have proceeded thus far in endeavouring to explain the nature of imagination; and we here turn aside from this general subject for the purpose of remarking on the utility of this power. And this appears to be necessary, since there are some who seem disposed to prejudice its claims in that respect. They warmly recommend the careful culture of the memory, the judgment, and the reasoning power, but look coldly and suspiciously on the imagination, and would rather encourage a neglect of it. But there is ground for apprehending that a neglect of this noble faculty in any person who aspires to a full developement and growth of the mind, cannot be justified either by considerations drawn from the nature of the mind itself, or by the practical results of such a course.

In speaking on the utility of the imagination, it is certainly a very natural reflection, that the Creator had some design or purpose in furnishing men with it, since we find universally that he does nothing in vain. And what design could he possibly have, if he did not intend that it should be employed, that it should be rendered active, and trained up with a suitable degree of culture? But if we are thus forced upon the conclusion that this faculty was designed to be rendered active, we must further suppose that its exercise was designed to promote some useful purpose. And such, although it has sometimes been perverted, has been the general result.

Nowhere is the power of imagination seen to better advantage than in the Prophets of the Old Testament. If it be said that those remarkable writers were inspired, it will still remain true that this was one of the faculties of the mind which inspiration especially honoured by the use which was made of it. And how many monuments may every civilized nation boast of, in painting, architecture, and sculpture, as well as in poetry, where the imagination, in contributing to the national glory, has at the same time contributed to the national happiness! Many an hour it has beguiled by the new situations it has depicted and the new views of human nature it has disclosed; many a pang of the heart it has subdued, either by introducing us to greater woes which others have suffered, or by intoxicating the memory with its luxuriance, and lulling it into a forgetfulness of ourselves; many a good resolution it has cherished, and subtending, as it were, a new and wider horizon around the intellectual being, has filled the soul with higher conceptions and inspired it with higher hopes. Conscious of its immortal destiny, and struggling against the bounds that limit it, the soul enters with joy into those new and lofty creations which it is the prerogative of the imagination to form; and they seem to it a congenial residence. Such are the views which obviously present themselves on the slightest consideration of this subject; and it is not strange, therefore, that we find in the writings of no less a judge than Addison, some remarks to this effect, that a refined imagination "gives a man a kind of property in everything he sees, and makes the most rude, uncultivated parts of nature administer to his pleasures; so that he looks upon the world, as it were, in another light, and discovers in it a multitude of charms that conceal themselves from the generality of mankind."

§ 316. Works of imagination give different degrees of pleasure.

Disposed as we are, however, to maintain the high rank of the imagination as compared with other powers of the mind, and not only its high rank, but its utility, we do not deny that different persons experience different degrees of pleasure from that source. Poetry, for instance, is one of the results of the imagination; and although it is generally regarded as a highly pleasing as well as useful art, we nevertheless find that all persons do not possess the same relish for its beauties. But the fault does not appear to be so much in the art, or the powers of imagination which give existence to the art, as in those to whom it is addressed. The pleasure which is felt by a reader of poetry (and similar remarks will apply to other efforts of the imagination) will in general depend upon three circumstances: (1.) the liveliness of his own imagination; (2.) the conformity of his experience to the things described; and (3.) the degree of aesthetic culture.

The pleasure which is felt by a reader of poetry will depend in part, in the first place, on the liveliness of his own imagination.—In poems the different parts are only imperfectly filled up; some describe more minutely than others; but the most minute describers only trace the outlines. These remain, therefore, to be filled up by the reader. But the ability to do this is found in very different degrees in different persons; some very rapidly and admirably finish the picture, and others do not. The latter, consequently, remain in a considerable degree unaffected, and perhaps condemn the poem as deficient in interest; while the former read it with great feeling and pleasure.

The pleasure will depend, in the second place, on the conformity of the reader's experience to the things described. If the scene of the poem is laid in the country, and deals exclusively in the toils, and sorrows, and joys of country life, it would not be unreasonable to anticipate that it might not excite any decided interest in those who never had any actual experience of that kind. It will probably be conceded that few poems, and perhaps none, have met with a more favourable reception, and have touched more deeply the universal sensibility, than the Cotter's Saturday Night of Burns. It is certainly a most admirable picture of domestic life, such as may sometimes be found among a poor and virtuous peasantry, with its little touching incidents of joy, and hope, and grief, of friendship and religious faith. It can hardly fail to be pleasing to all, but how much more so to those who had their birth and were brought up in the cottages of Scotland; who trod in early life her rugged hills, and mingled in the rural toils of her peasantry; and in whose bosoms every incident of the poem awakens some affecting recollections. Burns himself was by no means ignorant of the additional pleasure which arises under these circumstances. "He was passionately fond," says Dugald Stewart, "of the beauties of nature; and I recollect once he told me, when I was admiring a distant prospect in one of our morning walks, that the sight of so many smoking cottages gave a pleasure to his mind, which none could understand who had not witnessed, like himself, the happiness and the worth which they contained."*

And it remains further to be remarked, in connexion with the different results of poetic genius, that, while some poems are characterized by simplicity, there are others so elaborate in their finish, that a person who has not greatly cultivated the emotions of taste necessarily loses much of the pleasure he would otherwise experience. Those who are acquainted with the admirably artistic works of Virgil and Horace will understand what we mean; and among the illustrations furnished by English literature, it will be sufficient to mention the poems of Akenside, Campbell, and Rogers, which will be fully appreciated only by persons of great mental refinement.

While, therefore, we do not hesitate to assert the utility of the imagination and the adaptedness of its more successful creations to give a high degree of pleasure, we do not suppose, for the reasons mentioned in this section and for others which might be mentioned, that these views will answer equally well to the experience, or commend themselves equally to the judgment of all.

§ 317. Importance of the imagination in connexion with reasoning.

In remarking on the subject of the utility of the imagination, there is one important point of view in which it is capable of being considered; that of the relation of the imagination to the other intellectual powers. And, among other things, there is obviously

* See the letter of Mr. Stewart in Currie's Life of Burns.

ground for the remark, that a vigorous and well-disciplined imagination may be made subservient to promptness, and clearness, and success in reasoning. The remark is made, it will be noticed, on the supposition of the imagination being well disciplined, which implies that it is under suitable control; otherwise it will rather encumber and perplex than afford aid.

Take, for instance, two persons, one of whom has cultivated the reasoning power exclusive of the imagination. We will suppose him to possess very deservedly the reputation of an able and weighty dialectician; but it will be obvious to the slightest observation, that there is, in one respect, a defect and failure; there is an evident want of selection and vivacity in the details of his argument. He cannot readily appreciate the relation which the hearer's mind sustains to the facts which he wishes to present; and, accordingly, with much expense of patience on their part, he laboriously and very scrupulously takes up and examines everything which can come within his grasp, and bestows upon everything nearly an equal share of attention. And hence it is that many persons who are acknowledged to be learned, diligent, and even successful in argument, at the same time sustain the reputation, which is by no means an enviable one, of being dull, tiresome, and uninteresting.

Let us now look a moment at another person, who is not only a man of great powers of ratiocination, but has cultivated his imagination, and has it under prompt and judicious command. He casts his eye rapidly over the whole field of argument, however extensive it may be, and immediately perceives what facts are necessary to be stated and what are not; what are of prominent, and what of subordinate importance; what will be easily understood and possess an interest, and what will be difficult to be appreciated, and will also lose its due value from a want of attraction. And he does this on the same principle, and in virtue of the same mental training, which enables the painter, architect, sculptor, and poet to present the outlines of grand

and beautiful creations in their respective arts. There is a suitableness in the different parts of the train of reasoning; a correspondence of one part to another; a great and combined effect, enhanced by every suitable decoration, and undiminished by any misplaced excrescence, which undoubtedly implies a perfection of the imagination, in some degree kindred with that which projected the group of the Laocoon, crowned the hills of Greece with statues and temples, and lives in the works of renowned poets.

§ 318. Of misconceptions by means of the imagination.

But while it is safe to admit that the imagination may be made subservient to valuable purposes, it is no less true that it may sometimes mislead us. The following are instances, among others, where this is the result.

Our admiration of the great may be reckoned a prejudice of the imagination. We are apt to suppose them possessed of personal attractions, and of the highest happiness; and not only this, to invest them with every worthy moral attribute. "The misfortunes," says a late writer, "of Mary Queen of Scots, and of her descendant, Prince Charles Edward, commanded the sympathy, the love, and the enthusiasm of millions. In the cause of these princes, how many have joyfully sacrificed life, though neither of them was worthy or capable of reigning! How many labour still to blot out every stain from their memory! And yet every individual, in the circle of his own private friends and acquaintances, can undoubtedly find many persons more distinguished for virtue, for good principles, for integrity of character, than the prince for whom he is willing to lay down his life; but a friend, a private man, is invested with none of those attributes, always dazzling but often false, which are calculated to strike the imagination."

Our imaginations mislead us also in respect to war, whenever we contemplate it at a distance, and do not feel its effects at our own firesides and homes. We delight to dwell upon the idea of mighty power which it suggests; we recall to memory the homage and plaudits which have been given to the brave; we combine together conceptions of all that is stirring in music and brilliant in equipage. In a word, it is a kindling imagination, seizing upon some imposing circumstances, that leads multitudes into deplorable mistakes as to the character of that great scourge of the human race.—Again: the power of imagination often gives a wrong colouring to future life. It is here as in some prospects in natural scenery,

"'Tis distance lends enchántment to the view."

Whatever may be our present evils, we imagine there is good to come. We rush forward in the pursuit of it like children, who set out with spirited emulation, expecting to grasp in their hands the splendours of the rainbow, that appears to them to rest upon the neighbouring hills.

§ 319. **Explanation of the above misrepresentations of the imagination.**

But how happens it that this faculty, in these and other similar instances, sometimes misleads us? What explanation can be given?—The answer is, that the mind turns away with a natural aversion from whatever causes it pain or uneasiness; delighting to dwell on the elements of beauty and sublimity, and, in general, on all scenes which excite in it pleasant emotions. As there is, therefore, more or less in all actual situations which causes dissatisfaction, we shall always find, in every condition in which we are placed, something which detracts from what we imagine to be the sum of happiness. The evils which are around us and near us, we MUST know; our situation forbids an attempt at the concealment of them. Every day forces the lesson of human adversity on our attention. But when we look abroad from the reality which exists at home, from the cares and sorrows which are ever near at hand, to other scenes and prospects, we do not think of trial and disappointment, because we are not obliged to. We fix our attention upon those circumstances which appear most favourable and interesting; and, consequently, know nothing of the uneasiness and misery which actually exist in the imaginary paradise of our creation.—For instance, we are apt to associate, as has been remarked, with persons in very high stations of life, the ideas of unalloyed happiness, of moral excellence, of manliness and beauty of form; but while men in the most exalted stations have no less a share than others of bodily deformities and suffering, they have still greater anxieties; their hours of sorrow are often more numerous than those of any other class of persons. It was well inquired by King Henry in Shakspeare,

> "What infinite heart's ease must kings neglect,
> That private men enjoy?
> And what have kings, that privates have not too,
> Save ceremony, save general ceremony?"

And under the direction of the same mental tendency by which we are led to mark the elevations without noticing the depressions of the great men of the earth, we are led also to see the sublimities and hide from our sight the degradations and miseries of war, to behold the sunshine of the future, but no clouds.

§ 320. Feelings of sympathy aided by the imagination.

But where the imagination is not at liberty to fix itself exclusively upon pleasing circumstances, the results as to the degree of creative power are the same, although they are of a different kind. In the one case it forms creations of beauty, magnificence, sublimity; in the other it is equally efficacious in combining images of gloom and suffering. Hence a quick and powerful imagination is no small aid in the exercise of the sympathetic feelings. Accordingly, when two men (the one a person of imagination, the other not) meet a poor man who has suddenly been reduced to poverty, they will be found to have different degrees of sympathy for him. The latter, no doubt, will pity the unfortunate man; but the former will pity him more. He will think of his former situation; he will follow him to his dwelling; he will see in his "prophetic eye" the tears of his family; in a word, he will, as a general statement, have more feeling for all individuals in suffering, and, consequently, be more likely to lend his aid to alleviate it.

Thus, in Sterne's Sentimental Journey, he is led by some circumstance to think of a captive in one of the French State Prisons. He gives the reins to his imagination, "and looks through the twilight of the grated door to take the picture.—I beheld," says he, "his body half wasted with long expectation and confinement, and felt what kind of sickness of the heart it is which arises from hope deferred. Upon looking nearer, I saw him pale and feverish. In thirty years the western breeze had not fanned his blood. He had seen no sun, no moon, in all that time; nor had the voice of friend or kinsman breathed through his lattice.—His children—but here my heart began to bleed, and I was forced to go on with another part of the portrait."

CHAPTER XV.

COMPLEX IDEAS OF INTERNAL ORIGIN.

§ 321. Of complex ideas of external origin.

It will be recollected that, in considering that portion of our knowledge which has an external origin, our mental states were examined in relation to their Simplicity and Complexness. The names of colours, as red, white, yellow, green, and the like, were spoken of as being expressive of simple ideas, or, rather, of simple sensations. The character of simplicity belongs also to the original intimations of the touch, and to the original sensations of the hearing, smell, and taste. Other names, as loadstone, tree, sun, gold, and the like, were referred to as expressive of complex notions. It was laid down as characteristic of simple notions, that they are one and inseparable, while such as are complex embrace any number of simple ideas more than one.

But in respect to complex notions of an external origin, there is this further and obvious characteristic. When they are ascertained with suitable care, they are just what the forms of external nature have constituted them, being neither more nor less extensive. In our complex notions, for instance, of a loadstone, a tree, the sun, animal, man, horse, gold, &c., we embrace precisely what nature has allotted to the objects themselves; that is to say, if our complex ideas in these particular cases be properly and fully formed. Nature, as she exists external to the mind, has placed a limit on combinations of this kind which we are clearly not at liberty to disregard.

§ 322. Nature of complex ideas of internal origin.

But in considering, as we do at present, that portion of our knowledge which is not directly dependant on external objects, we are naturally led to remark on complex notions of internal origin. Complex ideas of this description are like all others, in being composed of elementary parts which are simple. Suggestion or Intuition, Consciousness, Relative Suggestion, and the Reasoning power, which are the great sources of internal knowledge, are all fountains of new simple views. A multitude of thoughts, unknown to the mind before, arise from these various sources, which are not susceptible of being resolved into others more elementary. But, while we cannot resolve, we are able to combine them in a variety of ways almost endless.

But the prominent characteristic of the complex mental states now under consideration is not that the elementary parts come in a great degree from these sources; it is rather the mind's agency in forming them. We are not limited, in the process of combination, by any precise complication of qualities in outward objects, which is the fact in respect to complex notions of external origin; but may bring together ideas of the same or of different kinds, and may form new wholes of every imaginable description. Such new notions, considered in reference to what they are in their complex state, are purely creatures of the mind, fashioned by the mind's choice, and capable of being altered, according to the mere dictates of that choice, into every degree of enlargement and diminution, and into every novelty of aspect.—It is on this ground chiefly that they are characterized as being of internal rather than of external origin.

§ 323. Of complex notions formed by the repetition of the same thing.

In some instances we find the same ideas repeated a greater or less number of times, and susceptible of enlargement and variety by the mere addition or multiplication of itself. By means of such repetition we become possessed of various complex notions, which are distinguished from others merely in being modifications of the same original thought, carried on to a greater or less extent, but without any intermixture of foreign materials.

Of the ideas of this class are such as are expressed by the words hour, day, week, month, and year; which are framed by the modification, and the adding together, as it were, of our elementary notions of time. Artificial measures of extension, such as an inch, foot, yard, furlong, and mile, although they are based upon something which is directly addressed to the outward senses, are nevertheless, in themselves considered, the arbitrary creations of the mind, and, of course, belong here.—To this class also belong the complex ideas of number, as a dozen, a score, a hundred, a thousand, which are formed by the repeated addition of units, as far as the collections specified by those names.

The origin of the elementary notion of unity or oneness was explained on a former occasion; and it is not only one of the earliest, but one of the most distinct notions men have. This simple elementary idea lays the foundation of all the numerous and diversified combinations of numbers. And it is worthy of remark, that these combinations, although they are carried to a wonderful extent, are exceedingly distinct in the mind's conception of them, so as to be but seldom confounded with each other, or attended with any perplexity. There is, for instance, no confusion and indistinctness in the complex idea expressed by the word MILLION, although it might not be unreasonable to expect it when we consider the vast number of subordinate parts embraced in it. But this is owing, in part, to certain facilities afforded to the mind by the numerical signs used, and by language in particular.

§ 324. Of the help afforded by names in the combination of numbers.

A certain writer remarks on the skilful formation of the names of numbers, and on the assistance afforded by them, in the following terms.—" And here we may take notice of a wonderful artifice made use of by the mind to facilitate and help itself forward in its conceptions. For, as the advance from number to number is endless, were they all to be distinguished by different denominations that had no connection or dependance one upon another, the multitude of them must soon overcharge the memory, and render it impossible for us to go any great way in the progress of numbering. For this reason it is so contrived, that the change of names is restrained to a few of the first combinations, all the rest that follow being marked by a repetition of the same terms, variously compounded and linked together. Thus thirteen is ten and three; fourteen, ten and four; and so on to twenty or two tens, when we begin again with one, two, &c., until we advance to thirty, or three tens. In this manner the progression continues; and when we arrive at ten tens, to prevent confusion by a too frequent repetition of the same word, that sum is distinguished by the name of a hundred. Again, ten hundred is called a thousand, at which period the computation begins anew, running through all the former combinations, as ten thousand, a hundred thousand, ten hundred thousand; which last collection, for the reasons mentioned above, has the name of million appropriated to it. With this million we can begin as before, until it is repeated a million of times; when, if we change the denomination to billions, and advance in the same manner through trillions, quartillions, &c., the series may be carried on without confusion to any length we please.

"This artful combination of names to mark the gradual increase of numbers is perhaps one of the greatest refinements of the human understanding, and particularly deserves our admiration for the manner of the composition; the several denominations being so contrived as to distinguish exactly the stages of the progression, and point out the distance from the beginning of the series. By this means it happens that our ideas of numbers are of all others the most accurate and distinct; nor does the multitude of units assembled together in the least puzzle or confound the understanding."*

§ 325. **Instances of complex notions made up of different simple ideas.**

The instances which have been given will perhaps be sufficient in illustration of those complex notions where the combination is limited to one original element. And we shall now proceed to the consideration of those cases where the act of combining is of a more complicated kind, and these are much more numerous than the others. Men are necessarily led, according to their manner of life, their situation and wants, to frame such permanent collections of simple ideas as experience has ascertained to be useful and necessary. They even frame such complex notions, in many cases, without waiting to be guided by expe-

* Duncan's Elements of Logic, bk. i., chap. iv.—The same subject is examined also and illustrated by Mr. Locke in that part of his Essay which treats of Mixed Modes.

rience, but in anticipation of what may possibly take place at some future time; or frame them, not unfrequently, as the mere exercise of invention. And as they advance in knowledge, and make improvements in the arts and sciences, they are necessarily led into complicated views of things, which would otherwise not offer themselves to their notice.

A few instances will help to illustrate what has been said.—The word THEFT is the name of a complex notion. It may perhaps be defined a change of property without the consent of the owner, and with fraudulent intentions on the part of the person who removes it. Consequently, it embraces, among other ideas differing from each other, those of ownership, evil design, transference, and the withholding of consent. If, however, we fully and minutely resolve it into its parts, we shall undoubtedly find elements not purely of an internal kind. And it is proper to make the general remark here, which has already been in part anticipated, that very many complex notions embrace elements, a part of which are addressed to the senses, and are, consequently, of an external origin, while others have their origin wholly in the mind. But while the elements, in many cases of internal complex notions, are partly of external origin, the selection and arrangement of them is wholly a mental work. Accordingly, while the complex terms GOLD, LOADSTONE, IRON, and others like them, embrace just what nature has allotted to the objects themselves, without the liability of increase or diminution from the mere arbitrary choice of men, the complex term THEFT, and all others like it, includes (whether it be more or less) what the human mind has agreed upon and assigned to it, and is liable to be modified from the same cause.—The word LEGISLATION also is the name of a complex idea of internal origin, implying the existence of a number of elements of thought, which are arbitrarily brought together and united by the mind, such as the existence of civil society, the formation of government, the delegation of power to certain individuals, and the exercise of that power in the making of laws.—The word TREASON implies the notions of country, government, law, obligation, agent, and violation of law; while PATRIOTISM, on the other hand, includes, in connexion with the ideas of country, government, and law, the notions of obedience, respect, and love, and the disposition to make great sacrifices in consequence of such love.

It is needless further to multiply instances in this place, since they make a great portion of every language, and will readily occur to the recollection. Notions thus formed, as they are the creations of the mind, are undoubtedly liable to be altered by it; and are, in fact, not unfrequently so, although there is in general a good degree of permanency. The combination, it will be recollected, is not formed in the first instance without a good reason; and while the circumstances which at first required its formation remain, the complex notion will be likely to remain also. And not only this; there is a great security of the permanency of the complex notion in the mere name itself. The name is fixed upon the thought, as the seal upon the wax; every time we see it, or have it brought to our notice in any other way, the precise combination of ideas which makes up the complex notion is suggested to the mind. Every repetition of this suggestion strengthens the bond of complexity, and diminishes the liability of its being rent asunder, or altered in any way whatever.

§ 326. Not the same internal complex ideas in all languages.

It is proper to repeat the remark here, that the origin of complex notions will depend in a great measure on the situation and the exigencies of men; and that, consequently, the words employed in different languages will often fail of precisely corresponding to each other. This is the natural and unavoidable result of the differences which, in different countries, exist in customs, habits, scenery, occupations, modes of thinking, and political institutions. Every language, therefore, as a matter of necessity, has not only its own terms and idioms expressive of the ordinary mass of ideas common to all men, but has some which are peculiar to itself, and to which there is nothing precisely corresponding in other languages. Thus the words CORBAN in the Hebrew, OSTRAKISMOS in the Greek, PROSCRIPTIO in the Latin, and ROTURIER in the French,* express ideas to which most other nations find nothing precisely answering, and, consequently, have no corresponding words.

This diversity will be manifest, not only in a few scattering terms, but will more or less be characteristic of whole departments of science. If, for instance, we make the laws of a country the subject of our examination, we shall readily see how mental perceptions and their combinations have been modified by circumstances; and that terms are used, expressive of such peculiarities in the people's views, principles, and practices, which cannot be understood without a particular study of their origin and their applications. It is certainly not too much to say that there are many languages in which an English book of law could not be written; and many of those who speak them would be unable to understand and appreciate it, if it could be. Their minds have not been cast in the mould of Englishmen; they have not been trained, from the moment they were capable of any mental discrimination whatever, to the recognition of personal rights, and the distinctions and rights of property.

This suggests a remark on the changes which take place in languages. It is well known that there are frequent alterations in the customs of a people, and also in their feelings and opinions, and hence there necessarily arise corresponding changes in the combinations of thought or ideas, and these must, in many cases, be expressed by new names. If people should be found unwilling or unable to invent new names

* "We have no English word," says Hallam, "that expresses the sense of *roturier*. How glorious is this deficiency in our political language, and how different are the ideas suggested by *commoner!*"

for the expression of new complex ideas, they would evidently be subjected to great inconvenience. This may be seen if we deprive ourselves of the benefit of any complex terms, for instance, *reprieve*, *appeal*, *inherit*, *adjudicate*, *legislate*, and the like, and then attempt to converse on the subjects where they naturally occur.

§ 327. Origin of the complex notion of a Supreme Being.

In connexion with the views of this chapter, it is proper to add, that we find here, more properly than anywhere else, the origin of the notion of a God. If there were any outward likeness of the Supreme Being; if he were addressed to our senses in the shape of the sun, moon, or stars, or anything else which the eyes of men have seen or the hands of men have fashioned, this would not be the appropriate place for the consideration of this topic, but it should have been treated of under the head of notions of an External origin. But it is far otherwise. God is a spirit, and his representative, or that which corresponds to him in others, is not in outward nature, but in the inward contemplation. His image arises and shines in the intellects he has created, and the emotions of the heart bow down and worship it.

The idea of the Supreme Being is a complex one, made up of many subordinate parts, such as the ideas of wisdom, truth, justice, power, benevolence, and causation; and all these enlarged and expanded to correspond with the notions of infinity. The mind gathers these subordinate conceptions from within and without; from the works of nature and from its own structure; from the world of intellect and feeling, and the world of matter. Ranging abroad in the great creation both of the spiritual and the material handiworks of the Most High, it finds one elementary thought here and another there; and perceiving the necessity of their approach and union in one independent existence, it is in this way that the vast and exalted conception we are considering results from their combination.

It is probably owing to this method of its origin that the complex notion of a Supreme being is so different in different nations. Where the moral views of the people are wanting in elevation, and the notions they form of truth, wisdom, and justice in particular, are low and inadequate, the combined or complex notion of a God, which embraces these elementary parts, will be depressed to a correspondence with its elements. And, on the other hand, wherever we find the perception of the human intellect not only highly purified and enlightened by human culture, but raised and guided also by the Holy Scriptures, we shall find a comprehensive and transcendent idea of the Deity, correspondent, in some good degree, to the glorious reality it expresses. For such a Being, and thus distinctively revealed to us in the soul, "we may cherish," in the words of Degerando, "the most august love which the heart of a creature can conceive; adoration, mingled with gratitude and confidence, finding its true and inexhaustible object in the source of infinite perfection, in the image of an eternal Benefactor."

CONCLUDING REMARKS.

Such is the view of the Intellect, in its normal action (not of the mind as a whole, but of the perceptive or intellective part of the mind), which seems to us accordant with the facts of personal consciousness, and with the record of the mind, as it discloses itself in the observation of others around us, and in human history. Not of the Will, and not of the Sensibilities, which remain to be considered, but of the Intellect alone, developing itself into the two great forms of the Sensuous and the Super-sensuous, otherwise known as Sensationalism and Intellectualism; and not only in the successive cognitive powers—all related to each other, and yet all comparatively independent—of Sensation, Perception, Conceptivity, Abstraction, Intuition, Consciousness, Relative Suggestion, and Reasoning, but also, closely related to, and yet discriminated from, the sources of cognition, in the great power of Imagination; together with the Auxiliary powers, which so greatly diversify and enhance the mental action, of Habit, Attention, Association, and Memory. If our inquiries stopped here, and we had nothing further to say, we could not fail to be impressed with the dignity and greatness of man's nature, and with the wisdom and goodness of the Being from whom he came.

DIVISION FIRST.

THE INTELLECT OR UNDERSTANDING.

INTELLECTIVE OR INTELLECTUAL STATES OF THE MIND.

PART THIRD.

IMPERFECT AND DISORDERED INTELLECTUAL ACTION.

CHAPTER I.

CONNEXION OF THE MIND AND BODY.

§ 328. Disordered intellectual action connected with the body.

Having completed our examination of the Intellect, so far as it presents itself to our notice in its more frequent and regular action, we now propose to conclude the subject by giving some instances of intellectual states which appear to take place in violation of its ordinary principles.* Whatever anticipations we might have been disposed to form À PRIORI, in relation to the action of the mind, it is a matter abundantly confirmed by painful experience and observation, that its operations are not always uniform; and that in some cases, as we shall have occasion to see, it exhibits an utter and disastrous deviation from the laws which commonly regulate it. The causes of these deviations it may not be easy always, and in all respects, to explain; but it is well understood that they are frequently connected with an irregular and diseased condition of the body. There may be, and there undoubtedly are, other causes more remote from common observation, and more intimately connected with the interior nature and the more secret springs of mental action; but this does not preclude a distinct and particular attention to one so obvious, and by general concession so powerful, as that which we now refer to. Accordingly, it will be the object of the few remarks embraced in this Chapter, and as introduc-

* Note.—The subject of Disordered Mental Action is one undoubtedly of great interest, but it is also one of no small difficulty. We have endeavoured in another volume (No. c. of Harpers' Family Library) to examine the subject at greater length. The chapters which are introduced here, together with some others having relation to the same general subject of Disordered Mental Action, are merely abridgments of what is to be found there. And to that volume, the reader who wishes for more particular information may perhaps properly be referred.

tory, in some degree, to what follows on the subject of disordered intellectual action, to show by some statements and illustrations the connexion existing between the body and mind, and the influence they reciprocally exert.

§ 329. The mind constituted on the principle of a connexion with the body.

In endeavouring to illustrate the subject of the intimate connexion and the reciprocal influence of the mind and body, the first remark is, that the mind is evidently constituted on the principle of such a connexion. Whatever expansion the mind may afterward attain to, whatever greatness of power it may exhibit in the progress of its subsequent developement, there is no doubt that it possesses the seeds of its power and the elements of its expansion in the very beginnings of its existence. They are there, although at first they do not manifest themselves. They have an existence, although they are in some sense invisible and unappreciable. They are not only in silence and in darkness, but, in themselves considered, and independently of aid from other sources, they appear to be destitute of any capability of quickening into action and of bursting forth into light.

And how does this happen? Evidently because the mind is constituted on the principle of a connexion with the body. The human mind (and this is probably true of every mind that is morally accountable) exists in the threefold nature or threefold division of the Intellect, the Sensibilities, and the Will. The action of the Will depends upon the antecedent action of the Sensibilities; and that of the sentimentive nature is based upon the antecedent action of the Intellect. The action of the Intellect or Understanding is twofold, External and Internal. And we have already endeavoured, on a former occasion, to show that the developement of the External Understanding is first in the order of time, as it is obviously first in the order of nature. It is here, so far as the mind is concerned, that we find the commencement of action; but it is well understood and is entirely undeniable, that all the action which takes place here, takes place in connexion with bodily action. The External intellect does not act, nor is it capable of acting, although the mind is so constituted that the movement of all the other parts depends upon movement here, without the antecedent affection of the outward or bodily senses.

In some remarks on this subject in a former chapter, we suggested that the soul, considered in its relationship to external objects, might be compared to a stringed instrument. That comparison may help to illustrate the subject here. In the essence of its own nature the soul is unseen and unsearchable, although it not only has an existence, but possesses the capacity and elements of mental harmony. But God has erected around it, unseen and intangible as it is, an outward structure of visible chords and artificial framework, such as the wonderful system of the nerves, the eye, the ear, and the senses generally. In accordance with this arrangement, the soul, although it has in itself the original and abundant source of harmony, will always be found (such is the law or principle on which it is constituted) to be utterly without music and without voice, until it is wakened into life and the utterance of appropriate sounds by an impulse communicated through the outward structure. The internal susceptibility must be interrogated through the openings of the exterior edifice; the tangible and visible chords must be smitten before the required response will be yielded by the mysterious and invisible agent beneath them.—These are the facts; but, as this topic has been particularly noticed upon a former occasion, we shall not further delay upon it here.

§ 330. Illustration of the subject from the effects of old age.

The existence of the connexion between the mind and body, and of their influence upon each other, appears, in the second place, from the effects which are witnessed in old age. The effects of old age, it is true, are first experienced in the bodily system. The outward senses become blunted and dim; the eye loses its keenness of sight; the ear its quickness of hearing; the palate its nice discriminations of taste; and in various other ways the whole bodily system shows the rapid diminution of its activity and power. But it is well known, since it is a matter of every day's observation, that these effects are not restricted to that part of the human system where they first show themselves. The mind also is unfavourably affected at the same time, and through the influence of the same causes.

These results, it is true, are not experienced to a great extent in the Internal Intellect, or that division of the intellect which operates in the discovery of truth, independent in a great measure of the outward senses; but they are seen and felt, perhaps we may say without a single exception, and in a high degree, in that department of the mind which we have proposed to designate, in consequence of its depending in its action on the external senses, as the External Intellect. As the senses one after another are prostrated, this portion of the intellective nature, which, as was noticed in the last section, was brought into action through their instrumentality, seems to fall and lie prostrate with them. It seems to be hardly less deaf and blind, hardly less sensible to the intimations of touch and taste, and to stand less in need of crutches to support it, than the bowed and superannuated body which it had formerly employed as the medium of its activity. The higher departments of the soul, as has been intimated, remain essentially firm and unshaken; but this, which has a particularly close connexion with the bodily nature, and is based, as it were, upon a foundation of materiality, is necessarily blunted and disordered in its action by the dislocation and breaking up of the earthy materials.

§ 331. The connexion of the bodily system with the mental shown from the effects resulting from diseases.

In addition to what has been said, it may be remarked further, in confirmation of the same general views, that violent corporeal diseases in youth and manhood, before any decays take place from age, often affect the powers of thought. Persons have been known, for instance, after a violent fever or violent attacks of some other form of disease, to lose entirely the power of recollection. Thucydides, in his account of the plague of Athens, makes mention of some persons who had survived that disease; but their intense bodily sufferings had affected their mental constitution so much, that they had forgotten their families and friends, and had lost all knowledge of their own former history.—It is a singular fact, also, that the result of violent disease is sometimes quite the reverse of what has now been stated. While in one case the memory is entirely prostrated, we find in others that, under the influence of such attacks, the memory is suddenly aroused, and restores the history of the past with a minuteness and vividness unknown before. But both classes of cases confirm what we are now attempting to show, viz., the existence of a connexion between the mind and body, and a reciprocal influence between them.

§ 332. Shown also from the effects of stimulating drugs and gases.

If there be not a close connexion between the body and mind, and if there be not various influences propagated from one to the other, how does it happen that many things of a stimulating nature, such as ardent spirits and opium, strongly affect the mind when taken into the system in considerable quantities? But, without delaying upon the effects of drugs of this description, which, unhappily, can hardly fail to be noticed every day, we would instance particularly the results which are found to follow from the internal use of the nitrous oxide gas. This gas, when it is received into the system, operates, in the first instance, on the body. The effect is a *physical* one. In particular, it quickens the circulation of the blood; and also, as is commonly supposed increases the volume of that fluid. But its effects, which are first felt in the body, are afterward experienced in the mind, and generally in a high degree. When it is inhaled in a considerable quantity, the sensations are more acute, the conceptions of absent objects are more vivid, associated trains of thought pass through the mind with increased rapidity, and emotions and passions, generally of a pleasant kind, are excited, corresponding in strength to the increased acuteness of sensations and the increased vividness of conceptions.

There is another gas, known in some writers as the FEBRILE MIASMA, which is found, on being inhaled, to affect the mind also, by first affecting the sanguineous fluid. But this gas diminishes instead of increasing the volume of blood, as is indicated by a small, contracted pulse, and an increasing constriction of the capillaries. As in the case of the nitrous oxide gas, the mental exercises are rendered intense and vivid by the febrile miasma; but the emotions which are experienced, instead of being pleasant, are gloomy and painful. The trains of thought which are at such times suggested, and the creations of the imagination, are all of an analogous character, strange, spectral, and terrifying.*—We may add as a general remark here, that, whenever the physical condition of the brain, which is a prominent organ in the process of sensation and external perception, is affected, whether it be from a more than common fulness of the bloodvessels or from some other cause, the mind itself will be found to be affected also, and oftentimes in a high degree.

§ 333. **Influence on the body of excited imagination and passion.**

The powers of the mind are not only liable to be powerfully affected by certain conditions of the corporeal system, but the body also, on the other hand, even to the functions of the vital principle itself, is liable to corresponding affections, superinduced by certain conditions of the mind. When the passions, for instance, are excited, particularly that of fear, the body

* See Hibbert's Philosophy of Apparitions, pt. ii., ch. i.

at once feels the influence; and instances have occurred where, under the influence of the last-named passion, even death itself has followed.—In the city of New-York a few years since, a little child was left in the evening in the care of a maid-servant, the mother having gone out. As the child was disposed to be troublesome and to cry after being placed at the usual time in bed in another room, the domestic resorted to the expedient of quieting it by making and placing before it the image of some frightful object. The fears of the little child were greatly excited; and when, in the latter part of the evening, the mother returned and went to the room, she found it dead; its eyes being open, and fixed with a singularly wild and maniac kind of stare on the frightful image which the girl had so cruelly placed before it.—In the time of the American Revolution, as the transaction was related by an officer who was present, a soldier, who had committed some crime, was condemned to be shot. He was finally pardoned, without a knowledge of the pardon being communicated to him, since it was thought advisable that he should be made to suffer as much as possible from the fear of death. In accordance with this plan, he was led at the appointed time to the place of execution; the bandage was placed over his eyes; and the soldiers were drawn out, but were privately ordered to fire over his head. At the discharge of their muskets, although nothing touched him, the man fell dead on the spot.—"A criminal was once sentenced in England to be executed, when a college of physicians requested liberty to make him the subject of an experiment connected with their profession. It was granted. The man was told that his sentence was commuted, and that he was to be bled to death. On the appointed day several physicians went to the prison, and made the requisite preparations in his presence; the lancet was displayed, bowls were in readiness to receive the blood, and the culprit was directed to place himself on his back, with his arm extended, ready to receive the fatal incision. When all this was done, his eyes were bandaged. In the mean time, a sufficient quantity of lukewarm water had been provided; his arm was merely touched with the lancet, and the water, poured slowly over it, was made to trickle down into the bowl below. One of the physicians felt his pulse, and the others frequently exchanged such remarks as, 'He is nearly exhausted—cannot hold out much longer—grows very pale,' &c.; and in a short time the criminal actually *died* from the force of imagination."*

§ 334. This doctrine of use in explaining mental phenomena.

These illustrations of the connexion existing between the body and mind, and of their influence on each other, are brought together here in order to prevent the necessity of hereafter interrupting our examination of other subjects by a particular recurrence to this. There might be a much more extended narration of facts, all tending to the same conclusion; but we take it for granted that it is unnecessary. We shall accordingly hereafter regard it as a settled principle, whenever a particular effect in the mind is ascribed to an influence from the body, that such bodily influence is at least *possible.* We may perhaps mistake, in a given case, in assigning the true corporeal cause; but this will not imply that there is no such thing as corporeal causes of mental action, or that such causes are inadequate to great effects. If we would understand the mind, we must also understand the body, not because they are identical, but because they are related. And for the same reason, if we would possess a sound mind, a mind capable of exertion corresponding to its capacity, we must endeavour to possess soundness of body. In another and future state of being, where the connexion which now exists will be broken, and the spiritual will be divorced from the material, it is possible that mental philosophy may be predicated on other principles; but, as matters now are, to attempt

* As the statement is given in the Work entitled Popular Superstitions.

to explain the phenomena of the soul without a recognition of its relationship to the body, is a violation of fact and an absurdity in reason.

CHAPTER II.

EXCITED CONCEPTIONS OR APPARITIONS.

§ 335. Of excited conceptions and of apparitions in general.

HAVING prepared the way by what has been said on the connexion existing between the mind and body, we shall now proceed in the examination of the painfully interesting subject before us, by giving some instances and explanations of EXCITED CONCEPTIONS or APPARITIONS. Conceptions, the consideration of which is to be resumed in the present chapter, are those ideas which we have of any absent object of perception. In their ordinary form they have already been considered in a former part of this Work. (See Chapter X., Part I.) But they are found to vary in degree of strength; and hence, when they are at the highest intensity of which they are susceptible, they may be denominated vivified or EXCITED CONCEPTIONS. They are otherwise called, particularly when they have their origin in the sense of sight, APPARITIONS.

Apparitions, therefore, are appearances which seem to be external and real, but which, in truth, have merely an interior or subjective existence; they are merely vivid or excited conceptions. Accordingly, there may be apparitions not only of angels and departed spirits, which appear to figure more largely in the history of apparitions than other objects of sight; but of landscapes, mountains, rivers, precipices, festivals, armies, funeral processions, temples; in a word, of all visual perceptions which we are capable of recalling. —Although there are excited conceptions both of the hearing and the touch, and sometimes, though less frequently, of the other senses, which succeed in reaching and controlling our belief with unreal intimations, those of the sight, in consequence of the great importance of that organ and the frequency of the deceptions connected with it, claim especial attention.

§ 336. Of the less permanent excited conceptions of sight.

Excited conceptions, which are not permanent, but have merely a momentary, although a distinct and real existence, are not uncommon. In explanation of these there are two things to be noticed.—I. They are sometimes the result of the natural and ordinary exercise of that power of forming conceptions which all persons possess in a greater or less degree. We notice them particularly in children, in whom the conceptive or imaginative power, so far as it is employed in giving existence to creations that have outline and form, is generally more active than in later life. Children, it is well known, are almost constantly projecting their inward conceptions into outward space, and erecting the fanciful creations of the mind amid the realities and forms of matter, beholding houses, men, towers, flocks of sheep, clusters of trees, and varieties of landscape in the changing clouds, in the wreathed and driven snow, in the fairy-work of frost, and in the embers and flickering flames of the hearth. This, at least, was the experience of the early life of Cowper, who has made it the subject of a fine passage in the poem of the Task.

"Me oft has fancy, ludicrous and wild,
Soothed with a waking dream of houses, towers,
Trees, churches, and strange visages express'd
In the red cinders, while, with poring eye,
I gazed, myself creating what I saw."

Beattie too, after the termination of a winter's storm, places his young Minstrel on the shores of the Atlantic, to view the heavy clouds that skirt the distant horizon.

"Where, 'mid the changeful scenery ever new,
Fancy a thousand wondrous forms descries,
More wildly great than ever pencil drew,
Rocks, torrents, gulfs, and shapes of giant size,
And glittering cliffs on cliffs, and fiery ramparts rise."

II. Again, excited conceptions which are not permanent are frequently called into existence in connexion with some anxiety and grief of mind, or some other modification of mental excitement. A person, for instance, standing on the sea-shore, and anxiously expecting the approach of his vessel, will sometimes see the image of it, and will be certain for the moment that he has the object of his anticipations in view, although, in truth, there is no vessel in sight. That is to say, the conception, idea, or image of the vessel, which it is evidently in the power of every one to form who has previously seen one, is rendered so intense by feelings of anxiety, as to be the same in effect as if the real object were present, and the figure of it were actually pictured on the retina.—It is in connexion with this view that we may probably explain a remark in the narrative of Mrs. Howe's captivity, who in 1775 was taken prisoner, together with her seven children, by the St. François Indians. In the course of her captivity, she was at a certain time informed by the Indians that two of her children were no more; one having died a natural death, and the other being knocked on the head. "I did not utter many words," says the mother, "but my heart was sorely pained within me, and *my mind exceedingly troubled with strange and awful ideas* [meaning conceptions or images]. I often imagined, for instance, that *I plainly saw* the naked carcasses of my children hanging upon the limbs of trees, as the Indians are wont to hang the raw hides of those beasts which they take in hunting."

§ 337. Of the less permanent excited conceptions of sound.

In regard to excited conceptions of sound (we may remark incidentally, as we intend to confine ourselves chiefly to those of sight), they are not, as was seen in a former part of this work (§ 115), so easily called into existence and so vivid as visual conceptions. Consequently, we have grounds for making a distinction, and for saying that only one of the remarks made in reference to the less permanent excited conceptions of sight will apply to those of sound. In other words, excited conceptions of sound (those which appear and depart suddenly without any permanent inconvenience to the subject of them) originate in connexion with a greater or less degree of mental excitement.—Persons, for instance, sitting alone in a room, are sometimes interrupted by the supposed hearing of a voice which calls to them. But, in truth, it is only their own internal conception of that particular sound, which, in consequence of some peculiar mental state, happens at the moment to be so distinct as to control their belief, and impose itself upon them for a reality. This is probably the whole mystery of what Boswell has related as a singular incident in the life of Dr. Johnson, that while at Oxford he distinctly heard his mother call him by his given name, although she was at the very time in Litchfield.—The same principle explains also what is related of Napoleon. Previously to his Russian expedition, he was frequently discovered half reclined on a sofa, where he remained several hours, plunged in profound meditation. Sometimes he started up convulsively, and with an ejaculation. Fancying he heard his name, he would exclaim, Who calls me? These are the sounds, susceptible of being heard at any time in the desert air, which started Robinson Crusoe from his sleep, when there was no one on his solitary island but himself:

> "The airy tongues, that syllable mens' names,
> On shores, in desert sands, and wildernesses."

§ 338. 1st cause of permanently vivid conceptions or apparitions. Morbid sensibility of the retina of the eye.

We have been led to see, particularly in a former chapter (§ 119), as well as in the preceding part of this, that our conceptions or renovated ideas may be so vivid as to affect our belief for a short time hardly less powerfully than the original perceptions. But, as in the cases referred to, there was not supposed to be an unsound or disordered state of the body, this extreme vividness of conception was exceedingly transitory. There are other cases of a comparatively permanent character, which are deserving of a more particular notice in the history of our mental nature. These last always imply a disordered state of the body, which we were led to see in the last chapter is often attended with very marked effects on the mind.

In attempting to give an explanation of the origin of permanently vivid conceptions, the first ground or cause of them which we shall notice is an unnatural and morbid sensibility of the retina of the eye, either the whole of the retina or only a part. This cause, it is true, is in some degree conjectural, in consequence of the retina being so situated as to render it difficult to make it a subject of observation and experiment. But knowing, as we do, that the nervous system generally is liable to be diseased, and that the disease of a particular portion is commonly productive of results having relation to the object or uses of that portion, we may for this reason, as well as for what we know directly and positively of the occasionally disordered affections of the optic nerve, give it a place in the explanations of the subject before us. In order to understand the applicability of this cause of permanently vivid conceptions or apparitions, it is necessary to keep in mind that, in conceptions of visible objects, there is probably *always* a slight sympathetic affection of the retina of the eye, analogous to what exists when the visible object is actually present. In a perfectly healthy state of the body, including the organ of visual sense, this affection of the retina is of course very slight. But, under the influence of a morbid sensibility, the mere conceptions of the mind may at times impart such an increased activity to the whole or a part of the retina as to give existence to visual or spectral illusions.

There is an account given in a foreign Medical Journal (the Medico-Chirurgical Repertory of Piedmont) of a young lady who attended for the first time the music of an orchestra, with which she was exceedingly pleased. She continued to hear the sounds distinctly and in their order for weeks and months afterward, till, her whole system becoming disordered in consequence of it, she died. Now we naturally suppose in this case that the nerve of the tympanum of the ear, which, both in a physiological point of view and in its relation to the mind, corresponds to the retina of the eye, continued actually to vibrate or reverberate with the sound, although she was no longer within hearing of it. In other words, it was diseased; it had become morbidly sensitive, and in this state was a source of action to itself, independently of any outward cause. And as the mental state or sensation of sound depends upon the actual condition of the auditory nerve, independently of the outward causes which may have been instrumental in producing that particular condition, we see how the sounds, which she at first heard for a few hours, continued for a number of months after to be generated and repeated.—And so in regard to the optic nerve. It may be so morbidly sensitive, that the mere conception of a man or of some other visible object may affect it as really and in the same way as if the man were actually present to the sight. And if so, the individual who is subject to this morbid affection has the power in himself of originating and sustaining the representation or pictures of objects, although no such objects are present. In other words, as these results depend upon the state of his physical system, and not upon volition, he is properly said to be subject to Apparitions.—We will only add, in confirmation of what has been said, that in one of the most interesting cases of spectral illusions or apparitions which has been published, the person who was the subject of them expressly states, that for some hours preceding their occurrence she had a peculiar feeling in the eyes, which was relieved as soon as they had passed away.*

* Brewster's Natural Magic, Letter iii.

§ 339. 2d cause of permanently excited conceptions or apparitions. Superabundance of blood in the system.

But there are other causes of the mental states under consideration, which, in some respects at least, are not so closely and exclusively connected with the eye. And one of these is connected with a superabundance of blood in the system, originating in some cases with a habit, which is not without its evil results, of periodical blood-letting. The following case, which is one of remarkable interest, will illustrate what is meant.

Nicolai, the name of the individual to whom the statements here given relate, was an inhabitant of Berlin, a celebrated bookseller, and naturally a person of a very vivid imagination. He was neither an ignorant man, nor superstitious; a fact which some undoubtedly will esteem it important to know, because it renders his statements the more reliable. The following account of the apparitions which appeared to him is given in his own words.—"My wife and another person came into my apartment in the morning in order to console me, but I was too much agitated by a series of incidents, which had most powerfully affected my moral feeling, to be capable of attending to them. On a sudden, I perceived, at about the distance of ten steps, a form like that of a deceased person. I pointed at it, asking my wife if she did not see it. It was but natural that she should not see anything; my question, therefore, alarmed her very much, and she immediately sent for a physician. The phantom continued about eight minutes. I grew at length more calm, and, being extremely exhausted, fell into a restless sleep, which lasted about half an hour. The physician ascribed the apparition to a violent mental emotion, and hoped there would be no return; but the violent agitation of my mind had in some way disordered my nerves, and produced further consequences, which deserve a more minute description.

"At four in the afternoon, the form which I had seen in the morning reappeared. I was by myself when this happened, and, being rather uneasy at the incident, went to my wife's apartment; but there likewise I was persecuted by the apparition, which, however, at intervals disappeared, and always presented itself in a standing posture. About six o'clock there appeared also several walking figures, which had no connexion with the first. After the first day the form of the deceased person no more appeared, but its place was supplied with many other phantasms, sometimes representing acquaintances, but mostly strangers; those whom I knew were composed of living and deceased persons, but the number of the latter was comparatively small. I observed the persons with whom I daily conversed did not appear as phantasms, these representing chiefly persons who lived at some distance from me.

"These phantasms seemed equally clear and distinct at all times and under all circumstances, both when I was by myself and when I was in company, as well in the day as in the night, and in my own house as well as abroad; they were, however, less frequent when I was in the house of a friend, and rarely appeared to me in the street. When I shut my eyes, these phantasms would sometimes vanish entirely, though there were instances when I beheld them with my eyes closed; yet, when they disappeared on such occasions, they generally returned when I opened my eyes. I conversed sometimes with my physician and my wife of the phantasms which at the moment surrounded me; they appeared more frequently walking than at rest, nor were they constantly present. They frequently did not come for some time, but always reappeared for a longer or shorter period, either singly or in company, the latter, however, being most frequently the case. I generally saw human forms of both sexes, but they usually seemed not to take the smallest notice of each other, moving as in a market-place, where all are eager to press through the crowd; at times, however, they seemed to be transacting business with each other. I also saw several times people on horseback, dogs, and birds. All these phantasms appeared to me in their natural size, and as distinct as if alive, exhibiting different shades of carnation in the uncovered parts, as well as different colours and fashions in their dresses, though the colours seemed somewhat paler than in real nature. None of the figures appeared particularly terrible, comical, or disgusting, most of them being of an indifferent shape, and some presenting a pleasing aspect. The longer these phantoms continued to visit me, the more frequently did they return; while, at the same time, they increased in number about four weeks after they had first appeared. I also began to hear them talk; these phantoms sometimes conversed among themselves, but more frequently addressed their discourse to me; their speeches were commonly short, and never of an unpleasant turn. At different times there appeared to me both dear and sensible friends of both sexes, whose addresses tended to appease my grief, which had not yet wholly subsided: their consolatory speeches were in general addressed to me when I was alone. Sometimes, however, I was accosted by these consoling friends while I was engaged in company, and not unfrequently while real persons were speaking to me. These consolatory addresses consisted sometimes of abrupt phrases, and at other times they were regularly executed."

§ 340. Methods of relief adopted in this case.

These are the leading facts in this case, as far as the mere appearance of the apparitions is concerned. But as Nicolai, besides possessing no small amount of acquired knowledge, was a person of a naturally philosophic turn of mind, he was able to detect and to assign the true cause of his mental malady.—He was, it is to be remembered, in the first place, a person of a very vivid fancy, and hence his mind was the more likely to be affected by any disease of the body. A number of years before the occurrences above related, he had been subject to a violent vertigo, which had been cured by means of leeches; and in consequence of this favourable experience, it had been his custom to lose blood twice a year; but, previously to the present attack, this evacuation had been neglected. Supposing, therefore, that the mental disorder might arise from a superabundance of blood and some irregularity in the circulation, he again resorted to the application of leeches. When the leeches were applied, no person was with him besides the surgeon; but, during the operation, his chamber was crowded with human phantasms of all descriptions. In the course of a few hours, however, they moved around the chamber more slowly; their colour began to fade, until, growing more and more obscure, they at last dissolved into air, and he ceased to be troubled with them afterward.*

§ 341. 3d cause of excited conceptions. Attacks of fever.

In violent attacks of fever there are sometimes excited conceptions; particularly those which have their origin in the sense of sight, and are known by way of distinction under the name of Apparitions. The conceptions which the sick person has, become increased in vividness, until the mind, seeming to project its own creations into the exterior space, peoples the room with living and moving phantoms. There is a statement, illustrative of this view, in the fifteenth volume of Nicholson's Philosophical Journal, a part of which will be here repeated. The fever in this instance, of which an acount is given by the patient himself, was of a violent character, originating in some deep-seated inflammation, and at first affecting the memory, although not permanently.

"Being perfectly awake," says this person, "in full possession of memory, reason, and calmness, conversing with those around me, and seeing without diffi-

* Memoir on the Appearance of Spectres or Phantoms occasioned by Disease, with Psychological Remarks, read by Nicolai to the Royal Society of Berlin on the 28th of February, 1799; as quoted by Hibbert, pt. i., ch. i.—Walter Scott, in his Demonology and Witchcraft, speaks of the apparitions of Nicolai as a leading case in this department of human knowledge. He also expresses the opinion that many others have had the same experience with Nicolai, but have been deterred by various causes from making it public.

culty or impediment every surrounding object, I was entertained and delighted with a succession of faces, over which I had no control, either as to their appearance, continuance, or removal.

"They appeared directly before me, one at a time, very suddenly, yet not so much so but that a second of time might be employed in the emergence of each, as if through a cloud or mist, to its perfect clearness. In this state each face continued five or six seconds, and then vanished, by becoming gradually fainter during about two seconds, till nothing was left but a dark opaque mist, in which almost immediately afterward appeared another face. All these faces were in the highest degree interesting to me for beauty of form, and for the variety of expression they manifested of every great and amiable emotion of the human mind. Though their attention was invariably directed to me, and none of them seemed to speak, yet I seemed to read the very soul which gave animation to their lovely and intelligent countenances. Admiration, and a sentiment of joy and affection when each face appeared, and regret upon its disappearance, kept my mind constantly riveted to the visions before it; and this state was interrupted only when an intercourse with the persons in the room was proposed or urged."

The apparitions which this person experienced were not limited to phantasms of the human countenance; he also saw phantasms of books, and of parchment and papers containing printed matter. Nor were these effects exclusively confined to ideas received from the sense of sight; at one time he seemed to himself to hear musical sounds; that is, his conceptions of sound were so exceedingly vivid, it was in effect the same as if he had really heard melodious voices and instruments.

§ 342. 4th cause of apparitions and other excited conceptions. Inflammation of the brain.

Apparitions, and excited conceptions in general, exist, in the fourth place, in consequence of inflammations and other diseases of the brain.—We may infer from certain passages which are found in his writings, that Shakspeare had some correct notions of the influence of a disordered condition of the brain on the mental operations. We allude, among others, to the passage where, in explanation of the apparition of the dagger which appeared to Macbeth, he says,

> "A dagger of the mind, a false creation,
> Proceeding from the heat-oppressed brain."

Whether the seat, or appropriate and peculiar residence of the soul be in the brain or not, it seems to be certain that this part of the bodily system is connected, in a very intimate and high degree, with the exercises of the mind, particularly with perception and volition. Whenever, therefore, the brain is disordered, whether by a contusion, or by a removal of part of it, by inflammation, or in other ways, the mind will in general be affected in a greater or less degree.—It may indeed be said, that the immediate connexion in the cases which we now have reference to is not between the mind and the substance of the brain, but between the mind and the blood which is thrown into that part of the system. It is, no doubt, something in favour of this notion, that so large a portion of the sanguineous fluid finds a circulation there; it being a common idea among anatomists, that at least one tenth of all the blood is immediately sent from the heart into the brain, although the latter is in weight only about the fortieth part of the whole body. It is to be considered, also, that the effects which are wrought upon the mind by the nitrous oxide and the febrile miasma gas are caused by an intermediate influence on the blood. On the other hand, it may be said that there cannot be a great acceleration of the blood's motion, or increase of its volume, without a very sensible effect on the cerebral substance. And, therefore, it may remain true, that very much may be justly attributed to the increase of quantity and motion in the blood, and still the brain be the proximate cause of alterations in the states of the mind.

§ 343. Facts having relation to the 4th cause of excited conceptions.

But here we stand in need of facts, as in all other parts of this investigation. The following statement, selected from a number of others not less authenticated, can be relied on.*—A citizen of Kingston-on-Hull had a quarrel with a drunken soldier, who attempted to enter his house by force at an unseasonable hour. In this struggle the soldier drew his bayonet, and, striking him across the temples, divided the temporal artery. He had scarcely recovered from the effects of a great loss of blood on this occasion, when he undertook to accompany a friend in his walking-match against time, in which he went forty-two miles in nine hours. He was elated by his success, and spent the whole of the following day in drinking.

The result of these things was an affection, probably an inflammation of the brain. And the consequence of this was the existence of those vivid states of mind which are termed apparitions. Accordingly, our shopkeeper (for that was the calling of this person) is reported to have seen articles of sale upon the floor, and to have beheld an armed soldier entering his shop, when there was nothing seen by other persons present. In a word, he was for some time constantly haunted by a variety of spectres or imaginary appearances; so much so, that he even found it difficult to determine which were real customers and which were mere phantasms of his own mind. The remedy in this case was blood-letting, and some other methods of cure which are practised in inflammations of the brain. The restoration of the mind to a less intense and more correct action was simultaneous with that of the physical system.

§ 344. 5th cause of apparitions. Hysteria.

It is further to be observed, that people are not unfrequently affected with apparitions in the paroxysms of the disease known as HYSTERIA or hysterics.—For the nature of this disease, which exists under a variety

* See the Edinburgh Medical and Surgical Journal, vol. vi., p. 288.

of forms, and is of a character so peculiar as to preclude any adequate description in the narrow limits we could properly allot to it, the reader is referred to such books as treat of medical subjects. This singular disease powerfully agitates the mind; and its effects are as various as they are striking. When the convulsive affections come on, the patient is observed to laugh and cry alternately, and altogether without any cause of a rational or moral nature, so that he has almost the appearance of fatuity, or of being delirious. But apparitions or intensely vivid conceptions are among its most striking attendants. The subjects of it distinctly see every description of forms: trees, houses, men, women, dogs, and other inferior animals, balls of fire, celestial beings, &c. We can, without doubt, safely refer to the experience of those who have been much conversant with instances of this disease, in confirmation of this.

The existence of the states of mind under consideration might, without much question, be found, on further examination, to connect itself with other forms of disease. The subject is certainly worthy, whether considered in relation to science or to human happiness, of such further developements as it is capable of receiving.

CHAPTER III.

PARTIAL INSANITY.

§ 345. Meaning of the term and kinds of insanity.

The term Insanity, etymologically considered, indicates simply a want of soundness or want of health. In its application to the mind, it indicates an unsound or disordered state of the mental action. As the mind is complicated in its structure, existing, as it were, in various departments and subdivisions of departments, the disordered action may pervade the whole mind, or exist exclusively in some one of its departments.

Accordingly, Insanity naturally resolves itself into the two species of Partial Insanity and Total Insanity, and it is under these two general heads that we shall now proceed to consider it.

Partial Insanity, which naturally comes first in order, is a disordered condition of one or more of the mental powers, but which leaves the mind essentially free and undisturbed in some of its departments and in some of its modes of action. The method which we propose to pursue in the investigation of this form of insanity is to consider it as it exhibits itself in the powers of the mind separately. And it is proper to add here, that we examine the subject of insanity at present only so far as it may naturally be supposed to exist in connexion with the Intellect, leaving the consideration of it, as it is occasionally found to exist in the Sensibilities, to a future time.

§ 346. Of disordered or alienated sensations.

Beginning with the External Intellect, the power which first presents itself to our notice is Sensation. It is well known that all the outward senses are liable to be disordered, and as the inward sensation corresponds to the condition of the outward or bodily organ, a disordered or irregular movement of the organ of sense necessarily communicates itself to the inward or mental state. A regular or healthy sensation always has reference to some outward cause (we mean here outward even in reference to the organ of sense), but a disease in the bodily organ disturbs this relation, and necessarily gives to the inward mental state the character, as compared with other sensations, of being unreal, visionary, and deceptive. Not unreal and deceptive in itself, but because it intimates a relation which is obliterated, and tends to force upon our belief an outward cause which has no existence.

There are diseased or disordered visual sensations existing in connexion with a morbid condition of the visual organ; but as this view of the subject was necessarily involved in some degree in what has already been said on the subject of excited conceptions or Apparitions, it is not necessary to enlarge upon it here. There are also diseased or disordered sensations of touch. A single instance, out of multitudes like it, will serve both to illustrate and confirm the remark. In the Natural Magic of Dr. Brewster is an account of a lady (the case which we have already had occasion to refer to) who was subject to spectral illusions, of whom it is expressly stated, in connexion with her remarkable mental affections, that she possesses "a naturally morbid imagination, so strongly affecting her corporeal impressions, that the story of any person having suffered severe pain by accident or otherwise will occasionally produce acute twinges in the corresponding part of her person. An account, for instance, of the amputation of an arm will produce an instantaneous and severe sense of pain in her own arm." There are also (and we might apply the statement to all the senses without exception) diseased or disordered sensations of hearing. The celebrated Mendelssohn was frequently subject to the attacks of a violent species of catalepsis. And it happened, if he had recently heard any lively conversation, a loud voice apparently repeated to him, while in the fit, the particular words which had been distinguished from others by being pronounced with an emphatic and raised tone of voice, and "in such a manner that his ear reverberated with the sound."

§ 347. Of disordered or alienated external perception.

We naturally proceed from sensation to a power closely connected with it, that of External Perception. Indeed, what has been said of sensation will apply in a considerable degree to the last-mentioned power, because sensation naturally precedes perception, and is always involved in it. But perception, while it involves sensation, implies also something more, something additional; it involves the reference of the inward mental state to the outward cause or object, and not unfrequently implies also acts of comparison, by which it distinguishes one cause from another. And particularly is this the case in respect to those perceptions which are designated as ACQUIRED perceptions, in order to distinguish them from ORIGINAL. So that, in view of what has been said, it would seem to be the fact, in the first place, that when our sensations are disordered, our perceptions will be so likewise. But this is not all. In consequence of some interior cause, such as an inability to attend to a thing for any length of time, or incapacity of instituting comparisons, disordered and false external perceptions will sometimes exist when there appears to be no unsoundness in the sensations.

Agreeably to these views, we find that persons, in whom the power of external perception is disordered from the first of the two causes just referred to, sometimes have perceptions of colour which do not accord with those of mankind generally, being entirely unable, for instance, to distinguish blue from green. Other persons, again, have no distinct perception of minute sounds, and take no more pleasure in the harmonies of a musical composition of truly great merit than they do in the most discordant screams. When the disordered action of the perceptive power originates from the second cause, the subjects of it are apt to confound times, persons, and places. They mistake, for instance, their friends and relations for others, and are at a loss as to the place where they are, although they may have been in it hundreds of times before. They exhibit particularly this species of alienated perception when they attempt to read a book. They no doubt see the letters no less than others, but the action of the mind in other respects not being such as to permit them to dwell upon them, and compare and combine them into words, they are unable to read; it is at least exceedingly difficult.

§ 348. Disordered state or insanity of intuition.

When we pass from the External to the Internal Intellect, from the region of sensation and external perception to the interior domain of Suggestion or Intuition, to the convictions involved in Consciousness, to the important powers of Relative Suggestion, Memory, and Reasoning, we are introduced, indeed, to a higher order of mental action, but we find no exemption from those disorders to which the human mind in all its great departments is occasionally exposed.—In regard to the Suggestional power, which comes first in order, a power which deals with original ideas and principles merely, without professing to ascertain the relations existing among them, it must be admitted that it does not give so frequent and decided indications of disordered action as we find elsewhere. Nevertheless, this is sometimes the case. The conviction, for instance, not only that we exist, but that we have personal identity, that we are now what we have been in times past in all that constitutes us rational and accountable beings, is obviously essential to a sound mind. But this elementary and important conviction, which obviously does not rest upon judgment nor the deductions of reasoning, but upon the higher basis of INTUITIONAL SUGGESTION, is sometimes annulled, either in whole or in part. To this head, so far as the conviction of the identity of the mind is concerned, we may refer the interesting case of the Reverend Simon Browne, an English clergyman, who fully believed for many years before his death that he had entirely lost his rational part or soul, and was the possessor merely of a corporeal or animal life, such as is possessed by the brutes. He was a man of marked ability both in conversation and writing; and this, too, on all subjects not connected with his malady, after his partial alienation. But so entirely was he convinced of the absence and of the probably actual extinction of his own soul, that, in a valuable Work which he dedicated to the Queen of England, he speaks of it in the dedication as the Work of one who "was once a man, of some little name, but of no worth, as his present unparalleled case makes but too manifest; for by the immediate hand of an avenging God, his very thinking substance has for more than seventeen years been gradually wasting away, till it is wholly perished out of him, if it be not utterly come to nothing."*

§ 349. Unsoundness or insanity of consciousness.

The basis of the various convictions or judgments of Consciousness, as that term is defined and illustrated by writers, is the antecedent idea and belief of personal identity. If this last conviction, therefore, be lost, as in the case mentioned in the last section, all that is involved in Consciousness goes with it. It is the business of Consciousness to connect the acts of the mind with the mind itself; to consolidate them, as it were, into one. But if, in our full belief, our mind is destroyed, if self or personality is obliterated, then it is clearly no longer within the power of consciousness to recognise our various acts of perception and reasoning as having a home and agency in our own bosoms. Self is destroyed; and the mental acts, which are appropriate to self, are mere entities, floating about, as it were, in the vacuities of space, without the possibility of being assigned to any locality or ascribed to any cause. The instance, therefore, mentioned in the preceding section, which may be regarded as of a mixed kind (that is to say, showing a perplexed action both of Intuitional Suggestion and Consciousness), will serve to illustrate what is said here. —Another instance not less striking is that of a celebrated watchmaker of Paris, who became insane during the period of the French Revolution. This man believed that he and some others had been beheaded, but that the heads were subsequently ordered to be restored to the original owners. Some mistake, however, as the insane person conceived, was committed in the process of restoration; in consequence of which, he had unfortunately been furnished with the head of one of his companions instead of his own. He was admitted into the Hospital Bicêtre, "where he was continually complaining of his misfortune, and lament-

* Conolly's Indications of Insanity, chap. x.

ing the fine teeth and wholesome breath he had exchanged for those of very different qualities."

Instances also have probably from time to time occurred, in which, although the conviction of personality and personal identity has remained, yet in the fixed belief of the insane person the bond of connexion between the mind and its powers has been dissolved; and the memory, perhaps, or the reasoning, or the imagination, which once belonged to himself, has been transferred by some mysterious agency to an intellect more favoured than his own.

§ 350. Insanity of the judgment or relative suggestion.

Pursuing this subject, in its connexion with the powers of the Internal Intellect, in the order in which they presented themselves to our notice in the Second Part of this Work, and which seems to be essentially the order of nature, we next proceed to Relative Suggestion. The power of Relative Suggestion, like that of Suggestion in its first or original form, is exceedingly simple in its action, being limited to the mere matter of perceiving relations; but it is different in this respect, that, while mental disorder but seldom reaches original suggestion, there is scarcely an instance of decidedly disordered intellect in which relative suggestion (that is to say, JUDGMENT in its simplest form) is not affected in a greater or less degree. And this seems to be unavoidable. For relations always imply the existence of something else; they cannot exist without the antecedent existence of other objects. And if mistakes, in consequence of a wrong mental action in other respects, exist in regard to those other things, whatever they may be, they necessarily either annul or greatly perplex the results of the power by which such relations are perceived.—Besides this, the power, in its own nature and independently of perplexities from other sources, is liable to be, and is, in fact, sometimes disordered. But, as this subject is closely connected with that of reasoning, and as they reciprocally throw light upon each other, we shall say nothing further here.

§ 351. Disordered or alienated association. Light-headedness.

The laws of the mind, the great principles which regulate its action, as well as its mere perceptions or states, may be disordered; for instance, the law of association. The irregular action of this important principle of our intellectual nature is sometimes greater, at others less. There is one of the slighter forms of mental alienation from this cause which may be termed LIGHT-HEADEDNESS; otherwise called by Pinel demence, and by Dr. Rush dissociation. Persons subject to this mental disease are sometimes designated as "flighty," "hair-brained;" and when the indications of it are pretty decided, as a "little cracked."—Their disorder seems chiefly to consist in a deficiency of the ordinary power over associated ideas. Their thoughts fly from one subject to another with great rapidity; and, consequently, one mark of this state of mind is great volubility of speech and almost constant motion of the body. This rapid succession of ideas and attendant volubility of tongue are generally accompanied with forgetfulness in a greater or less degree. And as the subject of this form of derangement is equally incapable of checking and reflecting upon his present ideas, and of recalling the past, he constantly forms incorrect judgments of things. Another mark which has been given is a diminished sensibility to external impressions.

§ 352. Illustrations of this mental disorder.

Dr. Rush, in his valuable work on the Diseases of the Mind, has repeated the account which an English clergyman, who visited Lavater the physiognomist, has given of that singular character. It accurately illustrates this mental disorder.—"I was detained," says he, "the whole morning by the strange, wild, eccentric Lavater, in various conversations. When once he is set a going, there is no such thing as stopping him, till he runs himself out of breath. He starts from subject to subject, flies from book to book, from picture to picture; measures your nose, your eye, your mouth, with a pair of compasses; pours forth a torrent of physiognomy upon you; drags you, for a proof of his dogma, to a dozen of closets, and unfolds ten thousand drawings; but will not let you open your lips to propose a difficulty, and crams a solution down your throat before you have uttered half a syllable of your objection.

"He is as meagre as the picture of famine; his nose and chin almost meet. I read him in my turn, and found little difficulty in discovering, amid great genius, unaffected piety, unbounded benevolence, and moderate learning, much caprice and unsteadiness; a mind at once aspiring by nature and grovelling through necessity; an endless turn to speculation and project; in a word, a clever, flighty, good-natured, necessitous man."

§ 353. Of partial insanity or alienation of the memory.

Among other exhibitions of partial insanity, using the terms in the manner already explained, we may include some of the more striking instances of weakened and disordered memory. Every other part of the intellect may be sound and regular in its action (for it will be recollected that we confine ourselves here to the disorders of the INTELLECT, without anticipating those of the Sensibilities), the powers of perception, of association, of imagination, of reasoning, at least so far as they are able to act independent of the memory, while the action of the latter power is either essentially obliterated, or is the subject of strange and unaccountable deviations. From the plan of this work we are obliged to content ourselves with the briefest possible notices, and can therefore only refer to one or two instances in illustration of what has been said. The instances of weakened and perverted memory are of three kinds: (1.) those where there is a general prostration, caused in various ways, such as grief and old age; (2.) those where there is a sudden and entire prostration, extending to particular subjects or through a particular period of time, generally caused by some sudden and violent affection of the body; and (3.) those where there is not so much an inordinate weakness or obliteration of the power under consideration, as a singularly perverse and irregular action of it.—It is probably not necessary to say anything of the first class. Of the second class is the case mentioned by Dr. Beattie, of a gentleman who, in consequence of a violent blow on the head, lost his knowledge of Greek, but did not appear to have lost anything else. Another instance is that mentioned by Dr. Abercrombie, of a lady who, in consequence of a protracted illness, lost the recollection of a period of about ten or twelve years, but spoke with perfect consistency of things as they stood before that time. Of the third class is the case of a man who always called tobacco a hogshead; and of another man, who, when he wanted coals put upon his fire, always called for paper, and when he wanted paper called for coals; and of another, who could not be made to understand the name of an object if it was spoken to him, but understood it perfectly when it was written. These three cases will be found more particularly detailed in Dr. Abercrombie's Inquiries into the Intellectual Powers. A case perhaps still more interesting is found in Dr. Conolly's Indications of Insanity as follows:

"A gentleman of considerable attainments, after long-continued attention to various subjects, found himself incapable of writing what he sat down to write; and, wishing to write a check, could get no farther than the first two words; he found that he wrote what he did not mean to write, but by no effort could he write what he intended. This impairment of his memory and attention lasted about half an hour, during which time his external senses were not impaired, but the only ideas which he had were such as the imagination dictated, without order and without object. He knew also, during this time, that when he spoke, the words he uttered were not the words he wished to utter. When he recovered, he found that in his attempt to write the check, he had, instead of the words 'fifty dollars, being one half year's rate,' put down 'fifty dollars through the salvation of Bra.'"

§ 354. Of the power of reasoning in the partially insane.

It will be noticed, so far as we have gone in the examination of the subject of insanity, that we have considered the powers of the mind separately. Probably every power of the mind, but particularly those of the intellect, may become more or less disordered. Having considered sensation, perception, the suggestional power, consciousness, judgment, association, and memory, we propose, as coming next in order, to examine the subject in its connexion with the reasoning power.—In some cases of insanity there is a total inability of reasoning. There is no power of attention, no power of comparison, and, of course, no ability in the mind to consolidate its action upon a particular subject, and to pass from the premises of an argument to the conclusion. In such cases the inability to reason may be spoken of as total; that is to say, it extends to all subjects alike. But it is more frequently the case, that the alienation of reasoning is not so extensive, but exists chiefly in relation to certain subjects, in respect to which the belief is affected. When the train of reasoning leads the person within the range of those particular subjects, whatever they are, we at once discover that the intellect is disordered. And this view has led to the common remark, which is obviously well founded, that the more common form of insane or alienated reason does not consist so much in the mode of connecting propositions, and in the conclusions drawn from them, as in the premises. The insane person believes, for instance, that he is a king. Accordingly, he reasons correctly in requiring for himself the homage suited to a king, and in expressing dissatisfaction on account of its being withheld; but he commits an essential error in the premises, which assume that he actually possesses that station.

§ 355. Instance of the above form of disordered reasoning.

We have an instance of the form of insanity just mentioned, the partially disordered action of the reasoning power in consequence of disordered belief, in the character of Don Quixote. Cervantes represents the hero of this work as having his naturally good understanding perverted by the perusal of certain foolish, romantic stories, falsely purporting to be a true record of knights and deeds of chivalry. These books, containing the history of dwarfs, giants, necromancers, and other preternatural extravagance, were zealously perused, until the head of Don Quixote was effectually turned by them. Although he was thus brought into a state of real mental derangement, it was limited to the extravagances which have been mentioned. We are expressly informed, that in all his conversations and replies, he gave evident proofs of a most excellent understanding, and never "lost the stirrups" except on the subject of chivalry. On this subject he "was crazed."—Accordingly, when the barber and curate visited him on a certain occasion, the conversation happened to turn on what are termed reasons of state, and on modes of administration; and Don Quixote spoke so well on every topic as to convince them that he was quite sound, and had recovered the right exercise of his judgment. But something being unadvisedly said about the Turkish war, the knight at once remarked, with much solemnity and seriousness, that his majesty had nothing to do but to issue a proclamation, commanding all the knights-errant in Spain to assemble at his court on a certain day; *and although not more than half a dozen should come, among them one would be found who would alone be sufficient to overthrow the whole Turkish power.*

When the subject of conversation turned upon war, which had so near a connexion with shields, and lances, and all the associations of chivalry, it came within the range of his malady, and led to the absurd remark, which showed at once the unsoundness of his mind, notwithstanding the sobriety and good sense which he had just before exhibited.

§ 356. Of readiness of reasoning in the partially insane.

Those who have been personally acquainted with the intellectual condition of the partially insane, have sometimes observed in them great quickness of thought in some little emergencies, and an unusual degree of cunning. When, for instance, an attempt has been made to seize and confine them, they steadily and promptly mark the motions of their pursuers; they rapidly decipher their intentions from their countenance, and cause them no small degree of perplexity. In particular, it has been observed in some instances that they discover more fluency of expression and rapidity of deduction than others of a perfectly sound mind, or than themselves could have exhibited before their derangement. This singular fact is to be briefly explained.

The unusual quickness of deduction and of expression which has sometimes been noticed in partially insane persons, may be referred to two causes: First, an uncommon excitation of the attention, and of all the intellectual powers; and, secondly, a removal of those checks which attend the sober and the rational in their reasonings.

Some of the checks which retard the process of reasoning in the case of men whose powers are in a good state, are these.—(1.) There is a distrust of phraseology, a fear of mistakes from the ambiguity and vagueness of language.—The object of a rational man is supposed to be to arrive at truth, and not merely to gain a victory. He therefore feels anxious not only to employ terms which appear to himself proper, but which shall be rightly understood by his opponent. But the irrational man, as might be expected, does not find himself embarrassed with considerations of this nature.—(2.) A second obstruction to facility and promptness in argumentation, in the case of the sober-minded and rational, is this: They fear that they may not be in possession of all those premises on which the solution will be found in the event to depend.—Many disputes are carried on without previously forming an acquaintance with those facts which are necessarily and prominently involved. While disputants of sound minds have any suspicion on this point, and know not but it will be labour lost, they of course feel their interest in the dispute very much diminished.—(3.) The third circumstance to which reference was had is this: The influence of certain feelings of propriety and of good sense, which ordinarily govern men in the full exercise of their powers.

The disputant feels himself under obligations to profess a deference for his opponent; it is due to the customary forms of society. He is sometimes restrained and embarrassed by what he considers due to those who are present to hear the argument. He is particularly careful to say nothing foolish, absurd, or uncharitable.—All these things weigh nothing with the insane person. He is not troubled about exactness of expression, or the observance of ceremonies, but strangely rushes, as it were, upon the main points of the controversy, regardless of all minor considerations.*

§ 357. Partial mental alienation by means of the imagination.

Men of sensibility and genius, by giving way to the suggestions of a melancholy imagination, sometimes become mentally disordered. Not that we are authorized to include these cases as among the more striking forms of insanity; they in general attract but little notice, although sources of exquisite misery to the subjects of them. But such are the extravagant dreams in which these persons indulge; such are the wrong views of the character and actions of men, which their busy and melancholy imaginations are apt to form, that they cannot be reckoned persons of truly sound minds. These instances, which are not rare, it is difficult fully to describe; but their most distinguishing traits will be recognised in the following sketch from Madame de Staël's Reflections on the Character and Writings of Rousseau.

* See Stewart's Philosophy of the Human Mind, vol. ii., ch. iii.

After remarking that he discovered no sudden emotions, but that his feelings grew upon reflection, and that he became impassioned in consequence of his own meditations, she adds as follows: "Sometimes he would part with you with all his former affection; but if an expression had escaped you which might bear an unfavourable construction, he would recollect it, examine it, exaggerate it, perhaps dwell upon it for a month, and conclude by a total breach with you. Hence it was that there was scarcely a possibility of undeceiving him; for the light, which broke in upon him at once, was not sufficient to efface the wrong impressions which had taken place so gradually in his mind. It was extremely difficult, too, to continue long on an intimate footing with him. A word, a gesture, furnished him with matter of profound meditation; he connected the most trifling circumstances like so many mathematical propositions, and conceived his conclusions to be supported by the evidence of demonstration.

"I believe," she further remarks, "that imagination was the strongest of his faculties, and that it had almost absorbed all the rest. He dreamed rather than existed; and the events of his life might be said more properly to have passed in his mind than without him: a mode of being, one should have thought, that ought to have secured him from distrust, as it prevented him from observation; but the truth was, it did not hinder him from attempting to observe; it only rendered his observations erroneous. That his soul was tender no one can doubt after having read his works; but his imagination sometimes interposed between his reason and his affections, and destroyed their influence; he appeared sometimes void of sensibility, but it was because he did not perceive objects such as they were. Had he seen them with our eyes, his heart would have been more affected than ours."

§ 358. Insanity or alienation of the power of belief.

The action of the various intellectual powers

brought to view in this chapter, which are cognitive in their character, terminates in the causation or production of Belief. In regard to that particular state of the intellect which is denominated belief, it is obvious that in a sound mind it is not an accident; but it has a natural and determinate relation to all the various cognitive susceptibilities, both External and Internal. This relation is sometimes disturbed; and the belief exists in a position altogether unsustained by the evidence which is presented. There are three classes of persons in whom this state of mind, or, in other words, the faculty or susceptibility of belief, if we may be permitted so to call it, appears to be disordered.—(1.) The first class are those who seem incapable of believing anything which they are required to receive on the testimony of others. They must see it with their own eyes; they must hear it or handle it for themselves; they must examine it by square, rule, and compass. They remind one of the Savage, who complained, when something was proposed for his belief, "that it would not believe for him." The causes of this singular inability are worthy of more inquiry than has hitherto been expended upon them. When it is very great, it is a mark of the approach or actual existence of idiocy.—(2.) There is another class of persons who plainly show a derangement of this power by their readiness to believe everything. No matter how incongruous or improbable a story is, it is received at once. They take no note of dates, characters, and circumstances; and as they find nothing too improbable to believe, they find nothing too strange, marvellous, and foolish to report. This state of mind is frequently an accompaniment of lightheadedness.—(3.) There are other cases where the alienation of belief is not general, but particular. There is nothing peculiar and disordered in its ordinary action, but only in respect to particular facts. That is, certain propositions, which are erroneous and absurd, are received by the disordered persons as certain, and nothing can convince them of the contrary.

One believes himself to be a king; another that he is the prophet Mohammed; and various other absurdities are received by them as undoubtedly true. On all other subjects they appear to be rational; but the alienation or insanity of belief is evident as soon as their cherished errors are mentioned.

CHAPTER IV.

TOTAL INSANITY OR DELIRIUM.

§ 359. Idea of total insanity or delirium.

We finish what we have to say on the subject of the Intellect, both in its regular and its disordered action, by a brief explanation of Total Insanity or Delirium. Partial insanity is so designated, because it exists in one only or a small number of intellectual powers; but total insanity, as the expression indicates, implies the perversion of all of them. It involves the idea of a total disorganization; of a chaotic mingling together of the mental elements, without regard to law or order; perception, consciousness, association, memory, reasoning, all conflicting with themselves and with each other in one wild mass of irretrievable ruin.

It may perhaps be intimated here, that the relation which total insanity holds to partial insanity precludes the necessity of saying much on the former, because we have only to unite the various evils which exist in partial insanity in one mind, in order to constitute the idea and the reality of total insanity. There is undoubtedly some foundation for this suggestion; but it is nevertheless true, that objects often assume a new character in virtue of the relations they sustain; and evils, which are great in themselves, may not only assume a new aspect, but an increased aggravation by being associated with other evils. And this is true in insanity. So long as only a part of the mind is disordered, there is some hope that the light which is unobscured may penetrate the darkness of the region which is insane. At any rate, we may well suppose that the insanity of the mind is favourably modified and kept in check by the elements that still remain unperverted. But when the contagion has spread through the whole mass; when every modifying and conservative influence is obliterated, the separate evils, which existed in the different departments and powers of the mind, are likely to become more intense than they would otherwise be.

§ 360. Of perception in cases of total or delirious insanity.

We may illustrate the general views of the last section by a reference to the power of perception. It will be recollected that perception involves something more than mere sensation; such as the reference of the sensation to the outward cause, and not unfrequently acts of judgment distinguishing one cause from another. Of course it follows, if the power of relative suggestion or judgment be disordered, as it is in all cases of delirium or total insanity, the disordered condition of the power of perception will be likely to be increased.—This is the case, in particular, in respect to what are called Acquired perceptions. In visual perception, for instance, all objects at first seem to touch the eye. Accordingly, our estimate of distance by the sight is not, properly speaking, original knowledge, but acquired. What we term perception of distance is not a mere act of the eye, a mere visual apprehension, but always presupposes certain preceding acts of the judgment. But in delirious insanity the power of judging is subverted and lost. Hence the delirious man necessarily mistakes in the perception of distance, and it is no uncommon thing to find him attempting to throw himself from the windows of an upper story or down the brink of a precipice. Such attempts can be accounted for on no other supposition than a mistake of sight, founded not so much on a false sensation as on a false or perverted judgment, involved in the complex act of visual perception.—The same causes which perplex his perceptions of distance, also confuse his notions of extension, of the form of bodies, and of the outlines of any object of sight whatever.

§ 361. Of association in delirious insanity.

In the form of insanity which is termed DELIRIOUS, the principle of association is not unfrequently found to be greatly affected. Rapidity of association was given as a characteristic of that form of partial insanity which was termed light-headedness or "demence." But in delirium it often exists in a far more striking degree. In light-headedness, the direct and indirect influence which is retained and exercised by the will over trains of thought, is only diminished; in delirium it seems to be wholly annulled. Every new object, every new countenance, every noise heard in the room where the delirious person is, or noises that are heard from without; indeed, everything with which thoughts and feelings have been formerly associated, revives those ancient trains of mental acts. They are poured in upon him like a flood; and it is easier to conceive than describe what a tumultuous chaos the mind in such a condition must be. When we consider that these uncalled-for trains of thought are thrown in upon the maniac when his system is in great nervous excitement, and that he is unable to resist or to regulate the instantaneous transference of the mind from subject to subject, it is no wonder that he should exhibit, as we often find that he does, much external agitation, wildness of countenance, violence of gestures, and outcries.

§ 362. Illustration of the above section.

The following account of the rapid mental transitions of an insane person in the New Bethlem Hospital, London, will go to confirm and illustrate what has been said. Like all characteristic sketches of insanity, it is a melancholy picture. Difficult as it is to conceive that such an endless series of topics should be crowded into the mind in a space so short, it is only what is realized in all cases of delirious insanity, where a derangement of the laws of association is the prominent trait.—"Wholly unlimited by the identities of time, place, or person, he instantly accommodates each to his fancy, and in a moment he is anywhere, and everywhere, and anybody, by turns. At one time he imagines himself to be the Lord Chancellor, or, as he emphatically styles himself, 'Young Baggs;' and no mortal tongue ever maintained the loquacity of the law, or talked with more incessant volubility, than his imaginary lordship. He would decide ten thousand causes in a day; he would accuse, try, condemn, and execute whole nations in a breath. His language was as wild and far-fetched as his fancy was various; topics of all kinds seemed to come tumbling into his mind without order or connexion. Of every name he heard mentioned he instantly became the personal representative, and says, 'I am he;' thus he is by turns Bonaparte, the King, the Duke of Wellington, Lord Londonderry, the Persian ambassador, Mr. Pope, Homer, Smollet, Hume, Gibbon, John Bunyan, &c.

"He is successively a Hottentot, a Lascar, a Spaniard, a Turk, a Jew, a Scotsman. He has been in all situations and occupations of life, according to his own account; a potboy at Hampstead, a shoeblack, a chimney-sweeper, an East India Director, a kennel-raker, a gold-finder, an oyster-woman, a Jew cast-clothesman, a police justice, a judge, a keeper of Newgate, and, as he styles it, 'His Majesty's law iron-monger for the home department;' nay, he has even been Jack Ketch, and has hung hundreds; he has been a soldier, and has killed thousands; a Portuguese, and poniarded scores; a Jew pedlar, and cheated all the world; a member of Parliament for London, and betrayed his constituents; a Lord Mayor, a bishop, an admiral, a dancing-master, a Rabbi, Grimaldi in the pantomime, and ten thousand other occupations, that no tongue or memory but his own could enumerate. The specimen just given may serve as a sample of what is passing in his fancy."

§ 363. Of the memory in connexion with delirious insanity.

The memory, too, whatever perversions it may suffer in partial insanity, is, as a general thing, still more unfavourably affected in delirium. The memory, it will be recollected, holds nearly the same relation to association that perception does to sensation. That is to say, it embraces something more; and this additional element is an act of the judgment, a process of comparison. If, therefore, the action of the judgment is annulled or greatly perplexed, as it always is in delirium, the malady of the memory, whatever it may happen to be, is unquestionably increased by that circumstance. Under such circumstances, the memory is not only like a ship without a rudder (a comparison which is frequently employed to illustrate its disordered action), but is coasting a shore where there are no buoys or lighthouses. The surrounding beacons of the mind are extinguished; the landmarks which nature had erected in other departments of the intellectual empire are obliterated; and there is nothing exterior to itself to indicate either the mistakes or the certainties of its position.

§ 364. Of the power of reasoning in total or delirious insanity.

If we further examine the subject of total insanity in connexion with the faculty of reasoning, we shall find results somewhat similar, or perhaps even more marked, more unfavourable. In partial insanity, it is true that the reasoning power is sometimes greatly impaired in every respect, whether we consider the mere act of comparison, or the elements which the act of comparison attempts to combine together. But it is not unfrequently the case, that in that form of insanity the deductive power remains essentially sound, so far as the process, or act of comparing and combining, is concerned; and is erroneous in its results merely in consequence of a mistake in the elements which it employs. In other words, the error is not so much in the acts of comparison as in the propositions which are compared together; the superstructure, in itself considered, is well enough, but the foundation is defective.—But in total insanity or delirium, there is, for the most part, neither the one nor the other; neither the basis of the building, nor the materials and requisite powers with which to erect it.

All reasoning, it is obvious, must have something to start from; some amount of knowledge, whether more or less, constituting its beginning, its antecedent position; but in total insanity, still more than in partial, the alienation that pervades the mind has infected and disordered the elements of thought, in addition to the inability of comparing them together. The ability to compare implies a healthy condition of the powers of association and relative suggestion, both of which are disordered in delirium. Of course, the two great conditions of sound reasoning, viz., sound knowledge to begin with and unimpaired powers of comparison, are wanting. Under these circumstances, we leave it to the reader to judge whether we may not reasonably anticipate that a disordered condition of the reasoning power in total insanity will be more aggravated and hopeless than at other times.—The statements which have been made sufficiently indicate, without our going further into the subject, the leading peculiarities of mental action which will be likely to attend a state of delirium or total insanity, in distinction from any other and lower form of disordered intellect.

§ 365. Of the form of insanity called furor or madness.

It is sometimes the case, that insanity of the intellectual powers, whether in whole or in part, is attended with a sort of dull and moping stupidity of the affections. The subject of it is averse to companionship, takes no interest in the ordinary concerns of life, and seems most to enjoy the little happiness which can be supposed to exist in his melancholy situation, when most remote from the observation of others. But sometimes it is otherwise. The fountains of the inner deep are broken up. There are sorrows profound and inextinguishable, sometimes borne and uttered with a degree of calmness, but not unfrequently venting themselves in impassioned expressions and furious acts. All the corporeal powers of the maniac, at such times, are put to the test; he makes war upon his own friends; he attacks his keepers; he assaults the bars and windows of his prison; and even turns, in the height of his uncontrolled vexation and anguish, upon his own person. It is this form of insanity which is commonly termed FUROR or MADNESS, and which we shall probably find occasion to illustrate more particularly when, as in the progress of this Work we shall be naturally led to do, we contemplate the subject in connexion with the Sensibilities.

§ 366. Of the causes of the different kinds of insanity.

In regard to the causes of insanity, which it may be proper here briefly to refer to, they are generally understood, whether the insanity is partial or delirious, to be of two kinds, viz., MORAL and PHYSICAL.—In the first place, all diseases which violently affect the physical system, such as epilepsy, fevers, apoplexy, also injuries of the brain, indirectly affect the mind, and may cause permanent insanity.—It is worthy of remark also in regard to an insane state of the mind, that it is in some degree hereditary; hence it is often said of particular families that they are predisposed to insanity. The father, son, and grandson have not only been known to become successively insane, but the derangement has sometimes taken place in each case in the same year of their life.

(II.) There are also various moral causes of mental alienation. It has been caused, among other circumstances of a moral nature, by disappointed ambition. Disappointment in mercantile and other speculations, and in any ardent expectations whatever, often has the same effect. Erroneous religious opinions, and great excitements of feeling on religious subjects, have contributed towards supplying lunatic hospitals. An unrestrained indulgence of any of the passions is found to be attended with the same results.

As an illustration of what has been said, it may be added, that we find a fruitful source of mental derangement in the vicissitudes of political events. A recent writer in a French medical work says that he could give a history of the political revolutions in France, from the taking of the Bastile down to the return of Bonaparte from Elba, by detailing the causes of certain cases of insanity.*—It appears from reports from insane hospitals, that moral causes of insanity are more numerous than physical. But in many cases the influence of both is combined together.

§ 367. Of moral accountability in mental alienation.

It is in some respects a difficult inquiry, Whether men who are in a state of mental alienation are morally accountable? Whether they are the subjects of merit or demerit? And, if so, in what cases and how far? In determining these questions, there ought to be a distinction made between cases of partial insanity, where the mind is deranged only in part, and cases of delirium or total insanity. In the last there is evidently no accountability. In the former instances, a judgment should be formed from the circumstances of the particular case under consideration.

Accordingly, this may be laid down as a general rule in respect to this subject, and perhaps it is the only one which can be; viz., Persons of an alienated mind, whether they be idiots or insane, are not to be considered accountable, are not subjects of praise or blame, whenever it appears that the mental alienation extends to and wholly annuls the power of correct judgment. And this is the case with all persons who are the subjects of total insanity.—When the insanity is partial, it would seem to follow, therefore, that the first inquiry should be, Whether the action committed comes within range of the malady. For a person who is insane on one subject merely, will probably be found to labour

* Dictionnaire des Sciences Medicales, Art. Folie (Esquirol). See also Des Causes Morales et Physiques des Maladies Mentales, par F. Voisin; Influence des Institutions Politiques.

under a perversion of judgment in respect to that particular subject no less than if the insanity were total or delirious. Consequently, a distinction may be justly set up, although it will require much caution in doing it, between those actions which can be clearly found within the limits of the person's insanity and those which evidently fall without it.

§ 368. Of the imputation of insanity to individuals.

While the existence of insanity, so far as materially to affect the power of judging, takes away accountability in whole or in part, it affects proportionably the relations which the subjects of it sustain to society. In all well-organized communities, it will be found to follow, from the terms of the civil compact, that those who exercise sovereignty are bound to afford protection to the citizens in general, and to individuals in particular, in certain cases. Hence they will be found to have taken precautionary measures, the nature of which all are acquainted with, to protect the community against the injuries which insane persons might commit, and also to alleviate that unhappiness which they necessarily bring, in a greater or less degree, on themselves and families.

Accordingly, it is implied, in the imputation of insanity to individuals, by an act of the civil authorities, that the insane person is deprived of that ability of self-government which is the common allotment of men; that the strong bonds of friendship, of family, and of country, which once kept him in his appropriate station in society, are loosened; and that he must find, in the substitution of the will and guardianship of the State, that oversight and protection which he has lost by the alienation of his own. While all must admit the propriety of this course, where the circumstances of the case justly demand it, it must be conceded that nothing can be more solemn and affecting than such a public imputation of derangement, which, whether just or unjust, practically annihilates the civil and social character of man, and seals his degradation in these respects. It is a right, therefore, which ought not to be exercised but upon good grounds, and the exercise of which ought to be understood to require and to imply a correct acquaintance with this difficult but practical and important subject. And the more so, because there have been depraved individuals who have endeavoured to fasten the charge of insanity upon others from some interested motives, in order to gratify malignant passions, or to control their persons or property. A suitable protection against the designs of such is to be had, not merely in the integrity of those who are to judge in these cases, but in their acquaintance with the laws and tendencies of the mind.

Before leaving this topic, one suggestion further remains. In forming an opinion as to the mental alienation of an individual, not only those particular facts are to be considered which are supposed to indicate insanity, but they are to be estimated in connexion with constitutional traits of character. That rapidity of association, that gay and heedless transition from subject to subject, which is natural in one and occasions no surprise, would be regarded in another as a positive indication of the disturbance of the mental powers.

§ 369. Of the treatment of the insane.

In closing this view of mental maladies, it is proper to make some suggestions on the treatment due to those of our fellow-beings who are thus afflicted. It is no uncommon thing to see them treated with unkindness. Although they may not, in general, so readily perceive and so intensely feel, as others, the injuries they receive, any cruelty of treatment towards them is very unjustifiable in the authors of it.

It is wrong on the general principle that we are bound not to cause and increase suffering unnecessarily in any case whatever, even in the animal creation. Men were designed to render each other happy, and not to increase each other's miseries. The poet Cowper uttered a sentiment, which finds a response in the bosoms of all kind and honourable men, when he declared he would not reckon in his list of friends the man who should needlessly set foot upon a worm.

It is wrong, also, on the principle that we should do to others as we ourselves wish to be done by.—The person of an alienated mind may not be able to reason on the subject of what is due him, but those who possess rational powers can. They cannot fail to see the application of the Scriptural principle which has been mentioned in the present instance. All persons whatever are subject to these mental evils; and it is presumed that no one would be easy in the anticipation of being left without care and assistance from others, when he should be unable to take care of himself. If, therefore, we take the ground that persons in the state of idiocy, or of delirium, or of any of the forms of mental alienation, are not entitled to care and kindness, we are probably treasuring up for ourselves a retribution of a similar fearful character.

Again: ill treatment of cases of this kind is a tacit reflection on the Supreme Being, which we cannot, without great self-ignorance, imagine ourselves authorized to make. He has, in his wisdom, permitted them to exist, as memorials of human weakness and as useful commentaries on pride of intellect; and perhaps, also, to give us an opportunity of exercising the noble virtues of charity and humanity. We are therefore bound to receive the instruction they impart, and to exercise the virtues which they give us an opportunity of exercising; otherwise we cast contempt on Him whose almighty hand orders the distinctions, and distributes the allotments both of bodily and intellectual life.

APPENDIX ON LANGUAGE.

APPENDIX ON LANGUAGE.

CHAPTER I.

NATURAL SIGNS.

§ 1. Of the natural and necessary communication of the mental states from one to another.

It requires but a slight acquaintance with the predominant traits and the history of the human race, to be fully satisfied of the intention of Providence, that our internal experiences, including both the suggestions of the intellect and the emotions of the heart, shall be communicated to others. The saying is not more common than true, that man is not born for himself alone. Not only his family, and the friends who share in his private personal intercourse, but his country and the whole human race, possess a positive degree of interest in him. He comes into existence in society; he is trained up in society; his home, his permanent residence, is in society. It is there that he finds the theatre of his sufferings and his joys; of all that he expects to endure, and of all that he permits himself to hope for, in the present life.

And if it were otherwise; if man had not, in fact, the society of his fellows, he would still not be in utter solitude. Let him be doomed to suffer the fate which is ascribed in biblical history to the king of Babylon; let him be driven out, and made to dwell with the beasts of the field, and he will not fail to make companions of them, and will take delight in it. He will even, where nothing else can be found to respond to the wants of his heart, converse with inanimate nature, with the flowers and trees, with the storms and the lightning; he will bless the fruit that nourishes him, and the shade that protects him; he will thank the blossom for its fragrance, and the distant waterfall for its pleasant sounds.—It may be asserted, therefore, with good reason, that a foundation is evidently laid in the human constitution for the intercourse of man with his fellow-man, and that such intercourse is essential to his existence and his happiness. And hence it happens that not merely our thoughts and feelings, in themselves considered, but the mode in which they are to be communicated from one to another, becomes an interesting subject of inquiry. The mode, or, rather, the instrument by which this communication takes place, is Language in its various forms.

§ 2. Mental states first expressed by gestures and the countenance.

The term LANGUAGE, which is employed here in its most general sense, and as standing for all signs of thought and feeling, embraces everything that proposes itself for consideration in this part of our inquiries. But, in order to render what we have to say the more easily understood, we shall consider the general subject under the distinct and important forms of Natural signs, Oral or spoken signs, and Written signs. And in the prosecution of this plan, we are first to consider NATURAL SIGNS, or such as a person would use who found himself incapable of employing either written signs or speech.

It is worthy of notice in respect to any individual who is separated in very early life from the human family, and permitted to grow up without any instruction in the use of the organs of speech, that he will be entirely ignorant in what way to employ such organs, with the unimportant exception of being able to utter a few inarticulate cries. The story of the wild boy found in the forests of Lithuania in 1695, which is introduced, with some comments of his own, in Part First of Condillac's Origin of Knowledge, may be referred to, among other instances, by way of confirming this remark. The same inability of articulate speech is noticed in those unfortunate individuals who are born deaf, and are commonly known under the designation of DEAF and DUMB persons.

But these persons are not without language, although they are incapable of articulate speech, and although we may suppose them ignorant of all artificial aids whatever in communicating thought. The kindness of nature has not failed to make a provision for them, which serves, although in a limited degree, to enable them to reveal to each other their thoughts and feelings. In the absence of other methods of mental communication, they are furnished with the visible and impressive language of gestures and of the countenance.

The expression of the countenance, exclusive of the eye, depends chiefly upon two things, the change of colour in the face, and the movement or play of the muscles. But in most cases we find the intimations of the face combined with movements of other parts of the body. Thus, the flushed countenance, with the hand uplifted, denotes in general an emotion of rage. In admiration or wonder, the countenance is animated with a quick play of the blood and muscles, the hand is elevated, and the body thrown back. A look, slightly illuminated with a smile, with none, or but a small motion of the body, is an indication of satisfaction or peace.—But, without entering into a full description of these signs, it may be said with great certainty, that fear, contempt, derision, grief, disappointment, malice, feelings of the ludicrous, anxiety, deep thought, terror, despair, have their natural signs. Without the aid either of written or spoken language, they can be distinctly expressed by means of gestures, inarticulate sounds, and changes in the countenance.

§ 3. Of the use made of natural signs by the deaf and dumb.

In proof of what has now been said of the capacity of natural signs for the expression of certain mental states, we may refer particularly to the DEAF and DUMB. As already intimated, these unfortunate persons have a language of their own; that is to say, they have a system of signs, partly natural and part of which they have been led to invent, either by their wants, or because they have found pleasure in the employment. Let any person who has been familiar with the deaf and dumb, and has paid attention to their modes of communicating their feeling, be introduced into the company of an individual afflicted with that calamity who is an utter stranger to him. They are no sooner met together than they have the appearance of old acquaintances, speaking a common language. The deaf and dumb person will enter readily, and with much earnestness, into the mute conversation which has been commenced; and by means of that language to which he has been accustomed, will answer the various questions that are put to him. But the system of signs brought into use on such an occasion is founded, in a considerable degree at least, in nature; it employs those elements of expression which God has given to all mankind, and seldom goes beyond mere bodily movements and the language of the looks.

There have been instances of a number of individuals in the same family unable to hear or to articulate. It is exceedingly pleasing to witness their quickness of invention in framing their vocabulary of gestures, and their readiness in conversing with each other by means of them. They interpret an inclination of the head, a movement of the hand or arm, a contraction of the muscles of the face, even the slightest motion of the finger, as readily as another person who is able to hear can interpret the most familiar words.—What a striking declaration do we here have, that, in the defect of oral and written signs of thought, nature has a resource which is antecedent to all other forms of language!

There are some slight gestures which appear to be arbitrary, but which are found to be susceptible of being traced back and resolved into others. Mr. Stewart remarks, that an instructer of Deaf and

Dumb informed him that his pupils (whatever part of the country they came from) agreed, in most instances, in expressing assent by holding up the thumb, and dissent by holding up the little finger. "It can be explained," he observes, "only by supposing that these gestures are abbreviations of those signs by which assent and dissent are generally expressed in the language of nature; and, in truth, the process by which they were introduced may be easily conceived. For the natural sign of assent is to throw the body open, by moving the hand from the breast with the palm towards the body and the thumb uppermost. The natural sign of dissent is the same movement, with the back of the hand towards the body and the little finger uppermost. The former conveys the idea of cordiality, of good-humour, and of inviting frankness; the latter of dislike and aversion. If two dumb persons were left to converse together, it is reasonable to suppose that they would gradually abridge their natural signs for the sake of despatch, and would content themselves with *hinting* at those movements, which could be easily anticipated from the commencement, and in this manner might raise those apparently arbitrary marks of assent or dissent which have just been mentioned."

§ 4. Further illustrations of the great power of natural signs.

The facts which have been already referred to are a sufficient proof of its having been wisely and kindly ordered that there should be a Natural language. The beneficial results of this provision cannot be misunderstood in the case of persons who are by some accident cast among a people whose oral or written language is unknown, and especially in its connection with the DEAF and DUMB. These persons come to their instructers not only weighed down by the pressure of other incidental evils, but ignorant, speechless, and wanting in confidence. The pupil and instructer have never before seen each other, and they are unable to communicate either by means of speech or of written signs. But nature speaks in the dialect of the countenance and of action; the pupil enters on his course of instruction, and in a single year learns, by the aid of signs, and chiefly by the aid of natural signs, the meaning of thousands of words. This is unquestionably ascribing great efficacy to natural signs, but not greater than seems to be warranted by the following authentic statements.

"In the summer of 1818, a Chinese young man passed through Hartford, Connecticut, in which place there is an Asylum for the education of the deaf and dumb. He was so ignorant of the English language that he could not express in it his most common wants. The principal of the Asylum invited the stranger to spend an evening within its walls, and introduced him to Mr. Laurent Clerc, the celebrated deaf and dumb pupil of the Abbé Sicard, and at that time an assistant teacher in the Asylum. The object of this introduction was to ascertain to what extent Mr. Clerc, who was entirely ignorant of the Chinese language, could conduct an intelligent conversation with the foreigner by signs and gestures merely. The result of the experiment surprised all who were present. Mr. Clerc learned from the Chinese many interesting facts respecting the place of his nativity, his parents and their family, his former pursuits in his own country, his residence in the United States, and his notions concerning God and a future state. By the aid of appropriate signs also, Mr. Clerc ascertained the meaning of about twenty Chinese words. When the conversation began, the stranger seemed to be bewildered with amazement at the novel kind of language that was addressed to him. Soon, however, he became deeply interested in the very expressive and significant manner which Mr. Clerc used to make himself understood; and, before one hour had expired, a very quick and lively interchange of thought took place between these so lately entire strangers to each other. The Chinese himself began to catch the spirit of his new deaf and dumb acquaintance, and to employ the language of the countenance and gestures with considerable effect to make himself understood.

"About a year afterward, the principal of the Asylum visited Cornwall, a small village in Connecticut, where upward of twenty heathen youths were receiving education under the patronage of the American Board of Commissioners for Foreign Missions. With the consent of the principal of that institution, the principal of the Asylum one evening gathered around him several of these interesting strangers, from the islands of the South Sea, and from different tribes of North American Indians. The object of this interview was to ascertain how far a conversation could be conducted with them merely by signs and gestures. The result was similar to that in the case of Mr. Clerc's intercourse with the Chinese. Questions were proposed to them on a variety of topics relating to their own individual history and that of their families, to the state of manners and morals in their respective countries, and to their early religious knowledge. For example, Thomas Hoopoo, a native of Owhyhee, was asked if his parents were living; how many brothers and sisters he had; when he left his native shores; whether his countrymen worshipped idols and sacrificed human victims; how the women were treated by the men; what was the climate of his country; what its productions; with many inquiries of a similar nature, all of which he well comprehended, and to many of which he replied by signs. The meaning, too, of a number of Owhyhee words was ascertained by signs merely, and found to correspond with the import which had been previously assigned to them in a dictionary which had been for some time preparing in the school; and, indeed, in a variety of instances, the most correct meaning of such words was established by the medium of signs in a more satisfactory way than had been previously attempted. Throughout this conversation the heathen youths appeared to take a deep interest, and to have a peculiar aptitude both in comprehending the signs which were proposed to them, and in inventing such as were necessary for a reply.

"On the testimony of several of the South Sea Islanders, it appeared that not a few of the signs employed in the instruction of the deaf and dumb are precisely the same which their countrymen use to supply the deficiency of, or to give emphasis to, their own comparatively barren language; a fact which had indeed been anticipated from the circumstance so often observed by the teachers of the deaf and dumb among their pupils, that mutes who meet for the first time are able to understand each other fully on many common topics; the Author of nature having laid the foundation in the very constitution of our species, and in the structure and processes of the visible creation, for a universal expression of the same ideas, on a vast variety of subjects, by similar signs."*

§ 5. Of the system of signs existing among the North American Savages.

It is an interesting fact in relation to the present subject, that a system of natural signs is affirmed, on the most respectable authority, to exist among the Savage tribes throughout North America, which is universally understood by them. A considerable catalogue of these signs has been given to the public by persons who have travelled and resided among the aboriginal inhabitants, and have thus had ample opportunities of knowing. The following, among others, are instances:

(1.) SUN. The forefinger and thumb are brought together at the tip so as to form a circle, and held up towards the sun's track. To indicate any particular time of the day, the hand with the sign of the sun is stretched out towards the east horizon, and then gradually elevated, to show the ascent of that luminary, until the hand arrives in a proper direction to indicate the part of the heavens in which the sun will be

* T. H. Gallaudet's Essay on the Language of Signs, in the (London) Christian Observer, Sept. and Oct., 1836.

at the given time.—(2.) NIGHT, or SLEEPING at night. The head, with the eyes closed, is laterally inclined for a moment upon the hand. As many times as this is repeated, so many nights, either with or without the additional notion of sleep, are indicated. And it will perhaps occur to the recollection here, that this is the sign for the same thing which is generally found to be adopted by deaf and dumb persons.—(3.) COMBAT. The clinched hands are held about as high as the neck, and five or six inches asunder, then waved two or three times laterally, to show the advances and retreats of the combatants; after which, the fingers of each hand are suffered to spring from the thumb towards each other, as in the act of sprinkling water, to represent the flight of the missile weapons which are used by them.—(4.) PRISONER. The forefinger and thumb of the left hand are held in the form of a semicircle, opening towards and near the breast; and the forefinger of the right, representing the prisoner, is placed upright within the curve, and passed from one side to the other, in order to show that it will not be permitted to pass out, &c.*

The epithet SYMBOLIC is sometimes applied to such combinations of gestures as these, but appears to be more generally applied to representative actions, which are either more formal and complicated, or in which the resemblance to the thing signified is less obvious, however simple the action may be in itself. So that SYMBOLS (if there be truly any distinction worthy of being retained) differ rather in degree than in kind; implying either greater complexity, or greater remoteness between the sentiment and the action, than in ordinary imitative gestures.

All travellers among our Savage tribes furnish illustrations of symbolic actions, although until recently they have not been generally aware of the existence of a system of imitative signs by mere gesture.

* See vol. i. of the Transactions of the American Philosophical Society, Long's Expedition from Pittsburg to the Rocky Mountains, and Flint's Valley of the Mississippi, Letter xv.

They accordingly tell us that friendly and peaceable sentiments are symbolically intimated when a stranger appears among a tribe carrying or smoking a large pipe of clay or marble, adorned with feathers, which the Indians call a CALUMET. The method of confirming a treaty of peace is also symbolical, it being done by means of what the Savages call a belt of WAMPUM. This belt is composed of shells of different colours, wrought into the shape of beads, which are strung upon thongs and strongly united together. The parties concerned hold the ends of the belt, and are thereby understood to signify reciprocal truth and sincerity.

§ 6. Of the symbolic exhibitions of the Hebrews.

Symbolical action is known to have been frequently employed in Oriental countries, owing in some measure to the great vivacity and bodily activity of the people. Those who are acquainted with the Bible know how frequently it was resorted to among the ancient Hebrews. It will be sufficient merely to allude to the following instances, which may be more fully understood by a reference to the Scriptures: Elisha directs Joash to shoot arrows out of a window eastward. Jeremiah, acting under divine direction, hides the linen girdle in the hole of a rock near Euphrates; he breaks a potter's vessel in the sight of the people; he puts on bonds and yokes, and casts a book into Euphrates. Ezekiel weighs his beard, delineates the siege of Jerusalem on a tile, &c.

It has sometimes been thought that such symbolic actions were below the dignity of the prophetic office; and there are not wanting those who are disposed to describe them as mean, absurd, and fanatical. But it ought to be remembered that it was the spirit of the times, the feeling of the people themselves, which dictated those exhibitions. It may further be said, that this is the spirit of all times and all countries where it is not controlled and subdued by civilization, and that even civilization does not always subdue and exclude it.

§ 7. Of the instinctive interpretation of certain natural signs.

The meaning of many of those signs which are called natural is learned from experience. The action being a representative or imitation of the thing itself, it necessarily suggests whatever is intended to be signified. But there are some which appear to be understood instinctively, and, of course, independently of experience; for instance, a smile, or frown, or the signs of terror. The opinion that there is to a certain extent an original or instinctive interpretation of signs, appears to be maintained by writers chiefly on the following grounds:

(1.) We are clearly led in all our inquiries, whether of an intellectual or a physical kind, to the conclusion, that the great Author of nature has some purpose or design in his works. Now there can be no dispute that he has furnished men with a large apparatus of natural signs. Almost every desire and passion of the human soul is capable of being expressed in that way. Peace of mind, the desire of knowledge, especially when quickened by any peculiar circumstances, the benevolent affections, intensity of thought, the passions of joy and grief, all have their appropriate language, beaming in the eye, quivering on the lips, contracting in the forehead, reddening and dimpling in the cheeks, and are rendered yet more emphatic by the attitude, the gestures, and the tones of voice. It being, therefore, an admitted fact, that his Creator has furnished man with a system of natural signs, it is but reasonable to suppose that he has furnished him also with a corresponding power of interpretation; and that man is thereby enabled, at the very earliest period, to avail himself of the price which has thus kindly been placed in his hands. It is maintained that this is the probability or presumption arising in the mere view of the facts; and also that such presumption is supported by the analogy of other cases. We not only find, for instance, in human nature, a love of the truth and a disposition to utter it, but a corresponding principle of belief; and, by analogy, we should be led to expect, in like manner, a corresponding power of interpretation, where we find a system of signs susceptible of being interpreted.

(2.) But there are other circumstances which seem to afford direct and positive proof of what we should thus be led to expect.—The power of interpreting natural signs is noticed at a very early period, long before the ability to interpret arbitrary signs. Children understand the meaning of smiles and frowns, of a soothing or threatening tone of voice, of the expressions of joy and grief, at a time of life when they cannot be supposed capable of so much observation as to remark the connexion between a passion and its external effect. While they are months learning the alphabet, and years elapse before they can read a book with facility, they read and understand the signs of nature as soon as their ears are opened to hear and their eyes to see, and without the aid of a laborious system of training.

§ 8. Further evidence of the instinctive interpretation of natural signs.

(3.) There is another train of thought tending to illustrate this subject. It is an undoubted matter of fact, that the knowledge of the intellectual operations and of the passions cannot be fully communicated to their pupils by instructers of the deaf and dumb in the ordinary modes. They cannot here, as in the case of external objects, write the name, and then point to the object in explanation of it. They are obliged to rely almost wholly on natural signs, particularly those of the countenance, in the explanation of what is taking place within. And when an instructer, who is well versed in the language of such signs, throws the workings of the soul into the looks, it is interesting to see with what avidity and ease his unfortunate pupils decipher this dialect of flesh and blood and muscular motion. It cannot be said here that the power of interpretation depends on the previous experience of the pupils, because we suppose the instructer (which is often the fact) is expressing mental acts and operations with which they have hitherto been unacquainted, or with which, as existing in the mind of another, they cannot possibly be made acquainted in any other way.

(4.) Those signs which are maintained to be susceptible of an instinctive interpretation affect us more than others. The passions of hatred, love, and anger interest us much more strongly when they are represented in the countenance than when they are expressed by mere written or spoken words. So that, unquestionably, we give to some natural signs a significancy which we do not and cannot give to others, and still less to those forms of language which are purely arbitrary. This being the case, it seems to be reasonable to conclude that the mind has an original power of interpreting to some extent.

(5.) This power seems to be necessary as an introductory step to the formation of all conventional language. Artificial language, whether we regard it as written or spoken, is arbitrary, and a matter of mere agreement. But if it were not of divine original, as many writers have contended, it is evident that there must have been some antecedent signs, by means of which such agreement was first formed. And we can think of no instrument which could have been employed to this end, except the instinctive power of interpreting those signs of gesture, tones of voice, and movements of the countenance, which we find, from the earliest period of life, to be expressive of emotions and the passions.

There is another consideration on this subject, in addition to those already alluded to, which it is proper to mention, although the train of thought cannot be pursued to any length.—The brute creation, as well as men, have their natural signs. They are destitute, it is true, of the natural language of the countenance, but they are rich in that of the voice. Every mountain and forest is vocal with the lowing of herds, the bleating of flocks, the threatening cries of animals of prey, and the infinitely varied notes of birds. By the sounds which are continually sent forth, they communicate to each other their joys and sorrows, their jealousies and hopes, their attachments and their aversions; and probably no one doubts that they are instinctively interpreted, for it is not easy to see in what other way they could be understood. But if the Creator has given this power of interpretation to brutes, we cannot well suppose that he has altogether withholden it from men, when he has given them the same natural signs, and with an originally equal necessity of their being interpreted.

§ 9. Considerations on the use of natural signs.

Before dismissing the subject of this chapter, it remains to be remarked, that it is one of no little practical importance, although it may often be thought otherwise.

An attention to natural signs could hardly fail to be of advantage in infant schools, and in all cases of instruction of very young children. The knowledge which is suited to their minds is that which we have already described as having an external origin. Consequently, the objects or actions, with which they are to be made acquainted, must be presented to the sight or some other of the senses. But, in the absence of objects, the instructer, if he has studied the language of natural signs, will be able to convey the meaning of many words by gestures; a method which will secure the purpose designed, and will not be wanting in interest to the little pupils. "Notwithstanding," says Dugald Stewart, "the decline of natural language in consequence of the use of artificial signs, the acquaintance we still have with the former (however imperfect) is of essential service in teaching children the meaning of the latter. This may be easily exemplified by first reading over to a child one of Æsop's fables without taking your eye from the book, or using any inflexion of voice; and afterward telling him the same story with the commentary of your face, and gestures, and tones."

Again, the doctrine of natural signs is deserving of

greater attention than it has received, when it is considered in connexion with the Deaf and Dumb. No small acquaintance with them is implied in being able to fix upon such as are suitable in the instruction of these unfortunate persons. And the worth of such acquaintance, therefore, can be conjectured from its subserviency to their improvement and happiness. If there were no other result, the labour attending the study of natural signs would be amply repaid by this.

Furthermore, some knowledge of natural signs might be found profitable to all travellers and sojourners among nations of an unknown tongue, and, among others, to Missionaries. It is one of the pleasing features of the present times, that men from almost all the civilized parts of the world are gone out to announce in heathen lands the glad news of the Gospel. One of the American missionaries in India, remarking on the acquisition of languages, observes that, in receiving lessons from his instructer, they were often compelled to resort to signs and gestures in order at all to understand each other.—Similar aids may be expected to be afforded from this source in all cases analogous to this. Lucian has somewhere made mention of a king, whose dominions bordered on the Euxine Sea, who, happening to be at Rome in the reign of Nero, and having seen a pantomime perform, begged him of the emperor as a present, in order that he might employ him as an interpreter among the nations in his neighbourhood, with whom he could have no intercourse on account of the diversity of language.*—These are not unimportant considerations; and there is ground for making this remark also, that a knowledge of natural signs is subservient, in some measure, to the success of the fine or liberal arts, particularly sculpture and painting, and also to the successful exhibition of the art of oratory.

The arts of sculpture and painting are addressed to the eye; and one great object in those arts is to express emotions. Those, therefore, who practise them,

* See Stewart's Philosophy of the Mind, part ii., chap. i., § 1.

must study the connexion between the illuminations of the eye, the colour and muscular movements of the face, and the general attitude, which are the natural outward signs, and the internal feelings which correspond to them. It is not possible that a single trait of character or even a single feeling should be conveyed by those admirable arts except by means of natural signs. And hence the obvious conclusion, that no man can excel in them without a knowledge of that form of language.—Similar remarks will apply to the orator. He addresses the eye as well as the ear; and, whenever he combines the language of looks, tones, and gestures with the arbitrary signs of articulate speech, he cannot fail to increase the interest of his hearers.

CHAPTER II.

ORAL SIGNS, OR SPEECH.

§ 10. Remarks on the original formation of oral signs.

Although we cannot but admire the wise provision of nature in furnishing men with natural signs, it ought to excite our gratitude that they are not left, in the communication of their thoughts and affections from one to another, to the assistances merely which are given them in that way. Possessed of the organs of speech, they are capable of forming signs, which are addressed to the ear, and which, from their very nature, are in a great degree conventional and arbitrary.—And we stop a moment to remark here, that we find, in this use of the organs of speech, a striking instance of the direction and power which the mental nature is capable of giving to the bodily action, and of the value of mental endowments in general. The brute animals are known to possess the physical requisites of articulation in a considerable degree; and some of their tribes have been frequently taught to utter the names of persons, and even distinctly to repeat whole sentences. Nevertheless, we do not find among the brute animals an oral language, a system of conventional sounds of their own making, and the general use and intercourse of speech. They are not only destitute of the preliminary requisite of the natural signs of the countenance, but the formation of a conventional language implies also the exercise of a degree of intellect, which they do not possess. Nothing short of the high capacities of the human mind is capable of securing this great result.

And such is the undeniable difficulty of employing the complicated machinery of articulation so as to form words, it is proper to remark in this place, that there has even been a doubt in the minds of some whether men, if wholly left to their own efforts, would ever have acquired this power. Such persons admit that others may acquire the power by a long and laborious process of imitating after it has been once attained (and, in fact, we daily see this in the case of children); but they cannot easily persuade themselves that the unaided faculties of the mind were equal to the original acquisition.

Hence it has been the opinion of the persons now alluded to, that we are indebted for the power of forming oral signs, or of speaking, to the direct interference of the Deity himself in behalf of our first parents. This is undoubtedly a matter of opinion, and we may even add, of probability, although it does not appear to be susceptible of clear and decided proof. The Bible, which is designed rather to subserve the moral and religious interests of mankind than to gratify antiquarian curiosity, does not entirely set us at rest on this point. It does indeed say that God brought the beasts of the field and the fowls of the air to Adam to see what he would call them, but it is not said that God gave the names himself, or that he directly aided Adam in giving them; although the supposition that such assistance was granted may be held to be supported by the circumstance that he either then or before obviously stood in need of it, and also by the consideration of that beneficence which is continually manifested in the dealings of the Supreme Being with his creatures.

§ 11. Of the possibility of forming an oral language without Divine aid.

With the assurance, which is so abundantly given in Revelation, that in ancient times the Supreme Being had communication with his creatures in diverse ways, no reasonable objection can be felt to the doctrine which makes God the direct author of oral language, provided there be found in the Scriptures sufficient evidence in favour of it. At the same time, notwithstanding the difficulties that beset the whole inquiry, it cannot be denied that some reasons may be proposed in support of the opinion that the formation of an oral language is within the unaided reach of the human faculties, of which God also is the author.

It is admitted, that if a man be placed in utter solitude, and be permitted to grow up in that situation, there is no reason to anticipate that he will ever have the command of articulate speech. The effort to obtain it is too great when he finds no one around him with whom to compare his labours, to sympathize in his discouragements, and to cheer him on to a successful termination. But his prospect is very different in the bosom of society; he there finds a multitude of incitements and assistances which in the other situation he would be destitute of, and, although it would cost him many a struggle, he would probably find himself rewarded at last for his labours in the possession of their object.

But if it be admitted that man, existing in society, would be able to acquire the power of articulate speech, the next inquiry is, What more is wanting in order to institute an oral language? Simply this: he must form a convention or agreement with his associates, by means of which distinct and separate sounds shall be made to stand for separate and definite objects. And, having arrived at this point in the inquiry, we shall no doubt be called upon to show how such convention or agreement could possibly be made. And it must be acknowledged there is but one answer; it can be made by means of Natural Signs, and in that way alone.

Natural signs are not only indispensable in the original formation of oral language, but, were it not for their assistance, it would be impossible to teach Oral language to children, even after it had been once formed. When a mother teaches her native tongue to her children, she utters a particular sound; the child himself, perhaps, utters the same sound; but how does the child know that the sound is to stand for a particular object, for a watch, a chair, a table, a man, &c.?—It is evident that he can form the association of the sign with the thing signified only through the agency of the antecedent language of natural signs. By means of tones of the voice, changes of the countenance, and gestures, the mother succeeds in awakening an interest in the child, and in communicating her general design; she then points to the object at the same time with the utterance of the sound or name; and she repeats this process till the child, by the aid of its instinctive power of interpreting natural signs, fully comprehends the meaning of the articulate sound.*

It will be remembered, that the inquiry which has been attended to in this section is not whether the original formation of oral language by man's unaided effort is probable, but merely whether it be *possible*. "Let us suppose," says Chateaubriand, "a Savage in possession of his senses, but not having speech; this man, pressed by hunger, meets in the forest some object proper to satisfy it; he utters a cry of joy at seeing it or at carrying it to his mouth. Is it not possible, that, having heard the cry, the sound, be it what it may, he retains it, and repeats it afterward every time he perceives the same object or is pressed with the same want? The cry will become the first word

* See Degerando's Histoire des Systèmes de Philosophie, tome i., chap. iii., note B.

of his vocabulary, and thus he will proceed on till he arrives at the expression of ideas purely intellectual."

§ 12. Oral signs or words are in general arbitrary.

In oral language, sounds stand for things, or, rather, the ideas of things; but there is no resemblance between the sign and the thing signified. The fact that articulated sounds or words are representative of the states of the mind, is founded on arbitrary agreement. And as this agreement necessarily involves the consent of the great mass of any people, by whom oral signs are employed, the alleged confession of the Emperor Augustus was made with good reason, that he was of himself unable to introduce a single new word into the Latin tongue.

If this statement were not correct; if words had any natural fitness for that purpose for which they are employed, and were not conventional, there would be but one language. Instead of the multiplied diversities in dialects and languages which we now witness, there would be the same words for things of the same nature throughout the world. But this is not the case. On the contrary, every body of men, as it happens to be separated from other communities by mountains, oceans, and other causes both physical and political, forms for itself its own arbitrary system of signs.

It ought to be observed, however, that there is a slight exception to this general view of the arbitrary nature of oral signs. We allude to a class of terms, of which the words CRASH, TWANG, BUZZ, WHISTLE, SHRILL, HISS, RATTLE, may be mentioned as specimens. There is evidently some resemblance between these words, as they are enunciated by the voice, and the things for which they stand; in other languages, some words similar to these, that is, having a like relation to the things for which they stand, are to be found. But with this exception, which is one of very limited extent, words are truly arbitrary and conventional sounds, formed in the progressive history of the human race, on such occasions of want or of convenience as seemed to call for them. These occasions, on which words were first employed, and their arrangement into classes (what grammarians call Parts of Speech), merit a brief consideration.

§ 13. Words at first few in number, and limited to particular objects.

In the infancy of the human race, men were without a knowledge of the arts; they had no laws but the dictates of conscience, no regularly instituted form of government; their food was the fruits of the earth, and they lived under the open sky, except when they retreated from the storm or the sunshine to the shade of trees or the cooler recesses of caverns. Their ideas, therefore, were few; the articulate sounds which either the active ingenuity of nature or the special interference of Providence had taught them not only to frame, but to employ as the instituted signs of things, must have been few also; even more so than their ideas.

The few names which they were able thus early to employ, related chiefly to the objects with which they were more immediately and particularly conversant. They gave a name to the sun that shone by day, and to the moon which ruled the night; they invented an oral sign for the tree under which they sat at noon; for the cavern to which they occasionally retired; for the fruit which relieved their hunger, and for the running water at which they slaked their thirst. Afterward they were led to form general names for a number of objects, and probably in the following manner.

§ 14. Of the formation of general names or appellatives.

Naturally possessed of too much activity of spirit to rest satisfied with remaining in one place, or to quiet their curiosity with a small number of objects, they engaged in some new enterprise, explored new tracts of country, and thus enlarged their knowledge. In going from place to place, they necessarily met again with those particular objects with which they had formed such an intimate acquaintance in their first residence. They met with other trees, with other animals, with other caves and fountains, which they at once perceived to be of the same kind with those that had previously come under their observation.

The recurrence of these new objects instantly called up the others. This happened by a law of their nature which they could not control; and the recollection was the more intense, as, in the infancy of things, curiosity is more alive, and astonishment more readily and deeply felt. The objects with which they had become first acquainted could not be recalled without a remembrance, at the same time, of the names which they had given them. As they perceived the objects which they now beheld to be the same in kind with those which they first knew, they at once concluded, and very naturally, that they had an equal right to the names with those to which those names were first appropriated. They therefore exclaimed, *a tree! a cave! a fountain!* whenever and wherever they met them. And thus what was at first a particular term, and was employed to express only an individual, had its meaning extended, and came in time to stand for a whole class of objects.

Such, there can hardly be a question, was the origin of general names; and the statement is not only agreeable to the natural course of things, but is indirectly confirmed by many incidents. When the Spaniards first arrived at a certain region bordering on the Gulf of Mexico, and found that the soil was rich, the dwellings good, the people numerous, they cried out, it is another Spain, and after that it bore the name of New Spain. When they first sailed along the coast of Columbia, they noticed an Indian village built on piles, to raise it above the stagnant water; and being, from that circumstance, reminded of the mistress of the Adriatic, they called that region VENEZUELA (Little Venice), which is the name of the province to this day.* And it is on the same princi-

* Amer. Quart. Review, March, 1831, p. 167.

ple that people so often find themselves in this country giving names to the objects around them in allusion to what exists on some other continent; calling a large river another Thames, and mountains of great altitude the American Alps. So readily does the mind connect together things which are remote, and seek for analogies between what is novel and what is familiar.

§ 15. The formation of appellatives implies the feeling of resemblance.

We discover, in the way which has just been mentioned, the origin of appellatives or common names (in treatises of a scientific nature more commonly termed GENERA and SPECIES), the formation of which has sometimes been considered a matter of difficult solution. If the statement which has been given in the preceding section be a correct one, the mental process, so far from being difficult, is definite and simple. Nature has made a provision which is prompt and easy in its applications, and abundantly successful in its results. There is, first, the perception of different objects of the same kind; then the suggestion or feeling of resemblance in respect to those objects; and, finally, the giving of the common name to such objects or parts of objects as are reached by the feeling of resemblance.

The feeling of resemblance is a distinct thing from the previous perception of the individual objects. If there had not been, between the perception of the objects and the giving of the common name, an intermediate feeling of resemblance, the primitive framers of language would have been as likely to have assigned the same appellative to the cave, and the mountain, and the river, or to any other things altogether dissimilar, as to those resembling objects to which it was assigned.

When, therefore, those persons who hold to the doctrine of the Nominalists assert that all general abstract ideas are but names, they appear to mistake. There is something more than the mere name, viz., the idea for which the name stands as it is modified by that feeling of resemblance which has been mentioned, and which, although it may be difficult to explain it, except it be by referring each one to his own intellectual experience, is clearly too important a circumstance to be hastily overlooked and thrown out of the question. (See the Chapter on General Abstract Ideas.)

§ 16. On the increase in the number of nouns or appellatives.

After a certain number of sounds had been selected and agreed upon as the signs or names of objects, the extension or increase of this part of oral language became comparatively easy. We may suppose that objects in nature were from time to time discovered, such as trees, plants, flowers, minerals, and others, which were unknown before; but, instead of uttering and agreeing upon altogether new sounds as their names, men searched among the treasures already in their possession, and found them there. This was particularly, and, we may suppose, almost uniformly the case, when there were words already existing which could be rendered, by their combination, descriptive of traits or qualities in the newly discovered objects. Nor are these statements wholly conjectural. They appear to be confirmed by what we notice every day in the history of languages. When, for instance, a new word is wanted in the English language to express some distinct idea not yet provided for, a sign entirely new is not invented for it. Every one knows that there is a great repugnance felt to coin new words out of sounds that have hitherto had no meaning attached to them. But the practice is to form a new word by a combination of others, or perhaps by an alteration, either in the beginning or the termination of the word, according to the settled analogy of the language. In case there are no words in the language which can either be compounded or altered so as to answer the purpose, resort is frequently had, in preference to framing a sound entirely new, to foreign languages. Many words in the English language have been introduced from the Greek, the French, and the Italian, although these are not its great and original sources.

It is this tendency to alter rather than invent new words which lays the foundation of the well-known fact, that there is a regular system of composition, of increase, and of diminution in words, running through every language. A single word (for instance, the verbs of the Latin, Greek, and Hebrew languages) may assume ten, twenty, or even fifty different forms, and every form is expressive of a distinct idea. And hence the primitive words of all languages, even those that are most copious, are comparatively few in number.

§ 17. Of the formation of verbs.

In the exercise of their power of appointing articulate sounds as signs of thought, we now suppose men to have proceeded so far as to form general nouns or appellatives, and to employ them with facility. But they soon find that there is need of another class of words, which are of great consequence both in the construction and the application of oral language, viz., VERBS.

As the ideas expressed by verbs concern actions rather than objects, and the attributes, affections, and relations of things rather than the things themselves, and cannot, therefore, be so easily defined to the understanding and fixed upon by it, words of this kind were not, we may suppose, so rapidly formed as appellatives, although some of them must have been of very early origin.

Their origin may be illustrated in this way. Let it be admitted that the primitive inhabitants have given names to certain wild animals; Condillac supposes that such names were given first, before those of trees, fountains, rivers, and other inanimate objects. It soon happens, as is very natural and reasonable to be imagined, that they see one of these animals advancing towards them with great speed and apparent ferocity. Certainly they would have an idea of the motion of the animal as something different from the animal itself; and if they could give a name to the animal, why not to the fact of his coming towards them or running from them, as the fact might be?

In the formation of the noun substantive or general term, they exclaimed, The tiger! The lion! and this exclamation became in time the common name. But now they discover a new attribute or action of the animal, which affects them strongly, and deserves a distinct appellation, and hence they utter some new exclamation; it may be conjectured, the word COMES or RUSHES; and the cry now is, tiger—rushes! lion—comes! The articulate sounds which, under such circumstances, are adopted, whatever they may be, are eventually fixed upon as the conventional and permanent representations of certain actions, attributes, and affections of things; and in the maturity of society and of knowledge, when man finds all that he has learned subjected to a more exact and scientific classification, they are accordingly classed as VERBS.

§ 18. Formation of adjectives and other parts of speech.

It has been conjectured that nouns and verbs were, in time of origin, the earliest of all the parts of speech, and, in truth, the hypothesis does not rest solely upon conjecture. It was the object of men at first to express their ideas as they could; and they reckoned it of but little consequence whether they did it with great precision or elegance. Adjectives, conjunctions, adverbs, prepositions, relative pronouns, were introduced by degrees, as they were found to be needed; but nouns and verbs could never be dispensed with. And, in addition to this consideration, that these classes of words could not at any time be dispensed with, there is much reason to suppose, from a variety of investigations, that adjectives and some other subordinate parts of speech were derived either from verbs or substantives, and, of course, they must have been subsequent in the period of their formation.

Agreeably to this statement, it is found that, in the dialect of some Savage tribes, those qualifying words which we call ADJECTIVES, or adnouns, do not exist. "The Mohegans," says an American writer, "have no adjectives in all their language. Although it may at first seem not only singular and curious, but impossible, that a language should exist without adjectives, yet it is an indubitable fact."* This fact, strange as it may seem at first, is undoubtedly consistent with what we notice in many of the most improved languages. Thus in the English we say, a *clay* colour, a *lead* colour, a *sea* fish, a *wine* vessel, a *gold* ring. But clay, lead, sea, wine, gold, are originally nouns, and are still used as such. We here call them adjectives, and not nouns, merely because they are employed as subordinate to other nouns, and for the purpose of qualifying them.

In other cases, adjectives can be traced back to verbs. Thus the adjective *proud* is ascertained to be the Anglo-Saxon PRUT, which is the past participle of PRYTIAN. The adjective TALL may also be traced to the Anglo-Saxon, being the past participle of the verb TILIAN, *to lift up*. The epithet RIGHT is from the past participle of the Latin verb REGO, *to govern* or *order*.

§ 19. The foregoing principles confirmed from the deaf and dumb.

The statements of the last section, introduced to show that some adjectives were originally nouns, are confirmed by what is almost invariably noticed in the Deaf and Dumb. Massieu, the celebrated pupil of the Abbé Sicard, is a proof.

He had acquired a clear conception of the qualities of objects, in distinction from the objects themselves to which they belonged. But when he first attempted to express those qualities in words, he invariably made use of other nouns, and not adjectives; selecting, of course, the names of such objects as were remarkable for the qualities in question.—If, for instance, he wished to express the quality or attribute

* Dr. Jonathan Edwards's Remarks on the Mohegan Indians.

of speed in one of his companions, instead of saying Albert is swift, he would say Albert is a BIRD. If he wished to express the quality of courage, instead of saying Paul is bold, he would say Paul is a LION. He would express his perception of sweetness of disposition in another, not by saying William is amiable, but William is a LAMB.*

§ 20. Of the formation of prepositions.

We should remember, in considering the subject of artificial language, that it was originally framed by comparatively artless men, and that its different parts appeared, not in obedience to a sort of prophetic invention merely, but as they were called for by an urgent necessity. There is good reason to suppose, in view of the considerations already advanced, that the earliest denominations or classes of speech were those which were subsequently called verbs and common nouns. But soon there were framed other parts or classes of speech, that were not permanently included under the names of verbs and appellatives, but in time assumed a distinct denomination. And this was the case not only with adjectives, but with prepositions.

Prepositions are the names of real objects, actions, attributes, and relations, not less than the parts of speech from which they are, in a great measure, derived. The preposition WITH, for instance, is asserted by etymologists to have been originally the imperative mode of a Saxon verb, which means to unite or join. The sun *with* his rays enlightens and warms the earth; that is, the sun, JOIN his rays, enlightens, &c. In like manner, the preposition *through* is said to have been originally the Teutonic substantive THURUH, meaning a door, gate, or passage. The beams of the sun pass *through* the air; that is, the beams of the sun pass; the air is their door or passage-way. The preposition *from* is the Anglo-Saxon FRUM, which means beginning or origin. In the proposition, The

* See Cours d'Instruction d'un Sourd-muet de Naissance, par Roch Ambroise Sicard, 2d ed., p. 47.

rays came from the sun, we have the two distinct propositions, viz., the rays came, and the sun their beginning or source. The lamp falls *from* the ceiling; that is, the lamp falls; the ceiling is its beginning, or the place where the falling begins.*

§ 21. Of the origin and original import of conjunctions.

The general doctrine that nouns were first formed, afterward verbs, and that these were the sources of other classes of words, is strengthened by what we know in respect to that species of connectives called conjunctions.

The conjunction IF was originally a verb in the imperative mode, viz., GIF, the imperative of the Saxon word GIFAN, which is the same with the modern English infinitive to GIVE. If we consider the original import of the words in this sentence, viz., If ye love me, ye will keep my commandments, it will stand thus: Give or grant this, viz., ye love me, ye will keep my commandments.

The conjunctions UNLESS, LEST, and ELSE, are derivatives from the Saxon verb LESAN, to dismiss. The meaning conveyed in this sentence, viz., Unless ye believe, ye shall not understand, may be thus analyzed: Dismiss, ye believe (the circumstance of belief being out of the way), ye shall not understand.

The conjunction THOUGH was originally a verb in the imperative, from the Saxon THAFIAN, meaning to grant or allow. The word was originally THAF or THOF, and is thus often pronounced by the people in some parts of England to this day. This sentence, Though he slay me, I will trust in him, may be thus explained, in conformity with the etymological derivation: Allow, grant this, he will slay me, I will trust in him.

* See this subject more fully considered in the EPEA PTEROENTA, or Diversions of Purley of Horne Tooke.

§ 22. Further remarks on the meaning of conjunctions and other particles.

Observations similar to those which have been made in reference to conjunctions and prepositions will apply to other subordinate parts of speech (which, including conjunctions and prepositions, are sometimes known under the names of particles). Accordingly, it will be found, on examination, that many adverbs were originally either nouns, verbs, or the participles of verbs. But this inquiry, interesting and important as it unquestionably is, cannot be further prosecuted here. It is proper, however, to guard the foregoing views by saying, that when a language is fully formed and settled upon, we would not advise a confident and indiscriminate reference to the etymology of particles, in order to determine their present significancy, although in many cases, as in those mentioned in the preceding section, such a reference throws light upon them. Whatever particles may have been at first, whether nouns or verbs, or whatever direct and positive significance they may have once had, they are at last, when the language is fully formed, evidently without meaning, except so far as they are connected with other words.

The proper use of them seems to be, to express the states of our mind as we pass from one clause of a sentence to another, or from one proposition to another; also the restriction, distinction, and opposition of our thoughts. Admitting, then, that, in some instances, we can derive considerable aid from etymology, the surest method of ascertaining the meaning of this class of words is by observing the operations of our own minds as we connect together our ideas in clauses, sentences, and consecutive propositions.

§ 23. Of the origin of particular or proper names.

Although general names or appellatives, as appeared in § 13, were first applied to particular objects, as soon as they became general and were employed to denote classes of objects, they were no longer of use in the specification of individuals. Their utility in that respect necessarily ceased. Hence arose the class of substances or nouns called particular or proper names, designed especially to indicate individual objects. In ascertaining to what objects terms of this kind shall be assigned, it can only be said that we give proper names to such things as we have frequent and urgent occasion to mention; no other rule can readily be laid down.—We accordingly give particular names to rivers, lakes, cataracts, mountains, because we have frequent occasion to speak of them individually; of the Mississippi, the La Plata, the Alps, and the Apennines. There is still greater reason why we should give names of this sort to our fellow-beings, with whom we constantly associate, and on whom our happiness is in no small degree dependent. But the assignation of proper names is far from being limited to men, or to rivers, or to mountains, or to cataracts. We continually meet with them.—The merchant gives names to his vessels, the farmer to his oxen, the hunter to his dogs, the jockey to his horses, on the same principles and for the same reason that one river is called Ganges and another Danube, and that one man is called John and another William.

§ 24. Principle of selection and significancy of proper names.

But a question arises, On what principle are the names themselves selected? Proper names undoubtedly were at first expressive of some qualities or events pertaining to the individuals or objects to which they were applied. Thus, in the Hebrew, certainly one of the most ancient of languages, the name Benjamin signifies a favourite or prosperous son; Joshua intimates help or deliverance; Samuel implies a disposition to hear or obey God; Moses, although perhaps not originally a Hebrew word, is supposed to denote a person drawn from the waters.

In the Gaelic language, Cairbar, the strong man; Morna, the well-beloved; Cathmor, great in battle; and a multitude of other significant names might be referred to, as illustrating and confirming this view.

In the Latin, the celebrated name of Brutus alludes to the fact that Lucius Junius acted the assumed part of a brutish or foolish person in order to conceal his patriotic designs. The renowned cognomen of Coriolanus was first given in reference to the assault of Corioli by a Roman soldier. The name of Publicola expressed the attachment of the first individual who bore it to the rights and interests of the people. Every reader of Roman history knows what splendid associations of an historical kind are connected with the names of Capitolinus and Africanus. And names were not only given by the Romans in reference to personal achievements and historical events, but as expressive of mental qualities, occupations, and situations in life. Accordingly, one man is called Egerius for his poverty; another is called Serranus in allusion to his business as a cultivator of the soil; another is called Cato out of regard to his wisdom.

§ 25. Of the origin and significancy of the names of places.

The names of places also have a meaning; it is sometimes a direct and positive significancy, at others only an allusion to historical facts. There is ample reason for believing that this is true almost without exception, although the original import is now, in many cases, lost.

The ancient Hebrews came to a mountainous ridge; they saw that it was plentifully watered, and that it was clothed, even to its summit, with oaks and firs, with laurels and olives; and they named it Mount Carmel, which means in the Hebrew tongue the mount of the *garden of God*. An early Christian teacher, according to the traditions of the country, having been put to death on a certain hill, it was thence called Montmartre; the name, to this day, of a celebrated eminence in the neighbourhood of Paris. When Columbus entered a capacious and safe harbour, with a rich and beautiful surrounding country, he called the place Puerto Bello, by a name descriptive of its predominant features. And so of instances without number.

On this subject a careful examination of the various dialects of the North American Savages would undoubtedly throw light. The meaning of very many proper names has already been ascertained, with a greater or less degree of probability, by careful inquirers into those languages. A company of Indians, seated on the banks of a river, and seeing it opposed and violently driven in different directions by the projecting rocks, would naturally enough call it the Kenaway, which means, in the Shawanese tongue, the river of whirlpools. Among many other similar instances, the words Mississippi and Niagara, which have no meaning for an Anglo-American, are accurately descriptive in the Aboriginal dialects; the former signifying the great river, and the latter the thunder of waters.

CHAPTER III.

WRITTEN SIGNS.

§ 26. Of the causes which led to the formation of written signs.

The formation of oral language preceded that of WRITTEN language, by which we understand those artificial signs which are addressed to the eye instead of the ear. With all the advantages of oral language, men could not long be insensible to the great convenience of a mode of communication which did not require personal presence. Previously to resorting to written signs, the transmission of commands from one place to another required the agency of persons especially commissioned for that purpose. Laborious and expensive as was this method of sending communications, it was not always a successful one. The most faithful messenger was liable to misunderstand the subject of his embassy, or to fail in communicating it with precision to others.

All history, likewise, during the period antecedent to the invention of written language, was necessarily imbodied in traditions. The father, who had himself participated in great national events, told them to the son, and the son repeated them in the ears of the succeeding generation. It was thus that the poems of Ossian are said to have been handed down. It was thus, according to Tacitus (DE MORIBUS GERMANORUM, § 2, 3), that the legends and heroic songs of the ancient tribes of Germany were transmitted. And it was from traditions, repeated through succeeding ages, that Garcillasso composed the history of the Incas of Peru.

Sometimes the rude nations of antiquity assisted their traditionary recollections by planting groves, throwing together monumental heaps of stones, and instituting games; but even these precautions did not avail. Various mistakes were found to arise; statements became confused and perplexed, till the unadorned truths of real history could no longer be separated from the embellishments of fiction.—Being, therefore, put upon some other artificial method of making their thoughts known to each other at the present time, and of transmitting their knowledge to future ages, men at last invented the different forms of written language.

§ 27. The first artificial signs addressed to the eye were pictures.

Although they did not find oral language suited to all their purposes, it seems to have been beyond their power immediately to invent alphabets. The object of their earliest efforts was exhausted in making visible sketches of actions and events precisely as they exist.

The expression of ideas in this method has been more or less practised in all nations during the early periods of their history, and has been of considerable aid to them in making out the record of their early annals. We are informed in the Pentateuch that figures were embroidered in the curtains of the HOLY OF HOLIES; and learn from the ancient poems of Homer that Helen wrought in embroidery the pictures of the battles in which the attractions of her own person had caused the Greeks and Trojans to be engaged.—The expression of ideas by painting in colours, or by pictorial writing in other ways, is found to exist among the Savages of North America. Bows and arrows, hatchets, animals of various kinds, are imprinted on the bodies of their chiefs, the indications of their calling, and of their heroic qualities. They go further, and are able to point out actions, situations, and events, although imperfectly. They often, in their journeyings, leave behind them figures, either painted or rudely carved, which convey much important information to those who happen afterward to come the same way.

A recent and somewhat striking illustration of this topic cannot well be omitted. It is found in the Journal of an expedition that was sent out in 1820 to explore the northwestern region of the United States. A part of the company, in passing across from the River St. Louis to Sandy Lake, had missed their way, together with their Indian attendants, and could not tell where they were. In consequence of being in this situation, the Indians, not knowing what might be the result, determined to leave, at a certain place, a memorial of their journey, for the information of such of their tribe as might happen to come in that direction afterward. In the party there was a military officer, a person whom the Indians understood to be an attorney, and a mineralogist; eight were armed; when they halted they formed three encampments. The Savages went to work and traced out with their knives upon a piece of birch bark a man with a sword for the officer, another human figure with a book in his hand for the lawyer, and a third with a hammer for the mineralogist; three ascending columns of smoke denoted the three encampments, and eight muskets the number of armed men, &c.*

We find pictorial delineations to have been practised, in particular, among the original inhabitants of Mexico. It is related by historians, that when the Spaniards first landed upon that coast, the natives

* Schoolcraft's Narrative Journal, chap. viii.

despatched messengers to the King Montezuma, with a representation painted on cloth of the landing and appearance of the Europeans. The events and appearances which they wished to describe were new to them, and these pictured representations were the methods which they adopted, in preference to any other, to express those ideas which they deemed it important the king should immediately possess.

Pictures, like the language of mere gesticulation, are a very imperfect mode of communicating ideas, as they must, from their very nature, be limited, in a great degree, to the description of external events. They fail in disclosing the connexions of those events, in developing dispositions, intricate trains of thought, and, in some measure, the passions. Attempts were therefore soon made to introduce another form of writing, called hieroglyphics.

§ 28. Of hieroglyphical writing.

Hieroglyphics (from the Greek words hieros, sacred, and glupho, to carve) are figures, sometimes painted or embroidered, and at others carved out, used to express ideas. They differ from pictorial writing chiefly in being an abridgment from it, and also in this particular, that they select, by the aid of analogies more or less remote, figures for the purpose of expressing the less obvious mental emotions and abstract truths.

Hieroglyphics were employed much more among the Egyptians than elsewhere, and the whole art probably arose in this way. The method of communicating thoughts by means of paintings, as among the Mexicans, and which undoubtedly existed among the Egyptians previous to the invention of Hieroglyphics, was found inconvenient. The work was difficult in the execution, and bulky when it was completed; and there was, accordingly, very soon an attempt at the abridgment of that method. Hence the head was used to designate a man; two or more hands, with weapons opposed, a battle; a scaling ladder set against a wall, a siege; a man's two feet in water, a fuller of clothes; a leafless tree, the winter.—Thus the first step towards the formation of a hieroglyphical system was taken.

But when those who depended upon this mode of expressing their thoughts came to certain classes of the passions, the moral qualities, and a variety of abstract truths, they were under the necessity of selecting certain visible objects, the delineation of which would be likely to suggest such truths and qualities. The eye was accordingly selected to signify wisdom; ingratitude was expressed by a viper biting the hand that gave it food; courage by a lion; imprudence by a fly; cunning by a serpent.—As the number of ideas among the people increased, and became more and more abstract, greater ingenuity was required in the invention of hieroglyphical characters to express them. Thus, a winged globe, with a serpent issuing from it, came to denote the universe, or universal nature.

In the opinion of Goguet, by no means an incompetent judge on any question of this kind, the methods of pictorial delineation and of hieroglyphics have prevailed, in a greater or less degree, in the early periods of almost every nation on earth. And he takes occasion to make the remark, which appears to be sufficiently sustained by the fact, that such a universal concurrence cannot be considered as the effect of accident or imitation; we must discern in it the voice of nature speaking, in a uniform tone, to the gross capacities of the first generations of men.*

§ 29. Of the written characters of the Chinese.

The third step in the progress of the human mind towards the invention of an alphabetical character was the framing of such arbitrary signs as are employed by the Chinese at the present day.

It is a peculiarity of the written language of the Chinese, that it employs artificial and arbitrary delineations. Thus, for the idea expressed by the English

* Goguet's Origin of Laws, Arts, and Sciences, bk. ii., chap. vi.

word PRISONER, we have this delineation, which is less complicated than many others, viz., a figure approaching in its form to a square, with another figure nearly in the shape of an equilateral triangle placed in the centre of it. The character, which, as it is articulated, is EUL, and answers to the English word ear, is somewhat in the shape of a PARALLELOGRAM, crossed at nearly equal distances from the ends by lines drawn at right angles to the sides.

§ 30. The Chinese character an improvement on the hieroglyphical.

As hieroglyphics are an improvement on the mode of expressing ideas by painting, the characters employed by the Chinese may, with good reason, be considered the next step in advance of hieroglyphics. It is a proof of this, that many of the characters, particularly those called elementary, bore originally an analogy or resemblance to the objects for which they stand. They were, of course, anciently hieroglyphics, although now arbitrary characters. The fact on which this conclusion is founded is ascertained by consulting ancient inscriptions on cups of serpentine stone, on vases of porcelain, on seals of agate, and the characters used in editions of very ancient books. The characters which at present stand for the sun, moon, a field, and the mouth, are quite arbitrary, and we discover no analogy between them and the object; but it was otherwise at first.—The sun was originally represented by a circle with a dot in the centre; the moon by the segment of a circle; a field by a figure resembling a square, set off into smaller divisions by two lines intersecting each other at right angles in the centre; a mouth by a figure intended to represent the projection of the lips.

The progress of the system of the Chinese from a hieroglyphical to a purely arbitrary character, may perhaps be better illustrated by the following story than by any abstract statement.

A tavern-keeper in Hungary, unable to write, kept account of the sums due to him by strokes chalked on his door; to each series of strokes was annexed a figure to denote the customer to whom they applied. The soldier was represented by the figure of a musket, the carpenter by a saw, the smith by a hammer. In a short time, for convenience, the musket was reduced to a straight line, the saw to a zigzag line, the hammer to a cross; and thus began to be formed a set of characters, gradually receding from the original figure. The resemblance might at last be entirely lost sight of, and the figures become mere arbitrary marks.

§ 31. Artificial delineations employed as signs of sound.

But it is to be recollected, that the artificial delineations, towards the formation of which the human mind has thus gradually advanced, were used to denote ideas merely, and not *sounds* or words as they are enunciated. The two systems of oral and written signs are supposed as yet to have been entirely independent of each other. It could not be long, however, before they would assume new relations, and written characters would gradually be employed as significant of sounds as well as of thought.

The idea which we express by the word PRISONER had its correspondent delineation, its appropriate arbitrary figure; it also had its appropriate oral sign or sound. The oral sign would, by association, call up both the thing itself and the written delineation. And, on the other hand, the written character would naturally suggest both the idea and the oral sign. It was in this way arbitrary written characters gradually gave up their original office, and came to stand as directly representative of sounds and indirectly of ideas. This was coming back to the original intention of nature, which seems to have framed the powers of the human voice with the design of making them the predominant instrument of intellectual communication, whatever aid might be derived to them from other sources.

§ 32. Formation of syllabic alphabets.

But it was desirable that every possible benefit

should be derived from this new application of arbitrary written marks as signs of words. The next step, therefore, was to fix upon such sounds as are elementary, and also upon certain characters to represent them. But to ascertain what sounds were elementary, and their exact number, was exceedingly difficult, and it is highly improbable that it was done at once.—The improvers of language, however, not only succeeded in detecting monosyllables in their vocabulary of words, and in distinguishing them from polysyllables, but also in resolving compound words into their monosyllabic parts. The first alphabets, therefore, as is generally supposed, were syllabic; that is, were single syllables, consisting of a consonant sound combined with a vowel sound. The base of these syllables being single consonants, variously modified by vowels, the distinction was at some subsequent period made between consonant and vowel sounds; characters and names were appropriated to each; and alphabets consequently assumed a new form.—Such, after many laborious investigations, seems to be the general sentiment as to the progress of human invention through the successive forms of pictures, hieroglyphics, the arbitrary delineations of the Chinese, and syllabic alphabets, to alphabets of letters. Abundant proofs are extant that these various methods of artificial writing have been employed at different periods; and such is their mutual relation, it is not difficult to conceive of the progress of the human mind from one to the other.

§ 33. The preceding views confirmed by recent researches.

The general views of the preceding sections receive some confirmation from the recent laborious and learned researches into the antiquities of Egypt. The prosecution of these researches, and the accumulation of light on the various monuments of that remarkable country, render it probable that the present inquiry will not always be regarded as a conjectural one, but that it may at last be satisfactorily settled. It appears to be even now sufficiently ascertained that there existed among the ancient Egyptians an alphabet, representative of simple sounds. The visible characters standing for the sounds are either the exact pictures or the hieroglyphics of objects. On examination, it appears that the pictures and hieroglyphics are taken from objects, the oral signs or names of which begin with the same articulate sounds which they are themselves destined to represent. Thus the image of an eagle, which in the Egyptian oral language is called ACHOM, became the sign of the vowel A. Hence it is probable they began in the examination of this subject with the names of objects. It was by the analysis of these names that ultimately the resolution of the human voice into its syllabic and primary elements was made. And, in giving signs to elementary sounds, they selected those pictures or hieroglyphics of objects, the names of which had particularly assisted them in their analysis.

The same is essentially true of other ancient languages. The names and forms of the Hebrew alphabet were, for the most part, designations of sensible objects. The first word of the alphabet is called ALEPH, which means an ox. It may be conjectured, therefore, that the broad sound of A was first separated from other elementary sounds in the analysis of that word. And, after such analysis and separation, the name and figure of the ox were retained as its permanent written and oral signs. Perhaps it should be added, that the resemblance between the written signs and their original archetypes is to be sought chiefly in the ancient Hebrew character, and not in that at present in use.

§ 34. On the recent formation of the Cherokee syllabic alphabet.

Great expectations have justly been directed towards the learned labours of Champollion and his associates; but it was probably not anticipated, that an uneducated North American Savage would throw light on these obscure inquiries. The Cherokees, like the other Aboriginal inhabitants of America, had their pictorial delineations, and probably some hieroglyphic characters, but nothing more; the sounds of their language had never been expressed by an alphabet either of single letters or of syllables. This was the work of the Cherokee See-qua-yah (known more generally by the English name of George Guess), who deserves to be remembered with honour.

About the time of the defeat of the American general St. Clair, when Guess was a young man, a letter fell into the hands of the Indians which greatly excited their curiosity. In some of their deliberations in respect to it, the question arose among them, Whether the mysterious power of the *talking leaf* was the gift of the Great Spirit to the white man, or the discovery of the white man himself? Most of his companions were of the former opinion, while Guess as strenuously maintained the latter. It was this incident which first directed the thoughts of Guess to the subject of written signs. The following statements were taken from his own lips in the winter of 1828, when he was on a visit to the city of Washington with some other persons of his tribe, and its accuracy can be relied on.*

§ 35. Facts relative to the invention of the Cherokee alphabet.

The letter, and the discussions connected with it, "frequently became a subject of contemplation with him afterward, as well as many other things which he knew, or had heard, that the white men could do; but he never sat down seriously to reflect on the subject, until a swelling in his knee confined him to his cabin, and which at length made him a cripple for life, by shortening the diseased leg. Deprived of the excitements of war and the pleasures of the chase, in the long nights of his confinement, his mind was again directed to the mystery of *speaking by letters*, the very name of which, of course, was not to be found in his language. From the cries of wild beasts, from the

* See Knapp's Lectures on American Literature, Lect. i.

talents of the mocking-bird, from the voices of his children and his companions, he knew that feelings and passions were conveyed by direct sounds from one intelligent being to another. The thought struck him to try and ascertain all the sounds in the Cherokee language. His own ear was not remarkably discriminating, and he called to his aid the more acute ears of his wife and children. He found great assistance from them.

"When he thought that he had distinguished all the different sounds in the language, he attempted to use pictorial signs, images of birds and beasts, to convey these sounds to others, or to mark them in his own mind. He soon dropped this method as difficult or impossible, and tried arbitrary signs, without any regard to appearances, except such as might assist him in recollecting them and distinguishing them from each other. At first these signs were very numerous; and when he got so far as to think his invention was nearly accomplished, he had about two hundred characters in his alphabet. By the aid of his daughter, who seemed to enter into the genius of his labours, he reduced them at last to eighty-six, the number he now uses. He then set to work to make these characters more comely to the eye, and succeeded. As yet he had not the knowledge of the pen as an instrument, but made his characters on a piece of bark with a knife or nail. At this time he sent to the Indian agent, or some trader in the nation, for paper and pen. His ink was easily made from some of the bark of the forest trees, whose colouring properties he had previously known; and after seeing the construction of the pen, he soon learned to make one, but at first he made it without a slit; this inconvenience was, however, quickly removed by his sagacity. His next difficulty was to make his invention known to his countrymen; for by this time he had become so abstracted from his tribe and their usual pursuits that he was viewed with an eye of suspicion. His former companions passed his wigwam without entering it, and mentioned his name as one who was practising improper spells, for notoriety or mischievous purposes; and he seems to think that he should have been hardly dealt with if his docile and unambitious disposition had not been so generally acknowledged by his tribe. At length he summoned some of the most distinguished of his nation, in order to make his communication to them; and, after giving the best explanation of his discovery that he could, stripping it of all supernatural influence, he proceeded to demonstrate to them, in good earnest, that he had made a discovery. His daughter, who was his only pupil, was ordered to go out of hearing, while he requested his friends to name a word or sentiment which he put down, and then she was called in and read it to them; then the father retired and the daughter wrote; the Indians were wonder-struck, but not entirely satisfied; See-qua-yah then proposed that the tribe should select several youths from among their best young men, that he might communicate the mystery to them. This was at length agreed to, although there was some lurking suspicion of necromancy in the whole business. John Maw (his Indian name I have forgotten), a full-blood, with several others, were selected for this purpose.—The tribe watched the youths for several months with anxiety, and when they offered themselves for examination, the feelings of all were wrought up to the highest pitch. The youths were separated from their master and from each other, and watched with great care. The uninitiated directed what master and pupil should write to each other, and the tests were viewed in such a manner as not only to destroy their infidelity, but most firmly to fix their faith."

§ 36. Conventional written signs as expressive of numbers and quantities.

The invention of written signs, as well as oral, gave increased power to the action of the mind; and the assistances thus rendered were so obvious and decisive, that the principle of expressing thoughts by conventional written signs was extended to other cases. Hence the origin of numerical and algebraic expressions. In the science of Algebra, the subjects of mathematical analysis, such as extension, quantities, forces, and their relations, instead of being expressed by words and sentences in the ordinary way, are represented by the letters of the alphabet. At first the large or capital, and afterward the small letters, being in some respects more convenient, were used for this purpose. And the system has been by degrees fully extended, not only to the quantities and forces thus represented, but to the operations performed in respect to them. It was regarded by scientific persons as an improvement worthy of some notice when the processes of adding and subtracting in algebra came to be expressed by the Latin terms *plus* and *minus*; it was considered a further improvement when these terms were in writing abridged into the initial letters *p* and *m*, and when they were subsequently altered into the signs + and −, &c.

The late Mr. Playfair, in his Historical Sketch of the Discoveries and Improvements in Science from the Revival of Letters to the present Century, has the following instructive remarks on the subject before us.—Speaking of some improvements by Des Cartes, he adds, "The leading principles of algebra were now unfolded, and the notation was brought, from a mere contrivance for abridging the common language, to a system of symbolical writing, admirably fitted to assist the mind in the exercise of thought.

"The happy idea, indeed, of expressing quantity and the operations on quantity by conventional symbols, instead of representing the first by real magnitudes, and enunciating the second in words, could not but make a great change in the nature of mathematical investigation. The language of mathematics, whatever may be its form, must always consist of two parts; the one denoting quantities simply, and the other denoting the manner in which the quantities are combined, or the operations understood to be performed on them. Geometry expresses the first of these by real magnitudes, or what may be called natural signs; a line by a line, an angle by an angle, an area by an area, &c.; and it describes the latter by words. Algebra, on the other hand, denotes both quantity and the operations on quantity by the same system of conventional symbols. Thus, in the expression $x^3 - ax^2 + b^2 = o$, the letters a b x denote quantities, but the terms x^3, ax^2, &c., denote certain operations performed on those quantities, as well as the quantities themselves; x^3 is the quantity x raised to the cube; and ax^2 the same quantity x raised to the square, and then multiplied into a, &c.; the combination, by addition or subtraction, being also expressed by the signs + and −.

"Now it is when applied to this latter purpose that the algebraic language possesses such exclusive excellence. The mere magnitudes themselves might be represented by figures, as in geometry, as well as in any way whatever; but the operations they are to be subjected to, if described in words, must be set before the mind slowly and in succession, so that the impression is weakened and the clear apprehension rendered difficult. In the algebraic expression, on the other hand, so much meaning is concentrated into a narrow space, and the impression made by all the parts is so simultaneous, that nothing can be more favorable to the exertion of the reasoning powers, to the continuance of their action, and their security against error."

CHAPTER IV.

CHARACTERISTICS OF LANGUAGES.

§ 37. All languages have their characteristic traits.

From the consideration of the origin and use of particular words and phrases, we naturally proceed to the characteristic peculiarities of languages. It is with nations, in some degree, as with individuals; every nation has a character, as each man has; and, in like manner, every language possesses its distinctive traits, not less than the mode of expression which is employed by individuals.

Let us, therefore, look a moment at this subject in reference to particular writers.—The style of a writer is understood to have relation chiefly to his choice of words and his manner of arranging them. Every writer of genius employs a style in some degree peculiar to himself. It cannot well be otherwise, since the mind of every individual is, in some respects, unlike that of all others. There are differences in situation; differences in intellect and feeling, in knowledge and taste, which necessarily lay the foundation for differences in style. Wherever, therefore, a writer attempts to imbody and set forth to others the series of his intellectual operations and feelings, such exposition will necessarily have a form and impress of its own. So true is this, that it is hardly more difficult to detect an author's style when it is once well-formed, than it is to distinguish one man's handwriting from another's.—And what is true of his manner of expression in the case of an individual, is equally so of national dialects. The languages of all nations have a style or peculiarity of manner. They are marked by certain prevailing characteristics, which readily distinguish them from those of other nations.

§ 38. Characteristics of the languages of uncivilized nations.

In the first place, there are certain general traits, which are characteristic of all languages that are spoken by the rude, uncultured tribes of men. As such uncivilized communities are in general ignorant of alphabetical writing, they cannot be expected to furnish us with numerous specimens of mental effort. Their glory is committed to the traditions of their country; and we rarely find among them anything more than some brief historical sketches, war songs, and speeches. But, even from these imperfect sources, we can form a judgment on the present subject.

The words which such tribes employ are generally few in number, compared with the vocabulary of civilized nations. Their knowledge is very limited; their ideas are few; and it is a necessary consequence that their words should be few likewise. Incapable of aiding their perceptions by remote deductions of reasoning, they draw instruction from the visible teachings of the woods, the waters, and the sky; but even the external world is very imperfectly learned, while they are almost wholly ignorant of the world within. And the range or compass of their language corresponds to the compass of their knowledge.

It is further worthy of remark, that only a small proportion of the words employed by uncivilized tribes are the signs of abstract ideas. Having but few abstract notions, and, consequently, but few names for them, they are under the necessity of resorting continually to figurative illustrations, so that their language seems to partake of the materiality of the external objects with which they are chiefly conversant. But aided, as they are, by metaphorical expressions, their stock of words still remains small, and the sentences which they utter must therefore, of necessity, be short.

These short and figurative sentences are inspirited by the infusion of the untamed passions of a savage mind. There is a vivacity in their griefs, their joys, and their anger, which is almost peculiar to uncivilized life.—"The bones of our countrymen," say the Chiefs, "lie uncovered; their bloody bed has not been washed clean; their spirits cry against us; they must be appeased; sit no longer inactive upon your mats; lift the hatchets; console the spirits of the dead."

§ 39. Characteristics of language in civilized and scientific nations.

As a nation advances in knowledge, its language becomes more strictly conventional, losing by degrees that metaphorical aspect which it presented in its earlier periods. A variety of new words are introduced, which previously had no existence, because the things for which they stand were not then known. New arts have their technical names and epithets, and new sciences furnish us with their novel nomenclatures.

The distiller speaks of the cohobation of liquors; the worker in mines of collieries; the chemist of sulphates and muriates; the botanist and mineralogist employ a variety of terms peculiar to their respective departments. An increased refinement and abstraction discovers itself in terms appropriated to moral, political, and literary subjects; and the language in all respects is more removed from the senses, and becomes more intellectual. But while it is, by a natural consequence of mental improvement, more exact and scientific, it is less directly and strikingly indicative of external objects and of the passions of men, and is, therefore, less poetical. As terms become more abstract, they are necessarily less picturesque. This is the natural consequence of their not being limited to particular objects, but extended over a vast surface of things. A Savage, if he had the most refined language of Europe at his command, would be at a loss to express in it the strong emotions which agitate him, and the outward and living beauties of his woodland scenery: he would choose for that purpose the dialect of his tribe.

§ 40. Characteristics of languages depend much on the people's habits.

Individual writers, as already observed, have a style, that is, characteristics of expression, of their own; for every one has a tendency to connect together thoughts, or words which are the signs of thought, agreeably to his peculiar intellectual habits and passions. But languages also, considered in their whole extent, have a style; because the nations, the whole mass of people that make use of those languages, have their characteristics as well as individuals.

It will be found, on inquiry, that the language of every people has words and combinations of words, evidently having their origin in the habits of the people and in the exigencies of their peculiar circumstances. Accordingly, we find the word CORBAN in Hebrew, OSTRAKISMOS in Greek, PROSCRIPTIO in Latin, ANGGAROS in Persian, ROTURIER in French, and many others, which are either wholly peculiar to their respective languages, or employed with some peculiarity of meaning not elsewhere acknowledged. No modern language had originally words precisely corresponding to the Latin terms TRIBUNUS, CONSUL, PROCONSUL, PRÆTOR, ÆDILIS, LICTOR, &c. The terms by which they are translated into the modern languages of Europe are the Latin words themselves, with only a slight alteration of form; and they can find their true interpretation and import only in the institutions of the Romans.

The single fact, without further delaying upon this topic, that no person can become fully acquainted with the true import and spirit of a language without an acquaintance with the geography of their country and its natural scenery, without a knowledge of the dress, buildings, arts, religion, customs, and history of the people, seems enough in support of the remark that languages take their character from the circumstances of those who speak them. If the fact on which the conclusion is founded be doubted, then we ask why instructers consider it so essential that their pupils should have a knowledge of the antiquities of the Romans, of the antiquities of the Greeks, of the antiquities of the Hebrews? and why this course is pursued, or is acknowledged to be requisite, in respect to every other dead language?*

§ 41. **Languages aid in forming correct ideas of national character.**

If the statements in the preceding section be true, it follows that a knowledge of languages very much helps us in acquiring a knowledge of the character of the people who speak them. The study of every language is the examination of a new chapter in the his-

* See, for some further illustrations of this subject, Heckewelder's and Duponceau's correspondence respecting the Languages of the American Indians, Letter viii.

tory and operations of the mind; that is, of the mind as it is modified by the peculiar circumstances, the climate, government, and habits of a people. Without an acquaintance, therefore, with their vernacular tongue, the critic will in vain take it upon him to judge of the philosophy of their literature and character. It is this, more than anything else, that breathes the national spirit; it fixes and retains it when all its other monuments and memorials are gone, and after the nation itself is extinct.

We may, perhaps, even go further, and assert that changes in languages are indices to particular events. In other words, that events of an extraordinary nature, whether they have relation to the sciences or politics, are often accompanied with corresponding effects on language. No one can be ignorant that great and radical changes in the sciences are usually attended with alterations, improvements, and accessions of this kind. Some years since, the French chemist Lavoisier laid the foundation of a new system of chemistry. In order to complete and sustain the revolution of which he had been so conspicuous an instrument, he and his associates invented a new nomenclature, which has since been pretty generally adopted.

Nearly at the same time happened the great political convulsions in France, which also had its effects on the French language. The patriotic Necker remarked this, and complained with no small degree of feeling of the barbarisms which he asserted had sprung up within a short time. He instanced, in particular, the words *influencer*, *utilizer*, *exceptioner*, *preconiser*, *fanatiser*, *patrioser*, *petitioner*, *vetoter*, *and harmonier*.

§ 42. Of the correspondence between national intellect and the progress of a language.

Whatever may have been at any time thought, it will be found, on examination, that those individuals who are looked up to as the eminent writers of a nation, seldom arise until its language is nearly or quite completed. They employ it as the people have formed it, and the people have formed it as their feelings and habits prompted.

The circumstance that language is a great and admirable instrument of intellectual power is of itself no small confirmation of the doctrine that developements of intellectual strength will correspond to the progressive improvement of a language, and that its great men, those who are to speak in it as long as it shall exist, will not make their appearance until it shall have arrived to some degree of perfection.

Let it be supposed that, in the midst of a Savage tribe, whose language is rude, a person is found of perfect mental organization, capable of remembering, separating, and comparing ideas with a quickness of invention and other qualities of genius above the common lot. He has influence over the minds of others; he is consulted in difficult emergencies; he is accounted wise; but how far he falls short of the mark, which is reached by others of originally no greater genius, who appear in a civilized community, and with the advantage of a perfect language!

"It is with languages," says Condillac, "as with geometrical signs; they give a new insight into things, and dilate the mind in proportion as they are more perfect. Sir Isaac Newton's extraordinary success was owing to the choice which had already been made of signs, together with the contrivance of methods of calculation. Had he appeared earlier, he might have been a great man for the age he would have lived in, but he would not have been the admiration of ours. It is the same in every other branch of learning. The success of geniuses who have had the happiness even of the best organization, depends entirely on the progress of the language in regard to the age in which they live; for words answer to geometrical signs, and the manner of using them to methods of calculation. In a language, therefore, defective in words, or whose construction is not sufficiently easy and convenient, we should meet with the same obstacles as occurred in geometry before the invention of algebra. The French tongue was for a long time so unfavourable to the progress of the mind, that if we could frame an idea of Corneille successively in the different ages of our monarchy, we should find him to have been possessed of less genius in proportion to his greater distance from the age in which he lived, till at length we should reach a Corneille who could not give the least mark of abilities."—*Origin of Knowledge*, pt. ii., § i.

This writer thinks it may be demonstrated that there can be no such thing as a superior genius (meaning probably a developement of superior genius) till the language of a nation has been considerably improved. And certainly it must be admitted, that the expectation of great and successful mental efforts of a literary kind, before the developement and organization of the national language, can hardly be better expected than the forming of statues, and the building of temples, and the execution of paintings, before men have invented those auxiliary instruments by which the trees of the forest are hewn into shape, and the marble is cut and drawn up from the quarry, and the colours are to be prepared and laid upon the canvass. There is soundness of thought as well as power of expression in the remark of a modern critic: "The first works of the imagination are poor and rude, not from the want of genius, but from the want of materials. Phidias could have done nothing with an old tree and a fish-bone, or Homer with the language of New Holland."*

§ 43. Different languages suited to different minds and to different kinds of subjects.

Some languages are more suited to certain minds than they are to others; more adapted also to the discussion of certain subjects than to others.—Accordingly, the French language is simple, clear, precise,

* Edinburgh Review, vol. xlvii., p. 11.

and, therefore, favourable to abstract investigations. And it is here, it may be conjectured, that we find one cause of the great excellence of the mathematicians and the philosophers of that nation. There is also a facility in its construction, and a conciseness and expressiveness in its particles, which render it eminently a *colloquial* language; and in this respect it is precisely such as the lively and sociable disposition of the French people requires it to be. The French themselves concede that other languages are better adapted to express the higher flights of imagination, and the more profound displays of the passions.

The Italian language, which has the Latin for its basis, although abundantly modified by the intermixture of the inflexions and phrases of the successive conquerors of Italy, is characterized by exceeding harmony. There is perhaps a want of diversity in its sounds, so much so that even its harmony is apt to prove tiresome. But it appears, notwithstanding, to be well suited to poetry of a plaintive and serious cast, particularly elegiac. It also furnishes a number of expressive and nicely discriminated terms, having a relation to the science of music.

The Spanish language seems to indicate, in its sonorous fulness, that dignified and measured solemnity which is so well known to be characteristic of the people who speak it. But it is as courteous as it is dignified. It has abundance of terms precisely suited to express every form and degree of deference, courtesy, and honour. The order of chivalry first arose among the Spaniards; and as all the members of that romantic institution were bound to practice the most refined courtesy as well as the most devoted heroism, it naturally happened that many expressions of respect and politeness were introduced in that way, which have since been retained.

§ 44. Such differences shown by attempts at translating.

The remarks of the preceding section lead us further to observe, that differences in their power of expression and other specific peculiarities of languages disclose themselves in all cases of a translation from one language to another. The remark has often been made, and probably with great correctness, that there are many languages into which the Paradise Lost of Milton could not be translated; and perhaps none where it could be done with perfect safety to the various and peculiar beauties of the original work.

But the difficulty of representing in a translation the entire shape and value of an original, is not limited to works of imagination. There are some languages which are almost wholly destitute of particular classes of terms, both of a scientific and of a moral and philosophic nature; a state of things which of course renders translation extremely difficult, so far as such classes of words are concerned. The Greek language is said to have been destitute of suitable terms in philosophy till after the time of Socrates; and it was the same with the Latin till after the time of Cicero, who introduced, by means of his philosophic writings, many new terms on those subjects. Both languages are destitute of a multitude of terms, which have a place in such abstract and experimental sciences as have received new developements and applications, or perhaps a new existence, in modern times.*—The Bohemian and the Swiss languages are spoken by nations that are shut up in inland and mountainous countries, and, being separated from the ocean, are ignorant of all navigation, excepting such as they are acquainted with on the limited scale of their own lakes and rivers. They are accordingly found to be greatly deficient in the terms that are employed in the building, rigging, and managing of ships.†

Sometimes whole classes of terms acquire a specific character, in consequence of the prevalent pursuits and habits of the people. In one country a high de-

* Degerando, Histoire des Systèmes de Philosophie, part i., chap. ix.

† See the Dissertation of Michaelis on the Influence of Language on Opinions, § 4.

gree of honour is attached to the life of a shepherd, as among the ancient Hebrews and the Arcadians; in another to that of a cultivator of the soil, as among the Romans; and in another to that of a merchant, as among the Tyrians and Carthaginians; and the supposed value of the calling becomes in time transferred to the terms having a relation to it. The Abbé de Lille translated the Georgics of Virgil into French; but he complains, in the preface of his work, that it was rendered difficult, in consequence of the ideas of want and meanness which the French are accustomed to associate with the life of a husbandman. The same difficulty is said to have been experienced by those who have attempted to translate the Seasons of Thomson into that language.

§ 45. Of the study of the Greek and Latin languages.

As incidental to this subject, it may not be out of place to say a few words in relation to the study of the Greek and Latin. Some of the reasons which are given for occupying a considerable portion of time in this way are briefly these.

(1.) Much information is locked up in these languages. The original Greek and Roman literature is of itself highly valuable; their poets, historians, and orators are worthy of being compared with those of any age or nation. In vigour of thought and purity of taste, in an enlightened freedom of inquiry, and in exaltation of moral and political sentiment, it is generally conceded that the original literature of no nations whatever, taken as a whole, presents more favourable claims to notice.—In addition to this, vast numbers of literary and other treatises have been written in the Latin language in later periods, particularly on the readings and interpretations of ancient authors, and on obscure and difficult points of history. A person ignorant of that language is shut out from the greater part of these important documents.

(2.) The intercourse of the world has been so much

increased in consequence of the spread of knowledge and the facilities of commerce, that an acquaintance with some of the modern languages, particularly the Spanish, Italian, and French, is considered highly desirable. An entire ignorance of all modern languages is thought to imply a very defective education. But the languages which have been mentioned, together with the Portuguese, have their origin in great part from the Latin, and can be more easily and perfectly learned by previously giving some attention to the parent dialect, than by attempting them without it.

(3.) No one who speaks the English language can deny the importance of a thorough knowledge of it. It imbodies and retains the vast wisdom of many good and learned men, and is the medium by which the thoughts and feelings of our own generation and of our own hearts are to be communicated. But in the knowledge of this language, the student will find himself assisted by an acquaintance with the Latin, since no inconsiderable proportion of the words in the English language are derived from that source.—The Greek, which is a source of many English words, has a similar argument in its favour, and the additional circumstance of being the original language of the New Testament.

(4.) The study of these languages answers a good purpose, as a sort of basis of education. During the period from eight to eleven years of age, the intellect may be supposed to be developing itself under the mere guidance of nature. It is a great point in education to aid this developement, to keep the mental powers in exercise, and to promote their growth. This object is known to be secured by the study of languages in a high degree. It is thought by many that it cannot be equally well secured by any other course of study.

(5.) It has also been strongly contended, that an acquaintance with any language is a valuable acquisition, because it opens new views of mental character. The language of every nation is modified by the exigencies of the people who speak it, and by individual and national traits. It imbodies their emotions, customs, prejudices, domestic and political history. No man, therefore, can make himself fully acquainted with a new language without having more correct and broader views of the developement of the mind, of the progress of men as they rise from barbarism to refinement, and of human nature in general. And these advantages can be secured by the study of the Greek and Latin languages, no less than by others.

§ 46. Of an universal language.

The question is sometimes asked, whether there will, or can be, an universal language? It may not be easy to give a definite and satisfactory answer. Nevertheless, when we remember that the system of natural signs is universal, and that the power of instinctive interpretation, in being an attribute of humanity, is universal also, and that this state of things lays the basis of conventional language both oral and written, we are thus furnished with some grounds of hope, that conventional language will also, at last, assume the same universality of character. And our hopes and anticipations are strengthened when we consider, that the elements of all languages, the parts of speech as we term them, are always and necessarily the same; nouns, for instance, are the names of things; verbs, of the activities of things; adjectives, of the attributes of things; and prepositions, and sometimes a change in the terminations of nouns, are expressive of relations. So that the foundations of conventional language, in the important matter of its grammatical construction, are deeply laid in the mental nature; and cannot be otherwise than they are, because the mind itself is not an accident, but a permanency; and gives forth its results, not accidentally, but by means of permanent principles. And further we find, that always, by some great law of being, the urgent wants of our nature, which ascend as earnest and persevering prayers to the great Source of supply, are at some time heard and answered. Can we well doubt, therefore, that an universal language, either written or spoken, or both, which will enable men everywhere to communicate with each other, is one of those things which the essential unity of human life, in its ceaseless prayer for the complete realization of itself, will verify, both as the means of its growth and the consummation of its happiness?

END OF VOL. I.

www.ingramcontent.com/pod-product-compliance
Lightning Source LLC
LaVergne TN
LVHW021234110826
845150LV00002B/334

* 9 7 8 1 4 2 5 5 6 2 3 0 4 *